Dynamic Asset Pricing Theory

Dynamic Asset Pricing Theory

Darrell Duffie

Princeton University Press
Princeton, New Jersey

Library of Congress Cataloging-in-Publication Data

Duffie, Darrell.
        Dynamic asset pricing theory / Darrell Duffie. — 2nd ed.
            p.   cm.
        Includes bibliographical references and index.
        ISBN 0-691-02125-2 (cl : alk. paper)
        1. Capital assets pricing model.   2. Portfolio management.   3. Uncertainty.   I. Title
HG4637.D84   1996
332.6–dc20   95–3212?
                                                                                                              CIP

This book was composed in ITC New Baskerville with LaTeX by Archetype Publishing Inc., 1₹
Turtle Pointe Road, Monticello, IL 61856.

For Colin

Contents

Preface

THIS BOOK IS an introduction to the theory of portfolio choice and asset pricing in multiperiod settings under uncertainty. An alternate title might be *Arbitrage, Optimality, and Equilibrium,* since the book is built around the three basic constraints on asset prices: absence of arbitrage, single-agent optimality, and market equilibrium. The most important unifying principle is that any of these three conditions implies that there are "state prices," meaning positive discount factors, one for each state and date, such that the price of any security is merely the state-price weighted sum of its future payoffs. This idea can be traced to Kenneth Arrow's (1953) invention of the general equilibrium model of security markets. Identifying the state prices is the major task at hand. Technicalities are given relatively little emphasis so as to simplify these concepts and to make plain the similarities between discrete and continuous-time models. All continuous-time models are based on Brownian motion, despite the fact that most of the results extend easily to the case of a general abstract information filtration.

To someone who came out of graduate school in the mid-eighties, the decade spanning roughly 1969–79 seems like a golden age of dynamic asset pricing theory. Robert Merton started continuous-time financial modeling with his explicit dynamic programming solution for optimal portfolio and consumption policies. This set the stage for his 1973 general equilibrium model of security prices, another milestone. His next major contribution was his arbitrage-based proof of the option pricing formula introduced by Fisher Black and Myron Scholes in 1973, and his continual development of that approach to derivative pricing. The Black-Scholes model now seems to be, by far, the most important single breakthrough of this "golden decade," and ranks alone with the Modigliani-Miller (1958) Theorem and the Capital Asset Pricing Model (CAPM) of Sharpe (1964) and Lintner (1965) in its overall importance for financial theory and practice. A tremendously influential simplification of the Black-Scholes model appeared in the "binomial" option pricing model of Cox, Ross, and Rubinstein (1979), who drew on an insight of Bill Sharpe.

Working with discrete-time models, LeRoy (1973), Rubinstein (1976), and Lucas (1978) developed multiperiod extensions of the CAPM. To this day, the "Lucas model" is the "vanilla flavor" of equilibrium asset pricing models. The simplest multiperiod representation of the CAPM finally appeared in Doug Breeden's continuous-time consumption-based CAPM, published in 1979. Although not published until 1985, the Cox-Ingersoll-Ross model of the term structure of interest rates appeared in the mid-seventies and is still the premier textbook example of a continuous-time general equilibrium asset pricing model with practical applications. It also ranks as one of the key breakthroughs of that decade. Finally, extending the ideas of Cox and Ross (1976) and Ross (1978), Harrison and Kreps (1979) gave an almost definitive conceptual structure to the whole theory of dynamic security prices.

The decade or so since 1979 has, with relatively few exceptions, been a mopping-up operation. On the theoretical side, assumptions have been weakened, there have been some noteworthy extensions, and the various problems have become much more unified under the umbrella of the Harrison-Kreps model. On the applied side, markets have experienced an explosion of new valuation techniques, hedging applications, and security innovation, much of this based on the Black-Scholes and related arbitrage models. No major investment bank, for example, lacks the experts or computer technology required to implement advanced mathematical models of the term structure.

Although it is difficult to predict where the theory will go next, in order to promote faster progress by people coming into the field it seems wise to have some of the basics condensed into a textbook. This book is designed to be a streamlined course text, not a research monograph. Much generality is sacrificed for expositional reasons, and there is relatively little emphasis on mathematical rigor or on the existence of general equilibrium. As its title indicates, I am treating only the theoretical side of the story. Although it might be useful to tie the theory to the empirical side of asset pricing, others more qualified than myself will surely follow with books specializing on the estimation and testing of asset pricing models. (Singleton [1987] and Campbell, Lo, and MacKinlay [1994] give useful surveys.) The story told by this book also leaves out some important aspects of functioning security markets such as asymmetric information, borrowing constraints, and transactions costs. I have chosen to develop only some of the essential ideas of dynamic asset pricing, and even these are more than enough to put into one book or into a one-semester course.

There are other books covering some of the topics treated here, such as those of Dana and Jeanblanc-Picqué (1994), Demange and Rochet (1992), Dewynne and Wilmott (1994), Dixit and Pindyck (1993), Dothan (1990), Duffie (1988), Harris (1987), Huang (1994), Huang and Litzenberger (1988), Ingersoll (1987), Jarrow (1988), Lamberton and Lapeyre (1991), Magill and Quinzii (1994), Malliaris (1982), Merton (1990b), and Stokey and Lucas (1989). Each has its own aims and themes. There are also survey articles by Constantinides (1989), Cox and Huang (1988), Huang (1987b), Karatzas (1987), Marimon (1987), Merton (1990a, 1993, 1994a,b), and Rothschild (1986). I hope that readers will find some advantage in having yet another perspective.

A reasonable way to teach a shorter course on continuous-time asset pricing out of this book is to begin with Chapter 1 as an introduction to the basic notion of state prices and then to go directly to Chapters 5 through 10. Chapter 11, on numerical methods, could be skipped at some cost in the student's ability to implement the results. There is no direct dependence of any results in Chapters 5 through 11 on the first four chapters.

For mathematical preparation, little beyond undergraduate analysis, as in Bartle (1976), and linear algebra, as in O'Nan (1976), is assumed. Further depth, for example, by study of Rudin (1973) or a similar text on functional analysis and measure theory, would be useful. Some background in microeconomics would be useful, at the level of Kreps (1990), Luenberger (1995), or Varian (1984). Familiarity with probability theory at a level approaching Billingsley (1986), for example, would also speed things along, although measure theory is not used heavily. In any case, a series of appendices supplies all of the required concepts and definitions from probability theory and stochastic calculus. Additional useful references in this regard are Arnold (1974), Chung and Williams (1990), Elliott (1982), Karatzas and Shreve (1988), Kopp (1984), Oksendal (1985), Rogers and Williams (1987), and Stroock and Varadhan (1979).

Students seem to learn best by doing problem exercises. Each chapter has exercises and notes to the literature. I have tried to be thorough in giving sources for results whenever possible and plead that any cases in which I have mistaken or missed sources be brought to my attention for correction. The notation and terminology throughout is fairly standard. I use $\mathbb{R}$ to denote the real line and $\overline{\mathbb{R}} = \mathbb{R} \cup \{-\infty, +\infty\}$ for the extended real line. For any set Z and positive integer n, I use Z^n for the set of n-tuples of the form $(z_1, \ldots, z_n)$ with z_i in Z for all i. For example, think of $\mathbb{R}^n$. The conventions used for inequalities in any context are

- $x \geq 0$ means that x is nonnegative. For x in $\mathbb{R}^n$, this is equivalent to $x \in \mathbb{R}^n_+$;
- $x > 0$ means that x is nonnegative and not zero, but not necessarily strictly positive in all coordinates;
- $x \gg 0$ means x is strictly positive in every possible sense. The phrase "x is strictly positive" means the same thing. For x in $\mathbb{R}^n$, this is equivalent to $x \in \mathbb{R}^n_{++} \equiv \text{int}(\mathbb{R}^n_+)$.

Although warnings will be given at appropriate times, it should be kept in mind that $X = Y$ will be used to mean equality almost everywhere or almost surely, as the case may be. The same caveat applies to each of the above inequalities. A function F on an ordered set (such as $\mathbb{R}^n$) is *increasing* if $F(x) \geq F(y)$ whenever $x \geq y$ and *strictly increasing* if $F(x) > F(y)$ whenever $x > y$. When the domain and range of a function are implicitly obvious, the notation "$x \mapsto F(x)$" means the function that maps x to $F(x)$; for example, $x \mapsto x^2$ means the function $F : \mathbb{R} \to \mathbb{R}$ defined by $F(x) = x^2$. Also, while warnings appear at appropriate places, it is worth pointing out again here that for ease of exposition, a continuous-time "process" will be defined throughout as a jointly measurable function on $\Omega \times [0, T]$, where $[0, T]$ is the given time interval and $(\Omega, \mathcal{F}, P)$ is the given underlying probability space.

I have many people to thank, in addition to those mentioned above who developed this theory. In 1982, Michael Harrison gave a class at Stanford that had a major effect on my understanding and research goals. Beside me in that class was Chi-fu Huang; we learned much of this material together, becoming close friends and collaborators. I owe him a lot. I am grateful to Niko and Vana Skiadas, who treated me with overwhelming warmth and hospitality at their home on Skiathos, where parts of the first draft were written. Useful comments on subsequent drafts have been provided by Howie Corb, Rui Kan, John Overdeck, Christina Shannon, Philippe Henrotte, Chris Avery, Pinghua Young, Don Iglehart, Rohit Rahi, Shinsuke Kambe, Marco Scarsini, Kerry Back, Heracles Polemarchakis, John Campbell, Ravi Myneni, Michael Intriligator, Robert Ashcroft, and Ayman Hindy. I thank Kingston Duffie, Ravi Myneni, Paul Bernstein, and Michael Boulware for coding and running some numerical examples. In writing the book, I have benefited from research collaboration over the years with George Constantinides, Larry Epstein, Mark Garman, John Geanakoplos, Chi-fu Huang, Matt Jackson, Pierre-Louis Lions, Andreu Mas-Colell, Andy McLennan, Philip Protter, Tony Richardson, Wayne Shafer, Ken Singleton, Costis Skiadas, Richard Stanton, and Bill Zame. At Princeton University

Press, Jack Repcheck was a friendly, helpful, and supportive editor. I owe a special debt to Costis Skiadas, whose generous supply of good ideas has had a big influence on the result. The errors are my own responsibility, and I hope to hear of them and any other comments from readers.

Although this preface is modified somewhat from that of the first edition, some additional remarks will clarify how the second edition differs from the first. What was Chapter 7 in the first edition has been split into two new chapters, one on term structure modeling, the other on derivative securities. The references have been thoroughly updated, and nontrivial changes have been made in most chapters. Extensive changes have been made to Chapter6 and Chapter11 (formerly Chapter10, Numerical Methods). Many corrections to and improvements of the first edition have been made with the helpful suggestions of Robert Ashcroft, Flavio Auler, Michael Boulware, Chin-Shan Chuan, Qiang Dai, Michelle Dick, Phil Dolan, Kian Esteghamat, John Fuqua, Ayman Hindy, Toshiki Honda, Ming Huang, Farshid Jamshidian, Ping Jiang, Allan Kulig, Yoichi Kuwana, Piero La Mura, Joe Langsam, Jun Liu, Lee Bath Nelson, Angela Ng, Kazuhiko Ōhashi, Amir Sadr, Martin Schneider, Lucie Tepla, Rajat Tewari, Steven Weinberg, Seth Weingram, and Guojun Wu. I am happy to have had access to research discussions here at Stanford, especially with Qiang Dai, Ayman Hindy, Ming Huang, Rui Kan, and Ken Singleton, and elsewhere with too many others to name. I am thankful to have had the chance to work on applied financial models with Mike Burger, Ken Knowles, and Elizabeth Glaeser of Mobil Corporation; Adam Duff, Craig Gustaffson, Joe Langsam, and Amir Sadr of Morgan Stanley and Company; Mark Williams and Wei Shi of Bank of America; Vince Kaminsky, Stenson Gibner, and Corwin Joy and Krishna Rao of Enron; and Matt Page and Aloke Majumdar of Susquehanna Investment Group. Peter Dougherty has been a wonderful editor. I am also grateful for the opportunity to have learned from new coauthors: Peter DeMarzo, Pierre-Yves Geoffard, Peter Glynn, Mike Harrison, Ming Huang, Rui Kan, Jin Ma, Rohit Rahi, Mark Schroeder, and Jiongmin Yong. Once again, I owe a special debt to Costis Skiadas for extensive suggestions. I rededicate this book to my son Colin.

Darrell Duffie

I
Discrete-Time Models

This first part of the book takes place in a discrete-time setting with a discrete set of states. This should ease the development of intuition for the models to be found in Part II. The three pillars of the theory, *arbitrage, optimality,* and *equilibrium,* are developed repeatedly in different settings. Chapter 1 is the basic single-period model. Chapter 2 extends the results of Chapter 1 to many periods. Chapter 3 specializes Chapter 2 to a Markov setting and illustrates dynamic programming as an alternate solution technique. The Ho-and-Lee and Black-Derman-Toy term-structure models are included as exercises. Chapter 4 is an infinite-horizon counterpart to Chapter 3 that has become known as the *Lucas model.*

The focus of the theory is the notion of state prices, which specify the price of any security as the state-price weighted sum or expectation of the security's state-contingent dividends. In a finite-dimensional setting, there exist state prices if and only if there is no arbitrage. The same fact is true in infinite-dimensional settings under mild technical regularity conditions. Given an agent's optimal portfolio choice, a state-price vector is given by that agent's utility gradient. In an equilibrium with Pareto optimality, a state-price vector is likewise given by a representative agent's utility gradient at the economy's aggregate consumption process.

1

An Introduction to State Pricing

THIS CHAPTER INTRODUCES the basic ideas of the course in a finite-state one-period setting. In some sense, each subsequent chapter merely repeats this one from a new perspective. The objective is a characterization of security prices in terms of "state prices," one for each state of the world. The price of a given security is simply the state-price weighted sum of its payoffs in the different states. One can treat a state-price as the "shadow price," or Lagrange multiplier, for wealth contingent on a given state of the world. We obtain a characterization of state prices, first based on the absence of arbitrage, then based on the first-order conditions for optimal portfolio choice of a given agent, and finally from the first-order conditions for Pareto optimality in an equilibrium with complete markets. State prices are connected with the "beta" model for excess expected returns, a special case of which is the Capital Asset Pricing Model (CAPM). Many readers will find this chapter to be a review of standard results. In most cases, here and throughout the book, technical conditions are imposed that give up much generality so as to simplify the exposition.

A. Arbitrage and State Prices

Uncertainty is represented here by a finite set $\{1, \ldots, S\}$ of states, one of which will be revealed as true. The N securities are given by an $N \times S$ matrix D, with D_{ij} denoting the number of units of account paid by security i in state j. The security prices are given by some q in $\mathbb{R}^N$. A *portfolio* $\theta \in \mathbb{R}^N$ has *market value* $q \cdot \theta$ and *payoff* $D^\top \theta$ in $\mathbb{R}^S$. An *arbitrage* is a portfolio θ in $\mathbb{R}^N$ with $q \cdot \theta \leq 0$ and $D^\top \theta > 0$, or $q \cdot \theta < 0$ and $D^\top \theta \geq 0$. An arbitrage is therefore, in effect, a portfolio offering "something for nothing." Not surprisingly, it will later be shown that an arbitrage is naturally ruled out, and this gives a characterization of security prices as follows: A *state-price* vector is a vector ψ

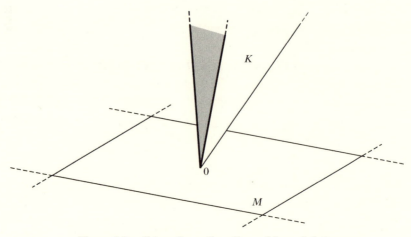

Figure 1.1.   *Separating a Cone from a Linear Subspace*

in $\mathbb{R}_{++}^S$ with $q = D\psi$. We can think of ψ_j as the marginal cost of obtaining an additional unit of account in state j.

Theorem.   *There is no arbitrage if and only if there is a state-price vector.*

Proof: The proof is an application of the Separating Hyperplane Theorem. Let $L = \mathbb{R} \times \mathbb{R}^S$ and $M = \{(-q \cdot \theta, D^{\top}\theta) : \theta \in \mathbb{R}^N\}$, a linear subspace of L. Let $K = \mathbb{R}_+ \times \mathbb{R}_+^S$, which is a cone (meaning that if x is in K, then λx is in K for each strictly positive scalar λ.) Both K and M are closed and convex subsets of L. There is no arbitrage if and only if K and M intersect precisely at 0, as pictured in Figure 1.1.

Suppose $K \cap M = \{0\}$. The Separating Hyperplane Theorem (in a version for closed cones that is found in Appendix B) implies the existence of a linear functional $F : L \to \mathbb{R}$ such that $F(z) < F(x)$ for all z in M and nonzero x in K. Since M is a linear space, this implies that $F(z) = 0$ for all z in M and that $F(x) > 0$ for all nonzero x in K. The latter fact implies that there is some $\alpha > 0$ in $\mathbb{R}$ and $\psi \gg 0$ in $\mathbb{R}^S$ such that $F(v, c) = \alpha v + \psi \cdot c$, for any $(v, c) \in L$. This in turn implies that $-\alpha q \cdot \theta + \psi \cdot (D^{\top}\theta) = 0$ for all θ in $\mathbb{R}^N$. The vector ψ/α is therefore a state-price vector.

Conversely, if a state-price vector exists, then there is clearly no arbitrage.   ∎

B. Risk-Neutral Probabilities

We can view any p in $\mathbb{R}_+^S$ with $p_1 + \cdots + p_S = 1$ as a vector of probabilities of the corresponding states. Given a state-price vector ψ for the dividend-price pair (D, q), let $\psi_0 = \psi_1 + \cdots + \psi_S$ and, for any state j, let $\hat{\psi}_j = \psi_j / \psi_0$. We now have a vector $(\hat{\psi}_1, \ldots, \hat{\psi}_S)$ of probabilities and can write, for an arbitrary security i,

$$\frac{q_i}{\psi_0} = \hat{E}(D_i) \equiv \sum_{j=1}^{S} \hat{\psi}_j D_{ij},$$

viewing the normalized price of the security as its expected payoff under specially chosen "risk-neutral" probabilities. If there exists a portfolio $\bar{\theta}$ with $D^\top \bar{\theta} = (1, 1, \ldots, 1)$, then $\psi_0 = \bar{\theta} \cdot q$ is the discount on riskless borrowing and, for any security i, $q_i = \psi_0 \hat{E}(D_i)$, showing any security's price to be its discounted expected payoff in this sense of artificially chosen probabilities.

C. Optimality and Asset Pricing

Suppose the dividend-price pair (D, q) is given and there is some portfolio θ with payoff $D^\top \theta > 0$. An *agent* is defined by a strictly increasing *utility function* $U : \mathbb{R}_+^S \rightarrow \mathbb{R}$ and an *endowment* e in $\mathbb{R}_+^S$. This leaves the *budget-feasible set*

$$X(q, e) = \left\{ e + D^\top \theta \in \mathbb{R}_+^S : \theta \in \mathbb{R}^N, \ q \cdot \theta \leq 0 \right\},$$

and the problem

$$\sup_{c \in X(q,e)} U(c). \tag{1}$$

Because U is strictly increasing and there is a portfolio θ with $D^\top \theta > 0$, the wealth constraint $q \cdot \theta \leq 0$ is binding. That is, if $C^* = e + D^\top \theta^*$ solves (1), then $q \cdot \theta^* = 0$.

Proposition. *If there is a solution to (1), then there is no arbitrage. If U is continuous and there is no arbitrage, then there is a solution to (1).*

Proof is left as an exercise.

Theorem. *Suppose that c^* is a strictly positive solution to (1) and that the vector $\partial U(c^*)$ of partial derivatives of U at c^* exists and is strictly positive. Then there is some scalar $\lambda > 0$ such that $\lambda \partial U(c^*)$ is a state-price vector.*

Proof: The first-order condition for optimality is that for any θ with $q \cdot \theta = 0$, the marginal utility for buying the portfolio θ is zero. This is expressed more precisely in the following way: The strict positivity of c^* implies that for any portfolio θ, there is some scalar $k > 0$ such that $c^* + \alpha D^\top \theta \geq 0$ for all α in $[-k, k]$. Let $g_\theta : [-k, k] \to \mathbb{R}$ be defined by

$$g_\theta(\alpha) = U(c^* + \alpha D^\top \theta).$$

Suppose $q \cdot \theta = 0$. The optimality of c^* implies that g_θ is maximized at $\alpha = 0$. The first-order condition for this is that $g'_\theta(0) = \partial U(c^*)^\top D^\top \theta = 0$. We can conclude that, for any θ in $\mathbb{R}^N$, if $q \cdot \theta = 0$, then $\partial U(c^*)^\top D^\top \theta = 0$. From this, there is some scalar μ such that $\partial U(c^*)^\top D^\top = \mu q$.

By assumption, there is some portfolio θ with $D^\top \theta > 0$. From the existence of a solution to (1), there is no arbitrage, implying that $q \cdot \theta > 0$. We have

$$\mu q \cdot \theta = \partial U(c^*)^\top D^\top \theta > 0.$$

Thus $\mu > 0$. We let $\lambda = 1/\mu$, obtaining

$$q = \lambda D \partial U(c^*), \tag{2}$$

implying that $\lambda \partial U(c^*)$ is a state-price vector. ∎

Although we have assumed that U is strictly increasing, this does not necessarily mean that $\partial U(c^*) \gg 0$. If U is concave and strictly increasing, however, it is always true that $\partial U(c^*) \gg 0$.

Corollary. *If U is concave and differentiable, then a budget-feasible consumption choice $c^* \gg 0$ is optimal if and only if $\lambda \partial U(c^*)$ is a state-price vector for some scalar $\lambda > 0$.*

This follows from the sufficiency of the first-order conditions for concave objective functions. The idea is illustrated in Figure 1.2. In that figure, there are only two states, and a state-price vector is a suitably normalized nonzero positive vector orthogonal to the set $B = \{D^\top \theta : q \cdot \theta = 0\}$ of budget-neutral consumption changes. The first-order condition for optimality of c^* is that movement in any feasible direction away from c^* has negative or zero marginal utility, which is equivalent to the statement that the budget-neutral set is tangent at c^* to the preferred set $\{c : U(c) \geq U(c^*)\}$, as shown in the figure. This is equivalent to the statement that $\partial U(c^*)$ is orthogonal to B, consistent with the last corollary. Figure 1.3 illustrates a strictly suboptimal consumption choice c, at which the derivative vector $\partial U(c)$ is not co-linear with the state-price vector ψ.

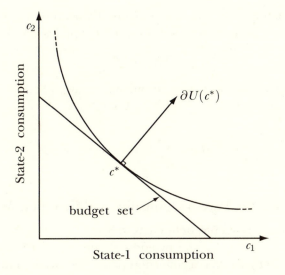

Figure 1.2. *First-Order Conditions for Optimal Consumption Choice*

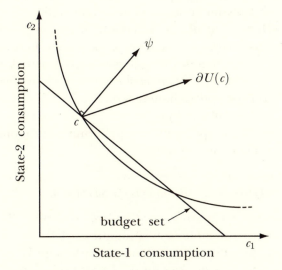

Figure 1.3. *A Strictly Suboptimal Consumption Choice*

We consider the special case of an *expected utility* function U, defined by a given vector p of probabilities and by some $u : \mathbb{R}_+ \to \mathbb{R}$ according to

$$U(c) = E\left[u(c)\right] \equiv \sum_{j=1}^{S} p_j u(c_j). \tag{3}$$

One can check that for $c \gg 0$, if u is differentiable, then $\partial U(c)_j = p_j u'(c_j)$. For this expected utility function, (2) therefore applies if and only if

$$q = \lambda E\left[Du'(c^*)\right], \tag{4}$$

with the obvious notational convention. As we saw in Section 1B, one can also write (2) or (4), with $\hat{\psi}_j = u'(c_j^*)p_j / E[u'(c^*)]$, as

$$\frac{q_i}{\psi_0} = \hat{E}(D_i) \equiv \sum_{j=1}^{S} D_{ij}\hat{\psi}_j, \qquad 1 \le i \le N. \tag{5}$$

D. Equilibrium, Pareto Optimality, and Complete Markets

Suppose there are m agents, defined as in Section 1C by strictly increasing utility functions $U_1, \ldots, U_m$ and by endowments $e^1, \ldots, e^m$. An *equilibrium* for the *economy* $[(U_i, e^i), D]$ is a collection $(\theta^1, \ldots, \theta^m, q)$ such that, given the security-price vector q, for each agent i, θ^i solves $\sup_\theta U_i(e^i + D^\top \theta)$ subject to $q \cdot \theta \le 0$, and such that $\sum_{i=1}^{m} \theta^i = 0$. The existence of equilibrium is treated in the exercises and in sources cited in the notes.

With $\mathrm{span}(D) \equiv \{D^\top \theta : \theta \in \mathbb{R}^N\}$ denoting the set of possible portfolio payoffs, markets are *complete* if $\mathrm{span}(D) = \mathbb{R}^S$, and are otherwise *incomplete*.

Let $e = e^1 + \cdots + e^m$ denote the aggregate endowment. A consumption *allocation* $(c^1, \ldots, c^m)$ in $\left(\mathbb{R}_+^S\right)^m$ is *feasible* if $c^1 + \cdots + c^m \le e$. A feasible allocation $(c^1, \ldots, c^m)$ is *Pareto optimal* if there is no feasible allocation $(\hat{c}^1, \ldots, \hat{c}^m)$ with $U_i(\hat{c}^i) \ge U_i(c^i)$ for all i and with $U_i(\hat{c}^i) > U_i(c^i)$ for some i. Complete markets and the Pareto optimality of equilibrium allocations are almost equivalent properties of any economy.

Proposition. *Suppose markets are complete and $(\theta^1, \ldots, \theta^m, q)$ is an equilibrium. Then the associated equilibrium allocation is Pareto optimal.*

This is sometimes known as *The First Welfare Theorem.* The proof, requiring only the strict monotonicity of utilities, is left as an exercise. We have established the sufficiency of complete markets for Pareto optimality. The necessity of complete markets for the Pareto optimality of equilibrium allocations does not always follow. For example, if the initial endowment allocation $(e^1, \ldots, e^m)$ happens by chance to be Pareto optimal, then any equilibrium allocation is also Pareto optimal, regardless of the span of securities. It would be unusual, however, for the initial endowment to be Pareto optimal. Although beyond the scope of this course, it can be shown that with incomplete markets and under natural assumptions on utility, for almost every endowment, the equilibrium allocation is not Pareto optimal.

E. Pareto Optimality and the Representative Agent

Aside from its allocational implications, Pareto optimality is also a convenient property for the purpose of security pricing. In order to see this, consider, for each vector $\lambda \in \mathbb{R}^m_+$ of "agent weights," the utility function $U_\lambda : \mathbb{R}^S_+ \to \mathbb{R}$ defined by

$$U_\lambda(x) = \sup_{(c^1,\ldots,c^m)} \sum_{i=1}^m \lambda_i U_i(c^i) \qquad \text{subject to } c^1 + \cdots + c^m \leq x. \qquad (6)$$

Lemma. *Suppose that for all i, U_i is concave. An allocation $(c^1,\ldots,c^m)$ that is feasible is Pareto optimal if and only if there is some nonzero $\lambda \in \mathbb{R}^m_+$ such that $(c^1,\ldots,c^m)$ solves (6) at $x = e = c^1 + \cdots + c^m$.*

Proof: Suppose that $(c^1,\ldots,c^m)$ is Pareto optimal. Let

$$\mathcal{U} = \{y \in \mathbb{R}^m : y_i \leq U_i(x^i) - U_i(c^i), \ x \in \mathcal{A}\},$$

where $\mathcal{A}$ is the set of feasible allocations. Let $J = \{y \in \mathbb{R}^m_+ : y \neq 0\}$. Since $\mathcal{U}$ is convex (by the concavity of utility functions) and $J \cap \mathcal{U}$ is empty (by Pareto optimality), the Separating Hyperplane Theorem (Appendix B) implies that there is a nonzero vector λ in $\mathbb{R}^m$ such that $\lambda \cdot y \leq \lambda \cdot z$ for each y in $\mathcal{U}$ and each z in J. Since $0 \in \mathcal{U}$, we know that $\lambda \geq 0$, proving the first part of the result. The second part is easy to show as an exercise. ∎

Proposition. *Suppose that for all i, U_i is concave. Suppose that markets are complete and that $(\theta^1,\ldots,\theta^m, q)$ is an equilibrium. Then there exists some nonzero $\lambda \in \mathbb{R}^m_+$ such that $(0, q)$ is a (no-trade) equilibrium for the single-agent economy $[(U_\lambda, e), D]$ defined by (6). Moreover, the equilibrium consumption allocation $(c^1,\ldots,c^m)$ solves the allocation problem (6) at the aggregate endowment. That is, $U_\lambda(e) = \sum_i \lambda_i U_i(c^i)$.*

Proof: Since there is an equilibrium, there is no arbitrage, and therefore there is a state-price vector ψ. Since markets are complete, this implies that the problem of any agent i can be reduced to

$$\sup_{c \in \mathbb{R}^S_+} U_i(c) \qquad \text{subject to } \psi \cdot c \leq \psi \cdot e^i.$$

We can assume that e^i is not zero, for otherwise $c^i = 0$ and agent i can be eliminated from the problem without loss of generality. By the Saddle Point Theorem of Appendix B, there is a Lagrange multiplier $\alpha_i \geq 0$ such that c^i solves the problem

$$\sup_{c \in \mathbb{R}^S_+} U_i(c) - \alpha_i \left(\psi \cdot c - \psi \cdot e^i \right).$$

(The Slater condition is satisfied since e^i is not zero and $\psi \gg 0$.) Since U_i is strictly increasing, $\alpha_i > 0$. Let $\lambda_i = 1/\alpha_i$. For any feasible allocation $(x^1, \ldots, x^m)$, we have

$$\sum_{i=1}^{m} \lambda_i U_i(c^i) = \sum_{i=1}^{m} \left[\lambda_i U_i(c^i) - \lambda_i \alpha_i \left(\psi \cdot c^i - \psi \cdot e^i \right) \right]$$

$$\geq \sum_{i=1}^{m} \lambda_i \left[U_i(x^i) - \alpha_i \left(\psi \cdot x^i - \psi \cdot e^i \right) \right]$$

$$= \sum_{i=1}^{m} \lambda_i U_i(x^i) - \psi \cdot \sum_{i=1}^{m} (x^i - e^i)$$

$$\geq \sum_{i=1}^{m} \lambda_i U_i(x^i).$$

This shows that $(c^1, \ldots, c^m)$ solves the allocation problem (6). We must also show that no trade is optimal for the single agent with utility function U_λ and endowment e. If not, there is some x in $\mathbb{R}^S_+$ such that $U_\lambda(x) > U_\lambda(e)$ and $\psi \cdot x \leq \psi \cdot e$. By the definition of U_λ, this would imply the existence of an allocation $(x^1, \ldots, x^m)$, not necessarily feasible, such that $\sum_i \lambda_i U_i(x^i) > \sum_i \lambda_i U_i(e^i)$ and

$$\sum_i \lambda_i \alpha_i \psi \cdot x^i = \psi \cdot x \leq \psi \cdot e = \sum_i \lambda_i \alpha_i \psi \cdot c^i.$$

Putting these two inequalities together, we have

$$\sum_{i=1}^{m} \lambda_i \left[U_i(x^i) - \alpha_i \psi \cdot (x^i - e^i) \right] > \sum_{i=1}^{m} \lambda_i \left[U_i(c^i) - \alpha_i \psi \cdot (c^i - e^i) \right],$$

which contradicts the fact that, for each agent i, (c^i, α_i) is a saddle point for that agent's problem. ∎

Corollary 1. *If, moreover, $e \gg 0$ and U_λ is differentiable at e, then λ can be chosen so that $\partial U_\lambda(e)$ is a state-price vector, meaning*

$$q = D\partial U_\lambda(e). \tag{7}$$

Corollary 2. *Suppose there is a fixed vector p of state probabilities such that for all i, $U_i(c) = E[u_i(c)] \equiv \sum_{j=1}^{S} p_j u_i(c_j)$, for some $u_i(\cdot)$. Then $U_\lambda(c) = E[u_\lambda(c)]$,* *where, for each y in* $\mathbb{R}_+$,

$$u_\lambda(y) = \max_{x \in \mathbb{R}_+^m} \sum_{i=1}^m \lambda_i u_i(x_i) \qquad \text{subject to } x_1 + \cdots + x_m \leq y.$$

In this case, (7) is equivalent to $q = E[Du'_\lambda(e)]$.

Extensions of this *representative-agent* asset pricing formula will crop up frequently in later chapters. Conditions for the differentiability of U_λ are given in an exercise. It is enough that the equilibrium allocation $(c^1, \ldots, c^m)$ is strictly positive and that for all i, U_i is of the expected utility form $U_i(c) = E[u_i(c)]$, where u_i is strictly concave and differentiable at c^i.

F. State-Price Beta Models

We fix a vector $p \gg 0$ in $\mathbb{R}^S$ of probabilities for this section, and for any x in $\mathbb{R}^S$ we write $E(x) = p_1 x_1 + \cdots + p_S x_S$. For any x and π in $\mathbb{R}^S$, we take $x\pi$ to be the vector $(x_1\pi_1, \ldots, x_S\pi_S)$. The following version of the *Riesz Representation Theorem* can be shown as an exercise.

Lemma. *Suppose* $F : \mathbb{R}^S \to \mathbb{R}$ *is linear. Then there is a unique* π *in* $\mathbb{R}^S$ *such that for all x in* $\mathbb{R}^S$, *we have* $F(x) = E(\pi x)$. *Moreover, F is strictly increasing if and only if* $\pi \gg 0$.

Corollary. *A dividend-price pair* (D, q) *admits no arbitrage if and only if there is some* $\pi \gg 0$ *in* $\mathbb{R}^S$ *such that* $q = E(D\pi)$.

Proof: Given a state-price vector ψ, let $\pi_s = \psi_s/p_s$. Conversely, if π has the assumed property, then $\psi_s = p_s \pi_s$ defines a state-price vector ψ. ∎

Given (D, q), we refer to any vector π given by this result as a *state-price deflator*. (The terms *state-price density* and *state-price kernel* are often used synonymously with state-price deflator.) For example, the representative-agent pricing model of Corollary 2 of Section 1E shows that we can take $\pi_s = u'_\lambda(e_s)$.

For any x and y in $\mathbb{R}^S$, the *covariance* $\text{cov}(x, y) \equiv E(xy) - E(x)E(y)$ is a measure of covariation between x and y that is useful in asset pricing applications. For any such x and y with $\text{var}(y) \equiv \text{cov}(y, y) \neq 0$, we can always represent x in the form $x = \alpha + \beta y + \epsilon$, where $\beta = \text{cov}(y, x)/\text{var}(y)$, where $\text{cov}(y, \epsilon) = E(\epsilon) = 0$, and where α is a scalar. This *linear regression* of x on y is uniquely defined. The coefficient β is called the associated *regression coefficient*.

Suppose (D, q) admits no arbitrage. For any portfolio θ with $q \cdot \theta \neq 0$, the *return* on θ is the vector R^θ in $\mathbb{R}^S$ defined by $R^\theta_s = (D^\top \theta)_s / q \cdot \theta$. Fixing a state-price deflator π, for any such portfolio θ, we have $E(\pi R^\theta) = 1$. Suppose there is a *riskless portfolio*, meaning some portfolio θ with constant return R^0. We then call R^0 the *riskless return*. A bit of algebra shows that for any portfolio θ with a return, we have

$$E(R^\theta) - R^0 = -\frac{\text{cov}(R^\theta, \pi)}{E(\pi)}.$$

Thus, covariation with π has a negative effect on expected return, as one might expect from the interpretation of state prices as shadow prices for wealth.

The *correlation* between any x and y in $\mathbb{R}^S$ is zero if either has zero variance, and is otherwise defined by

$$\text{corr}(x, y) = \frac{\text{cov}(x, y)}{\sqrt{\text{var}(x)\,\text{var}(y)}}.$$

There is always a portfolio θ^* solving the problem

$$\sup_\theta \text{corr}(D^\top \theta, \pi). \qquad (8)$$

If there is such a portfolio θ^* with a return R^* having nonzero variance, then it can be shown as an exercise that for any return R^θ,

$$E(R^\theta) - R^0 = \beta_\theta \left[E(R^*) - R^0\right], \qquad (9)$$

where

$$\beta_\theta = \frac{\text{cov}(R^*, R^\theta)}{\text{var}(R^*)}.$$

If markets are complete, then R^* is of course perfectly correlated with the state-price deflator.

Formula (9) is a *state-price beta model*, showing excess expected returns on portfolios to be proportional to the excess return on a portfolio having maximal correlation with a state-price deflator, where the constant of proportionality is the associated regression coefficient. The formula can be extended to the case in which there is no riskless return. Another exercise carries this idea, under additional assumptions, to the *Capital Asset Pricing Model*, or *CAPM*.

Exercises

1.1 The dividend-price pair (D, q) of Section 1A is defined to be *weakly arbitrage-free* if $q \cdot \theta \geq 0$ whenever $D^\top \theta \geq 0$. Show that (D, q) is weakly arbitrage-free if and only if there exists ("weak" state prices) $\psi \in \mathbb{R}_+^S$ such that $q = D\psi$. This fact is known as *Farkas's Lemma*.

1.2 Prove the assertion in Section 1A that (D, q) is arbitrage-free if and only if there exists some $\psi \in \mathbb{R}_{++}^S$ such that $q = D\psi$. Instead of following the proof given in Section 1A, use the following result, sometimes known as the *Theorem of the Alternative*.

Stiemke's Lemma. *Suppose A is an $m \times n$ matrix. Then one and only one of the following is true:*

    (a) There exists x in $\mathbb{R}_{++}^n$ with $Ax = 0$.
    (b) There exists y in $\mathbb{R}^m$ with $y^\top A > 0$.

1.3 Show for $U(c) \equiv E[u(c)]$ as defined by (3) that (2) is equivalent to (4).

1.4 Prove the existence of an equilibrium as defined in Section 1D under these assumptions: There exists some portfolio θ with payoff $D^\top \theta > 0$ and, for all i, $e^i \gg 0$ and U_i is continuous, strictly concave, and strictly increasing. This is a demanding exercise, and calls for the following general result.

Kakutani's Fixed Point Theorem. *Suppose Z is a nonempty convex compact subset of $\mathbb{R}^n$, and for each x in Z, $\varphi(x)$ is a nonempty convex compact subset of Z. Suppose also that $\{(x, y) \in Z \times Z : x \in \varphi(y)\}$ is closed. Then there exists x^* in Z such that $x^* \in \varphi(x^*)$.*

1.5 Prove Proposition 1D. Hint: The maintained assumption of strict monotonicity of $U_i(\cdot)$ should be used.

1.6 Suppose that the endowment allocation $(e^1, \ldots, e^m)$ is Pareto optimal.

(A) Show, as claimed in Section 1D, that any equilibrium allocation is Pareto optimal.

(B) Suppose that there is some portfolio θ with $D^\top \theta > 0$ and, for all i, that U_i is concave and $e^i \gg 0$. Show that $(e^1, \ldots, e^m)$ is itself an equilibrium allocation.

1.7 Prove Proposition 1C. Hint: A continuous real-valued function on a compact set has a maximum.

1.8 Prove Corollary 1 of Proposition 1E.

1.9   Prove Corollary 2 of Proposition 1E.

1.10   Suppose in addition to the assumptions of Proposition 1E that

>   (a) $e = e^1 + \cdots + e^m$ is in $\mathbb{R}^S_{++}$;
>   (b) for all i, U_i is concave and twice continuously differentiable in $\mathbb{R}^S_{++}$;
>   (c) for all i, c^i is in $\mathbb{R}^S_{++}$ and the Hessian matrix $\partial^2 U(c^i)$, which is negative semi-definite by concavity, is in fact negative definite.

Property (c) can be replaced with the assumption of *regular preferences*, as defined in a source cited below in the Notes.

(A) Show that the assumption that $\partial U_\lambda(e)$ exists is justified and, moreover, that for each i there is a scalar $\gamma_i > 0$ such that $\partial U_\lambda(e) = \gamma_i \partial U_i(c^i)$. (This co-linearity is known as "equal marginal rates of substitution," a property of any Pareto optimal allocation.) Hint: Use the following:

Implicit Function Theorem. Suppose for given m and n that $f : \mathbb{R}^m \times \mathbb{R}^n \to \mathbb{R}^n$ is C^k (k times continuously differentiable) for some $k \geq 1$. Suppose also that the Jacobian matrix $\partial f(a, b)$ of f at some (a, b) is nonsingular. If $f(a, b) = 0$, then there exist scalars $\epsilon > 0$ and $\delta > 0$ and a C^k function $Z : \mathbb{R}^m \to \mathbb{R}^n$ such that if $\|x - a\| < \epsilon$, then $f[x, Z(x)] = 0$ and $\|Z(x) - b\| < \delta$.

(B) Show that the negative definite part of condition (c) is satisfied if $e \gg 0$ and, for all i, U_i is an expected utility function of the form $U_i(c) = E[u_i(c)]$, where u_i is strictly concave with an unbounded derivative on $(0, \infty)$.

(C) Obtain the result of Part (A) without assuming the existence of second derivatives of the utilities. (You would therefore not exploit the Hessian matrix or Implicit Function Theorem.)

1.11   (Binomial Option Pricing)   As an application of the results in Section 1A, consider the following two-state ($S = 2$) option-pricing problem. There are $N = 3$ securities:

>   (a) a stock, with initial price $q_1 > 0$ and dividend $D_{11} = Gq_1$ in state 1 and dividend $D_{12} = Bq_1$ in state 2, where $G > B > 0$ are the "good" and "bad" gross returns, respectively;
>   (b) a riskless bond, with initial price $q_2 > 0$ and dividend $D_{21} = D_{22} = Rq_2$ in both states (that is, R is the riskless return and R^{-1} is the discount);
>   (c) a *call option* on the stock, with initial price $q_3 = C$ and dividend $D_{3j} = (D_{1j} - K)^+ \equiv \max(D_{1j} - K, 0)$ for both states $j = 1$ and

$j = 2$, where $K \geq 0$ is the *exercise price* of the option. (The call option gives its holder the right, but not the obligation, to pay K for the stock, with dividend, after the state is revealed.)

(A) Show necessary and sufficient conditions on G, B, and R for the absence of arbitrage involving only the stock and bond.

(B) Assuming no arbitrage for the three securities, calculate the call-option price C explicitly in terms of q_1, G, R, B, and K. Find the state-price probabilities $\hat{\psi}_1$ and $\hat{\psi}_2$ referred to in Section 1B in terms of G, B, and R, and show that $C = R^{-1}\hat{E}(D_3)$, where $\hat{E}$ denotes expectation with respect to $(\hat{\psi}_1, \hat{\psi}_2)$.

1.12 (CAPM) In the setting of Section 1D, suppose $(c^1, \ldots, c^m)$ is a strictly positive equilibrium consumption allocation. For any agent i, suppose utility is of the expected-utility form $U_i(c) = E[u_i(c)]$. For any agent i, suppose there are fixed positive constants $\bar{c}$ and b_i such that for any state j, we have $c_j^i < \bar{c}$ and $u_i(x) = x - b_i x^2$ for all $x \leq \bar{c}$.

(A) In the context of Corollary 2 of Section 1E, show that $u_\lambda'(e) = k - Ke$ for some positive constants k and K. From this, derive the CAPM

$$q = AE(D) - B\operatorname{cov}(D, e), \tag{10}$$

for positive constants A and B, where $\operatorname{cov}(D, e) \in \mathbb{R}^N$ is the vector of covariances between the security dividends and the aggregate endowment.

Suppose for a given portfolio θ that each of the following is well defined:

- the return $R^\theta \equiv D^\top \theta / q \cdot \theta$;
- the return R^M on a portfolio M with payoff $D^\top M = e$;
- the return R^0 on a portfolio θ^0 with $\operatorname{cov}(D^\top \theta^0, e) = 0$;
- $\beta_\theta = \operatorname{cov}(R^\theta, R^M) / \operatorname{var}(R^M)$.

The return R^M is sometimes called the *market return*. The return R^0 is called the *zero-beta return* and is the return on a riskless bond if one exists. Prove the "beta" form of the CAPM

$$E(R^\theta - R^0) = \beta_\theta E(R^M - R^0). \tag{11}$$

(B) Part (A) relies on the completeness of markets. Without any such assumption, but assuming that the equilibrium allocation $(c^1, \ldots, c^m)$ is strictly positive, show that the same beta form (11) applies, provided we extend the definition of the market return R^M to be the return on any portfolio solving

$$\sup_{\theta \in \mathbb{R}^N} \operatorname{corr}(R^\theta, e). \tag{12}$$

For complete markets, corr $(R^M, e) = 1$, so the result of part (A) is a special case.

(C) The CAPM applies essentially as stated without the quadratic expected-utility assumption provided that each agent i is *strictly variance-averse*, in that $U_i(x) > U_i(y)$ whenever $E(x) = E(y)$ and $\text{var}(x) < \text{var}(y)$. Formalize this statement by providing a reasonable set of supporting technical conditions.

We remark that a common alternative formulation of the CAPM allows security portfolios in initial endowments $\hat{\theta}^1, \ldots, \hat{\theta}^m$ with $\sum_{i=1}^{m} \hat{\theta}^i_j = 1$ for all j. In this case, with the total endowment e redefined by $e = \sum_{i=1}^{m} e^i + D^\top \theta^i$, the same CAPM (11) applies. If $e^i = 0$ for all i, then even in incomplete markets, corr $(R^M, e) = 1$, since (12) is solved by $\theta = (1, 1, \ldots, 1)$. The Notes below provide references.

1.13   An *Arrow-Debreu equilibrium* for $[(U_i, e^i), D]$ is a nonzero vector ψ in $\mathbb{R}^S_+$ and a feasible consumption allocation $(c^1, \ldots, c^m)$ such that for each i, c^i solves $\sup_c U_i(c)$ subject to $\psi \cdot c^i \le \psi \cdot e^i$. Suppose that markets are complete, in that $\text{span}(D) = \mathbb{R}^S$. Show that $(c^1, \ldots, c^m)$ is an Arrow-Debreu consumption allocation if and only if it is an equilibrium consumption allocation in the sense of Section 1D.

1.14   Suppose (D, q) admits no arbitrage. Show that there is a unique state-price vector if and only if markets are complete.

1.15   (Aggregation)   For the "representative-agent" problem (6), suppose for all i that $U_i(c) = E[u(c)]$, where $u(c) = c^\gamma/\gamma$ for some nonzero scalar $\gamma < 1$.

(A) Show for any nonzero agent weight vector $\lambda \in \mathbb{R}^m_+$ that $U_\lambda(c) = E[kc^\gamma/\gamma]$ for some scalar $k > 0$ and that (6) is solved by $c^i = k_i x$ for some scalar $k_i \ge 0$ that is nonzero if and only if λ_i is nonzero.

(B) With this special utility assumption, prove, with the assumption that $e^i \in \text{span}(D)$ for all i, that there is an equilibrium consumption allocation that is Pareto optimal.

1.16   (State-Price Beta Model)   This exercise is to prove and extend the state-price beta model (9) of Section 1F.

(A) Show problem (8) is solved by any portfolio θ such that $\pi = D^\top \theta + \epsilon$, where $\text{cov}(\epsilon, D^j) = 0$ for any security j, where $D^j \in \mathbb{R}^S$ is the payoff of security j.

(B) Given a solution θ to (8) such that R^θ is well defined with nonzero variance, prove (9).

(C) Reformulate (9) for the case in which there is no riskless return by redefining R^0 to be the expected return on any portfolio θ such that R^θ is well defined and $\operatorname{cov}(R^\theta, \pi) = 0$, assuming such a portfolio exists.

1.17 Prove the Riesz representation lemma of Section 1F. The following hint is perhaps unnecessary in this simple setting but allows the result to be extended to a broad variety of spaces called *Hilbert spaces*. Given a vector space L, a function $(\cdot \mid \cdot) : L \times L \to \mathbb{R}$ is called an *inner product* for L if for any x, y, and z in L and any scalar α we have the five properties:

(a) $(x \mid y) = (y \mid x)$
(b) $(x + y \mid z) = (x \mid z) + (y \mid z)$
(c) $(\alpha x \mid y) = \alpha(x \mid y)$
(d) $(x \mid x) \geq 0$
(e) $(x \mid x) = 0$ if and only if $x = 0$.

Suppose a finite-dimensional vector space L has an inner product $(\cdot \mid \cdot)$. (This defines a special case of a Hilbert space.) Two vectors x and y are defined to be *orthogonal* if $(x \mid y) = 0$. For any linear subspace H of L and any x in L, it can be shown that there is a unique y in H such that $(x - y \mid z) = 0$ for all z in H. This vector y is the orthogonal projection in L of x onto H, and solves the problem $\min_{h \in H} \|x - h\|$. Let $L = \mathbb{R}^S$. For any x and y in L, let $(x \mid y) = E(xy)$. We must show that given a linear functional F, there is a unique π with $F(x) = (\pi \mid x)$ for all x. Let $J = \{x : F(x) = 0\}$. If $J = L$, then F is the zero functional, and the unique representation is $\pi = 0$. If not, there is some z such that $F(z) = 1$ and $(z \mid x) = 0$ for all x in J. Show this using the idea of orthogonal projection. Then show that $\pi = z/(z \mid z)$ represents F, using the fact that for any x, we have $x - F(x)z \in J$.

Notes

The basic approach of this chapter follows Arrow (1953), taking a general-equilibrium perspective originating with Walras (1874–77). Black (1993) offers a persepctive on the general equilibrium approach and a critique of other approaches. The state-pricing implications of no arbitrage found in Section 1A originate with Ross (1978). The idea of "risk-neutral" probabilities apparently originates with Arrow (1970: 131), a revision of Arrow (1953), and appears as well in Drèze (1971). Proposition 1D is the First Welfare Theorem of Arrow (1951) and Debreu (1954). The generic inoptimality of incomplete markets equilibrium allocations can be gleaned from sources cited by Geanakoplos (1990). Indeed, Geanakoplos and Polemarchakis (1986) show that even a reasonable notion of constrained optimality generically fails in certain incomplete markets settings. See, however, Kajii (1994) and references cited in the Notes of Chapter 2 for mitigating results. Mas-Colell (1987) and Werner (1991) also treat constrained optimality.

The "representative-agent" approach goes back, at least, to Negishi (1960). The existence of a representative agent is no more than an illustrative simplification in this setting, and should not be confused with the more demanding notion of aggregation of Gorman (1953) found in Exercise 1.15. In Chapter 9, the existence of a representative agent with smooth utility, based on Exercise 1.11, is important for technical reasons.

Debreu (1972) provides preference assumptions that substitute for the existence of a negative-definite Hessian matrix of each agent's utility function at the equilibrium allocation. For more on regular preferences and the differential approach to general equilibrium, see Mas-Colell (1985) and Balasko (1989). Kreps (1988) reviews the theory of choice and utility representation of preferences. For Farkas's and Stiemke's Lemmas, and other forms of the Theorem of the Alternative, see Gale (1960).

Arrow and Debreu (1954) and, in a slightly different model, McKenzie (1954) are responsible for a proof of the existence of complete-markets equilibria. Debreu (1982) surveys the existence problem. Standard introductory treatments of general equilibrium theory are given by Debreu (1959) and Hildenbrand and Kirman (1989). In this setting, with incomplete markets, Polemarchakis and Siconolfi (1991) address the failure of existence unless one has a portfolio θ with payoff $D^\top \theta > 0$. Geanakoplos (1990) surveys other literature on the existence of equilibria in incomplete markets, some of which takes the alternative of defining security payoffs in nominal units of account, while allowing consumption of multiple commodities. Most of the literature allows for an initial period of consumption before the realization of the uncertain state. For related results in multiperiod settings, references are cited in the Notes of Chapter 2.

Hellwig (1991), Mas-Colell and Monteiro (1991), and Monteiro (1991) have recently shown existence with a continuum of states. Geanakoplos and Polemarchakis (1986) and Chae (1988) show existence in a model closely related to that studied in this chapter. Grodal and Vind (1988) and Yamazaki (1991) show existence with alternative formulations. With multiple commodities or multiple periods, existence is not guaranteed under any natural conditions, as shown by Hart (1975), who gives a counterexample. For these more delicate cases, the literature on generic existence is cited in the Notes of Chapter 2.

The CAPM is due to Sharpe (1964) and Lintner (1965). The version without a riskless asset is due to Black (1972). Allingham (1991),

Berk (1992), and Nielsen (1990a,b) address the existence of equilibrium in the CAPM. Characterization of the mean-variance model and two-fund separation is provided by Bottazzi, Hens, and Löffler (1994), and Nielsen (1993a,b). Löffler (1994) provides sufficient conditions for variance aversion in terms of mean-variance preferences. Ross (1976) introduced the *arbitrage pricing theory*, a multifactor model of asset returns that in terms of expected returns can be thought of as an extension of the CAPM. In this regard, see also Bray (1994a,b) and Gilles and LeRoy (1991). Balasko and Cass (1986) and Balasko, Cass, and Siconolfi (1990) treat equilibrium with constrained participation in security trading. See, also, Hara (1994).

The binomial option-pricing formula of Exercise 1.11 is from an early edition of William Sharpe's text, *Investments* (1985), and is extended in Chapter 2 to a multiperiod setting. The hint given for the demonstration of the Riesz representation exercise is condensed from the proof given by Luenberger (1969) of the *Riesz-Frechet Theorem*: For any Hilbert space H with inner product $(\cdot \mid \cdot)$, any continuous linear functional $F : H \to \mathbb{R}$ has a unique π in H such that $F(x) = (\pi \mid x)$, $x \in H$. The Fixed Point Theorem of Exercise 1.4 is from Kakutani (1941).

2

The Basic Multiperiod Model

THIS CHAPTER EXTENDS the results of Chapter 1 on arbitrage, optimality, and equilibrium to a multiperiod setting. A connection is drawn between state prices and martingales for the purpose of representing security prices. The exercises include the consumption-based capital asset pricing model and the multiperiod "binomial" option pricing model.

A. Uncertainty

As in Chapter 1, there is some finite set, say Ω, of states. In order to handle multiperiod issues, however, we will treat uncertainty a bit more formally as a *probability space* $(\Omega, \mathcal{F}, P)$, with $\mathcal{F}$ denoting the *tribe* of subsets of Ω that are *events* (and can therefore be assigned a probability), and with P a *probability measure* assigning to any event B in $\mathcal{F}$ its probability $P(B)$. Those not familiar with the definition of a probability space can consult Appendix A.

There are $T + 1$ dates: $0, 1, \ldots, T$. At each of these, a tribe $\mathcal{F}_t \subset \mathcal{F}$ denotes the set of events corresponding to the information available at time t. That is, if an event B is in $\mathcal{F}_t$, then at time t this event is known to be true or false. (A definition of tribes in terms of "partitions" of Ω is given in Exercise 2.11.) We adopt the usual convention that $\mathcal{F}_t \subset \mathcal{F}_s$ whenever $t \leq s$, meaning that events are never "forgotten." For simplicity, we also take it that every event in $\mathcal{F}_0$ has probability 0 or 1, meaning roughly that there is no information at time $t = 0$. Taken altogether, the *filtration* $\mathbb{F} = \{\mathcal{F}_0, \ldots, \mathcal{F}_T\}$ represents how information is revealed through time. For any random variable Y, we let $E_t(Y) = E(Y \mid \mathcal{F}_t)$ denote the conditional expectation of Y given $\mathcal{F}_t$. (Appendix A provides definitions of random variables and of conditional expectation.) An *adapted process* is a sequence $X = \{X_0, \ldots, X_T\}$ such that for each t, X_t is a random variable with respect to $(\Omega, \mathcal{F}_t)$. Informally, this means that at time t, the outcome of X_t is known.

21

An adapted process X is a *martingale* if, for any times t and $s > t$, we have $E_t(X_s) = X_t$. As we shall see, martingales are useful in the characterization of security prices. In order to simplify things, for any two random variables Y and Z, we always write $Y = Z$ if the probability that $Y \neq Z$ is zero.

B. Security Markets

A security is a claim to an adapted *dividend process*, say δ, with δ_t denoting the dividend paid by the security at time t. Each security has an adapted *security-price process* S, so that S_t is the price of the security, *ex dividend*, at time t. That is, at each time t, the security pays its dividend δ_t and is then available for trade at the price S_t. This convention implies that δ_0 plays no role in determining ex-dividend prices. The *cum-dividend* security price at time t is $S_t + \delta_t$.

Suppose there are N securities defined by the $\mathbb{R}^N$-valued adapted dividend process $\delta = (\delta^1, \ldots, \delta^N)$. These securities have some adapted price process $S = (S^1, \ldots, S^N)$. A *trading strategy* is an adapted process θ in $\mathbb{R}^N$. Here, $\theta_t = (\theta_t^1, \ldots, \theta_t^N)$ represents the portfolio held after trading at time t. The dividend process δ^θ *generated* by a trading strategy θ is defined by

$$\delta_t^\theta = \theta_{t-1} \cdot (S_t + \delta_t) - \theta_t \cdot S_t, \tag{1}$$

with "θ_{-1}" taken to be zero by convention.

C. Arbitrage, State Prices, and Martingales

Given a dividend-price pair (δ, S) for N securities, a trading strategy θ is an *arbitrage* if $\delta^\theta > 0$. Let Θ denote the space of trading strategies. For any θ and φ in Θ and scalars a and b, we have $a\delta^\theta + b\delta^\varphi = \delta^{a\theta + b\varphi}$. Thus the *marketed subspace* $M = \{\delta^\theta : \theta \in \Theta\}$ of dividend processes generated by trading strategies is a linear subspace of the space L of adapted processes.

Proposition. *There is no arbitrage if and only if there is a strictly increasing linear function $F : L \to \mathbb{R}$ such that $F(\delta^\theta) = 0$ for any trading strategy θ.*

Proof: The proof is almost identical to the first part of the proof of Theorem 1A. Let $L_+ = \{c \in L : c \geq 0\}$. There is no arbitrage if and only if the cone L_+ and the linear subspace M intersect precisely at zero. Suppose there is no arbitrage. The Separating Hyperplane Theorem, in a form given in Appendix B for cones, implies the existence of a nonzero linear functional F such that $F(x) < F(y)$ for each x in M and each nonzero y in L_+. Since M is a linear subspace, this implies that $F(x) = 0$ for each x in M, and thus that $F(y) > 0$ for each nonzero y in L_+. This implies that F is strictly increasing. The converse is immediate. ∎

The following result gives a convenient *Riesz representation* of a linear function on the space of adapted processes. Proof is left as an exercise, extending the single-period Riesz representation lemma of Section 1F.

Lemma. *For each linear function $F : L \to \mathbb{R}$ there is a unique π in L, called the Riesz representation of F, such that*

$$F(x) = E\left(\sum_{t=0}^{T} \pi_t x_t\right), \qquad x \in L.$$

If F is strictly increasing, then π is strictly positive.

For convenience, we call any strictly positive adapted process a *deflator*. A deflator π is a *state-price deflator* if, for all t,

$$S_t = \frac{1}{\pi_t} E_t\left(\sum_{j=t+1}^{T} \pi_j \delta_j\right). \tag{2}$$

For $t = T$, the right-hand side of (2) is zero, so $S_T = 0$ whenever there is a state-price deflator. The notion here of a state-price deflator is thus a natural extension of that of Chapter 1. It can be shown as an exercise that a deflator π is a state-price deflator if and only if, for any trading strategy θ,

$$\theta_t \cdot S_t = \frac{1}{\pi_t} E_t\left(\sum_{j=t+1}^{T} \pi_j \delta_j^\theta\right), \qquad t < T, \tag{3}$$

meaning roughly that the market value of a trading strategy is, at any time, the state-price discounted expected future dividends generated by the strategy.

The *gain process* G for (δ, S) is defined by $G_t = S_t + \sum_{j=1}^{t} \delta_j$. Given a deflator γ, the *deflated gain process* G^γ is defined by $G_t^\gamma = \gamma_t S_t + \sum_{j=1}^{t} \gamma_j \delta_j$. We can think of deflation as a change of numeraire. One can show as an easy exercise that π is a state-price deflator if and only if $S_T = 0$ and the state-price-deflated gain process G^π is a martingale.

Theorem. *The dividend-price pair (δ, S) admits no arbitrage if and only if there is a state-price deflator.*

Proof: Suppose there is no arbitrage. Then $S_T = 0$, for otherwise the strategy θ is an arbitrage when defined by $\theta_t = 0$, $t < T$, $\theta_T = -S_T$. The previous proposition implies that there is some strictly increasing linear function $F : L \to \mathbb{R}$ such that $F(\delta^\theta) = 0$ for any strategy θ. By the previous lemma, there is some deflator π such that $F(x) = E(\sum_{t=0}^{T} x_t \pi_t)$ for all x in L. This implies that $E(\sum_{t=0}^{T} \delta_t^\theta \pi_t) = 0$ for any strategy θ.

We must prove (2), or equivalently, that G^π is a martingale. From Appendix A, an adapted process X is a martingale if and only if $E(X_\tau) = X_0$ for any finite-valued stopping time $\tau \le T$. Consider, for an arbitrary security n and an arbitrary finite-valued stopping time $\tau \le T$, the trading strategy θ defined by $\theta^k = 0$ for $k \ne n$ and $\theta_t^n = 1$, $t < \tau$, with $\theta_t^n = 0$, $t \ge \tau$. Since $E(\sum_{t=0}^{T} \pi_t \delta_t^\theta) = 0$, we have

$$E\left(-S_0^n \pi_0 + \sum_{t=1}^{\tau} \pi_t \delta_t^n + \pi_\tau S_\tau^n \right) = 0,$$

implying that the deflated gain process $G^{n\pi}$ of security n satisfies $G_0^{n\pi} = E(G_\tau^{n\pi})$. Since τ is arbitrary, $G^{n\pi}$ is a martingale, and since n is arbitrary, G^π is a martingale.

This shows that absence of arbitrage implies the existence of a state-price deflator. The converse is easy. ∎

D. Individual Agent Optimality

We introduce an agent, defined by a strictly increasing utility function U on the set L_+ of nonnegative adapted "consumption" processes, and by an *endowment process* e in L_+. Given a dividend-price process (δ, S), a trading strategy θ leaves the agent with the total consumption process $e + \delta^\theta$. Thus the agent has the *budget-feasible consumption set*

$$X = \{ e + \delta^\theta \in L_+ : \theta \in \Theta \},$$

and the problem

$$\sup_{c \in X} U(c). \tag{4}$$

The existence of a solution to (4) implies the absence of arbitrage. Conversely, it is shown as an exercise that if U is continuous, then the absence of arbitrage implies that there exists a solution to (4). (For purposes of checking continuity or the closedness of sets in L, we will say that c_n converges to c if $c_n(\omega, t) \to c(\omega, t)$ for all ω and t. Then U is continuous if $U(c_n) \to U(c)$ whenever $c_n \to c$.)

Suppose that (4) has a strictly positive solution c^* and U is differentiable at c^*. We can use the first-order conditions for optimality (which can be reviewed in Appendix B) to characterize security prices in terms of the derivatives of the utility function U at c^*. Specifically, for any c in L, the derivative of U at c^* in the direction c is the derivative $g'(0)$, where $g(\alpha) = U(c^* + \alpha c)$ for any scalar α sufficiently small in absolute value. That is, $g'(0)$ is the marginal rate of improvement of utility as one moves in the direction c away from c^*. This derivative is denoted $\nabla U(c^*; c)$. By saying that U is differentiable at c^*, we mean that this derivative exists for any c in L and that the function $c \mapsto \nabla U(c^*, c)$ is a linear function on L into $\mathbb{R}$. Since δ^θ is a budget-feasible direction of change for any trading strategy θ, the first-order conditions for optimality of c^* imply that

$$\nabla U(c^*; \delta^\theta) = 0, \qquad \theta \in \Theta.$$

We now have a characterization of a state-price deflator.

Proposition. *Suppose that (4) has a strictly positive solution c^* and that $\nabla U(c^*)$ exists and is strictly increasing. Then there is no arbitrage and a state-price deflator is given by the Riesz representation π of $\nabla U(c^*)$:*

$$\nabla U(c^*; x) = E\left(\sum_{t=0}^{T} \pi_t x_t\right), \qquad x \in L.$$

Despite our standing assumption that U is strictly increasing, $\nabla U(c^*)$ need not in general be strictly increasing, but is so if U is concave.

As an example, suppose U has the *additive* form

$$U(c) = E\left[\sum_{t=0}^{T} u_t(c_t)\right], \qquad c \in L_+, \tag{5}$$

for some $u_t : \mathbb{R}_+ \to \mathbb{R}$, $t \geq 0$. It is then an exercise to show that if $\nabla U(c)$ exists, then

$$\nabla U(c; x) = E\left[\sum_{t=0}^{T} u_t'(c_t)x_t\right]. \tag{6}$$

If, for all t, u_t is concave with an unbounded derivative and e is strictly positive, then any solution c^* to (4) is strictly positive.

Corollary. *Suppose U is defined by (5). Under the conditions of the Proposition, for any times t and $\tau \geq t$,*

$$S_t = \frac{1}{u_t'(c_t^*)} E_t\left[S_\tau u_\tau'(c_\tau^*) + \sum_{j=t+1}^{\tau} \delta_j u_j'(c_j^*)\right].$$

For the case $\tau = t + 1$, this result is often called the *stochastic Euler equation*. Extending this classical result for additive utility, the exercises include other utility examples such as *habit-formation* utility and *recursive* utility. As in Chapter 1, we now turn to the multi-agent case.

E. Equilibrium and Pareto Optimality

Suppose there are m agents; agent i is defined as above by a strictly increasing utility function $U_i : L_+ \rightarrow \mathbb{R}$ and an endowment process $e^i \in L_+$. An *equilibrium* is a collection $(\theta^1, \ldots, \theta^m, S)$, where S is a security-price process and, for each i, θ^i is a trading strategy solving

$$\sup_{\theta \in \Theta} \; U_i(c) \qquad \text{subject to } c = e^i + \delta^\theta \in L_+, \tag{7}$$

with $\sum_{i=1}^m \theta^i = 0$.

We define markets to be *complete* if, for each process x in L, there is some trading strategy θ with $\delta_t^\theta = x_t$, $t \geq 1$. Complete markets thus means that any consumption process x can be obtained by investing some amount at time 0 in a trading strategy that generates the dividend x_t in each period t after 0. With the same definition of Pareto optimality, Proposition 1D carries over to this multiperiod setting. Any equilibrium $(\theta^1, \ldots, \theta^m, S)$ has an associated feasible consumption allocation $(c^1, \ldots, c^m)$ defined by letting $c^i - e^i$ be the dividend process generated by θ^i.

Proposition. *Suppose $(\theta^1, \ldots, \theta^m, S)$ is an equilibrium and markets are complete. Then the associated consumption allocation is Pareto optimal.*

The completeness of markets depends on the security-price process S itself. Indeed, the dependence of the marketed subspace on S makes the existence of an equilibrium a nontrivial issue. We ignore existence here and refer to the Notes for some relevant sources.

F. Equilibrium Asset Pricing

Again following the ideas in Chapter 1, we define for each λ in $\mathbb{R}_+^m$ the utility function $U_\lambda : L_+ \rightarrow \mathbb{R}$ by

$$U_\lambda(x) = \sup_{(c^1, \ldots, c^m)} \; \sum_{i=1}^m \lambda_i U_i(c^i) \qquad \text{subject to } c^1 + \cdots + c^m \leq x. \tag{8}$$

Proposition. *Suppose for all i that U_i is concave and strictly increasing. Suppose that $(\theta^1, \ldots, \theta^m, S)$ is an equilibrium and that markets are complete. Then there* *exists some nonzero* $\lambda \in \mathbb{R}_+^m$ *such that* $(0, S)$ *is a (no-trade) equilibrium for the one-agent economy* $[(U_\lambda, e), \delta]$, *where* $e = e^1 + \cdots + e^m$. *With this* λ *and with* $x = e = e^1 + \cdots + e^m$, *problem (8) is solved by the equilibrium consumption allocation.*

Proof is assigned as an exercise. The result is essentially the same as Proposition 1E. A method of proof, as well as the intuition for this proposition, is that with complete markets, a state-price deflator π represents Lagrange multipliers for consumption in the various periods and states for all of the agents simultaneously, as well as for the *representative agent* (U_λ, e).

Corollary 1. *If, moreover,* U_λ *is differentiable at* e, *then* λ *can be chosen so that for any times* t *and* $\tau \geq t$, *there is a state-price deflator* π *equal to the Riesz representation of* $\nabla U_\lambda(e)$.

Differentiability of U_λ at e can be shown by exactly the arguments used in Exercise 1.10.

Corollary 2. *Suppose for each* i *that* U_i *is of the additive form*

$$U_i(c) = E\left[\sum_{t=0}^T u_{it}(c_t)\right].$$

Then U_λ *is also additive, with*

$$U_\lambda(c) = E\left[\sum_{t=0}^T u_{\lambda t}(c_t)\right],$$

where

$$u_{\lambda t}(y) = \sup_{x \in \mathbb{R}_+^m} \sum_{i=1}^m \lambda_i u_{it}(x_i) \qquad \text{subject to } x_1 + \cdots + x_m \leq y.$$

In this case, the differentiability of U_λ *at* e *implies that for any times* t *and* $\tau \geq t$,

$$S_t = \frac{1}{u'_{\lambda t}(e_t)} E_t\left[u'_{\lambda \tau}(e_\tau)S_\tau + \sum_{j=t+1}^\tau u'_{\lambda j}(e_j)\delta_j\right]. \tag{9}$$

G. Arbitrage and Equivalent Martingale Measures

This section shows the equivalence between the absence of arbitrage and the existence of a probability measure Q with the property, roughly speaking, that discounted gain processes are martingales under Q.

There is *short-term riskless borrowing* at a given time $t < T$ if there is a trading strategy θ with

(a) $\delta_s^\theta = 0$, $s < t$;
(b) $\delta_{t+1}^\theta = 1$; and
(c) $\delta_s^\theta = 0$, $s > t + 1$.

In that case, the *discount* at period t is defined as $d_t = -\delta_t^\theta$.

Let us suppose throughout this section that for each $t < T$, there is short-term riskless borrowing at a strictly positive discount d_t. We can define, for any times t and $\tau < T$,

$$R_{t,\tau} = (d_t d_{t+1} \cdots d_{\tau-1})^{-1},$$

the payback at time τ of one unit of account borrowed risklessly at time t and rolled over in short-term borrowing repeatedly until date τ.

It would be a simple situation, both computationally and conceptually, if any security's price were merely the expected discounted dividends of the security. Of course, this is unlikely to be the case in a market with risk-averse investors. We can nevertheless come close to this sort of characterization of security prices by adjusting the original probability measure P. For this, we define a new probability measure Q to be *equivalent* to P if Q and P assign zero probabilities to the same events. An equivalent probability measure Q is an *equivalent martingale measure* if

$$S_t = E_t^Q \left(\sum_{j=t+1}^T \frac{\delta_j}{R_{t,j}} \right), \qquad t < T,$$

where E^Q denotes expectation under Q, and likewise $E_t^Q(x) = E^Q(x \mid \mathcal{F}_t)$ for any random variable x.

It is easy to show that Q is an equivalent martingale measure if and only if, for any trading strategy θ,

$$\theta_t \cdot S_t = E_t^Q \left(\sum_{j=t+1}^T \frac{\delta_j^\theta}{R_{t,j}} \right), \qquad t < T. \tag{10}$$

If interest rates are deterministic, (10) is merely the total discounted expected dividends, after substituting Q for the original measure P. We will show that the absence of arbitrage is equivalent to the existence of an equivalent martingale measure.

The deflator γ defined by $\gamma_t = R_{0,t}^{-1}$ defines the *discounted gain process* G^γ. The word "martingale" in the term "equivalent martingale measure" comes from the following equivalence.

Lemma. *A probability measure Q equivalent to P is an equivalent martingale measure for (δ, S) if and only if $S_T = 0$ and the discounted gain process G^γ is a martingale with respect to Q.*

We already know from Theorem 2C that the absence of arbitrage is equivalent to the existence of a state-price deflator π. Let Q be the probability measure defined, as explained in Appendix A, by the Radon-Nikodym derivative given by

$$\xi_T = \frac{\pi_T R_{0,T}}{\pi_0}.$$

That is, Q is defined by letting $E^Q(Z) = E(\xi_T Z)$ for any random variable Z. Because ξ_T is strictly positive, Q and P are equivalent probability measures. The *density process* ξ for Q is defined by $\xi_t = E_t(\xi_T)$. Relation (A.2) of Appendix A implies that for any times t and $j > t$ and any $\mathcal{F}_j$-measurable random variable Z_j,

$$E_t^Q(Z_j) = \frac{1}{\xi_t} E_t(\xi_j Z_j). \tag{11}$$

Fixing some time $t < T$, consider a trading strategy θ that invests one unit of account at time t and repeatedly rolls the value over in short-term riskless borrowing until time T, with final value $R_{t,T}$. That is, $\theta_t \cdot S_t = 1$ and $\delta_T^\theta = R_{t,T}$. Relation (3) then implies that

$$\pi_t = E_t(\pi_T R_{t,T}) = \frac{E_t(\pi_T R_{0,T})}{R_{0,t}} = \frac{E_t(\xi_T \pi_0)}{R_{0,t}} = \frac{\xi_t \pi_0}{R_{0,t}}. \tag{12}$$

From (11), (12), and the definition of a state-price deflator, (10) is satisfied, so Q is indeed an equivalent martingale measure. We have shown the following result.

Theorem. *There is no arbitrage if and only if there exists an equivalent martingale measure. Moreover, π is a state-price deflator if and only if an equivalent martingale measure Q has the density process ξ defined by $\xi_t = R_{0,t}\pi_t/\pi_0$.*

Proposition. *Suppose that $\mathcal{F}_T = \mathcal{F}$ and there is no arbitrage. Then markets are complete if and only if there is a unique equivalent martingale measure.*

Proof: Suppose that markets are complete and let Q_1 and Q_2 be two equivalent martingale measures. We must show that $Q_1 = Q_2$. Let A be any event. Since markets are complete, there is a trading strategy θ with dividend process δ^θ such that $\delta^\theta_T = R_{0,T} 1_A$ and $\delta^\theta_t = 0$, $0 < t < T$. By (10), we have $\theta_0 \cdot S_0 = Q_1(A) = Q_2(A)$. Since A is arbitrary, $Q_1 = Q_2$.

Exercise 2.18 outlines a proof of the converse part of the result. ∎

This martingale approach simplifies many asset-pricing problems that might otherwise appear to be quite complex, such as the American option-pricing problem to follow in Section I. This martingale approach also applies much more generally than indicated here. For example, the assumption of short-term borrowing is merely a convenience. More generally, one can typically obtain an equivalent martingale measure after normalizing prices and dividends by the price of some particular security.

H. Valuation of Redundant Securities

Suppose that the given dividend-price pair (δ, S) is arbitrage-free, with an associated state-price deflator π. Now consider the introduction of a new security with dividend process $\hat{\delta}$ and price process $\hat{S}$. We say that $\hat{\delta}$ is *redundant* given (δ, S) if there exists a trading strategy θ, with respect to only the original securities, that *replicates* $\hat{\delta}$, in the sense that $\delta^\theta_t = \hat{\delta}_t, t \geq 1$. The absence of arbitrage implies that

$$\hat{S}_t = V_t \equiv \frac{1}{\pi_t} E_t \left(\sum_{j=t+1}^{T} \pi_j \hat{\delta}_j \right), \qquad t < T.$$

If this were not the case, there would be an arbitrage, as follows. For example, suppose that for some stopping time τ, we have $\hat{S}_\tau > V_\tau$, and that $\tau \leq T$ with strictly positive probability. We can then define the strategy:

  (a) Sell the redundant security $\hat{\delta}$ at time τ for $\hat{S}_\tau$, and hold this position until T.
  (b) Invest $\theta_\tau \cdot S_\tau$ at time τ in the replicating strategy θ, and follow this strategy until T.

Since the dividends generated by this combined strategy (a)–(b) after τ are zero, the only dividend is at τ for the amount $\hat{S}_\tau - V_\tau > 0$, which means that this is an arbitrage. Likewise, if $\hat{S}_\tau < V_\tau$ for some finite-valued stopping time τ, the opposite strategy is an arbitrage. We have shown the following.

Proposition. *Suppose* (δ, S) *is arbitrage-free with state-price deflator* π. *Let* $\hat{\delta}$ *be a redundant dividend process with price process* $\hat{S}$. *Then the combined dividend-price pair* $[(\delta, \hat{\delta}), (S, \hat{S})]$ *is arbitrage-free if and only if it has* π *as a state-price deflator.*

In applications, it is often assumed that (δ, S) generates complete markets, in which case any additional security is redundant. Exercise 2.1 gives an example in which the redundant security is an option on one of the original securities.

I. American Exercise Policies and Valuation

We will now extend our pricing framework to include a family of securities, called "American," for which there is discretion regarding the timing of cash flows.

Given an adapted process X, each finite-valued stopping time τ generates a dividend process δ^τ defined by $\delta_t^\tau = 0$, $t \neq \tau$, and $\delta_\tau^\tau = X_\tau$. In this context, a finite-valued stopping time is an *exercise policy*, determining the time at which to accept payment. Any exercise policy τ is constrained by $\tau \leq \bar{\tau}$, for some *expiration time* $\bar{\tau} \leq T$. We say that $(X, \bar{\tau})$ defines an *American security*. The exercise policy is selected by the holder of the security. Once exercised, the security has no remaining cash flows. A standard example is an American put option on a security with price process p. The American put gives the holder of the option the right, but not the obligation, to sell the underlying security for a fixed exercise price at any time before a given expiration time $\bar{\tau}$. If the option has an exercise price K and expiration time $\bar{\tau} < T$, then $X_t = (K - p_t)^+$, $t \leq \bar{\tau}$, and $X_t = 0$, $t > \bar{\tau}$.

We will suppose that in addition to an American security $(X, \bar{\tau})$, there are securities with an arbitrage-free dividend-price process (δ, S) that generates complete markets. The assumption of complete markets will dramatically simplify our analysis since it implies that the dividend process δ^τ of the American security is redundant given (δ, S), regardless of the exercise policy τ. For notational convenience, we assume that $0 < \bar{\tau} < T$.

Let π be a state-price deflator associated with (δ, S). From Proposition 2H, given any exercise policy τ, the American security's dividend process δ^τ has an associated cum-dividend price process, say V^τ, which, in the absence of arbitrage, satisfies

$$V_t^\tau = \frac{1}{\pi_t} E_t \left(\pi_\tau X_\tau \right), \qquad t \leq \tau.$$

This value does not depend on which state-price deflator is chosen since with complete markets, state-price deflators are all equal up to a positive rescaling, as one can see from the theorem and proposition of Section 2G.

We consider the optimal stopping problem

$$V_0^* \equiv \max_{\tau \in \mathcal{T}(0)} \quad V_0^\tau, \tag{13}$$

where, for any time $t \leq \overline{\tau}$, we let $\mathcal{T}(t)$ denote the set of stopping times taking values in $\{t, t+1, \ldots, \overline{\tau}\}$. A solution to (13) is called a *rational exercise policy* for the American security X, in the sense that it maximizes the initial arbitrage-free value of the security.

We claim that in the absence of arbitrage, the actual initial price V_0 for the American security must be V_0^*. In order to see this, suppose first that $V_0^* > V_0$. Then one could buy the American security, adopt for it a rational exercise policy τ, and also undertake a trading strategy replicating $-\delta^\tau$. Since $V_0^* = E(\pi_\tau X_\tau)/\pi_0$, this replication involves an initial payoff of $-\delta_0^\tau = V_0^*$, and the net effect is a total initial dividend of $V_0^* - V_0 > 0$ and zero dividends after time 0, which defines an arbitrage. Thus the absence of arbitrage easily leads to the conclusion that $V_0 \geq V_0^*$. It remains to show that the absence of arbitrage also implies the opposite inequality $V_0 \leq V_0^*$.

Suppose that $V_0 > V_0^*$. One could sell the American security at time 0 for V_0. We will show that for an initial investment of V_0^*, one can "super-replicate" the payoff at exercise demanded by the holder of the American security, *regardless of the exercise policy used.* Specifically, a *super-replicating trading strategy* for $(X, \overline{\tau}, \delta, S)$ is a trading strategy θ involving only the securities with dividend-price process (δ, S) with the properties

(a) $\delta_t^\theta = 0$ for $0 < t < \overline{\tau}$, and
(b) $V_t^\theta \geq X_t$ for all $t \leq \overline{\tau}$,

where $V_t^\theta = \theta_{t-1} \cdot (S_t + \delta_t)$ is the cum-dividend value of the trading strategy at time t. Regardless of the exercise policy τ used by the holder of the security, the payment of X_τ demanded at time τ is covered by the market value V_t^θ of a super-replicating strategy θ. (In effect, one modifies θ by liquidating the portfolio θ_τ at time τ, so that the actual trading strategy φ associated with the arbitrage is defined by $\varphi_t = \theta_t$ for $t < \tau$ and $\varphi_t = 0$ for $t \geq \tau$.) By these properties (a)–(b), if $V_0 > V_0^*$ then the strategy of selling the American security and adopting a super-replicating strategy is an arbitrage provided $V_0^\theta = V_0^*$.

This notion of arbitrage for American securities, an extension of the notion of arbitrage used earlier in the chapter, is reasonable because a super-replicating strategy does not depend on the exercise policy adopted by the holder (or sequence of holders over time) of the American security. It would be unreasonable to call a strategy involving a short position in the American

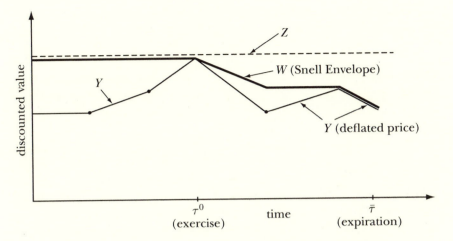

Figure 2.1. *Snell Envelope and Optimal Stopping Rule: Deterministic Case*

security an "arbitrage" if, in carrying it out, one requires knowledge of the exercise policy for the American security that will be adopted by other agents that hold the security over time, who may after all act "irrationally."

Proposition. *There is a super-replicating trading strategy θ for $(X, \bar{\tau}, \delta, S)$ with the initial value $V_0^{\theta} = V_0^*$.*

In order to construct a super-replicating strategy, we will make a short excursion into the theory of optimal stopping. Let Y be the process defined by $Y_t = X_t \pi_t$, and let

$$W_t = \max_{\tau \in \mathcal{T}(t)} E_t(Y_\tau), \qquad 0 \leq t \leq \bar{\tau}.$$

The process W defined in this manner (up to time $\bar{\tau}$) is the *Snell envelope* of Y. It can be shown as an exercise that for any $t < \bar{\tau}$, $W_t = \max[Y_t, E_t(W_{t+1})]$. Thus $W_t \geq E_t(W_{t+1})$, implying that W is a supermartingale, meaning that we can decompose W in the form $W = Z - A$ for some martingale Z and some increasing adapted process A with $A_0 = 0$. This decomposition is illustrated in Figure 2.1 for the case in which Y is a deterministic process, which implies that W, Z, and A are also deterministic.

By the definition of complete markets, there is a trading strategy θ with the property that

- $\delta_t^{\theta} = 0$ for $0 < t < \bar{\tau}$;
- $\delta_{\bar{\tau}}^{\theta} = Z_{\bar{\tau}} / \pi_{\bar{\tau}}$;
- $\delta_t = 0$ for $t > \bar{\tau}$.

Property (a) of a super-replicating strategy is satsifed by this strategy θ. From (3) and the fact that Z is a martingale,

$$\pi_t \theta_t \cdot S_t = E_t(\pi_{\bar{T}} \delta^\theta_{\bar{T}}) = E_t(Z_{\bar{T}}) = Z_t, \qquad t \le \bar{T}. \tag{14}$$

From (14) and the fact that $A_0 = 0$, we know that $V^\theta_0 = V^*_0$ because $Z_0 = W_0 = \pi_0 V^*_0$. Since $Z_t - A_t = W_t \ge Y_t$ for all t, from (14) we also know that

$$\theta_t \cdot S_t = \frac{Z_t}{\pi_t} \ge \frac{1}{\pi_t}(Y_t + A_t) = X_t + \frac{A_t}{\pi_t} \ge X_t, \qquad t \le \bar{T},$$

the last inequality following from the fact that $A_t \ge 0$ for all t. Thus property (b) is also satisfied, and θ is indeed a super-replicating strategy with $V^\theta_0 = V^*_0$. This proves the proposition and implies that unless there is an arbitrage, the initial price V_0 of the American security is equal to the market value V^*_0 associated with a rational exercise policy.

The Snell envelope W is also the key to finding a rational exercise policy. As for the deterministic case illustrated in Figure 2.1, a rational exercise policy is given by $\tau^0 = \min\{t : W_t = Y_t\}$. We now give a sketch of the optimality of τ^0. First, we know that if τ is a rational exercise policy, then $W_\tau = Y_\tau$. (This can be seen from the fact that $W_\tau \ge Y_\tau$, and if $W_\tau > Y_\tau$ then τ cannot be rational.) From this fact, any rational exercise policy τ has the property that $\tau \ge \tau^0$. For any such τ, we have

$$E_{\tau^0}(Y_\tau) \le W_{\tau^0} = Y_{\tau^0},$$

and the law of iterated expectations implies that $E(Y_\tau) \le E(Y_{\tau^0})$, so τ^0 is rational.

We have shown the following result.

Theorem. *Let W be the Snell envelope of $X\pi$ up to the expiration time $\bar{T}$, where π is a state-price deflator for (δ, S). Then a rational exercise policy for $(X, \bar{T}, \delta, S)$ is given by $\tau^0 = \min\{t : W_t = \pi_t X_t\}$.*

J. Is Early Exercise Optimal?

With the equivalent martingale measure Q defined in Section 2G, we can also write the optimal stopping problem (13) in the form

$$V^*_0 = \max_{\tau \in \mathcal{T}(0)} E^Q\left(\frac{X_\tau}{R_{0,\tau}}\right). \tag{15}$$

This representation of the rational exercise problem is sometimes convenient. For example, let us consider the case of an American call option on a security with price process p. We have $X_t = (p_t - K)^+$ for some exercise price K. Suppose the underlying security has no dividends before or at the expiration time $\bar{\tau}$. We suppose positive interest rates, meaning that $R_{t,s} \geq 1$ for all t and $s \geq t$. With these assumptions, we will show that it is never optimal to exercise the call option before its expiration date $\bar{\tau}$. This property is sometimes called "no early exercise," or "better alive than dead."

We define the "discounted price process" p^* by $p_t^* = p_t / R_{0,t}$. The fact that the underlying security pays dividends only after the expiration time $\bar{\tau}$ implies, by Lemma 2G, that p^* is a Q-martingale at least up to the expiration time $\bar{\tau}$. That is, for any $s \leq \bar{\tau}$ and $t \leq s$, we have $E_t^Q(p_s^*) = p_t^*$.

Jensen's Inequality can be used to show the following fact about convex functions of martingales.

Lemma. *Suppose $f : \mathbb{R} \times \mathbb{R} \to \mathbb{R}$ is convex with respect to its first argument, Y is a martingale, $\tau(1)$ and $\tau(2)$ are two stopping times with $\tau(2) \geq \tau(1)$, and Z is an adapted process. Then $f(Y_{\tau(1)}, Z_{\tau(1)}) \leq E_{\tau(1)}[f(Y_{\tau(2)}, Z_{\tau(1)})]$. Moreover, the law of iterated expectations implies that $E[f(Y_{\tau(1)}, Z_{\tau(1)})] \leq E[f(Y_{\tau(2)}, Z_{\tau(1)})]$.*

With the benefit of this lemma and positive interest rates, we have, for any stopping time $\tau \leq \bar{\tau}$,

$$
\begin{aligned}
E^Q\left[\frac{1}{R_{0,\tau}}(p_\tau - K)^+\right] &= E^Q\left[\left(p_\tau^* - \frac{K}{R_{0,\tau}}\right)^+\right] \\
&\leq E^Q\left[\left(p_{\bar{\tau}}^* - \frac{K}{R_{0,\tau}}\right)^+\right] \\
&\leq E^Q\left[\left(p_{\bar{\tau}}^* - \frac{K}{R_{0,\bar{\tau}}}\right)^+\right] \\
&= E^Q\left[\frac{1}{R_{0,\bar{\tau}}}(p_{\bar{\tau}} - K)^+\right].
\end{aligned}
$$

It follows that $\bar{\tau}$ is a rational exercise policy. In typical cases, $\bar{\tau}$ is the unique rational exercise policy.

If the underlying security pays dividends before expiration, then early exercise of the American call is, in certain cases, optimal. From the fact that the put payoff is increasing in the strike price (as opposed to decreasing for the call option), the second inequality in (16) is reversed for the case of a put option, and one can guess that early exercise of the American put is sometimes optimal.

Exercise 2.1 gives a simple example of American security valuation in a complete-markets setting. Chapter 3 presents the idea in a Markovian setting, which offers computational advantages in solving for the rational exercise policy and market value of American securities. In Chapter 3 we also consider the case of American securities that offer dividends before expiration.

The real difficulties with analyzing American securities begin with incomplete markets. In that case, the choice of exercise policy may play a role in determining the marketed subspace, and therefore a role in pricing securities. If the state-price deflator depends on the exercise policy, it could even turn out that the notion of a rational exercise policy is not well defined.

Exercises

2.1   Suppose in the setting of Section 2B that S is the price process of a security with zero dividends before T. We assume that

$$S_{t+1} = S_t H_{t+1}; \qquad t \geq 0; \qquad S_0 > 0,$$

where H is an adapted process such that for all $t \geq 1$, H_t has only two possible outcomes $U > 0$ and $D > 0$, each with positive conditional probability given $\mathcal{F}_{t-1}$. Suppose β is the price process of a security, also with no dividends before T, such that

$$\beta_{t+1} = \beta_t R; \qquad t \geq 1; \qquad \beta_0 > 0,$$

where $R > 1$ is a constant. We can think of β as the price process of a riskless bond. Consider a third security, a *European call option* on S with *expiration* at some fixed date $\tau < T$ and exercise price $K \geq 0$. This means that the price process C^τ of the third security has expiration value

$$C^\tau_\tau = (S_\tau - K)^+ \equiv \max\left(S_\tau - K, 0\right),$$

with $C^\tau_t = 0$, $t > \tau$. That is, the option gives its holder the right, but not the obligation, to purchase the stock at time τ at price K.

(A)   Assuming no arbitrage, show that for $0 \leq t < \tau$,

$$C^\tau_t = \frac{1}{R^{\tau-t}} \sum_{i=0}^{\tau-t} b(i; \tau - t, p)(U^i D^{\tau-t-i} S_t - K)^+, \qquad (16)$$

where $p = (R - D)/(U - D)$ and where

$$b(i; n, p) = \frac{n!}{i!(n - i)!} p^i (1 - p)^{n-i} \tag{17}$$

is the probability of i successes, each with probability p, out of n independent binomial trials. One can thus view (16) as the discounted expected exercise value of the option, with expectation under some probability measure constructed from the stock and bond returns. In order to model this viewpoint, let $\hat{S}$ be the process defined by

$$\hat{S}_{t+1} = \hat{S}_t \hat{H}_{t+1}; \qquad t \geq 0; \qquad \hat{S}_0 = S_0, \tag{18}$$

where $\{\hat{H}_0, \hat{H}_1, \ldots\}$ is a sequence of independent random variables with outcomes U and D of probability p and $1 - p$, respectively. Then (18) implies that

$$C_0^\tau = E \left[\frac{(\hat{S}_\tau - K)^+}{R^\tau} \right]. \tag{19}$$

(B)   We take it that $\mathbb{F}$ is the filtration generated by the return process H, meaning that for all $t \geq 1$, $\mathcal{F}_t$ is the tribe generated by $\{H_1, \ldots, H_t\}$. We extend the definition of the option described in part (A) by allowing the expiry date τ to be a stopping time. Show that (19) is still implied by the absence of arbitrage.

(C)   An *American call option* with expiration date $\bar{\tau} < T$ is merely an option of the form described in part (A), with the exception that the exercise date τ is a finite-valued stopping time selected by the holder of the option from the set $\mathcal{T}(0)$ of all stopping times bounded by $\bar{\tau}$. Show that the rational exercise problem

$$\sup_{\tau \in \mathcal{T}(0)} C_0^\tau \tag{20}$$

is solved by $\tau = \bar{\tau}$. In other words, the holder of the American call option maximizes its value by holding the option to expiration. Hint: Jensen's Inequality states that for f a convex function, X a random variable on $(\Omega, \mathcal{F}, P)$, and $\mathcal{G}$ a sub-tribe of $\mathcal{F}$, we have $E[f(X) \mid \mathcal{G}] \geq f[E(X \mid \mathcal{G})]$.

(D)   Show that the unique arbitrage-free price of the American call described in part (C) is at any time t equal to $C_t^{\bar{\tau}}$, which is the corresponding European call price.

(E)   A *European put option* is defined just as is the European call, with the exception that the exercise value is $(K - S_\tau)^+$ rather than $(S_\tau - K)^+$. That is, the put gives its holder the right, but not the obligation, to sell (rather than buy) the stock at τ for the exercise price K. Let F^τ denote the European put price process for expiration at τ. The *American put* with expiration $\bar{\tau}$, analogous to the case of calls, has an exercise date τ selected by the holder from the set $\mathcal{T}(\bar{\tau})$ of stopping times bounded by $\bar{\tau}$. Show by counterexample that the problem

$$\sup_{\tau \in \mathcal{T}(\bar{\tau})} F_0^\tau \tag{21}$$

is not, in general, solved by $\tau = \bar{\tau}$, and that the arbitrage-free American put price process is not generally the same as the corresponding arbitrage-free European put price process $F^{\bar{\tau}}$, contrary to the case of American call options on stocks with no dividends before expiration. An easy algorithm for computing the value of the American put in this setting is given in Chapter 3.

(F)   Show that markets are complete.

2.2   Suppose in the context of problem (4) that (δ, S) admits no arbitrage and that U is continuous. Show the existence of a solution. Hint: A continuous function on a compact set has a maximum. In this setting, a set is compact if it is closed and bounded.

2.3   Suppose in the context of problem (4) that $e \gg 0$ and that U has the additive form (5), where for each t, u_t is concave with an unbounded derivative. Show that any solution c^* is strictly positive. Show that the same conclusion follows if the assumption that $e \gg 0$ is replaced with the assumption that markets are complete and that e is not zero.

2.4   Prove Lemma 2C. Hint: For any x and y in L, let

$$(x \mid y) = E\left(\sum_{t=0}^T x_t y_t\right).$$

Then follow the hint given for Exercise 1.17, remembering that we write $x = y$ whenever $x_t = y_t$ for all t almost surely.

2.5   For U of the additive form (5), show that the gradient $\nabla U(c)$, if it exists, is represented as in (6).

2.6   Suppose $(c^1, \dots, c^m)$ is a strictly positive equilibrium consumption allocation and that for all i, U_i is of the additive form: $U_i(c) = E[\sum_{t=0}^T u_{it}(c_t)]$. Assume there is a constant $\bar{c}$ larger than c_t^i for all i and t such that for all i and t, $u_{it}(x) = A_{it}x - B_{it}x^2$, $x \le \bar{c}$, for some positive constants A_{it} and B_{it}. That is, utility is quadratic in the relevant range.

(A) In the context of Corollary 2 of Section 2F, show that for each t, there are some constants k_t and K_t such that $u'_{\lambda_t}(e_t) = k_t + K_t e_t$. Suppose for a given trading strategy θ and time t that the following are well defined:

- $R_t^\theta = \theta_{t-1} \cdot (S_t + \delta_t)/\theta_{t-1} \cdot S_{t-1}$, the return on θ at time t;
- R_t^M, the return at time t on a strategy φ maximizing $\mathrm{corr}_{t-1}(R_t^\varphi, e_t)$, where $\mathrm{corr}_t(\cdot)$ denotes $\mathcal{F}_t$-conditional correlation;
- $\beta_{t-1}^\theta = \mathrm{cov}_{t-1}(R_t^\theta, R_t^M)/\mathrm{var}_{t-1}(R_t^M)$, the conditional beta of the trading strategy θ with respect to the market return, where $\mathrm{cov}_t(\cdot)$ denotes $\mathcal{F}_t$-conditional covariance and $\mathrm{var}_t(\cdot)$ denotes $\mathcal{F}_t$-conditional variance;
- R_t^0, the return at time t on a strategy η with $\mathrm{corr}_{t-1}(R_t^\eta, e_t) = 0$.

Derive the following beta-form of the *consumption-based CAPM*:

$$E_{t-1}(R_t^\theta - R_t^0) = \beta_{t-1}^\theta E_{t-1}(R_t^M - R_t^0). \tag{22}$$

(B) Prove the same beta-form (22) of the CAPM holds in equilibrium even without assuming complete markets.

(C) Extend the state-price beta model of Section 1F to this setting, as follows, without using the assumptions of the CAPM. Let π be a state-price deflator. For each t, suppose R_t^* is the return on a trading strategy solving

$$\sup_\theta \mathrm{corr}_{t-1}(R_t^\theta, \pi_t).$$

Assume that $\mathrm{var}_{t-1}(R_t^*)$ is nonzero almost surely. Show that for any return R_t^θ,

$$E_{t-1}(R_t^\theta - R_t^0) = \beta_{t-1}^\theta E_{t-1}(R_t^* - R_t^0), \tag{23}$$

where $\beta_{t-1}^\theta = \mathrm{cov}_{t-1}(R_t^\theta, R_t^*)/\mathrm{var}_{t-1}(R_t^*)$ and $\mathrm{corr}_{t-1}(R_t^0, \pi_t) = 0$.

2.7 Prove Proposition 2E.

2.8 In the context of Section 2D, suppose that U is the *habit-formation* utility function defined by $U(c) = E[\sum_{t=0}^T u(c_t, h_t)]$, where $u : \mathbb{R}_+ \times \mathbb{R} \to \mathbb{R}$ is differentiable on the interior of its domain and, for any t, the "habit" level of consumption is defined by $h_t = \sum_{j=0}^t \alpha_j c_{t-j}$ for some $\alpha \in \mathbb{R}^T$. For example, we could take $\alpha_j = \gamma^j$ for $\gamma \in (0, 1)$, which gives geometrically declining weights on past consumption. Calculate the Riesz representation of the gradient of U at a strictly positive consumption process c.

2.9 Consider a utility function U defined by $U(c) = V_0$, where the *utility process* V is defined recursively, backward from T in time, by $V_T = J(c_T, h(0))$

and, for $t < T$, by $V_t = J(c_t, E_t[h(V_{t+1})])$, where $J : \mathbb{R}_+ \times \mathbb{R} \to \mathbb{R}$ is increasing and continuously differentiable on the interior of its domain and $h : \mathbb{R} \to \mathbb{R}$ is increasing and continuously differentiable. This is a special case of what is known as *recursive utility*, and also a special case of what is known as *Kreps-Porteus* utility. Note that the utility function can depend nontrivially on the filtration $\mathbb{F}$, which is not true for additive or habit-formation utility functions. This utility model is reconsidered in an exercise in Chapter 3.

(A) Give an expression for the gradient of U at a strictly positive consumption process c.

(B) Suppose that h and J are concave and increasing functions. Show that U is concave and increasing.

2.10 In the setting of Section 2E, an Arrow-Debreu equilibrium is a feasible consumption allocation $(c^1, \ldots, c^m)$ and a nonzero linear function $\Psi : L \to \mathbb{R}$ such that for all i, c^i solves $\max_{c \in L_+} U_i(c)$ subject to $\Psi(c^i) \le \Psi(e^i)$. Suppose that $(c^1, \ldots, c^m)$ and Ψ form an Arrow-Debreu equilibrium and that π is the Riesz representation of Ψ. Let S be defined by $S_T = 0$ and by taking π to be a state-price deflator. Suppose, given (δ, S), that markets are complete. Show the existence of trading strategies $\theta^1, \ldots, \theta^m$ such that $(\theta^1, \ldots, \theta^m, S)$ is an equilibrium with the same consumption allocation $(c^1, \ldots, c^m)$.

2.11 Given a finite set Ω of states, a *partition* of Ω is a collection of disjoint nonempty subsets of Ω whose union is Ω. For example, a partition of $\{1, 2, 3\}$ is given by $\{\{1\}, \{2, 3\}\}$. The tribe on a finite set Ω generated by a given partition p of Ω, denoted $\sigma(p)$, is the smallest tribe $\mathcal{F}$ on Ω such that $p \subset \mathcal{F}$. Conversely, for any tribe $\mathcal{F}$ on Ω, the partition $\mathcal{P}(\mathcal{F})$ generated by $\mathcal{F}$ is the smallest partition p of Ω such that $\mathcal{F} = \sigma(p)$. For instance, the tribe $\{\emptyset, \Omega, \{1\}, \{2, 3\}\}$ is generated by the partition in the above example. Since partitions and tribes on a given finite set Ω are in one-to-one correspondence, we could have developed the results of Chapter 2 in terms of an increasing sequence $p_0, p_1, \ldots, p_T$ of partitions of Ω rather than a filtration of tribes, $\mathcal{F}_0, \mathcal{F}_1, \ldots, \mathcal{F}_T$. (In the infinite-state models of Part II, however, it is more convenient to use tribes than partitions.)

Given a subset B of Ω and a partition p of Ω, let $n(B, p)$ denote the minimum number of elements of p whose union contains B. In a sense, this is the number of distinct nonempty events that might occur if B is to occur. For $t < T$, let

$$n_t = \max_{B \in p_t} \ n(B, p_{t+1}).$$

Finally, the *spanning number* of the filtration $\mathbb{F}$ generated by $p_0, \ldots, p_T$ is

$n(\mathbb{F}) \equiv \max_{t<T} n_t$. In a sense, $n(\mathbb{F})$ is the maximum number of distinct events that could be revealed between two periods.

Show that complete markets requires at least $n(\mathbb{F})$ securities, and that given the filtration $\mathbb{F}$, there exists a set of $n(\mathbb{F})$ dividend processes and associated arbitrage-free security-price processes such that markets are complete. This issue is further investigated in sources indicated in the Notes.

2.12 Given securities with a dividend-price pair (δ, S), extend Theorem 2G to show, in the presence of riskless borrowing at a strictly positive discount at each date, the equivalence of these statements:

    (a) There exists a state-price deflator.
    (b) There exists a deflator π such that (3) holds for any trading strategy θ.
    (c) $S_T = 0$ and there exists a deflator π such that the deflated gain process G^π is a martingale.
    (d) There is no arbitrage.
    (e) There is an equivalent martingale measure.

2.13 Show, from (11) and (12), that (10) is indeed satisfied, confirming that Q is an equivalent martingale measure.

2.14 Show, as claimed in Section 2I, that if τ^* is a rational exercise policy for the American security X and if V^* is the price process for the American security with this rational exercise policy, then $V_\tau^* \geq X_\tau$ for any stopping time $\tau \leq \tau^*$.

2.15 (Aggregation Revisited)   Suppose, in the context of problem (8), that $x \gg 0$ and, for all i, $U_i(c) = E[\sum_{t=0}^{T} u_t(c_t)]$, where, for all t, $u_t(x) = k_t x^{\gamma(t)}/\gamma(t)$, where k_t and $\gamma(t) < 1$, $\gamma(t) \neq 0$, are constants (depending on t). Show that U_λ is of the same form. Replace the assumption of complete markets in Proposition 2F with the assumption that $e \gg 0$ and, for all i, there is a trading strategy θ such that $\delta_t^\theta = e_t^i$, for $t \geq 1$. Demonstrate the same conclusion. Show that the equilibrium consumption allocation is Pareto optimal.

2.16 (Put-Call Parity)   In the general setting explained in Section 2B, suppose there exist the following securities:

    (a) a "stock," with price process X;
    (b) a European call option on the stock with exercise price K and expiration date τ;
    (c) a European put option on the stock with exercise price K and expiration date τ;

(d) a τ-period zero-coupon riskless bond.

Let X_0, C_0, P_0, and B_0 denote the initial respective prices of the securities. Suppose there is no arbitrage. Solve for C_0 explicitly in terms of X_0, P_0, and B_0.

2.17   (Futures-Forward Price Equivalence)   This exercise defines (in ideal terms) a *forward contract* and a *futures contract*, and gives simple conditions under which the *futures price* and the *forward price* coincide. We adopt the setting of Section 2B, in the absence of arbitrage. Fixed throughout are a *delivery date* τ and a *settlement amount* W_τ (an $\mathcal{F}_\tau$-measurable random variable).

Informally speaking, the associated forward contract made at time t is a commitment to pay an amount F_t (the forward price), which is agreed upon at time t and paid at time τ, in return for the amount W_τ at time τ. Formally speaking, this means that the forward contract is a security whose price process is zero and whose dividend process δ is defined by $\delta_t = 0$, $t \neq \tau$, and $\delta_\tau = W_\tau - F_t$.

(A) Suppose that Q is an equivalent martingale measure and that there is riskless short-term borrowing at any date t at a discount d_t that is deterministic. Show that $\{F_0, F_1, \ldots, F_\tau\}$ is a Q-martingale, in that $F_t = E_t^Q(F_\tau)$ for all $t \leq \tau$.

A futures contract differs from a forward contract in several practical ways that depend on institutional details. One of the details that is particularly important for pricing purposes is *resettlement*. For theoretical modeling purposes, we can describe resettlement as follows: A futures-price process $\Phi = \{\Phi_0, \ldots, \Phi_\tau\}$ for delivery of W_τ at time τ is taken as given. At any time t, an investor can adopt a position of θ futures contracts by agreeing to accept the resettlement payment $\theta(\Phi_{t+1} - \Phi_t)$ at time $t+1$, $\theta(\Phi_{t+2} - \Phi_{t+1})$ at time $t+2$, and so on, until the position is changed (or eliminated). This process of paying or collecting any changes in the futures price, period by period, is called *marking to market*, and serves in practice to reduce the likelihood or magnitude of potential defaults. Formally, all of this means simply that the dividend process δ of the futures contract is defined by $\delta_t = \Phi_t - \Phi_{t-1}$, $1 \leq t \leq \tau$.

For our purposes, it is natural to assume that the delivery value Φ_τ is contractually equated with W_τ. (In a more detailed model, we could equate Φ_τ and W_τ by the absence of *delivery arbitrage*.)

(B) Suppose Q is an equivalent martingale measure and show that for all $t \leq \tau$, $\Phi_t = E_t^Q(W_\tau)$.

It follows from parts (A) and (B) that with deterministic interest rates and the absence of arbitrage, futures and forward prices coincide.

We now suppose that W_τ is the market value S_τ of a security with dividend process δ.

(C) Suppose that δ and the discount process $d = \{d_1, \ldots, d_T\}$ on riskless borrowing are both deterministic. Calculate the futures and forward prices, Φ_t and F_t, explicitly in terms of S_t, d, and δ.

2.18 Provide details fleshing out the following outline of a proof of the converse part of Proposition 2G.

Let $J = \{(x_1, \ldots, x_T) : x \in L\}$ and $H = \{(\delta_1^\theta, \ldots, \delta_T^\theta) : \theta \in \Theta\}$. Markets are complete if and only if $J = H$. By Theorem 2G, there is a unique equivalent martingale measure if and only if there is a unique state-price deflator π such that $\pi_0 = 1$. Suppose $H \neq J$. Since H is a linear subspace of J, there is some nonzero y in J "orthogonal" to H, in the sense that $E(\sum_{t=1}^T y_t h_t) = 0$ for all h in H. Let $\hat{\pi} \in L$ be defined by $\hat{\pi}_0 = 1$ and $\hat{\pi}_t = \pi_t + \alpha y_t$, $t \geq 1$, where $\alpha > 0$ is a scalar small enough that $\hat{\pi} \gg 0$. Then $\hat{\pi}$ is a distinct state-price deflator with $\hat{\pi}_0 = 1$. This shows that if there is a unique state-price deflator π with $\pi_0 = 1$, then markets must be complete. Hint: Let

$$(y \mid h) \equiv E\left(\sum_{t=1}^T y_t h_t\right), \qquad h \in H$$

define an inner $(\cdot \mid \cdot)$ for H in the sense of Exercise 1.17.

2.19 It is asserted in Section 2I that if W is the Snell envelope of Y, then $W_t = \max(Y_t, E_t(W_{t+1}))$. Prove this natural property.

2.20 Prove Lemma 2J.

2.21 Given a dividend-price process (δ, S) for N securities and a deflator γ, let $\delta_t^\gamma = \delta_t \gamma_t$ and $S_t^\gamma = S_t \gamma_t$ define the deflated dividend-price process $(\delta^\gamma, S^\gamma)$. Show that (δ, S) admits no arbitrage if and only if $(\delta^\gamma, S^\gamma)$ admits no arbitrage. This is one aspect of what is sometimes called *numeraire irrelevance*.

Notes

The model of uncertainty and information is standard. The model of uncertainty is equivalent to that originated in the general equilibrium model of Debreu (1953), which appears in Chapter 7 of Debreu (1959). For more details in a finance setting, see Dothan (1990). The connection between arbitrage and martingales given in Sections 2C and 2G is from the more general model of Harrison and Kreps (1979). Girotto and Ortu (1993) present general results, in this finite-dimensional setting, on the equivalence between no arbitrage and the existence of an equivalent martingale measure. The spirit of the results on optimality and state prices is also from Harrison and Kreps (1979). The habit-formation utility model was developed by Dunn and Singleton (1986) and in continuous time by Ryder and Heal (1973). An application of habit formation to state-pricing in this setting appears in Chapman (1994). The recursive-utility model, in various forms, is due to Selden (1978), Kreps and Porteus (1978), and Epstein and Zin (1989), and is surveyed by Epstein (1992). Koopmans (1960) presented an early precursor. The recursive-utility model allows for preference for earlier or later resolution of uncertainty (which have no impact on additive utility). This is relevant, for example, in the context of the remarks by Ross (1989), as shown by Skiadas (1991a) and Duffie, Schroder, and Skiadas (1993). For a more general form of recursive utility than that appearing in Exercise 2.9, the von Neumann-Morgenstern function h can be replaced with a function of the conditional distribution of next-period utility. Examples are the local-expected-utility model of Machina (1982) and the *betweenness certainty equivalent* model of Chew (1983, 1989), Dekel (1987), and Gul and Lantto (1992). The equilibrium state-price associated with recursive utility is computed in a Markovian version of this setting by Kan (1993). For further justification and properties of recursive utility, see Chew and Epstein (1991) and Skiadas (1991a,b). For further implications for asset pricing, see Epstein (1988, 1992), Epstein and Zin (1991), and Giovannini and Weil (1989).

Radner (1967, 1972) originated the sort of dynamic equilibrium model treated in this chapter. The basic approach to existence given in Exercise 2.11 is suggested by Kreps (1982), and is shown to work for "generic" dividends and endowments, under technical regularity conditions, in McManus (1984), Repullo (1986), and Magill and Shafer (1990), provided the number of securities is at least as large as the spanning number of the filtration $\mathbb{F}$ (as suggested in Exercise 2.11). This literature is reviewed in depth by Geanakoplos (1990). See Duffie and Huang (1985) for the definition of spanning number in more general settings and for a continuous-time version of a similar result. Duffie and Shafer (1985, 1986a) show generic existence of equilibrium in incomplete markets; Hart (1975) gives a counterexample. Bottazzi (1995) has a somewhat more advanced version of this result in its single-period multiple-commodity version. Related existence topics are studied by Bottazzi and Hens (1993), Hens (1991), and Zhou

(1993). Dispersed expectations, in a temporary equilibrium variant of the model, is shown to lead to existence by Henrotte (1994) and by Honda (1992). Alternative proofs of existence of equilibrium are given in the 2-period version of the model by Geanakoplos and Shafer (1990), Hirsch, Magill, and Mas-Colell (1990), and Husseini, Lasry, and Magill (1990); and in a T-period version by Florenzano and Gourdel (1994). If one defines security dividends in nominal terms, rather than in units of consumption, then equilibria always exist under standard technical conditions on preferences and endowments, as shown by Cass (1984), Werner (1985), Duffie (1987), and Gottardi and Hens (1994), although equilibrium may be indeterminate, as shown by Cass (1989) and Geanakoplos and Mas-Colell (1989). On this point, see also Kydland and Prescott (1991), Mas-Colell (1991), and Cass (1991). Likewise, one obtains existence in a one-period version of the model provided securities have payoffs in a single commodity (the framework of most of this book), as shown by Chae (1988) and Geanakoplos and Polemarchakis (1986). Surveys of general equilibrium models in incomplete markets setting are given by Cass (1991), Duffie (1992), Geanakoplos (1990), Magill and Quinzii (1994b), and Magill and Shafer (1991). In the presence of price-dependent options, existence can be more problematic, as shown by Polemarchakis and Ku (1990), but variants of the formulation will suffice for existence in many cases, as shown by Huang and Wu (1994) and Krasa and Werner (1991). Detemple and Selden (1991) examine the implications of options for asset pricing in a general equilibrium model with incomplete markets. Bajeux-Besnainou and Rochet (1992) explore the dynamic spanning implications of options. The importance of the timing of information in this setting is described by Berk and Uhlig (1993). Hindy and Huang (1993) show the implications of linear collateral constraints on security valuation. Hara (1993) treats the role of "redundant" securities in the presence of transactions costs.

Hahn (1992, 1994) raises some philosophical issues regarding the possibility of complete markets and efficiency. The Pareto inefficiency of incomplete markets equilibrium consumption allocations, and notions of constrained efficiency, are discussed by Hart (1975), Kreps (1979) (and references therein), Citanna, Kajii, and Villanacci (1994), Citanna and Villanacci (1993), and Pan (1992, 1993).

The optimality of individual portfolio and consumption choices in incomplete markets in this setting is given a dual interpretation by He and Pearson (1991b). (Girotto and Ortu [1994] offer related remarks.) Methods for computation of equilibrium with incomplete markets are developed by Brown, DeMarzo, and Eaves (1993a,b) and DeMarzo and Eaves (1993).

The representative agent state-pricing model for this setting was shown by Constantinides (1982). An extension of this notion to incomplete markets, where one cannot exploit Pareto optimality, is given by Cuoco and He (1992a). Kraus and Litzenberger (1975) and Stapleton and Subrahmanyam (1978) present parametric examples of equilibrium. Hansen and Richard (1987) explore the state-price beta model in a much more general multiperiod setting. Ross (1987) and Prisman (1985) show the impact of taxes and transactions costs on the state-pricing model. Hara (1993) discusses the role of redundant securities in the presence of transactions costs. The consumption-based CAPM of Exercise 2.6 is found, in a different form, in Rubinstein (1976). The aggregation result of Exercise 2.15 is based on Rubinstein (1974b). Rubinstein (1974a) has a detailed treatment of asset pricing results in the setting of this chapter. Rubinstein (1987) is a useful expository treatment of derivative asset pricing in this setting.

The role of production is considered by Duffie and Shafer (1986b) and Naik (1993). The Modigliani-Miller Theorems are reconsidered in this setting by DeMarzo (1988), Duffie and Shafer (1986b), and Gottardi (1995).

The modeling of American security valuation given here is similar to the continuous-time treatments of Bensoussan (1984) and Karatzas (1988), who does not formally connect the valuation of American securities with the absence of arbitrage, but rather deal with the notion of "fair price." Merton (1973b) was the first to attack American option valuation systematically using arbitrage-based methods and to point out the inoptimality of early exercise of certain American options in a Black-Scholes style setting. American option valuation is reconsidered in Chapters 3 and 8, whose literature notes cite many additional references.

3

The Dynamic Programming
Approach

THIS CHAPTER PRESENTS portfolio choice and asset pricing in the framework of dynamic programming, a technique for solving dynamic optimization problems with a recursive structure. The asset-pricing implications go little beyond those of the previous chapter, but there are computational advantages. After introducing the idea of dynamic programming in a deterministic setting, we review the basics of a finite-state Markov chain. The Bellman equation is shown to characterize optimality in a Markov setting. The first-order condition for the Bellman equation, often called the "stochastic Euler equation," is then shown to characterize equilibrium security prices. This is done with additive utility in the main body of the chapter, and extended to more general recursive forms of utility in the exercises. The last sections of the chapter show the computation of arbitrage-free derivative security values in a Markov setting, including an application of Bellman's equation for optimal stopping to the valuation of American securities such as the American put option. An exercise presents algorithms for the numerical solution of term-structure derivative securities in a simple binomial setting.

A. The Bellman Approach

To get the basic idea, we start in the T-period setting of the previous chapter, with no securities except those permitting short-term riskless borrowing at any time t at the discount $d_t > 0$. The endowment process of a given agent is e. Given a consumption process c, it is convenient to define the agent's *wealth process* W^c by $W_0^c = 0$ and

$$W_t^c = \frac{W_{t-1}^c + e_{t-1} - c_{t-1}}{d_{t-1}}, \qquad t \geq 1. \tag{1}$$

Given a utility function $U : L_+ \to \mathbb{R}$ on the set L of nonnegative adapted processes, the agent's problem can be rewritten as

$$\sup_{c \in L_+} U(c) \qquad \text{subject to (1) and } c_T \leq W_T^c + e_T. \tag{2}$$

Dynamic programming is only convenient with special types of utility functions. One example is an additive utility function U, defined by

$$U(c) = E\left[\sum_{t=0}^{T} u_t(c_t)\right], \tag{3}$$

with $u_t : \mathbb{R}_+ \to \mathbb{R}$ strictly increasing and continuous for each t. Given this utility function, it is natural to consider the problem at any time t of maximizing the "remaining utility," given current wealth $W_t^c = w$. In order to keep things simple at first, we take the case in which there is no uncertainty, meaning that $\mathcal{F}_t = \{\Omega, \emptyset\}$ for all t. The maximum remaining utility at time t is then written, for each w in $\mathbb{R}$, as

$$V_t(w) = \sup_{c \in L_+} \sum_{s=t}^{T} u_s(c_s),$$

subject to $W_t^c = w$, the wealth dynamic (1), and $c_T \leq W_T^c + e_T$. If there is no budget-feasible consumption choice (because w is excessively negative), we write $V_t(w) = -\infty$.

Clearly $V_T(w) = u_T(w + e_T)$ for $w \geq -e_T$, and it is shown as an exercise that for $t < T$,

$$V_t(w) = \sup_{\bar{c} \in \mathbb{R}_+} u_t(\bar{c}) + V_{t+1}\left(\frac{w + e_t - \bar{c}}{d_t}\right), \tag{4}$$

the *Bellman equation*. It is also left as an exercise to show that an optimal consumption policy c is defined inductively by $c_t = C_t(W_t^c)$, where $C_t(w)$ denotes a solution to (4) for $t < T$, and where $C_T(w) = w + e_T$. From (4), the *value function* V_{t+1} thus summarizes all information regarding the "future" of the problem that is required for choice at time t.

B. First-Order Conditions of the Bellman Equation

Throughout this section, we take the additive model (3) and assume in addition that for each t, u_t is strictly concave and differentiable on $(0, \infty)$. Extending Exercise 2.2, there exists an optimal consumption policy c^*. We assume that c^* is strictly positive. Let W^* denote the wealth process associated with c^* by (1).

Lemma. *For any t, V_t is strictly concave and continuously differentiable at W_t^*, with $V_t'(W_t^*) = u_t'(c_t^*)$.*

Proof is left as Exercise 3.3, which gives a broad hint. The first-order conditions for the Bellman equation (4) then imply, for any $t < T$, that the one-period discount is

$$d_t = \frac{u_{t+1}'(c_{t+1}^*)}{u_t'(c_t^*)}. \tag{5}$$

The same equation is easily derived from the general characterization of equilibrium security prices given by equation (2.9). More generally, the price $\Lambda_{t,\tau}$ at time t of a unit riskless bond maturing at any time $\tau > t$ is

$$\Lambda_{t,\tau} \equiv d_t\, d_{t+1} \cdots d_{\tau-1} = \frac{u_\tau'(c_\tau^*)}{u_t'(c_t^*)}, \tag{6}$$

which, naturally, is the marginal rate of substitution of consumption between the two dates.

Since the price of a coupon-bearing bond, the only kind of security in a deterministic setting, is merely the sum of the prices of its coupons and principal, (6) provides a complete characterization of security prices in this setting.

C. Markov Uncertainty

We take the easiest kind of Markov uncertainty, a *time-homogeneous Markov chain*. Let the elements of a fixed set $Z = \{1, \ldots, k\}$ be known as *shocks*. For any shocks i and j, let $q_{ij} \in [0,1]$ be thought of as the probability, for any t, that shock j occurs in period $t+1$ given that shock i occurs in period t. Of course, for each i, $q_{i1} + \cdots + q_{ik} = 1$. The $k \times k$ *transition matrix q* is thus a complete characterization of transition probabilities. This idea is formalized with the following construction of a probability space and filtration of tribes. It is enough to consider a state of the world as some particular sequence $(z_0, \ldots, z_T)$ of shocks that might occur. We therefore let $\Omega = Z^{T+1}$ and let $\mathcal{F}$ be the set of all subsets of Ω. For each t, let $X_t : \Omega \to Z$ (the random shock at time t) be the random variable defined by $X_t(z_0, \ldots, z_T) = z_t$. Finally, for each i in Z, let P_i be the probability measure on $(\Omega, \mathcal{F})$ uniquely defined by two conditions:

$$P_i(X_0 = i) = 1 \tag{7}$$

and, for all $t < T$,

$$P_i[X(t+1) = j \mid X(0), X(1), X(2), \ldots, X(t)] = q_{X(t),j}. \tag{8}$$

Relations (7) and (8) mean that under probability measure P_i, X starts at i with probability 1 and has the transition probabilities previously described informally. In particular, (8) means that $X = \{X_0, \ldots, X_T\}$ is a *Markov process*: the conditional distribution of X_{t+1} given $X_0, \ldots, X_t$ depends only on X_t. To complete the formal picture, for each t, we let $\mathcal{F}_t$ be the tribe generated by $\{X_0, \ldots, X_t\}$, meaning that the information available at time t is that obtained by observing the shock process X until time t.

Lemma. *For any time t, let $f : Z^{T-t+1} \to \mathbb{R}$ be arbitrary. Then there exists a fixed function $g : Z \to \mathbb{R}$ such that for any i in Z,*

$$E^i\left[f(X_t, \ldots, X_T) \mid \mathcal{F}_t\right] = E^i[f(X_t, \ldots, X_T) \mid X_t] = g(X_t),$$

where E^i denotes expectation under P_i.

This lemma gives the complete flavor of the Markov property.

D. Markov Asset Pricing

Taking the particular Markov source of uncertainty described in Section 3C, we now consider the prices of securities in a single- or representative-agent setting with additive utility of the form (3), where, for all t, u_t has a strictly positive derivative on $(0, \infty)$. Suppose, moreover, that for each t there are functions $f_t : Z \to \mathbb{R}^N$ and $g_t : Z \to \mathbb{R}$ such that the dividend is $\delta_t = f_t(X_t)$ and the endowment is $e_t = g_t(X_t)$. Then Lemma 3C and the general gradient solution (2.9) for equilibrium security prices imply the following characterization of the equilibrium security price process S. For each t there is a function $\mathcal{S}_t : Z \to \mathbb{R}^N$ such that $S_t = \mathcal{S}_t(X_t)$. In particular, for any initial shock i and any time $t < T$,

$$\mathcal{S}_t(X_t) = \frac{1}{\pi_t} E^i\left(\pi_{t+1}\left[f_{t+1}(X_{t+1}) + \mathcal{S}_{t+1}(X_{t+1})\right] \,\Big|\, X_t\right), \tag{9}$$

where π is the state-price deflator given by $\pi_t = u_t'[g_t(X_t)]$. This has been called the *stochastic Euler equation* for security prices.

E. Security Pricing by Markov Control

We will demonstrate (9) once again, under stronger conditions, using instead Markov dynamic programming methods. Suppose that $\{X_t\}$ is the shock process already described. For notational simplicity, we take it that the transition matrix q is strictly positive and that for all t,

- u_t is continuous, strictly concave, increasing, and differentiable on $(0, \infty)$;
- $e_t = g_t(X_t)$ for some $g_t : Z \to \mathbb{R}_{++}$; and
- $\delta_t = f_t(X_t)$ for some $f_t : Z \to \mathbb{R}^N_{++}$.

We assume, naturally, that $\mathcal{S}_t : Z \to \mathbb{R}^N_{++}$, $t < T$, and that there is no arbitrage. We let Θ denote the space of trading strategies and L_+ the space of nonnegative adapted processes (for consumption). For each $t \leq T$, consider the value function $V_t : Z \times \mathbb{R} \to \overline{\mathbb{R}}$ defined by

$$V_t(i, w) = \sup_{(c,\theta) \in L_+ \times \Theta} E\left[\sum_{j=t}^{T} u_j(c_j) \,\Big|\, X_t = i\right], \qquad (10)$$

subject to

$$W_j^\theta = \theta_{j-1} \cdot \left[\mathcal{S}_j(X_j) + f_j(X_j)\right], \qquad j > t; \qquad W_t^\theta = w, \qquad (11)$$

and

$$c_j + \theta_j \cdot \mathcal{S}_j(X_j) \leq W_j^\theta + g_j(X_j), \qquad t \leq j \leq T.$$

The conditional expectation in (10), which is well defined since $q \gg 0$, does not depend on the initial state X_0 according to Lemma 3C, so we abuse the notation by simply ignoring the initial state in this sort of expression. For sufficiently negative w, there is no (θ, c) that is feasible for (10), in which case we take $V_t(i, w) = -\infty$. For initial wealth $w = 0$ and time $t = 0$, (10) is equivalent to problem (2.4) with $S_j = \mathcal{S}_j(X_j)$ for any time j.

We now define a sequence $F_0, \ldots, F_T$ of functions on $Z \times \mathbb{R}$ into $\overline{\mathbb{R}}$ that will eventually be shown to coincide with the value functions $V_0, \ldots, V_T$. We first define $F_{T+1} \equiv 0$. For $t \leq T$, we let F_t be given by the Bellman equation

$$F_t(i, w) = \sup_{(\overline{\theta}, \overline{c}) \in \mathbb{R}^N \times \mathbb{R}_+} G_{it}(\overline{\theta}, \overline{c}) \qquad \text{subject to } \overline{c} + \overline{\theta} \cdot \mathcal{S}_t(i) \leq w + g_t(i), \quad (12)$$

where

$$G_{it}(\overline{\theta}, \overline{c}) = u_t(\overline{c}) + E\left[F_{t+1}\left(X_{t+1}, \overline{\theta} \cdot \left[\mathcal{S}_{t+1}(X_{t+1}) + f_{t+1}(X_{t+1})\right]\right) \,\Big|\, X_t = i\right].$$

The following technical conditions extend those of Lemma 3B, and have essentially the same proof.

Proposition. For any i in Z and $t \leq T$, the function $F_t(i, \cdot) : \mathbb{R} \to \overline{\mathbb{R}}$, restricted to its domain of finiteness $\{w : F_t(i, w) > -\infty\}$, is strictly concave and increasing. If $(\overline{c}, \overline{\theta})$ solves (12) and $\overline{c} > 0$, then $F_t(i, \cdot)$ is continuously differentiable at w with derivative $F_{tw}(i, w) = u'_t(\overline{c})$.

It can be shown as an exercise that unless the constraint is infeasible, a solution to (12) always exists. In this case, for any i, t, and w, let $[\Phi_t(i, w), C_t(i, w)]$ denote a solution. We can then define the associated wealth process W^* recursively by $W^*_0 = 0$ and

$$W^*_t = \Phi_{t-1}(X_{t-1}, W^*_{t-1}) \cdot [S_t(X_t) + f_t(X_t)], \qquad t \geq 1.$$

Let (c^*, θ^*) be defined, at each t, by $c^*_t = C_t(X_t, W^*_t)$ and $\theta^*_t = \Phi_t(X_t, W^*_t)$. The fact that (c^*, θ^*) solves (10) for $t = 0$ and $w = 0$ can be shown as follows: Let (c, θ) be an arbitrary feasible policy. We have, for each t from the Bellman equation (12),

$$F_t(X_t, W^\theta_t) \geq u_t(c_t) + E\left[F_{t+1}\left(X_{t+1}, \theta_t \cdot [S_{t+1}(X_{t+1}) + f_{t+1}(X_{t+1})]\right) \,\middle|\, X_t\right].$$

Rearranging this inequality and applying the law of iterated expectations,

$$E[F_t(X_t, W^\theta_t)] - E\left[F_{t+1}\left(X_{t+1}, W^\theta_{t+1}\right)\right] \geq E[u_t(c_t)]. \tag{13}$$

Adding equation (13) from $t = 0$ to $t = T$ shows that $F_0(X_0, W_0) \geq U(c)$. Repeating the same calculations for the special policy $(c, \theta) = (c^*, \theta^*)$ allows us to replace the inequality in (13) with an equality, leaving $F_0(X_0, W_0) = U(c^*)$. This shows that $U(c^*) \geq U(c)$ for any feasible (θ, c), meaning that (θ^*, c^*) indeed solves equation (10) for $t = 0$. An optimal policy can thus be captured in *feedback* form in terms of the functions C_t and Φ_t, $t \leq T$. We also see that for all $t \leq T$, $F_t = V_t$, so V_t inherits the properties of F given by the last proposition.

We can now recover the stochastic Euler equation (9) directly from the first-order conditions to (12), rather than from the more general first-order conditions developed in Chapter 2 based on the gradient of U.

Theorem. A feasible policy (c^*, θ^*) with c^* strictly positive solves (10) for $t = 0$ and $w = 0$ if and only if, for all $t < T$,

$$S_t(X_t) = \frac{1}{u'_t(c^*_t)} E\left[u'_{t+1}(c^*_{t+1}) [S_{t+1}(X_{t+1}) + f_{t+1}(X_{t+1})] \,\middle|\, X_t\right]. \tag{14}$$

The theorem follows from the necessity and sufficiency of the first-order conditions for (12), relying on the last proposition for the fact that $F_{t+1,w}(X_{t+1}, W_{t+1}^*) = u'_{t+1}(c_{t+1}^*)$.

In a single-agent model, we define a sequence $\{S_0, \ldots, S_T\}$ of security-price functions to be a *single-agent equilibrium* if $(e, 0)$ (no trade) solves (10) for $t = 0$, $w = 0$, and any initial shock i.

Corollary. $\{S_0, \ldots, S_T\}$ *is a single-agent equilibrium if and only if* $S_T = 0$ *and, for all* $t < T$, *the stochastic Euler equation (9) is satisfied taking* $c^* = e$.

F. Arbitrage-Free Valuation in a Markov Setting

Taking the setting of Markov uncertainty described in Section 3C, but assuming no particular optimality properties or equilibrium, suppose that security prices and dividends are given, at each t, by functions S_t and f_t on Z into $\mathbb{R}^N$. It can be shown as an exercise that the absence of arbitrage is equivalent to the existence of a state-price deflator π given by $\pi_t = \psi_t(X_t)$ for some $\psi_t : Z \to \mathbb{R}$. With this, we have, for $0 < t \leq T$,

$$S_{t-1}(X_{t-1}) = \frac{1}{\psi_{t-1}(X_{t-1})} E\left(\psi_t(X_t)\left[f_t(X_t) + S_t(X_t)\right] \big| X_{t-1}\right). \qquad (15)$$

In the special setting of Section 3E, for example, (9) tells us that we can take $\psi_t(i) = u'_t[g(i)]$.

Since $Z = \{1, \ldots, k\}$ for some integer k, we can abuse the notation by treating any function such as $\psi_t : Z \to \mathbb{R}$ interchangeably as a vector in $\mathbb{R}^k$ denoted ψ_t, with i-th element $\psi_t(i)$. Likewise, S_t can be treated as a $k \times N$ matrix, and so on. In this sense, (15) can also be written

$$S_{t-1} = \Pi_{t-1}(f_t + S_t), \qquad (16)$$

where Π_{t-1} is the $k \times k$ matrix with (i, j)-element $q_{ij}\psi_t(j)/\psi_{t-1}(i)$. For each t and $s > t$, we let $\Pi_{t,s} = \Pi_t\Pi_{t+1}\cdots\Pi_{s-1}$. Then (16) is equivalent to, for any t and $\tau > t$,

$$S_t = \Pi_{t,\tau}S_\tau + \sum_{s=t+1}^{\tau} \Pi_{t,s}f_s. \qquad (17)$$

As an example, consider the "binomial" model of Exercise 2.1. We can let $Z = \{0, 1, \ldots, T\}$, with shock i having the interpretation: "There have so far occurred i 'up' returns on the stock." From the calculations in

Exercise 2.1, it is apparent that for any t, we may choose $\Pi_t = \Pi$, where

$$\Pi_{ij} = \frac{p}{R}, \qquad j = i + 1,$$

$$= \frac{1 - p}{R}, \qquad j = i,$$

$$= 0, \qquad \text{otherwise,}$$

where $p = (R - D)/(U - D)$, for constant coefficients R, U, and D, with $0 < D < R < U$. For a given initial stock price x and any $i \in Z$, the stock-price process S of Exercise 2.1 can indeed be represented at each time t by $S_t : Z \to \mathbb{R}$, where $S_t(i) = xU^iD^{t-i}$.

We can recover the "binomial" option-pricing formula (2.16) by noting that the European call option with strike price K and expiration time τ may be treated as a security with dividends only at time τ given by the function $g : Z \to \mathbb{R}$, with $g(i) = [S_\tau(i) - K]^+$. From (17), the arbitrage-free value of the option at time t is $C_t^\tau = \Pi^{\tau-t}g$, where Π^t denotes the t-th power of Π. This same valuation formula applies to an arbitrary security paying a dividend at time τ defined by some payoff function $g : Z \to \mathbb{R}$.

G. Early Exercise and Optimal Stopping

In the setting of Section 3F, consider an "American" security, defined by some payoff functions $g_t : Z \to \mathbb{R}$, $t \in \{0, \dots, T\}$. As explained in Section 2I, the security is a claim to the dividend $g_\tau(X_\tau)$ at any stopping time τ selected by the owner. Expiration of the security at some time $\bar{\tau}$ is handled by defining g_t to be zero for $t > \bar{\tau}$. Given the state-price deflator π defined by $\pi_t = \psi_t(X_t)$, as outlined in the previous section, the rational exercise problem (2.13) for the American security, with initial shock i, is given by

$$J_0(i) \equiv \max_{\tau \in \mathcal{T}} \frac{1}{\psi_0(i)} E^i \left[\psi_\tau(X_\tau) g(X_\tau) \right], \tag{18}$$

where $\mathcal{T}$ is the set of stopping times bounded by T. As explained in Section 2I, if the American security is redundant and there is no arbitrage, then $J_0(i)$ is its cum-dividend value at time 0 with initial shock i. Provided the transition matrix q is strictly positive, the Bellman equation for (18) is

$$J_t(i) \equiv \max \left(g_t(i), \frac{1}{\psi_t(i)} E \left[\psi_{t+1}(X_{t+1}) J_{t+1}(X_{t+1}) \mid X_t = i \right] \right). \tag{19}$$

If q is not strictly positive, a slightly more complicated expression applies. It is left as an exercise to show that J_0 is indeed determined inductively, backward in time from T, by (19) and $J_T = g_T$. Moreover, as demonstrated in Section 2I, problem (18) is solved by the stopping time

$$\tau^* = \min \left[t : J_t(X_t) = g_t(X_t) \right]. \tag{20}$$

In our alternate notation that treats J_t as a vector in $\mathbb{R}^k$, we can rewrite the Bellman equation (19) in the form

$$J_t = \max \left(g_t, \Pi_t J_{t+1} \right), \tag{21}$$

where, for any x and y in $\mathbb{R}^k$, $\max(x, y)$ denotes the vector in $\mathbb{R}^k$ that has $\max(x_i, y_i)$ as its i-th element. This form (21) of the Bellman equation applies even if q is not strictly positive.

Equation (21) leads to a simple recursive solution algorithm for the American put valuation problem of Exercise 2.1. Given an expiration time $\overline{\tau} < T$ and exercise price K, we have $J_T = 0$ and

$$J_t = \max \left[(K - S_t)^+, \ \Pi_t J_{t+1} \right], \tag{22}$$

or more explicitly: For any t and $i \le t$,

$$J_t(i) = \max \left([K - S_t(i)]^+, \ \frac{p J_{t+1}(i+1) + (1 - p) J_{t+1}(i)}{R} \right), \tag{23}$$

where $S_t(i) = x U^i D^{t-1}$ and $p = (R - D)/(U - D)$, for constant coefficients R, U, and D, with $0 < D < R < U$.

More generally, consider an *American security* defined by dividend functions $h_0, \ldots, h_T$ and exercise payoff functions $g_0, \ldots, g_T$. For a given expiration time $\overline{\tau}$, we have $h_t = g_t = 0$, $t > \overline{\tau}$. The owner of the security chooses a stopping time τ at which to exercise, generating the dividend process δ^τ defined by

$$
\begin{aligned}
\delta_t^\tau &= h_t(X_t), \qquad t < \tau, \\
&= g_t(X_t), \qquad t = \tau, \\
&= 0, \qquad\quad t > \tau.
\end{aligned}
$$

Assuming that δ^τ is redundant for any exercise policy τ, the security's arbitrage-free cum-dividend value is defined recursively by $J_T = 0$ and the extension of (21):

$$J_t = \max \left(g_t, \ h_t + \Pi_t J_{t+1} \right). \tag{24}$$

Exercises

3.1   Prove the Bellman equation (4).

3.2   For each t and each w such that there exists a feasible policy, let $C_t(w)$ solve equation (4). Let W^* be determined by equation (1) with $c_{t-1} = C_{t-1}(W^*_{t-1})$ for $t > 0$. Show that an optimal policy c^* is given by $c_t^* = C_t(W_t^*)$, $t < T$, and $c_T^* = e_T + W_T^*$.

3.3   Prove Lemma 3B. Hint: If $f : \mathbb{R} \to \mathbb{R}$ is concave, then for each x there is a number β such that $\beta(x - y) \ge f(x) - f(y)$ for all x and y. If f is also differentiable at x, then $\beta = f'(x)$. If f is differentiable and strictly concave, then f is continuously differentiable. Let $w^* = W_t^*$. If $c_t^* > 0$, there is an interval $I = (\underline{w}, \overline{w}) \subset \mathbb{R}$ with $w^* \in I$ such that $v : I \to \mathbb{R}$ is well defined by

$$v(w) = u_t(c_t^* + w - w^*) + V_{t+1}(W^*_{t+1}).$$

Now use the differentiability of v, the definition of a derivative, and the fact that $v(w) \le V_t(w)$ for all $w \in I$.

3.4   Prove equation (9).

3.5   Prove Proposition 3E.

3.6   Prove Theorem 3E and its corollary.

3.7   Consider the case of securities in positive supply, which can be taken without loss of generality to be a supply of 1 each. Equilibrium in the context of Section 3E is thus redefined by the following: $\{S_0, \dots, S_T\}$ is an equilibrium if (c^*, θ^*) solves (10) at $t = 0$ and $w = \mathbf{1} \cdot [S_0(X_0) + f_0(X_0)]$, where $\mathbf{1} = (1, \dots, 1)$ and, for all t, $\theta_t^* = \mathbf{1}$, and $c_t^* = g_t(X_t) + \mathbf{1} \cdot f_t(X_t)$. Demonstrate a new version of the stochastic Euler equation (9) that characterizes equilibrium in this case.

3.8   (Recursive Utility Revisited)   The objective in this exercise is to extend the basic results of the chapter to the case of a recursive-utility function that generalizes additive utility. Rather than assuming a typical additive-utility function U of the form

$$U(c) = E\left[\sum_{t=0}^{T} \rho^t u(c_t)\right], \tag{25}$$

we adopt instead the more general recursive definition of utility given by $U(c) = Y_0$, where Y is a process defined by $Y_{T+1} = 0$ and, for any $t \le T$,

$$Y_t = J\left(c_t, E_t[h(Y_{t+1})]\right), \tag{26}$$

where $J : \mathbb{R}_+ \times \mathbb{R} \to \mathbb{R}$ and $h : \mathbb{R} \to \mathbb{R}$. This is the special case treated in Exercise 2.9 of what is known as recursive utility. (In an even more general recursive-utility model, the von Neumann-Morgenstern criterion $E[h(\cdot)]$ is replaced by a general functional on distributions, but we do not deal with this further generalization.) Note that the special case $J(q, w) = u(q) + \rho w$ and $h(y) = y$ gives us the additively separable criterion (25). The conventional additive utility has the disadvantage that the elasticity of intertemporal substitution (as measured in a deterministic setting) and relative risk aversion are fixed in terms of one another. The recursive criterion, however, allows one to examine the effects of varying risk aversion while holding fixed the utility's elasticity of intertemporal substitution in a deterministic setting.

(A)   (Dynamic Programming)   Provide an extension of the Bellman equation (12) for optimal portfolio and consumption choice, substituting the recursive utility for the additive utility. That is, state a revised Bellman equation and regularity conditions on the utility primitives (J, h) under which a solution to the Bellman equation implies that the associated feedback policies solving the Bellman equation generate optimal consumption and portfolio choice. (State a theorem with proof.) Also, include conditions under which there exists a solution to the Bellman equation. For simplicity, among your conditions you may wish to impose the assumptions that J and h are continuous and strictly increasing.

(B)   (Asset Pricing Theory)   Suppose that J and h are differentiable, increasing, and concave, with either h or J (or both) strictly concave. Provide any additional regularity conditions that you feel are called for in order to derive an analogue to the stochastic Euler equation (9) for security prices.

(C)   (An Investment Problem)   Let $G : Z \times \mathbb{R}_+ \to \mathbb{R}_+$ and consider the capital-stock investment problem defined by

$$\sup_{c \in L_+} U(c) \tag{27}$$

subject to $0 \leq c_t \leq K_t$ for all t, where $K_0, K_1, \ldots,$ is a capital-stock process defined by $K_t = G(X_t, K_{t-1} - c_{t-1})$, and where $X_0, \ldots, X_T$ is the Markov process defined in Section 3C. The utility function U is the recursive function defined above in terms of (J, h). Provide reasonable conditions on (J, h, G) under which there exists a solution. State the Bellman equation.

(D)   (Parametric Example)   For this part, in order to obtain closed-form solutions, we depart from the assumption that the shock takes only a finite number of possible values, and replace this with a normality assumption. Solve the problem of part (C) in the following case:

(a) X is the real-valued shock process defined by $X_{t+1} = A + BX_t + \epsilon_{t+1}$, where A and B are scalars and $\epsilon_1, \epsilon_2, \ldots$ is an *i.i.d.* sequence of normally distributed random variables with $E(\epsilon_t) = 0$ and $\text{var}(\epsilon_t) = \sigma^2$.

(b) $G(x, a) = a^\gamma e^x$ for some $\gamma \in (0, 1)$.

(c) $J(q, w) = \log(q) + \rho \log(w^{1/\alpha})$ for some $\alpha \in (0, 1)$.

(d) $h(v) = e^{\alpha v}$ for $v \geq 0$.

Hint: You may wish to conjecture a solution to the value function of the form $V_t(x, k) = A_1(t) \log(k) + A_2(t)x + A_3(t)$, for time-dependent coefficients A_1, A_2, and A_3. This example is unlikely to satisfy the regularity conditions that you imposed in part (C).

(E) (Term Structure) For the consumption endowment process e defined by the solution to part (D), return to the setting of part (B), and calculate the price $\Lambda_{t,s}$ at time t of a pure discount bond paying one unit of consumption at time $s > t$. Note that α is a measure of risk tolerance that can be studied independently of the effects of intertemporal substitution in this model, since, for deterministic consumption processes, utility is independent of α, with $J[q, h(v)] = \log(q) + \rho \log(v)$.

3.9 Show equation (5) directly from equation (2.9).

3.10 Consider, as in the setup described in Section 3F, securities defined by the dividend-price pair (δ, S), where, for all t, there are functions f_t and S_t on Z into $\mathbb{R}^N$ such that $\delta_t = f_t(X_t)$ and $S_t = S_t(X_t)$. Show that there is no arbitrage if and only if there is a state-price deflator π such that, for each time t, $\pi_t = \psi_t(X_t)$ for some function $\psi_t : Z \to (0, \infty)$.

3.11 (Binomial Term-Structure Algorithms) This exercise asks for a series of numerical solutions of term-structure valuation problems in a setting with binomial changes in short-term interest rates. In the setting of Section 3F, suppose that short-term riskless borrowing is possible at any time t at the discount d_t. The one-period interest rate at time t is denoted r_t, and is given by its definition:

$$d_t = \frac{1}{1 + r_t}.$$

The underlying shock process X has the property that either $X_t = X_{t-1} + 1$ or $X_t = X_{t-1}$. That is, in each period, the new shock is the old shock plus a 0-1 binomial trial. An example is the binomial stock-option pricing model of Exercise 2.1, which is reconsidered in Section 3F. As opposed to that example, we do not necesarily assume here that interest rates are constant. Rather, we allow, at each time t, a function $\rho_t : Z \to \mathbb{R}$ such that $r_t = \rho_t(X_t)$. For simplicity, however, we take it that at any time t the pricing matrix Π_t defined in Section 3F is of the form

$$(\Pi_t)_{ij} = \frac{p}{1 + \rho_t(i)}, \qquad j = i + 1,$$

$$= \frac{1 - p}{1 + \rho_t(i)}, \qquad j = i,$$

$$= 0, \qquad \text{otherwise},$$

where $p \in (0, 1)$ is the "risk-neutral" probability that $X_{t+1} - X_t = 1$. Literally, there is an equivalent martingale measure Q under which, for all t, we have

$$Q(X_{t+1} - X_t = 1 \mid X_0, \dots, X_t) = p.$$

It may help to imagine the calculation of security prices at the nodes of the "tree" illustrated in Figure 3.1. The horizontal axis indicates the time periods; the vertical axis corresponds to the possible levels of the shock, assuming that $X_0 = 0$. At each time t and at each shock level i, the price of a given security at the (i, t)-node of the tree is given by a weighted sum of its value at the two successor nodes $(i + 1, t + 1)$ and $(i, t + 1)$. Specifically,

$$S_t(i) = \frac{1}{1 + \rho_t(i)} \left[p(S_{t+1}(i + 1) + f_{t+1}(i + 1)) + (1 - p)(S_{t+1}(i) + f_{t+1}(i)) \right].$$

Two typical models for the short rate are obtained by taking $p = 1/2$ and either

(a) the *Ho-Lee model*: For each $t < T$, $\rho_t(i) = a_t + b_t i$ for some constants a_t and b_t; or

(b) the *Black-Derman-Toy model*: For each t, $\rho_t(i) = a_t \exp(b_t i)$ for some constants a_t and b_t.

(A)   For case (b), prepare computer code to calculate the arbitrage-free price $\Lambda_{0,t}$ of a zero-coupon bond of any given maturity t, given the coefficients a_t and b_t for each t. Prepare an example taking $b_t = 0.01$ for all t and $a_0, a_1, \dots, a_T$ such that $E^Q(r_t) = 0.01$ for all t. (These parameters are of a typical order of magnitude for monthly periods.) Solve for the price $\Lambda_{0,t}$ of a unit zero-coupon riskless bond maturing at time t, for all t in $\{1, \dots, 50\}$.

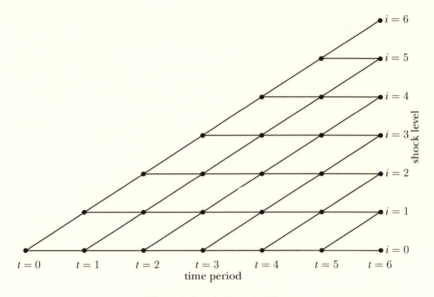

Figure 3.1.   *A Binomial Tree*

(B) Consider, for any i and t, the price $\psi(i, t)$ at time 0 of a security that pays one unit of account at time t if and only if $X_t = i$.

Show that ψ can be calculated recursively by the forward difference equation

$$
\begin{aligned}
\psi(i, t+1) &= \frac{\psi(i, t)}{2[1 + \rho_t(i)]} + \frac{\psi(i-1, t)}{2[1 + \rho_t(i-1)]}, && 0 < i < t+1, \\
&= \frac{\psi(i-1, t)}{2[1 + \rho_t(i-1)]}, && i = t+1, \qquad\qquad (28) \\
&= \frac{\psi(i, t)}{2[1 + \rho_t(i)]}, && i = 0.
\end{aligned}
$$

The initial condition is $\psi(0,0) = 1$ and $\psi(i,0) = 0$ for $i > 0$.

Knowledge of this "shock-price" function ψ, often called *Green's function*, is useful. For example, the arbitrage-free price at time 0 of a security that pays the dividend $f(X_t)$ at time t (and nothing otherwise) is given by $\sum_{i=0}^{t} \psi_t(i) f(i)$.

(C)   In practice, the coefficients a_t and b_t are often fitted to match the initial term structure $\Lambda_{0,1}, \ldots, \Lambda_{0,T}$, given the "volatility" coefficients $b_0, \ldots, b_T$.

The following algorithm has been suggested for this purpose, using the fact that $\Lambda_{0,t} = \sum_{i=0}^{t} \psi_t(i)$.

(a) Let $\psi(0,0) = 1$ and let $t = 1$.

(b) Fixing ψ_{t-1} and b_t, let $\lambda_t(a_{t-1}) = \sum_{i=0}^{t} \psi_t(i)$, where ψ_t is given by the forward difference equation (28). Only the dependence of the t-maturity zero-coupon bond price $\lambda_t(a_{t-1})$ on a_{t-1} is notationally explicit. Since $\lambda_t(a_{t-1})$ is strictly monotone in a_{t-1}, we can solve numerically for that coefficient a_{t-1} such that $\Lambda_{0,t} = \lambda_t(a_{t-1})$. (A Newton-Raphson search will suffice.)

(c) Let t be increased by 1. Return to step (b) if $t \leq T$. Otherwise, stop.

Prepare computer code for this algorithm (a)–(b)–(c). Given $b_t = 0.01$ for all t, solve for a_t for all t, using the Black-Derman-Toy model, given an initial term structure that is given by $\Lambda_{0,t} = \alpha^t$, where $\alpha = 0.99$.

(D) Extend your code as necessary to give the price of American call options on coupon bonds of any given maturity. For the coefficients $a_0, \ldots,$ a_{T-1} that you determined from part (C), calculate the initial price of an American option on a bond that pays coupons of 0.011 each period until its maturity at time 20, at which time it pays 1 unit of account in addition to its coupon. The option has an exercise price of 1.00 and expiration at time 10. Do this for the Black-Derman-Toy model only.

Notes

Bellman's principle of optimality is due to Bellman (1957). Freedman (1983) covers the theory of Markov chains. For general treatments of dynamic programming in a discrete-time Markov setting, see Bertsekas (1976) and Bertsekas and Shreve (1978). The proof for Lemma 3B that is sketched in Exercise 3.3, on the differentiability of the value function, is from Benveniste and Scheinkman (1979), and easily extends to general state spaces; see, for example, Duffie (1988b) and Stokey and Lucas (1989). The *semigroup* pricing approach implicit in equation (17) is from Duffie and Garman (1991). Exercise 3.8, treating asset pricing with the recursive utility of Exercise 2.9, is extended to the infinite-horizon setting of Epstein and Zin (1989) in Exercise 4.12. See the Notes of Chapter 2 for additional references on recursive utility and Streufert (1991a,b,c) for more on dynamic programming with a recursive-utility function. For additional work on recursive utility and asset pricing in a discrete-time Markovian setting, see Kan (1993, 1995) and Ma (1991a, 1994b).

The extensive exercise on binomial term-structure models is based almost entirely on Jamshidian (1991c), who emphasizes the connection between the solution ψ of the difference equation (28) and *Green's function*. This connection is reconsidered in Chapters 7 and 11 for continuous-time applications. The two particular term-structure models appearing in this exercise are based, respectively, on Ho and Lee (1986) and Black, Derman, and Toy (1990). The parametric form shown here for the Ho-Lee model is slightly more general than the form actually appearing in Ho and Lee (1986). Most authors take the convention that X_{t+1} is $X_t + 1$ or $X_t - 1$, which generates a slightly different form for the same model. The two forms are equivalent after a change of the parameters. Pye (1966), whose work predates the notion of "risk-neutral valuation" provides a remarkably early precursor to these discrete-time Markovian models of the term structure. Continuous-time versions of these models are considered in Chapter 7. Chapter 11 also deals in more detail with algorithms designed to match the initial term structure. Exercise 11.5 demonstrates convergence, with a decreasing length of time period, of the discrete-time Black-Derman-Toy model to its continuous-time version. Jamshidian (1991c) considers a larger class of examples.

Derman and Kani (1994), Dupire (1994), and Rubinstein (1994, 1995) provide various methods for calibrating a "binomial" Markov stock price process, similar to that of Section 3F, to the available prices of options of various strike prices and, in some cases, of various maturities. This is part of a literature devoted to the *smile curve*, which refers to the shape often found for a plot of the "implied volatilities" of option prices derived from the Black-Scholes formula against the exercise prices of the respective options. If the assumptions underlying the Black-Scholes formula are correct, the implied volatility does not depend on the strike price. The smile curve is discussed once again in Chapter 8, under the topic of stochastic volatility. Related literature is cited in the Notes of Chapter 8. A related approach to calibration of the stochastic behavior of the underlying asset price to the prices of options is considered by Shimko (1993).

4

The Infinite-Horizon Setting

THIS CHAPTER PRESENTS infinite-period analogues of the results of Chapters 2 and 3. Although it requires additional technicalities and produces few new insights, this setting is often deemed important for reasons of elegance or for serving the large-sample theory of econometrics, which calls for an unbounded number of observations. We start directly with a Markov dynamic programming extension of the finite-horizon results of Chapter 3, and only later consider the implications of no arbitrage or optimality for security prices without using the Markov assumption. Finally, we return to the stationary Markov setting to review briefly the large-sample approach to estimating asset pricing models. Only Sections 4A and 4B are essential; the remainder could be skipped on a first reading.

A. The Markov Dynamic Programming Solution

Suppose $X = \{X_0, X_1, X_2, \ldots\}$ is a time-homogeneous Markov chain of shocks valued in a finite set $Z = \{1, \ldots, k\}$, defined exactly as in Section 3C, with the exception that there is an infinite number of time periods. Given a $k \times k$ nonnegative matrix whose columns sum to 1, sources given in the Notes explain the existence of a probability space $(\Omega, \mathcal{F}, P_i)$, for each initial shock i, satisfying the defining properties $P_i(X_0 = i) = 1$ and

$$P_i(X_{t+1} = j \mid X_0, \ldots, X_t) = q_{X(t),j}.$$

As in Chapter 3, $\mathcal{F}_t$ denotes the tribe generated by $\{X_0, \ldots, X_t\}$. That is, the source of information is the Markov chain $\{X_t\}$. This is the first appearance in the book of a set Ω of states that need not be finite, but because there is only a finite number of events in $\mathcal{F}_t$ for each t, most of this chapter can be easily understood without referring to Appendix C for a review of general probability spaces.

Let L denote the space of sequences of random variables of the form $c = \{c_0, c_1, c_2, \ldots\}$ such that there is a constant k with the property that for all t, c_t is $\mathcal{F}_t$-measurable with $|c_t| \leq k$. In other words, L is the space of bounded adapted processes. Agents choose a consumption process from the set L_+ of nonnegative processes in L. There are N securities; security n is defined by a dividend process δ^n in L and has a price process S^n in L. A trading strategy is some $\theta = (\theta^1, \ldots, \theta^N) \in \Theta \equiv L^N$. Each strategy θ in Θ generates a dividend process δ^θ in L defined, just as in Chapter 2, by

$$\delta_t^\theta = \theta_{t-1} \cdot (S_t + \delta_t) - \theta_t \cdot S_t, \qquad t \geq 0,$$

with "θ_{-1}" $= 0$ by convention. A given agent has an endowment process e in L_+ and, given a particular initial shock i, a utility function $U^i : L_+ \to \mathbb{R}$. The agent's problem is

$$\sup_{\theta \in \Theta(e)} \quad U^i(e + \delta^\theta),$$

where $\Theta(e) = \{\theta \in \Theta : e + \delta^\theta \geq 0\}$.

In order to develop a time-homogeneous Markov model, we restrict ourselves initially to utility functions, endowments, and security dividends with special time-homogeneous properties. Given an initial shock i, consider the utility function $U^i : L_+ \to \mathbb{R}$ defined by a discount $\rho \in (0, 1)$ and a strictly increasing, bounded, concave, and continuous $u : \mathbb{R}_+ \to \mathbb{R}$ according to

$$U^i(c) = E^i \left[\sum_{t=0}^\infty \rho^t u(c_t) \right], \tag{1}$$

where E^i denotes expectation under the probability measure P_i associated with the initial shock $X_0 = i$. Suppose that $g : Z \to \mathbb{R}_{++}$ and $f : Z \to \mathbb{R}_{++}^N$ are such that for all t, the endowment is $e_t = g(X_t)$ and the dividend vector is $\delta_t = f(X_t)$. Finally, suppose that security prices are given by some fixed $S : Z \to \mathbb{R}_{++}^N$ so that for all t, $S_t = \mathcal{S}(X_t)$.

We fix a portfolio b in $\mathbb{R}_{++}^N$ and think of $-b$ as a lower bound on short positions. This restriction will later be removed. For now, however, wealth is bounded below by

$$\underline{w} = \min_{i \in Z} \; -b \cdot [\mathcal{S}(i) + f(i)].$$

Let $D = Z \times [\underline{w}, \infty)$. A function $F : D \to \mathbb{R}$ is defined to be in the space denoted $B(D)$ if, for each i in Z, $F(i, \cdot) : [\underline{w}, \infty) \to \mathbb{R}$ is bounded, continuous, and concave. We are looking for some V in $B(D)$ as the *value* of the agent's control problem. That is, we want some V in $B(D)$ with

$$V(i, w) = \sup_{(c,\theta) \in L_+ \times \Theta} U^i(c), \tag{2}$$

subject to

$$W_0^\theta = w, \tag{3}$$

$$W_t^\theta = \theta_{t-1} \cdot [S(X_t) + f(X_t)], \qquad t \geq 1, \tag{4}$$

$$c_t + \theta_t \cdot S(X_t) \leq W_t^\theta + g(X_t), \qquad t \geq 0, \tag{5}$$

$$\theta_t \geq -b, \qquad t \geq 0. \tag{6}$$

We will solve for the value function V by taking an arbitrary F in $B(D)$ and, from this candidate, construct a new candidate denoted UF that is described below. Our method will show that if $F = UF$, then $F = V$. In fact, this approach also leads to an algorithm, called *value iteration*, for calculating V. This algorithm is laid out below. For any F in $B(D)$, let $UF : D \to \mathbb{R}$ be defined by

$$UF(i, w) = \sup_{(\bar{\theta}, \bar{c}) \in \mathbb{R}^N \times \mathbb{R}_+} u(\bar{c}) + \rho E^i \left[F\left(X_1, \bar{\theta} \cdot [S(X_1) + f(X_1)]\right) \right], \tag{7}$$

subject to

$$\bar{c} + \bar{\theta} \cdot S(i) \leq w + g(i), \tag{8}$$

$$\bar{\theta} \geq -b. \tag{9}$$

In other words, $UF(i, w)$ is the supremum utility that can be achieved at (i, w), assuming that the value function in the next period is F.

Proofs of the next three results are left as exercises.

Fact. *If F is in $B(D)$, then UF is in $B(D)$.*

For any F and G in $B(D)$, let

$$d(F, G) = \sup\{|F(i, w) - G(i, w)| : (i, w) \in D\},$$

giving a notion of the *distance* between any two such functions. Clearly $F = G$ if and only if $d(F, G) = 0$.

Lemma. *For any F and G in $B(D)$, $d(UF, UG) \leq \rho\, d(F, G)$.*

Using this lemma, we can construct the unique solution F to the equation $UF = F$, which is known as the *Bellman equation* for problem (2)–(6). The solution F is called the *fixed point* of U and, as shown by the following result, can be constructed as the limit of the finite-horizon versions of the value functions as the horizon goes to infinity.

Proposition. *Let $F_{-1}(i, w) = 0$ for all (i, w) in D, and let $F_t = \mathcal{U}F_{t-1}$, $t \geq 0$. Then $F(i, w) \equiv \lim_{t \to \infty} F_t(i, w)$ exists for all (i, w) in D and defines the unique function F in $B(D)$ satisfying $F = \mathcal{U}F$.*

We take F to be the unique fixed point of $\mathcal{U}$. We will show that F is the value function V of problem (2)–(6). Let $C : D \to \mathbb{R}_+$ and $\Phi : D \to \mathbb{R}^N$ be functions defined by letting $[C(i, w), \Phi(i, w)]$ solve (7)–(9). Given the initial conditions (i, w) of (2)–(6), let W^* be defined by $W_0^* = w$ and $W_t^* = \Phi(X_{t-1}, W_{t-1}^*) \cdot [\mathcal{S}(X_t) + f(X_t)]$, $t \geq 1$. Then let (c^*, θ^*) be defined by $c_t^* = C(X_t, W_t^*)$ and $\theta_t^* = \Phi(X_t, W_t^*)$, $t \geq 0$. We refer to (θ^*, c^*) as the *optimal feedback policy.*

Theorem. *The value function V of (2)–(6) is the unique fixed point of $\mathcal{U}$. The optimal feedback policy (c^*, θ^*) solves (2)–(6).*

Proof: Let F be the unique solution of the Bellman equation $\mathcal{U}F = F$. Fix any initial shock i in Z and initial wealth w in $[\underline{w}, \infty)$. Let (θ, c) be an arbitrary feasible policy. For any time t, by the Bellman equation (7)–(9),

$$F(X_t, W_t^\theta) \geq u(c_t) + \rho E^i \left[F(X_{t+1}, W_{t+1}^\theta) \mid X_t \right].$$

Multiplying through by ρ^t and rearranging,

$$\rho^t F(X_t, W_t^\theta) - \rho^{t+1} E^i \left[F(X_{t+1}, W_{t+1}^\theta) \mid X_t \right] \geq \rho^t u(c_t). \qquad (10)$$

Taking expectations on each side, and using the law of iterated expectations,

$$E^i \left[\rho^t F(X_t, W_t^\theta) \right] - \rho^{t+1} E^i \left[F(X_{t+1}, W_{t+1}^\theta) \right] \geq E^i [\rho^t u(c_t)].$$

Calculating the sum of this expression from $t = 0$ to $t = T$, for any time $T \geq 1$, causes telescopic cancellation on the left-hand side, leaving only

$$E^i \left[F(X_0, W_0^\theta) \right] - \rho^{T+1} E^i \left[F(X_{T+1}, W_{T+1}^\theta) \right] \geq E^i \left[\sum_{t=0}^{T} \rho^t u(c_t) \right].$$

Since F is a bounded function and $\rho \in (0, 1)$, the limit of the left-hand side as $T \to \infty$ is $F(i, w)$. By the Dominated Convergence Theorem (Appendix C), the limit of the right-hand side is $U^i(c)$. Thus $F(i, w) \geq U^i(c)$, implying that $F(i, w) \geq V(i, w)$ for any i and w. All of the above calculations apply for the feedback policy (c^*, θ^*), for which we can replace the inequality in (10) with an equality, using the definition of C and Φ. This leaves $F(i, w) = U^i(c^*)$. It follows, since (i, w) is arbitrary, that V is indeed the value function and that (c^*, θ^*) is an optimal policy, proving the result. ∎

B. Markov Dynamic Programming and Equilibrium

Section 4A shows the existence of optimal control in feedback form, given by *policy functions* C and Φ that specify optimal consumption and portfolio choices in terms of the current shock–wealth pair (i, w). In order to characterize an equilibrium by the same approach, we adopt stronger utility conditions for this section. In addition to our standing assumption that u is strictly increasing, bounded, concave, and continuous, we add the following regularity condition.

Assumption A. *The function u is strictly concave and differentiable on $(0, \infty)$.*

We define S to be a single-agent *Markov equilibrium* if associated optimal feedback policies C and Φ can be chosen so that for any shock i, $C(i, 0) = g(i)$ and $\Phi(i, 0) = 0$. With this, the consumption and security markets always clear if the agent is originally endowed with no wealth beyond that of his or her private endowment. The short sales restriction on portfolios is superfluous in equilibrium since this short sales constraint is not binding at the solution $(e, 0)$, and since the equilibrium shown (which is the unique equilibrium) does not depend on the particular lower bound $-b$ chosen. (It is assigned as an exercise to verify this fact.) Our main objective is to demonstrate the following characterization of equilibrium.

Proposition. *S is a Markov equilibrium if and only if, for all i,*

$$S(i) = \frac{1}{u'[g(i)]} E^i \left(\sum_{t=1}^{\infty} \rho^t \, u'[g(X_t)] f(X_t) \right). \tag{11}$$

The law of iterated expectations implies the following equivalent form of (11), sometimes called the stochastic Euler equation.

Corollary. *S is a Markov equilibrium if and only if, for any time t and any initial shock i,*

$$S(X_t) = \frac{1}{u'[g(X_t)]} E^i \left(\rho u'[g(X_{t+1})] \left[S(X_{t+1}) + f(X_{t+1}) \right] \Big| X_t \right). \tag{12}$$

We will demonstrate these results by exploiting the properties of the value function V.

Fact 1. *For each i, $V(i, \cdot) : [\underline{w}, \infty) \to \mathbb{R}$ is increasing and strictly concave.*

Fact 2. *Fixing S arbitrarily, let (C, Φ) be the optimal feedback policies, as above. Suppose, at a given i and $\hat{w} > \underline{w}$, that $\hat{c} = C(i, \hat{w}) > 0$. Then $V(i, \cdot)$ is continuously differentiable at $\hat{w}$ with derivative $V_w(i, \hat{w}) = \rho \, u'(\hat{c})$.*

These two facts, proved in a manner similar to their analogues in Chapter 3, imply, from the first-order conditions of the Bellman equation (7) and the fact that V solves the Bellman equation, that C and Φ can be chosen with $C(i, 0) = g(i)$ and $\Phi(i, 0) = 0$ for all i if and only if

$$S(i) = \frac{1}{u'[g(i)]} E^i \left(\rho \, u'[g(X_1)] \, [S(X_1) + f(X_1)] \right), \qquad i \in Z. \qquad (13)$$

Then (13) is equivalent to (11) and (12), proving the Proposition and Corollary.

C. Arbitrage and State Prices

We turn away from the special case of Markov uncertainty in order to investigate the implications of lack of arbitrage and of optimality for security prices in an abstract infinite-horizon setting. Suppose Ω is a set, $\mathcal{F}$ is a tribe on Ω, and, for each nonnegative integer t, $\mathcal{F}_t$ is a finite sub-tribe with $\mathcal{F}_t \subset \mathcal{F}_s$ for $s \geq t$. We also fix a probability measure P on $(\Omega, \mathcal{F})$. As usual, we assume that $\mathcal{F}_0$ includes only events of probability 0 or 1. We again denote by L the space of bounded adapted processes. There are N securities; security n is defined by a dividend process δ^n in L and has a price process S^n in L. A trading strategy is some $\theta = (\theta^1, \ldots, \theta^N) \in \Theta \equiv L^N$.

An *arbitrage* is a trading strategy θ with $\delta^\theta > 0$. If there is no arbitrage, then for any T, there is no *T-period arbitrage*, meaning an arbitrage θ with $\theta_t = 0$, $t \geq T$. Fixing T momentarily, if there is no T-period arbitrage, then the results of Chapter 2 imply that there is a *T-period state-price deflator*, a strictly positive process π^T in L with $\pi_0^T = 1$ such that for any trading strategy θ with $\theta_t = 0$, $t \geq T$, we have $E(\sum_{t=0}^T \pi_t^T \delta_t^\theta) = 0$. Likewise, there is a $(T+1)$-period state-price deflator π^{T+1}. It can be checked that the process $\hat{\pi}$ defined by $\hat{\pi}_t = \pi_t^T$, $t \leq T$, and $\hat{\pi}_t = \pi_t^{T+1}$, $t > T$, is also a $(T+1)$-period state-price deflator. By induction in T, this means that there is a strictly positive adapted process π such that for any trading strategy θ with $\theta_t = 0$ for all t larger than some T, we have $E(\sum_{t=0}^\infty \pi_t \delta_t^\theta) = 0$. In particular, π has the property that for any times t and $\tau \geq t$, we have the now-familiar state-pricing relationship

$$S_t = \frac{1}{\pi_t} E_t \left(\pi_\tau S_\tau + \sum_{j=t+1}^\tau \pi_j \delta_j \right). \qquad (14)$$

Equation (14) even holds when τ is a bounded stopping time. Unfortunately, there is no reason (yet) to believe that there is a state-price deflator, a strictly positive adapted process π such that (14) holds for τ an unbounded stopping time, or that for any t,

$$S_t = \frac{1}{\pi_t} E_t \left(\sum_{j=t+1}^{\infty} \pi_j \, \delta_j \right). \tag{15}$$

Indeed, the right-hand side of (15) may not even be well defined. We need some restriction on π!

We call an adapted process x *mean-summable* if $E\left(\sum_{t=0}^{\infty} |x_t|\right) < \infty$, and let L^* denote the space of mean-summable processes. If $\pi \in L^*$ and $c \in L$, then the Dominated Convergence Theorem (Appendix C) implies that $E\left(\sum_{t=0}^{\infty} \pi_t \, c_t\right)$ is well defined and finite, so L^* may be a natural space of candidate state-price deflators if (15) is to work.

D. Optimality and State Prices

An agent is defined by an endowment process e in the space L_+ of nonnegative processes in L, and by a strictly increasing utility function $U : L_+ \to \mathbb{R}$. Given the dividend-price pair $(\delta, S) \in L^N \times L^N$, the agent has the budget-feasible set $X(S, e) = \{e + \delta^\theta \in L_+ : \theta \in \Theta\}$ and faces the problem

$$\sup_{c \in X(S,e)} U(c). \tag{16}$$

We say that the utility function U is L^*-*smooth* at c if the gradient $\nabla U(c)$ exists and moreover has a unique Riesz representation π in L^* defined by

$$\nabla U(c; x) = E\left(\sum_{t=0}^{\infty} \pi_t \, x_t \right),$$

for any feasible direction x in L. (See Appendix B for the definition of the gradient and feasible directions.) For example, suppose that U is defined by $U(c) = E\left[\sum_{t=0}^{\infty} \rho^t u(c_t)\right]$, where $u : \mathbb{R}_+ \to \mathbb{R}$ is strictly increasing and continuously differentiable on $(0, \infty)$, and where $\rho \in (0, 1)$. Then, for any c in L_+ that is bounded away from zero, U is L^*-smooth at c, any x in L is a feasible direction at c, and

$$\nabla U(c; x) = E\left[\sum_{t=0}^{\infty} \rho^t \, u'(c_t) \, x_t \right], \qquad x \in L, \tag{17}$$

implying that the Riesz representation of the utility gradient is in this case the process π defined by $\pi_t = \rho^t u_t'(c_t)$.

More generally, we have the following characterization of state-price deflators.

Proposition. *Suppose c^* solves (16), c^* is bounded away from zero, and U is L^*-smooth at c^*. Then the Riesz representation π of $\nabla U(c^*)$ is a state-price deflator.*

Corollary. *Suppose, moreover, that U is defined by*

$$U(c) = E\left[\sum_{t=0}^{\infty} \rho^t u(c_t)\right],$$

where $\rho \in (0,1)$ and u has a strictly positive derivative on $(0,\infty)$. Then π, defined by $\pi_t = \rho^t u'(c_t^*)$, is a state-price deflator and, for any time t and stopping time $\tau > t$,

$$S_t = \frac{1}{u'(c_t^*)} E_t\left[\rho^{\tau-t} u'(c_\tau^*) S_\tau + \sum_{j=t+1}^{\tau} \rho^{j-t} u'(c_j^*)\delta_j\right].$$

This corollary gives a necessary condition for optimality that when specialized to the case of equilibrium, recovers the stochastic Euler equation (12) as a necessary condition on equilibrium without relying on Markov uncertainty or dynamic programming. For sufficiency, we should give conditions under which the stochastic Euler equation implies that S is an equilibrium. For this, we define S to be a single-agent equilibrium if e solves (16) given S.

Theorem. *Suppose that U is strictly increasing, concave, and L^*-smooth at the endowment process e. Suppose that the endowment process e is bounded away from zero. Let $\pi \in L^*$ be the Riesz representation of $\nabla U(e)$. It is necessary and sufficient for S to be a single-agent equilibrium that π is a state-price deflator.*

The assumption that e is bounded away from zero is automatically satisfied in the Markovian example of Section 4A. Proof of the theorem is assigned as an exercise.

E. Method-of-Moments Estimation

Although it is not our main purpose to delve into econometrics, it seems worthwhile to illustrate here why the infinite-horizon setting is deemed useful for empirical modeling.

Suppose, for some integer $m \geq 1$, that $B \subset \mathbb{R}^m$ is a set of parameters. Each b in B corresponds to a different Markov economy with the same state space Z. In particular, the transition matrix $q(b)$ of the Markov process X may vary with b. For instance, we could take a single agent with utility given by a discount factor $\rho \in (0,1)$ and a reward function $u_\alpha(x) = x^\alpha/\alpha$ for $\alpha < 1$ (with $u_0(x) = \log x$). We could then take $m = 2$ and $b = (\rho, \alpha) \in$

$B = (0, \infty) \times (-\infty, 1)$. In this example, the transition matrix $q(b)$ does not depend on b.

We fix some b_0 in B, to be thought of as the "true" parameter vector governing the economy. Our goal is to estimate the unknown parameter vector b_0.

For simplicity, we will assume that the transition matrix $q(b_0)$ of X is strictly positive. With this, a result known as the *Frobenius-Perron Theorem* implies that there is a unique vector $p \in \mathbb{R}^k_{++}$ whose elements sum to 1 with the property that $q(b_0)^\top p = p$. Letting $q(b_0)^t$ denote the t-fold product of $q(b_0)$, we see that $P_i(X_t = j) = q(b_0)^t_{ij}$, so that $q(b_0)^t$ is the t-period transition matrix. It can be shown that p is given by any row of $\lim_t q(b_0)^t$. Thus, regardless of the initial shock i, $\lim_t P_i(X_t = j) = p_j$. Indeed, the convergence to the "steady-state" probability vector p is exponentially fast, in the sense that there is a constant $\beta > 1$ such that for any i and j,

$$\beta^t[p_j - P_i(X_t = j)] \to 0. \tag{18}$$

From this, it follows immediately that for any $H : Z \to \mathbb{R}$, we have $E^i[H(X_t)] \to \sum_{i=1}^k p_i H(i)$, and again convergence is exponentially fast. The *empirical distribution vector* p_T of X at time T is defined by

$$p_{Ti} = \frac{1}{T} \#\{t < T : X_t = i\},$$

where $\#A$ denotes the number of elements in a finite set A. That is, p_{Ti} is the average fraction of time, up to T, spent in state i. From the law of large numbers for *i.i.d.* sequences of random variables, it is not hard to show that p_T converges almost surely to the steady-state distribution vector p. Proof of this fact is assigned as Exercise 4.14, which includes a broad hint. From this, we have the following form of the *law of large numbers for Markov chains.*

The Strong Law of Large Numbers for Markov Chains. *For any $H : Z \to \mathbb{R}$, the empirical average $\sum_{t=0}^T H(X_t)/T$ converges almost surely to the steady-state mean $\sum_{i=1}^k p_i H(i)$.*

Proof: Since $\sum_{t=0}^T H(X_t)/T = \sum_{i=1}^k p_{Ti} H(i)$, the result follows from the fact that $p_T \to p$ almost surely. ∎

Suppose that there is some integer $\ell \geq 0$ such that for each time t, the econometrician observes at time $t + \ell$ the data $h(Y_t)$, where $Y_t = (X_t, X_{t+1}, \ldots, X_{t+\ell})$ and $h : Z^{\ell+1} \to \mathbb{R}^n$. For example, the data could be in the form of security prices, dividends, endowments, or functions of these. It is easy to check that the strong law of large numbers would apply even if $q(b_0)$ were not strictly positive, provided the t-period transition matrix $q(b_0)^t$ is strictly positive for some t. From this fact, Y also satisfies the strong law of large numbers, since Y can be treated as a Markov process whose $(\ell + 1)$-period transition matrix is strictly positive. In particular, for any $G : Z^{\ell+1} \to \mathbb{R}$, the empirical average $\sum_{t=1}^{T} G(Y_t)/T$ converges almost surely to the corresponding steady-state mean, which is also equal to $\lim_t E^i[G(Y_t)]$, a quantity that is independent of the initial shock i.

We now specify some *test moment function* $K : \mathbb{R}^n \times B \to \mathbb{R}^M$, for some integer M, with the property that for all t, $E_t(K[h(Y_t), b_0]) = 0$. For a simple example, we could take the single-agent Markov equilibrium described by the stochastic Euler equation (13), where the utility function is specified as above by the unknown parameter vector $b_0 = (\rho_0, \alpha_0)$. For this example, we can let $Y_t = (X_t, X_{t+1})$ and let $h(Y_t) = (R_{t+1}, e_{t+1}, e_t)$, where $e_t = g(X_t)$ is the current endowment and R_t is the $\mathbb{R}^N$-valued return vector defined by

$$R_{it} = \frac{S_i(X_t) + f_i(X_t)}{S_i(X_{t-1})}, \qquad i \in \{1, \ldots, N\}.$$

With $M = N$ and $b = (\rho, \alpha)$, we can let

$$K_i[h(Y_t), b] = \frac{\rho e_{t+1}^{\alpha-1} R_{i,t+1}}{e_t^{\alpha-1}} - 1. \tag{19}$$

From (13), we confirm that $E_t[K(Y_t, b_0)] = 0$.

We know from the strong law of large numbers that for each b in B, the empirical average $\overline{K}_T(b) \equiv \sum_{t=1}^{T} K(Y_t, b)/T$ converges almost surely to a limit denoted $\overline{K}_\infty(b)$. By the law of iterated expectations, for any initial state i,

$$E^i[K(Y_t, b_0)] = E^i(E_t[K(Y_t, b_0)]) = 0.$$

From this, we know that $\overline{K}_\infty(b_0) = 0$ almost surely. A natural estimator of b_0 at time t is then given by the problem

$$\inf_{b \in B} \| \overline{K}_t(b) \|. \tag{20}$$

Under conditions, one can show that if b_t solves (20) for each t, then $\{b_t\}$ is a *consistent estimator*, in the sense that $b_t \to b_0$ almost surely. The sequence $\{b_t\}$, if it exists, is called a *generalized-method-of-moments*, or *GMM*, estimator of b_0. A sufficient set of technical conditions is as follows.

GMM Regularity Conditions. *The parameter set B is compact. For any b in B other than b_0, $\overline{K}_\infty(b) \neq 0$. The function K is Lipschitz with respect to b, in the sense that* *there is a constant k such that for any y in $Z^{\ell+1}$ and any b_1 and b_2 in B, we have*

$$\| K(y, b_1) - K(y, b_2) \| \leq k \| b_1 - b_2 \|.$$

Theorem. *Under the GMM regularity conditions, a GMM estimator exists and any GMM estimator is consistent.*

The proof follows immediately from the following proposition.

Uniform Strong Law of Large Numbers. *Under the GMM regularity conditions,*

$$\sup_{b \in B} |\overline{K}_T(b) - \overline{K}_\infty(b)| \to 0 \qquad \text{almost surely.}$$

Proof: The following proof is adapted from a source indicated in the Notes. Without loss of generality for the following arguments, we can take $M = 1$. Since B is a compact set and K is Lipschitz with respect to b, for each $\epsilon \in (0, \infty)$ there is a finite set $B_\epsilon \subset B$ with the following property: For any b in B there is some b_ϵ and b^ϵ in B_ϵ satisfying, for all y,

$$K(y, b_\epsilon) \leq K(y, b) \leq K(y, b^\epsilon), \qquad |K(y, b_\epsilon) - K(y, b^\epsilon)| \leq \epsilon. \qquad (21)$$

As is customary, for any sequence $\{x_n\}$ of numbers we let

$$\underline{\lim}_n \, x_n = \sup_n \inf_{k \geq n} x_k.$$

For a given $\epsilon > 0$,

$$\underline{\lim}_t \, \inf_b \left[\overline{K}_t(b) - \overline{K}_\infty(b) \right] \geq \underline{\lim}_t \, \inf_b \left[\overline{K}_t(b_\epsilon) - \overline{K}_\infty(b) \right]$$

$$\geq \underline{\lim}_t \, \inf_b \left[\overline{K}_t(b_\epsilon) - \overline{K}_\infty(b_\epsilon) \right]$$

$$+ \inf_b \left[\overline{K}_\infty(b_\epsilon) - \overline{K}_\infty(b) \right]$$

$$\geq -\epsilon \qquad \text{almost surely,}$$

by the strong law of large numbers, (21), and the fact that B_ϵ is finite. Let $A_\epsilon \subset \Omega$ be the event of probability 1 on which this inequality holds, and let $A = A_1 \cap A_{1/2} \cap A_{1/3} \cdots$. Then A also has probability 1, and on A we have

$$\underline{\lim}_t \, \inf_b \left[\overline{K}_t(b) - \overline{K}_\infty(b) \right] \geq 0. \qquad (22)$$

Likewise, by using b^ϵ in place of b_ϵ and $-\overline{K}$ in place of $\overline{K}$, we have

$$\underline{\lim}_t \, \inf_b \left[-\overline{K}_t(b) + \overline{K}_\infty(b) \right] \geq 0 \qquad \text{almost surely.} \qquad (23)$$

The claim follows from (22) and (23). ∎

The Notes cite papers that prove the consistency of GMM estimators under weaker conditions and analyze the theoretical properties of this estimator. Included in these are conditions for the normality of the limit of the distribution of $(b_t - b_0)/\sqrt{t}$ and the form of covariance matrix Σ of this asymptotic distribution. As shown in these references, the efficiency properties of the GMM estimator, in terms of this asymptotic covariance matrix Σ, can be improved by replacing the criterion function $b \mapsto \| \overline{K}_t(b) \|$ in (20) with the criterion function $b \mapsto \overline{K}_t(b)^\top W_t \overline{K}_t(b)$, for a particular adapted sequence $\{W_t\}$ of positive semi-definite "weighting" matrices. Other papers cited in the Notes apply GMM estimators in a financial setting.

Exercises

4.1 Prove Fact 4A.

4.2 Prove Lemma 4A.

4.3 Prove Proposition 4A.

4.4 Prove Fact 1 of Section 4B.

4.5 Prove Fact 2 of Section 4B.

4.6 Show that (13) is necessary and sufficient for optimality of $C(i,0) = g(i)$ and $\Phi(i,0) = 0$, that is, for equilibrium.

4.7 Show that (11), (12), and (13) are equivalent.

4.8 Show that the constraint (9), placing a lower bound on portfolios, is not binding in a Markov equilibrium.

4.9 Suppose there is a single security with price process $S \equiv 1$ and with dividend process δ satisfying $\delta_t > -1$ for all t. The utility function U is defined by (1), where $u(x) = x^\alpha/\alpha$ for $\alpha < 1$ and $\alpha \neq 0$. The endowment process e is given by $e_t = 0$, $t > 1$, and $e_0 = w > 0$. Let $\mathcal{L}_+$ denote the space of nonnegative adapted processes. With a nonnegative wealth constraint and no other bounding restrictions, the agent's problem is modified to

$$\sup_{c \in \mathcal{L}_+} U(c) \qquad \text{subject to } W_t^c \geq 0, \ t \geq 0, \tag{24}$$

where $W_0^c = w$ and $W_t^c = (W_{t-1}^c - c_{t-1})(1 + \delta_t)$, $t > 1$.

(A)   Suppose $\delta_t = \epsilon$ for all t, where $\epsilon > -1$ is a constant. Provide regularity conditions on α, ρ, and ϵ under which there exists a solution to (24). Solve for the value function and the optimal consumption policy. Hint: Use dynamic programming and conjecture that the value function is of the form $V(w) = kw^\alpha/\alpha$ for some constant k. Solve the Bellman equation explicitly for V, and then show that the Bellman equation characterizes optimality by showing that $V(w) \geq U(c)$ for any feasible c, and that $V(w) = U(c^*)$, where c^* is your candidate policy. Note that this will require a demonstration that $\rho^t V(W_t^c) \to 0$ for any feasible c.

(B) Suppose that δ is an *i.i.d.* process. Provide regularity conditions on $\beta = \rho E[(1 + \delta_1)^\alpha]$, ρ, and α under which there exists a solution to (24). Solve for the value function and the optimal consumption policy.

(C) Solve parts (A) and (B) once again for $u(x) = \log(x)$, $x > 0$, and $u(0) = -\infty$. The utility function U may now take $-\infty$ as a value.

4.10 Extend the solutions to parts (D) and (E) of Exercise 3.8 to the infinite-horizon case, adding any additional regularity conditions on the parameters $(\gamma, \alpha, \rho, A, B, \sigma^2)$ that you feel are called for.

4.11 Demonstrate the Riesz representation (17) of the gradient of the additive discounted utility function. Hint: Use the Dominated Convergence Theorem.

4.12 Prove Theorem 4D.

4.13 Prove relation (18), showing exponential convergence of probabilities to their steady-state counterparts.

4.14 Prove the version of the strong law of large numbers shown in Section 4E. Hint: Prove the almost sure convergence of the empirical distribution vector p_T to p by using the strong law of large numbers for *i.i.d.* random variables with finite expectations. For this, given any $l \in Z$, let $\tau_n(l)$ be the n-th time $t \geq 0$ that $X_t = l$. Note that

$$Q_{nlj} \equiv \#\{t : X_t = j, \, \tau_n(l) \leq t < \tau_{n+1}\}$$

has a distribution that does not depend on n or the initial state i, and that for each l and j, the sequences $\{Q_{1lj}, Q_{2lj}, \ldots\}$ and $\{t_n\}$, with $t_n = \tau_{n+1}(l) - \tau_n(l)$, are each *i.i.d.* with distributions that do not depend on the initial state i. Complete the proof from this point, considering the properties, for each l and j in Z, of

$$\frac{N^{-1} \sum_{n=1}^N Q_{nlj}}{N^{-1} \sum_{n=1}^N t_n}.$$

Notes

Freedman (1983) covers the theory of Markov chains. Revuz (1975) is a treatment of Markov processes on a general state space. Sections 4A and 4B are based on Lucas (1978), although the details here are different. LeRoy (1973) gives a precursor of this model. The probability space, on which the Markov process X is defined, is constructed in Bertsekas and Shreve (1978). The fixed-point approach of Section 4A is based on Blackwell (1965); Lemma 4A, in more general guises, is called Blackwell's Theorem. The results extend easily to a general compact metric space Z of shocks, as, for example, in Lucas (1978), Duffie (1988b), or Stokey and Lucas (1989). Smoothness of the policy function or the value function is addressed by Benveniste and Scheinkman (1979). Santos (1991, 1994) has recent results on smoothness and provides references to the extensive related literature. Versions of some of the results for this chapter that include production are found in Brock (1979, 1982), Duffie (1988b), and Stokey and Lucas (1989). The recursive-utility model was introduced into this setting by Epstein and Zin (1989). See also Becker and Boyd (1992), Hong and Epstein (1989), Kan (1992, 1993), Ma (1991a, 1994a), and Streufert (1991a,b,c). Wang (1991, 1993b) shows the generic ability to distinguish between additive and nonadditive recursive utility from security-price data. Sections 4C and 4D are slightly unconventional, and are designed merely to bridge the gap from the finite-dimensional results of Chapter 2 to this infinite-dimensional setting. Strong assumptions are adopted here in order to guarantee the "transversality" conditions. Much weaker conditions suffice. See, for example, Kocherlakota (1990). Schachermayer (1994) and Santos and Woodford (1994) give conditions for the existence of a state-price deflator in this and more general settings.

Kandori (1988) gives a proof of Pareto optimality and a representative agent in a complete-markets general equilibrium model. Examples are given by Abel (1986), Campbell (1984), Donaldson, Johnson, and Mehra (1987), and Dumas and Luciano (1990). Further characterization of equilibrium is given by Prescott and Mehra (1980) and Donaldson and Mehra (1984). Hernandez and Santos (1994), Levine (1989), Magill and Quinzii (1993, 1994a), and Levine and Zame (1992) show conditions for the existence of equilibrium with incomplete markets.

Conditions for the existence of a stationary Markov equilibrium (with incomplete markets and heterogeneous agents) are given by Duffie, Geanakoplos, Mas-Colell, and McLennan (1994).

The role of debt constraints in promoting existence of equilibria in this setting is developed by Florenzano and Gourdel (1993), Kehoe and Levine

(1993), Levine and Zame (1992), and Magill and Quinzii (1993, 1994a). The related issue of speculative bubbles is addressed by Gilles and LeRoy (1992a,b), Magill and Quinzii (1993), and Santos and Woodford (1994). Kurz (1992, 1993) develops the implications of stationarity and rationality in this setting. Shannon (1993) gives conditions for determinacy. Hansen and Sargent (1990) have worked out extensive examples for equilibrium in this setting with quadratic utilities and linear dynamics.

A recent spate of literature has addressed the issue of asset pricing with heterogeneous agents and incomplete markets, partly spurred by the *equity premium puzzle* pointed out by Mehra and Prescott (1985), showing the difference in expected returns between equity and riskless bonds to be far in excess of what one would find from a typical representative-agent model. Bewley (1982) and Mankiw (1986) have seminal examples of the effects of incomplete markets. The more recent literature includes Acharya and Madan (1993a,b), Aiyagari and Gertler (1990), Constantinides and Duffie (1991), Duffie (1992), Haan (1994), Heaton and Lucas (1992), Lucas (1991), Marcet and Singleton (1991), Mehrling (1990), Scheinkman (1989), Scheinkman and Weiss (1986), Telmer (1990), and Weil (1992). Others have attempted to resolve the perceived equity premium puzzle by turning to more general utility functions, such as the habit-formation model (see, for example, Constantinides [1990] and Hansen and Jaganathan [1990]) or the recursive model (see Epstein and Zin [1989, 1991]). For the effect of first-order risk aversion or Knightian uncertainty, see Epstein and Wang (1994), and for empirical results, Bekaert, Hodrick, and Marshall (1994).

Section 4E gives a "baby version" of the estimation technique used in Hansen and Singleton (1982, 1983). Brown and Gibbons (1985) give an alternative exposition of this model. The generalized method of moments, in a much more general setting than that of Section 4E, is shown by Hansen (1982) to be consistent. We have used the exponential convergence of probabilities given by equation (18) to avoid the assumption that the shock process X is stationary. This extends to a more general Markov setting under regularity conditions. The proof given for the uniform strong law of large numbers is based on Pollard (1984). A general treatment of method-of-moments estimation can be found in Gallant and White (1988). Duffie and Singleton (1993), Lee and Ingram (1991), McFadden (1986), and Pakes and Pollard (1986) extend the GMM to a setting with simulated estimation of moments. General treatments of dynamic programming are given by Bertsekas and Shreve (1978) and Dynkin and Yushkevich (1979). Exercise 4.11 is based on Samuelson (1969) and Levhari and Srinivasan (1969), and is extended by Hakansson (1970), Blume, Easley, and O'Hara (1982), and others. For a related *turnpike* theorem, see Hakansson (1974). Many further results in the vein of Chapter 4 are summarized in Duffie (1988b) and, especially, Stokey and Lucas (1989).

II

Continuous-Time Models

Part II is a continuous-time counterpart to Part I in which uncertainty is generated by Brownian motion. The results are somewhat richer and more delicate than those in Part I, with a greater dependence on mathematical technicalities. It is wiser to focus on the parallels than on these technicalities. Once again, the three basic forces behind the theory are arbitrage, optimality, and equilibrium.

Chapter 5 introduces the continuous-trading model and develops the Black-Scholes partial differential equation (PDE) for arbitrage-free prices of derivative securities. The Harrison-Kreps model of equivalent martingale measures is presented in Chapter 6 in parallel with the theory of state prices in continuous time. Chapter 7 presents models of the term structure of interest rates, including the Black-Derman-Toy, Vasicek, Cox-Ingersoll-Ross, and Heath-Jarrow-Morton models, as well as extensions. Chapter 8 presents specific classes of derivative securities, such as futures, forwards, American options, and lookback options. Chapter 8 also introduces models of option pricing with stochastic volatility. Chapter 9 is a summary of optimal continuous-time portfolio choice, using both dynamic programming and an approach involving equivalent martingale measures or state prices. Chapter 10 is a summary of security pricing in an equilibrium setting. Included are such well-known models as Breeden's consumption-based capital asset pricing model and the general equilibrium version of the Cox-Ingersoll-Ross model of the term structure of interest rates. Chapter 11 outlines three numerical methods for calculating derivative security prices in a continuous-time setting: binomial approximation, Monte Carlo simulation of a discrete-time approximation of security prices, and finite-difference solution of the associated PDE for the asset price or the Green's function.

5

The Black-Scholes Model

THIS CHAPTER PRESENTS the basic Black-Scholes model of arbitrage pricing in continuous time, as well as extensions to a nonparametric multivariate Markov setting. We first introduce the Brownian model of uncertainty and continuous security trading, and then derive partial differential equations for the arbitrage-free prices of derivative securities. The classic example is the Black-Scholes option-pricing formula. Chapter 6 extends to a non-Markovian setting using more general techniques.

A. Trading Gains for Brownian Prices

We fix a probability space $(\Omega, \mathcal{F}, P)$. A *process* is a measurable function on $\Omega \times [0, \infty)$ into $\mathbb{R}$. (For a definition of measurability with respect to a product space of this variety, see Appendix C.) The value of a process X at time t is the random variable variously written as X_t, $X(t)$, or $X(\cdot, t) : \Omega \to \mathbb{R}$. A *standard Brownian motion* is a process B defined by the following properties:

(a) $B_0 = 0$ almost surely;

(b) for any times t and $s > t$, $B_s - B_t$ is normally distributed with mean zero and variance $s - t$;

(c) for any times $t_0, \ldots, t_n$ such that $0 \le t_0 < t_1 < \cdots < t_n < \infty$, the random variables $B(t_0)$, $B(t_1) - B(t_0)$, $\ldots, B(t_n) - B(t_{n-1})$ are independently distributed; and

(d) for each ω in Ω, the *sample path* $t \mapsto B(\omega, t)$ is continuous.

It is a nontrivial fact, whose proof has a colorful history, that the probability space $(\Omega, \mathcal{F}, P)$ can be constructed so that there exist standard Brownian motions. By 1900, in perhaps the first scientific work involving Brownian motion, Louis Bachelier proposed Brownian motion as a model of stock prices. We will follow his lead for the time being and suppose that a given standard Brownian motion B is the price process of a security. Later we consider more general classes of price processes.

The tribe $\mathcal{F}_t^B$ generated by $\{B_s : 0 \leq s \leq t\}$ is, on intuitive grounds, a reasonable model of the information available at time t for trading the security, since $\mathcal{F}_t^B$ includes every event based on the history of the price process B up to that time. For technical reasons, however, one must be able to assign probabilities to the *null sets* of Ω, the subsets of events of zero probability. For this reason, we will fix instead the *standard filtration* $\mathbb{F} = \{\mathcal{F}_t : t \geq 0\}$ of B, with $\mathcal{F}_t$ defined as the tribe generated by the union of $\mathcal{F}_t^B$ and the null sets. The probability measure P is also extended by letting $P(A) = 0$ for any null set A. This *completion* of the probability space is defined in more detail in Appendix C.

A *trading strategy* is an adapted process θ specifying at each state ω and time t the number $\theta_t(\omega)$ of units of the security to hold. If a strategy θ is a constant, say $\overline{\theta}$, between two dates t and $s > t$, then the total gain between those two dates is $(B_s - B_t)\overline{\theta}$, the price change multiplied by the quantity held. So long as the strategy is piecewise constant, we would have no difficulty in defining the total gain between any two times. In order to make for a good model of trading gains when we do not necessarily require piecewise constant trading, a trading strategy θ is required to satisfy $\int_0^T \theta_t^2 \, dt < \infty$ almost surely for each T. Let $\mathcal{L}^2$ denote the space of adapted processes satisfying this integrability restriction. For each θ in $\mathcal{L}^2$ there is an adapted process with continuous sample paths, denoted $\int \theta \, dB$, that is called the *stochastic integral* of θ with respect to B. The definition of $\int \theta \, dB$ is outlined in Appendix D. The value of the process $\int \theta \, dB$ at time T is usually denoted $\int_0^T \theta_t \, dB_t$, and represents the total gain generated up to time T by trading the security with price process B according to the trading strategy θ.

An interpretation of $\int_0^T \theta_t \, dB_t$ can be drawn from the discrete-time analogue $\sum_{t=0}^T \theta_t \Delta^1 B_t$, where $\Delta^1 B_t \equiv B_{t+1} - B_t$, that is, the sum (over t) of the shares held at t multiplied by the change in price between t and $t + 1$. More generally, let $\Delta^n B_t = B_{(t+1)/n} - B_{t/n}$. In a sense that we shall not make precise, $\int_0^T \theta_t \, dB_t$ can be thought of as the limit of $\sum_{t=0}^{Tn} \theta_{t/n} \Delta^n B_t$, as the number n of trading intervals per unit of time goes to infinity. This statement is literally true, for example, if θ has continuous sample paths, taking "limit" to mean limit in probability. The definition of $\int_0^T \theta_t \, dB_t$ as a limit in probability of the discrete-time analogue extends to a larger class of θ, but not large enough to capture some of the applications in later chapters. The definition of $\int_0^T \theta_t \, dB_t$ given in Appendix D therefore admits any θ in $\mathcal{L}^2$.

The stochastic integral has some of the properties that one would expect from the fact that it is a good model of trading gains. For example, suppose a trading strategy θ is piecewise constant on $[0, T]$ in that for some stopping times $t_0, \ldots, t_N$ with $0 = t_0 < t_1 < \cdots < t_N = T$, and for any n, we have $\theta(t) = \theta(t_{n-1})$ for all $t \in [t_{n-1}, t_n)$. Then

$$\int_0^T \theta_t \, dB_t = \sum_{n=1}^N \theta(t_{n-1})[B(t_n) - B(t_{n-1})].$$

One of the advantages of the continuous-time model is that it allows us to consider trading strategies that are not necessarily piecewise constant. A second natural property of stochastic integration as a model for trading gains is linearity: For any θ and φ in $\mathcal{L}^2$ and any scalars a and b, the process $a\theta + b\varphi$ is also in $\mathcal{L}^2$, and, for any time $T > 0$,

$$\int_0^T (a\theta_t + b\varphi_t) \, dB_t = a \int_0^T \theta_t \, dB_t + b \int_0^T \varphi_t \, dB_t.$$

B. Martingale Trading Gains

The properties of standard Brownian motion imply that B is a martingale. (This follows basically from the property that its increments are independent and of zero expectation, but a proof is not offered here.) A process θ is bounded if there is a fixed constant k such that $|\theta(\omega, t)| \leq k$ for all (ω, t). For any bounded θ in $\mathcal{L}^2$, the law of iterated expectations and the "martingality" of B imply, for any integer times t and $\tau > t$, that $E_t(\sum_{s=t}^\tau \theta_s \Delta^1 B_s) = 0$. This means that the discrete-time gain process X, defined by $X_0 = 0$ and $X_t = \sum_{s=0}^{t-1} \theta_s \Delta^1 B_s$, is itself a martingale with respect to the discrete-time filtration $\{\mathcal{F}_0, \mathcal{F}_1, \ldots\}$, an exercise for the reader. The same is also true in continuous time: For any bounded θ in $\mathcal{L}^2$, $\int \theta \, dB$ is a martingale. This is natural; it should be impossible to generate an expected profit by trading a security that never experiences an expected price change. If one places no bounding restriction on θ, however, the expectation of $\int_0^T \theta_t \, dB_t$ may not even exist. The following proposition assists in determining whether the expectation or the variance of $\int_0^T \theta_t \, dB_t$ is finite, and whether $\int \theta \, dB$ is indeed a martingale. Consider the spaces

$$\mathcal{H}^1 = \left\{ \theta \in \mathcal{L}^2 : E\left[\left(\int_0^T \theta_t^2 \, dt \right)^{1/2} \right] < \infty, \qquad T > 0 \right\}$$

$$\mathcal{H}^2 = \left\{ \theta \in \mathcal{L}^2 : E\left(\int_0^T \theta_t^2 \, dt \right) < \infty, \qquad T > 0 \right\}.$$

Proposition. *If θ is in $\mathcal{H}^1$ or $\mathcal{H}^2$, then $\int \theta \, dB$ is a martingale. If $\int \theta \, dB$ is a martingale, then*

$$\text{var}\left(\int_0^T \theta_t \, dB_t \right) = E\left(\int_0^T \theta_t^2 \, dt \right). \qquad (1)$$

A proof is cited in the Notes.

C. Ito Prices and Gains

As a model of security-price processes, standard Brownian motion is too restrictive for most purposes. Consider, instead, a process of the form

$$S_t = x + \int_0^t \mu_s \, ds + \int_0^t \sigma_s \, dB_s, \qquad t \geq 0, \qquad (2)$$

where x is a real number, σ is in $\mathcal{L}^2$, and μ is in $\mathcal{L}^1$, meaning that μ is an adapted process such that $\int_0^t |\mu_s| \, ds < \infty$ almost surely for all t. We call a process S of this form (2) an *Ito process*, a sufficiently general type of security-price process for all that follows in this chapter. It is common to write (2) in the informal "differential" form

$$dS_t = \mu_t \, dt + \sigma_t \, dB_t; \qquad S_0 = x.$$

One often thinks intuitively of dS_t as the "increment" of S at time t, made up of two parts, the "dt" part and the "dB_t" part. In order to further interpret this differential representation of an Ito process, suppose that σ and μ are in $\mathcal{H}^2$. It is then literally the case that for any time t,

$$\left. \frac{d}{d\tau} E_t(S_\tau) \right|_{\tau=t} = \mu_t \qquad \text{almost surely} \qquad (3)$$

and

$$\left. \frac{d}{d\tau} \text{var}_t(S_\tau) \right|_{\tau=t} = \sigma_t^2 \qquad \text{almost surely}, \qquad (4)$$

where the derivatives are taken from the right, and where, for any random variable X with finite variance, $\text{var}_t(X) \equiv E_t(X^2) - [E_t(X)]^2$ is the $\mathcal{F}_t$-conditional variance of X. In this sense of (3) and (4), we can interpret μ_t as the conditional expected rate of change of S at time t and σ_t^2 as the rate of change of the conditional variance of S at time t. One sometimes reads the associated abuses of notation "$E_t(dS_t) = \mu_t \, dt$" and "$\text{var}_t(dS_t) = \sigma_t^2 \, dt$." Of course, dS_t is not even a random variable, so this sort of characterization is not rigorously justified and is used purely for its intuitive content. We will refer to μ and σ as the *drift* and *diffusion* processes of S, respectively. Many authors reserve the term "diffusion" for σ_t^2 or other related quantities.

For an Ito process S of the form (2), let $\mathcal{L}(S)$ denote the space consisting of any adapted process θ with $\{\theta_t \mu_t : t \geq 0\}$ in $\mathcal{L}^1$ and $\{\theta_t \sigma_t : t \geq 0\}$ in $\mathcal{L}^2$. For θ in $\mathcal{L}(S)$, we define the stochastic integral $\int \theta \, dS$ as the Ito process given by

$$\int_0^T \theta_t \, dS_t = \int_0^T \theta_t \mu_t \, dt + \int_0^T \theta_t \sigma_t \, dB_t, \qquad T \geq 0. \qquad (5)$$

We also refer to $\int \theta \, dS$ as the *gain process generated by* θ, given the price process S. If $\theta \in \mathcal{L}(S)$ is such that $\{\theta_t \sigma_t : t \geq 0\}$ is in $\mathcal{H}^2$ and $E\left[\left(\int_0^T \theta_t \mu_t \, dt\right)^2\right] < \infty$ we write that θ is in $\mathcal{H}^2(S)$. By Proposition 5B, if θ is in $\mathcal{H}^2(S)$ then $\int \theta \, dS$ is a finite-variance process.

We will have occasion to refer to adapted processes θ and φ that are equal *almost everywhere,* by which we mean that $E(\int_0^\infty |\theta_t - \varphi_t| \, dt) = 0$. In fact, we shall write "$\theta = \varphi$" whenever $\theta = \varphi$ almost everywhere. This is a natural convention, for suppose that X and Y are Ito processes with $X_0 = Y_0$ and with $dX_t = \mu_t \, dt + \sigma_t \, dB_t$ and $dY_t = a_t \, dt + b_t \, dB_t$. Since stochastic integrals are defined for our purposes as continuous sample path processes, it turns out that $X_t = Y_t$ for all t almost surely if and only if $\mu = a$ almost everywhere and $\sigma = b$ almost everywhere. We call this the *unique decomposition property* of Ito processes.

D. Ito's Lemma

More than any other result, *Ito's Lemma* is the basis for explicit solutions to asset-pricing problems in a continuous-time setting.

Ito's Lemma. *Suppose X is an Ito process with $dX_t = \mu_t \, dt + \sigma_t \, dB_t$, and let $f : \mathbb{R}^2 \to \mathbb{R}$ be twice continuously differentiable. Then the process Y, defined by $Y_t = f(X_t, t)$, is an Ito process with*

$$dY_t = \left[f_x(X_t, t)\mu_t + f_t(X_t, t) + \frac{1}{2} f_{xx}(X_t, t)\sigma_t^2 \right] dt + f_x(X_t, t)\sigma_t \, dB_t. \qquad (6)$$

A generalization of Ito's Lemma appears later in the chapter. Expression (6) is known as *Ito's formula.*

E. The Black-Scholes Option-Pricing Formula

Consider a security, to be called a *stock*, with price process

$$S_t = x \exp(\alpha t + \sigma B_t), \qquad t \geq 0, \tag{7}$$

where $x > 0$, α, and σ are constants. Such a process, called a *geometric Brownian motion*, is often called *log-normal* because, for any t, $\log(S_t) = \log(x) + \alpha t + \sigma B_t$ is normally distributed. Moreover, since $X_t \equiv \alpha t + \sigma B_t = \int_0^t \alpha \, ds + \int_0^t \sigma \, dB_s$ defines an Ito process X with constant drift α and diffusion σ, and since $y \mapsto x e^y$ is a C^2 function, Ito's Lemma implies that S is an Ito process and that

$$dS_t = \mu S_t \, dt + \sigma S_t \, dB_t; \qquad S_0 = x,$$

where $\mu = \alpha + \sigma^2/2$. From (3) and (4), at any time t, S has the conditional expected rate of change μS_t and conditional rate of change of variance $\sigma^2 S_t^2$, so that per dollar invested in this security at time t, one may think of μ as the "instantaneous" expected rate of return, and σ as the "instantaneous" standard deviation of the rate of return. This sort of characterization abounds in the literature, and one often reads the associated abuses of notation "$E(dS_t/S_t) = \mu \, dt$" and "$\mathrm{var}(dS_t/S_t) = \sigma^2 \, dt$." The coefficient σ is also known as the *volatility* of S. In any case, a geometric Brownian motion is a natural two-parameter model of a security-price process because of these simple interpretations of μ and σ.

Consider a second security, to be called a *bond*, with the price process β defined by

$$\beta_t = \beta_0 \, e^{rt}, \qquad t \geq 0, \tag{8}$$

for some constants $\beta_0 > 0$ and r. We have the obvious interpretation of r as the *continually compounding interest rate*, that is, the exponential rate at which riskless deposits accumulate with interest. Throughout, we will also refer to r as the *short rate*. Since $\{rt : t \geq 0\}$ is trivially an Ito process, β is also an Ito process with

$$d\beta_t = r\beta_t \, dt. \tag{9}$$

We can also view (9) as an ordinary differential equation with initial condition β_0 and solution (8).

We allow any trading strategies a in $\mathcal{H}^2(S)$ for the stock and b in $\mathcal{H}^2(\beta)$ for the bond. Such a trading strategy (a, b) is said to be *self-financing* if it generates no dividends (either positive or negative), meaning that for all t,

$$a_t S_t + b_t \beta_t = a_0 S_0 + b_0 \beta_0 + \int_0^t a_\tau \, dS_\tau + \int_0^t b_\tau \, d\beta_\tau. \tag{10}$$

The self-financing condition (10) is merely a statement that the current portfolio value (on the left-hand side) is precisely the initial investment plus any trading gains, and therefore that no dividend "inflow" or "outflow" is generated.

Now consider a third security, an *option*. We begin with the case of a European call option on the stock, giving its owner the right, but not the obligation, to buy the stock at a given exercise price K on a given expiry date T. The option's price process Y is as yet unknown except for the fact that $Y_T = (S_T - K)^+ \equiv \max(S_T - K, 0)$, which follows from the fact that the option is rationally exercised if and only if $S_T > K$. (See Exercise 2.1 for a discrete-time analogue.)

Suppose there exists a self-financing trading strategy (a, b) in the stock and bond with $a_T S_T + b_T \beta_T = Y_T$. If $a_0 S_0 + b_0 \beta_0 < Y_0$, then one could sell the option for Y_0, make an initial investment of $a_0 S_0 + b_0 \beta_0$ in the trading strategy (a, b), and at time T liquidate the entire portfolio $(-1, a_T, b_T)$ of option, stock, and bond with payoff $-Y_T + a_T S_T + b_T \beta_T = 0$. The initial profit $Y_0 - a_0 S_0 - b_0 \beta_0 > 0$ is thus riskless, so the trading strategy $(-1, a, b)$ would be an arbitrage. Likewise, if $a_0 S_0 + b_0 \beta_0 > Y_0$, the strategy $(1, -a, -b)$ is an arbitrage. Thus, if there is no arbitrage, $Y_0 = a_0 S_0 + b_0 \beta_0$. The same arguments applied at each date t imply that in the absence of arbitrage, $Y_t = a_t S_t + b_t \beta_t$. A full definition of continuous-time arbitrage is given in Chapter 6, but for now we can proceed without much ambiguity at this informal level. Our objective now is to show the following.

The Black-Scholes Formula. *If there is no arbitrage, then, for all $t < T$, $Y_t = C(S_t, t)$, where*

$$C(x, t) = x\Phi(z) - e^{-r(T-t)} K\Phi\left(z - \sigma\sqrt{T - t}\right), \tag{11}$$

with

$$z = \frac{\log(x/K) + (r + \sigma^2/2)(T - t)}{\sigma\sqrt{T - t}}, \tag{12}$$

where Φ is the cumulative standard normal distribution function.

F. A First Attack on the Black-Scholes Formula

We will eventually see many different ways to arrive at the Black-Scholes formula (11)–(12). Although it is not the shortest argument, the following is perhaps the most obvious and constructive. We start by assuming that

$Y_t = C(S_t, t)$, $t < T$, without knowledge of the function C aside from the assumption that it is twice continuously differentiable on $(0, \infty) \times [0, T)$ (allowing an application of Ito's Lemma). This will lead us to deduce (11)–(12), justifying the assumption and proving the result at the same time.

Based on our assumption that $Y_t = C(S_t, t)$ and Ito's Lemma,

$$dY_t = \mu_Y(t)\, dt + C_x(S_t, t)\sigma S_t\, dB_t, \qquad t < T, \tag{13}$$

where

$$\mu_Y(t) = C_x(S_t, t)\mu S_t + C_t(S_t, t) + \frac{1}{2} C_{xx}(S_t, t)\sigma^2 S_t^2.$$

Now suppose there is a self-financing trading strategy (a, b) with

$$a_t S_t + b_t \beta_t = Y_t, \qquad t \in [0, T], \tag{14}$$

as outlined in Section E. This assumption will also be justified shortly. Equations (10) and (14), along with the linearity of stochastic integration, imply that

$$dY_t = a_t\, dS_t + b_t\, d\beta_t = (a_t \mu S_t + b_t \beta_t r)\, dt + a_t \sigma S_t\, dB_t. \tag{15}$$

One way to choose the trading strategy (a, b) so that both (13) and (15) are satisfied is to "match coefficients separately in both dB_t and dt." In fact, the unique decomposition property of Ito processes explained at the end of Section 5C implies that this is the only way to ensure that (13) and (15) are consistent. Specifically, we choose a_t so that $a_t \sigma S_t = C_x(S_t, t)\sigma S_t$; for this, we let $a_t = C_x(S_t, t)$. From (14) and $Y_t = C(S_t, t)$, we then have $C_x(S_t, t)S_t + b_t \beta_t = C(S_t, t)$, or

$$b_t = \frac{1}{\beta_t}\left[C(S_t, t) - C_x(S_t, t)S_t\right]. \tag{16}$$

Finally, "matching coefficients in dt" from (13) and (15) leaves, for $t < T$,

$$-rC(S_t, t) + C_t(S_t, t) + rS_t C_x(S_t, t) + \frac{1}{2}\sigma^2 S_t^2 C_{xx}(S_t, t) = 0. \tag{17}$$

In order for (17) to hold, it is enough that C satisfies the PDE

$$-rC(x, t) + C_t(x, t) + rxC_x(x, t) + \frac{1}{2}\sigma^2 x^2 C_{xx}(x, t) = 0,$$

$$(x, t) \in (0, \infty) \times [0, T). \tag{18}$$

The fact that $Y_T = C(S_T, T) = (S_T - K)^+$ supplies the *boundary condition*:

$$C(x, T) = (x - K)^+, \qquad x \in (0, \infty). \tag{19}$$

By direct calculation of derivatives, one can show as an exercise that (11)–(12) is a solution to (18)–(19). All of this seems to confirm that $C(S_0, 0)$, with C defined by the Black-Scholes formula (11)–(12), is a good candidate for the initial price of the option. In order to make this solid, suppose that $Y_0 > C(S_0, 0)$. Consider the strategy $(-1, a, b)$ in the option, stock, and bond, with $a_t = C_x(S_t, t)$ and b_t given by (16) for $t < T$. We can choose a_T and b_T arbitrarily so that (14) is satisfied; this does not affect the self-financing condition (10) because the value of the trading strategy at a single point in time has no effect on the stochastic integral. (For this, see the implications of equality "almost everywhere" at the end of Section 5C.) The result is that (a, b) is self-financing by construction and that $a_T S_T + b_T \beta_T = Y_T = (S_T - K)^+$. This strategy therefore nets an initial riskless profit of

$$Y_0 - a_0 S_0 - b_0 \beta_0 = Y_0 - C(S_0, 0) > 0,$$

which defines an arbitrage. Likewise, if $Y_0 < C(S_0, 0)$, the trading strategy $(+1, -a, -b)$ is an arbitrage. Thus, it is indeed a necessary condition for the absence of arbitrage that $Y_0 = C(S_0, 0)$. Sufficiency is a more delicate matter. We shall see in Chapter 6 that under mild technical conditions on trading strategies, the Black-Scholes formula for the option price is also sufficient for the absence of arbitrage. One last piece of business is to show that the "option-hedging" strategy (a, b) is such that a is in $\mathcal{H}^2(S)$ and b is in $\mathcal{H}^2(\beta)$. This is true, and is left to show as an exercise.

Transactions costs play havoc with the sort of reasoning just applied. For example, if brokerage fees are any positive fixed fraction of the market value of stock trades, the stock-trading strategy a constructed above would call for infinite total brokerage fees, since, in effect, the number of shares traded is infinite! This fact and the literature on transactions costs in this setting is reviewed in the Notes of Chapters 6 and 9.

G. The PDE for Arbitrage-Free Derivative Security Prices

The expression $dS_t = \mu S_t \, dt + \sigma S_t \, dB_t$ for the log-normal stock-price process S of Section E is a special case of a *stochastic differential equation* (SDE) of the form

$$dS_t = \mu(S_t, t) \, dt + \sigma(S_t, t) \, dB_t; \qquad S_0 = x, \tag{20}$$

where $\mu : \mathbb{R} \times [0, \infty) \rightarrow \mathbb{R}$ and $\sigma : \mathbb{R} \times [0, \infty) \rightarrow \mathbb{R}$ are given functions. Under regularity conditions on μ and σ reviewed in Appendix E, there is a unique Ito process S solving (20) for each starting point x in $\mathbb{R}$. Assuming that such a solution S defines a stock-price process, consider the bond-price process β defined by

$$\beta_t = \beta_0 \exp \left[\int_0^t r(S_u, u) \, du \right], \tag{21}$$

where $r : \mathbb{R} \times [0, \infty) \rightarrow \mathbb{R}$ is well enough behaved for the existence of the integral in (21). A trivial application of Ito's Lemma implies that

$$d\beta_t = \beta_t r(S_t, t) \, dt; \qquad \beta_0 > 0. \tag{22}$$

Rather than restricting attention to the option payoff $Y_T = (S_T - K)^+$, consider a *derivative security* defined by the payoff $Y_T = g(S_T)$ at time T, for some continuous $g : \mathbb{R} \rightarrow \mathbb{R}$. Arguments like those in Section F lead one to formulate the arbitrage-free price process Y of the derivative security as $Y_t = C(S_t, t), \, t \in [0, T]$, where C solves the PDE

$$- r(x, t) C(x, t) + C_t(x, t) + r(x, t) x C_x(x, t) + \frac{1}{2} \sigma(x, t)^2 C_{xx}(x, t) = 0, \tag{23}$$

for $(x, t) \in \mathbb{R} \times [0, T)$, with the boundary condition

$$C(x, T) = g(x), \qquad x \in \mathbb{R}. \tag{24}$$

In order to tie things together, suppose that C solves (23)–(24). If $Y_0 \neq C(S_0, 0)$, then an obvious extension of our earlier arguments implies that there is an arbitrage. (This extension is left as an exercise.) This is true even if C is not twice continuously differentiable, but merely $C^{2,1}(\mathbb{R} \times [0, T))$, meaning that the derivatives C_x, C_t, and C_{xx} exist and are continuous in $\mathbb{R} \times (0, T)$, and extend continuously to $\mathbb{R} \times [0, T)$. (Ito's Lemma also applies to any function in this class.)

This PDE characterization of the arbitrage-free price of derivative securities is useful if there are convenient methods for solving PDEs of the form (23)–(24). Numerical solution techniques are discussed in Chapter 11. One of these techniques is based on a probabilistic representation of solutions given in the next section.

H. The Feynman-Kac Solution

A potential simplification of the PDE problem (23)–(24) is obtained as follows. For each (x, t) in $\mathbb{R} \times [0, T]$, let $Z^{x,t}$ be the Ito process defined by $Z_s^{x,t} = x$, $s \leq t$, and

$$dZ_s^{x,t} = r(Z_s^{x,t}, s)Z_s^{x,t}\, ds + \sigma(Z_s^{x,t}, s)\, dB_s, \qquad s > t. \tag{25}$$

That is, $Z^{x,t}$ starts at x at time t and continues from there by following the SDE (25).

Condition FK. *The functions σ, r, and g satisfy one of the technical sufficient conditions given in Appendix E for Feynman-Kac solutions.*

The FK (for "Feynman-Kac") conditions here cited from Appendix E are indeed only technical, and can be viewed as smoothness conditions limiting how quickly the functions σ, r, and g can grow or change direction. Referring to Appendix E, we have the following solution to the PDE (23)–(24) as an expectation of the discounted payoff of the derivative security, modified by replacing the original price process S with a *pseudo-price process* $Z^{x,t}$ whose expected rate of return is the riskless interest rate. This is sometimes known as *risk-neutral valuation*. This is not to say that agents are risk-neutral, but rather that risk-neutrality is without loss of generality for purposes of pricing derivative securities.

The Feynman-Kac Solution. *Under Condition FK, if there is no arbitrage, then the derivative security defined by the payoff $g(S_T)$ at time T has the price process Y with $Y_t = C(S_t, t)$, where C is the solution to (23)–(24) given by*

$$C(x, t) = E\left(\exp\left[-\int_t^T r(Z_s^{x,t}, s)\, ds \right] g\left(Z_T^{x,t} \right) \right), \qquad (x, t) \in \mathbb{R} \times [0, T]. \tag{26}$$

It can be checked as an exercise that (26) recovers the Black-Scholes option-pricing formula (11). Calculating this expectation directly is a simpler way to solve the corresponding PDE (17)–(18) than is the method originally used in discovering the Black-Scholes formula. Chapter 11 presents numerical methods for solving (23)–(24), one of which involves Monte Carlo simulation of the Feynman-Kac solution (26), which bears a close resemblance to the discrete-time equivalent-martingale-measure arbitrage-free price representation of Chapter 2. This is more than a coincidence, as we shall see in Chapter 6.

I. The Multidimensional Case

Suppose that $B^1, \ldots, B^d$ are d independent standard Brownian motions on a probability space $(\Omega, \mathcal{F}, P)$. The process $B = (B^1, \ldots, B^d)$ is known as a *standard Brownian motion in* $\mathbb{R}^d$. The standard filtration $\mathbb{F} = \{\mathcal{F}_t : t \geq 0\}$ of B is defined just as in the one-dimensional case. Given $\mathbb{F}$, the subsets $\mathcal{L}^1, \mathcal{L}^2$, $\mathcal{H}^1$, and $\mathcal{H}^2$ of adapted processes are also as defined in Sections A and B.

In this setting, X is an Ito process if, for some x in $\mathbb{R}$, some μ in $\mathcal{L}^1$, and some $\theta^1, \ldots, \theta^d$ in $\mathcal{L}^2$,

$$X_t = x + \int_0^t \mu_s \, ds + \sum_{i=1}^d \int_0^t \theta_s^i \, dB_s^i, \qquad t \geq 0. \tag{27}$$

For convenience, (27) is also written

$$X_t = x + \int_0^t \mu_s \, ds + \int_0^t \theta_s \, dB_s, \qquad t \geq 0, \tag{28}$$

or in the convenient stochastic differential form

$$dX_t = \mu_t \, dt + \theta_t \, dB_t; \qquad X_0 = x. \tag{29}$$

If $X^1, \ldots, X^N$ are Ito processes, then we call $X = (X^1, \ldots, X^N)$ an *Ito process in* $\mathbb{R}^N$, which can be written

$$X_t = x + \int_0^t \mu_s \, ds + \int_0^t \theta_s \, dB_s, \qquad t \geq 0, \tag{30}$$

or

$$dX_t = \mu_t \, dt + \theta_t \, dB_t; \qquad X_0 = x \in \mathbb{R}^N, \tag{31}$$

where μ and θ are valued in $\mathbb{R}^N$ and $\mathbb{R}^{N \times d}$, respectively. (Here, $\mathbb{R}^{N \times d}$ denotes the space of real matrices with N rows and d columns.) Ito's Lemma extends as follows.

Ito's Lemma. *Suppose X is the Ito process in $\mathbb{R}^N$ given by (30) and f is in $C^{2,1}(\mathbb{R}^N \times [0, \infty))$. Then $\{f(X_t, t) : t \geq 0\}$ is an Ito process and, for any time t,*

$$f(X_t, t) = f(X_0, 0) + \int_0^t \mathcal{D}_X f(X_s, s) \, ds + \int_0^t f_x(X_s, s)\theta_s \, dB_s,$$

where

$$\mathcal{D}_X f(X_t, t) = f_x(X_t, t)\mu_t + f_t(X_t, t) + \frac{1}{2}\text{tr}\left[\theta_t \theta_t^\top f_{xx}(X_t, t)\right].$$

Here, f_x, f_t, and f_{xx} denote the obvious partial derivatives of f valued in $\mathbb{R}^N$, $\mathbb{R}$, and $\mathbb{R}^{N \times N}$ respectively, and $\text{tr}(A)$ denotes the *trace* of a square matrix A (the sum of its diagonal elements).

If X and Y are real-valued Ito processes with $dX_t = \mu_X(t)\,dt + \sigma_X(t)\,dB_t$ and $dY_t = \mu_Y(t)\,dt + \sigma_Y(t)\,dB_t$, then Ito's Lemma (for $N = 2$) implies that the product $Z = XY$ is an Ito process, with drift μ_Z given by

$$\mu_Z(t) = X_t\,\mu_Y(t) + Y_t\mu_X(t) + \sigma_X(t) \cdot \sigma_Y(t). \tag{32}$$

Provided that μ_X, μ_Y, σ_X, and σ_Y are all in $\mathcal{H}^2$, an application of Fubini's Theorem (Appendix C) implies that

$$\frac{d}{ds}\,\text{cov}_t\,(X_s, Y_s)\,\bigg|_{s=t} = \sigma_X(t) \cdot \sigma_Y(t) \qquad \text{almost surely}, \tag{33}$$

where $\text{cov}_t(X_s, Y_s) = E_t(X_s Y_s) - E_t(X_s)E_t(Y_s)$ and where the derivative is taken from the right, extending the intuition developed with (3) and (4).

If X is an Ito process in $\mathbb{R}^N$ with $dX_t = \mu_t\,dt + \sigma_t\,dB_t$ and $\theta = (\theta^1, \ldots, \theta^N)$ is a vector of adapted processes such that $\theta \cdot \mu$ is in $\mathcal{L}^1$ and, for each i, $\theta \cdot \sigma^i$ is in $\mathcal{L}^2$, then we say that θ is in $\mathcal{L}(X)$, which implies that

$$\int_0^T \theta_t\,dX_t \equiv \int_0^T \theta_t \cdot \mu_t\,dt + \int_0^T \theta_t^\top \sigma_t\,dB_t, \qquad T \geq 0$$

is well defined as an Ito process. If $E[(\int_0^T \theta_t \cdot \mu_t\,dt)^2] < \infty$ and, for each i, $\theta \cdot \sigma^i$ is also in $\mathcal{H}^2$, then we say that θ is in $\mathcal{H}^2(X)$, which implies that $\int \theta\,dX$ is a finite-variance process.

Suppose that $S = (S^1, \ldots, S^N)$ is an Ito process in $\mathbb{R}^N$ specifying the prices of N given securities, and that S satisfies the stochastic differential equation:

$$dS_t = \mu(S_t, t)\,dt + \sigma(S_t, t)\,dB_t; \qquad S_0 = x \in \mathbb{R}^N, \tag{34}$$

where $\mu : \mathbb{R}^N \times [0, \infty) \to \mathbb{R}^N$ and $\sigma : \mathbb{R}^N \times [0, \infty) \to \mathbb{R}^{N \times d}$ satisfy enough regularity (conditions are given in Appendix E) for existence and uniqueness of a solution to (34). Let

$$\beta_t = \beta_0 \exp\left[\int_0^t r(S_u, u)\,du\right]; \qquad \beta_0 > 0, \tag{35}$$

define the price process of a bond, where $r : \mathbb{R}^N \times [0, \infty) \to \mathbb{R}$ defines a continuously compounding short rate, sufficiently well behaved that (35) is a well-defined Ito process. We can also use Ito's Lemma to write

$$d\beta_t = \beta_t r(S_t, t)\,dt; \qquad \beta_0 > 0. \tag{36}$$

Finally, let some continuous $g : \mathbb{R}^N \to \mathbb{R}$ define the payoff $g(S_T)$ at time T of a derivative security whose price at time zero is to be determined.

   Once again, the arguments of Section F can be extended to show that under technical regularity conditions and in the absence of arbitrage, the price process Y of the derivative security is given by $Y_t = C(S_t, t)$, where C solves the PDE:

$$\mathcal{D}_Z C(x, t) - r(x, t) C(x, t) = 0, \qquad (x, t) \in \mathbb{R}^N \times [0, T), \qquad (37)$$

with boundary condition

$$C(x, T) = g(x), \qquad x \in \mathbb{R}^N, \qquad (38)$$

where

$$\mathcal{D}_Z C(x, t) = C_x(x, t) r(x, t) x + C_t(x, t)$$
$$+ \frac{1}{2} \operatorname{tr} \left[\sigma(x, t) \sigma(x, t)^\top C_{xx}(x, t) \right]. \qquad (39)$$

We exploit once again the technical condition FK on (r, σ, g) reviewed in Appendix E for existence of a probabilistic representation of solutions to the PDE (37)–(38).

The Feynman-Kac Solution. *Under Condition FK, if there is no arbitrage, then the derivative security with payoff $g(S_T)$ at time T has the price process Y given by $Y_t = C(S_t, t)$, where C is the solution to the PDE (37)–(38) given by*

$$C(x, t) = E \left[\exp \left(- \int_t^T r(Z_s^{x,t}, s) \, ds \right) g \left(Z_T^{x,t} \right) \right],$$
$$(x, t) \in \mathbb{R}^N \times [0, T], \qquad (40)$$

where $Z^{x,t}$ is the Ito process defined by $Z_s^{x,t} = x$, $s \le t$, and

$$dZ_s^{x,t} = r(Z_s^{x,t}, s) Z_s^{x,t} \, ds + \sigma(Z_s^{x,t}, s) \, dB_s, \qquad s \ge t. \qquad (41)$$

   The exercises provide applications and additional extensions of this approach to the arbitrage-free valuation of derivative securities, allowing for intermediate dividends and for an underlying Markov-state process. Chapter 6 further extends arbitrage-free pricing to a non-Markovian setting using martingale methods. Chapters 7 and 8 give further applications, including futures, forwards, American options, and the term structure of interest rates.

Exercises

5.1 Fixing a probability space and a filtration $\{\mathcal{F}_t : t \geq 0\}$, a process X is *Markov* if, for any time t and any integrable random variable Y that is measurable with respect to the tribe generated by $\{X_s : s \geq t\}$, we have $E(Y \mid \mathcal{F}_t) = E(Y \mid X_t)$ almost surely. In particular, for any measurable $f : \mathbb{R} \to \mathbb{R}$ such that $f(X_t)$ has finite expectation, we have $E[f(X_t) \mid \mathcal{F}_s] = E[f(X_t) \mid X_s]$ for $s \leq t$. It is a fact, which we shall not prove, that standard Brownian motion B is a Markov process with respect to its standard filtration. Use this fact to show that B is a martingale with respect to its standard filtration. Suppose that θ is a bounded adapted process. Show, as stated in Section B, that the discrete-time process X defined by $X_0 = 0$ and $X_t = \sum_{s=0}^{t-1} \theta_s \Delta^1 B_s$, $t \geq 1$, is a martingale with respect to $\{\mathcal{F}_0, \mathcal{F}_1, \ldots\}$.

5.2 Suppose that S is defined by (7). Use Ito's Lemma to show that as claimed, $dS_t = \mu S_t \, dt + \sigma S_t \, dB_t$, where $\mu = \alpha + \sigma^2/2$.

5.3 Verify that the ordinary differential equation (9), with initial condition β_0, is solved by (8).

5.4 Verify by direct calculation of the derivatives that the PDE (18)–(19) is solved by the Black-Scholes formula (11).

5.5 Derive the PDE (23) for the arbitrage-free value of the derivative security. Hint: Use arguments analogous to those used to derive the PDE (18) for the Black-Scholes formula.

5.6 Suppose the PDE (37) for the arbitrage-free value of the derivative security is not satisfied, in that the initial price Y_0 of the security is not equal to $C(S_0, 0)$, where C solves (37)–(38). Construct an arbitrage that nets an initial risk-free profit of m units of account, where m is an arbitrary number chosen by you.

5.7 Suppose that the stock, whose price process S is given by (20), pays dividends at a rate $\delta(S_t, t)$ at time t, where a continuous function $\delta : \mathbb{R} \times [0, \infty) \to \mathbb{R}$ defines a *cumulative dividend process* D by $D_t = \int_0^t \delta(S_u, u) \, du$. The total gain process G for the security is defined by $G_t = S_t + D_t$, and a trading strategy θ in $\mathcal{L}(G)$ generates the gain process $\int \theta \, dG$, the sum of capital and dividend gains. Derive a new PDE generalizing (23) for the arbitrage-free value of the derivative security defined by g. Provide regularity conditions for the associated Feynman-Kac solution, extending (25)–(26).

5.8   Suppose that S is a stock-price process defined by (20), β is a bond-price process defined by (21), and a derivative security is defined by the lump-sum payoff $g(S_T)$ at time T, as in Section G, and also by the cumulative dividend process H defined by $H_t = \int_0^t h(S_\tau, \tau)\, d\tau$, for some continuous $h : \mathbb{R} \times [0, T] \to \mathbb{R}$. By definition, a trading strategy (a, b) in $\mathcal{H}^2(S, \beta)$ *finances* this derivative security if

$$a_t S_t + b_t \beta_t = a_0 S_0 + b_0 \beta_0 + \int_0^t a_u\, dS_u + \int_0^t b_u\, d\beta_u - H_t, \qquad t \le T, \quad (42)$$

and

$$a_T S_T + b_T \beta_T = g(S_T). \tag{43}$$

Relation (42) means that the current value of the portfolio is, at any time, the initial value, plus trading gains to date, less the payout to date of the derivative dividends. If (a, b) finances the derivative security in this sense and the derivative security's initial price Y_0 is not equal to $a_0 S_0 + b_0 \beta_0$, then there is an arbitrage. For example, if $Y_0 > a_0 S_0 + b_0 \beta_0$, then the strategy $(-1, a, b)$ in derivative security, stock, and bond generates the cumulative dividend process $-H + H = 0$ and the final payoff $-g(S_T) + g(S_T) = 0$, with the initial riskless profit $Y_0 - a_0 S_0 - b_0 \beta_0 > 0$. Derive an extension of the PDE (23)–(24) for the derivative security price, as well as an extension of the Feynman-Kac solution (25)–(26).

5.9   Suppose that X is the Ito process in $\mathbb{R}^K$ solving the SDE

$$dX_t = \mu(X_t, t)\, dt + \sigma(X_t, t)\, dB_t; \qquad X_0 = x.$$

We could refer to X, by analogy with Chapter 3, as the "shock process." Suppose the price process S for the N "stocks" is defined by $S_t = \mathcal{S}(X_t, t)$, where $\mathcal{S}$ is in $C^{2,1}(\mathbb{R}^K \times [0, \infty))$, and that the bond-price process β is the Ito process defined by $d\beta_t = \beta_t r(X_t, t)\, dt$, $\beta_0 > 0$, where $r : \mathbb{R}^K \times [0, \infty) \to \mathbb{R}$ is bounded and continuous.

(A)   State regularity conditions that you find appropriate in order to derive a PDE analogous to (37)–(38) for the price of an additional security defined by the payoff $g(X_T)$ at time T, where $g : \mathbb{R}^K \to \mathbb{R}$. Then provide the Feynman-Kac solution, analogous to (40)–(41), including a sufficient set of technical conditions based on Appendix E.

(B)   Extend part (A) to the case in which the stocks pay a cumulative dividend process D that is an Ito process in $\mathbb{R}^N$ well defined by $D_t = \int_0^t \delta(X_s, s)\, ds$, where $\delta : \mathbb{R}^K \times [0, \infty) \to \mathbb{R}^N$, and in which the additional security has the lump-sum payoff of $g(X_T)$ at time T, as well as a cumulative dividend Ito process H well defined by $H_t = \int_0^t h(X_s, s)\, ds$, where $h : \mathbb{R}^K \times [0, T] \to \mathbb{R}$.

5.10 Suppose the short-rate process r is given by a bounded continuous function $r : [0, T] \to \mathbb{R}$. Consider a security with price process S defined by

$$dS_t = \mu(S_t) \, dt + \sigma(S_t) \, dB_t,$$

where μ and σ satisfy a Lipschitz condition. Suppose this security has the cumulative dividend process D defined by $D_t = \int_0^t \delta_u S_u \, du$, where $\delta : [0, T] \to \mathbb{R}$ is a continuous function. (Such a function δ is often called the "dividend yield.")

(A)   (Put-Call Parity)   Suppose there are markets for European call and put options on the above security with exercise price K and expiry date T. Let C_0 and P_0 denote the call and put prices at time zero. Give an explicit expression for P_0 in terms of C_0, in the absence of arbitrage and transactions costs.

(B)   Suppose, for all t, that $r_t = 0.10$ and that $\delta_t = 0.08$. Consider a European option expiring in $T = 0.25$ years. Suppose that $K = 50$ and $S_0 = 45$. If the call sells for 3.75, what is the put price? (Give a specific dollar price, to the nearest penny, showing how you calculated it.)

(C)   Suppose, instead, that the dividend process D is defined by $D_t = \int_0^t \delta_\tau \log(S_\tau) S_\tau \, d\tau$. Suppose $\sigma(x) = \epsilon x$, for some constant $\epsilon > 0$. Solve part (A) again. Then calculate the price of a European call with exercise price $K = 35$ given initial stock price $S_0 = 40$, assuming, for all t, that $\delta_t = 0.08$, $r_t = 0.10$, and $\epsilon = 0.20$. Assume expiry in 0.25 years. Justify your answer.

5.11 Suppose the price of haggis (an unusually nasty food served in Scotland) follows the process H defined by

$$dH_t = H_t \mu_H \, dt + H_t \sigma_H \, dB_t; \qquad H_0 > 0,$$

in British pounds per pint, where μ_H is a constant, σ_H is a constant vector in $\mathbb{R}^2$, and B is a standard Brownian motion in $\mathbb{R}^2$. A trader at a Wall Street investment bank, Gold in Sacks, Incorporated, has decided that since there are options on almost everything else, there may as well be options on haggis. Of course, there is the matter of selling the options in the United States, denominated in U.S. dollars. It has been noted that the price of the U.S. dollar, in British pounds per dollar, follows the process

$$dD_t = D_t \mu_D \, dt + D_t \sigma_D \, dB_t; \qquad D_0 > 0,$$

where μ_D is a constant and σ_D is a constant vector in $\mathbb{R}^2$. The continuously compounding short rate in U.S. funds is r_D, a constant. Although there are liquid markets in Edinburgh for haggis and for U.S. dollars, there is not a liquid market for haggis options. Gold in Sacks has therefore decided to sell call options on haggis at a U.S. dollar strike price of 6.50 per pint expiring in 3 months, and cover its option position with a replicating strategy in the other instruments, so as to earn a riskless profit equal to the markup in the sale price of the options over the initial investment cost to Gold in Sacks for the replicating strategy.

(A)   What replicating strategy would you recommend?

(B)   If the options are sold at a 10 percent profit markup, give an explicit formula for the option price Gold in Sacks should charge its customers.

(C)   Suppose borrowing in U.S. funds is too clumsy, since the other two parts of the strategy (dollar and haggis trading) are done at Gold in Sacks's Edinburgh office. If the British pound borrowing rate is r_P, a constant, can you still answer parts (A) and (B), using British pound borrowing (and lending) rather than U.S. dollar borrowing (and lending)? If so, do so. If not, say why not. If you find it useful, you may use any arbitrage conditions relating the various coefficients $(\mu_H, \mu_D, \sigma_H, \sigma_D, r_D, r_P)$, if indeed there are any such coefficients precluding arbitrage.

5.12   Show, in the setting of Section E, that (26) recovers the Black-Scholes formula (11)–(12).

5.13   Show that the Black-Scholes option-hedging strategy (a, b) of Section F is such that $a \in \mathcal{H}^2(S)$ and $b \in \mathcal{H}^2(\beta)$, as assumed.

Notes

The material in this chapter is standard. Proposition 5B is from Protter (1990). The Brownian model was introduced to the study of option pricing by Bachelier (1900). The Black-Scholes (1973) formula was extended by Merton (1973b, 1977) and subsequently given literally hundreds of further extensions and applications. Cox and Rubinstein (1985) is a standard reference on options, while Hull (1993) has further applications and references. The basic approach of using continuous-time self-financing strategies as the basis for making arbitrage arguments is due to Merton (1977) and Harrison and Kreps (1979). The basic idea of risk-neutral valuation, via adjustment of the underlying stock-price process, is due to Cox and Ross (1976). This is extended to the notion of equivalent martingale measures, found in Chapter 6, by Harrison and Kreps (1979). The impact of variations in the "volatility" on the Black-Scholes option-pricing formula is shown, in two different senses, by El Karoui, Jeanblanc-Picqué, and Viswanathan (1991), Grundy and Wiener (1995), Johnson and Shanno (1987), and Reisman (1986). For "stochastic volatility" models, see Section 8H and references cited in the Notes to Chapter 8.

Alternative approaches to the standard methods of stochastic calculus have been developed by Cutland, Kopp, and Willinger (1991, 1993a,b), who apply nonstandard analysis; by Bick and Willinger (1994) and Willinger and Tacqu (1989), who use a path-wise integral established by Föllmer (1981); and by Kunitomo (1993) and Cutland, Kopp, and Willinger (1991, 1993b), who exploit fractional Brownian motion.

Part (C) of Exercise 5.10 was related to the author by Bruce Grundy. The line of exposition in this chapter is based on Gabay (1982) and Duffie (1988a). For the case of transactions costs and other market "imperfections," see the Notes of Chapter 6.

6

State Prices and Equivalent
Martingale Measures

THIS CHAPTER SUMMARIZES the theory of arbitrage-free security prices in the continuous-time setting introduced in Chapter 5. The main idea is the equivalence between no arbitrage, the existence of state prices, and the existence of an equivalent martingale measure, paralleling the discrete-state theory of Chapter 2. This extends the Markovian results of Chapter 5, which are based on PDE methods. For those interested mainly in applications, the first sections of Chapters 7 and 8 summarize the major conclusions of this chapter as a "black box," making it possible to skip this chapter on a first reading.

The existence of a state-price deflator is shown to imply the absence of arbitrage. Then a state-price "beta" model of expected returns is derived. Turning to equivalent martingale measures, we begin with the sufficiency of an equivalent martingale measure for the absence of arbitrage. Girsanov's Theorem (Appendix D) gives conditions under which there exists an equivalent martingale measure. This approach generates yet another proof of the Black-Scholes formula. State prices are then connected with equivalent martingale measures; the two concepts are more or less the same. Technical conditions are given under which the absence of arbitrage leads to the existence of an equivalent martingale measure, showing the essential equivalence of these two properties. (They are literally equivalent in the analogous finite-state model of Chapter 2, and the distinction here is purely technical.) The last few sections are relatively difficult; it is up to the reader where to stop.

A. Arbitrage

We fix a standard Brownian motion $B = (B^1, \ldots, B^d)$ in $\mathbb{R}^d$, restricted to some time interval $[0, T]$, on a given probability space $(\Omega, \mathcal{F}, P)$. We also fix the standard filtration $\mathbb{F} = \{\mathcal{F}_t : t \in [0, T]\}$ of B, as defined in Section 5I. For simplicity, we take $\mathcal{F}$ to be $\mathcal{F}_T$. Suppose the price processes of N given securities form an Ito process $X = (X^1, \ldots, X^N)$ in $\mathbb{R}^N$. We assume that $\text{var}(X_t^i) < \infty$ for all i and t.

A trading strategy θ, as we recall from Chapter 5, is an $\mathbb{R}^N$-valued process θ in $\mathcal{L}(X)$, as defined in Section 5I. This means simply that the stochastic integral $\int \theta \, dX$ defining trading gains is well defined. A trading strategy θ is *self-financing* if

$$\theta_t \cdot X_t = \theta_0 \cdot X_0 + \int_0^t \theta_s \, dX_s, \qquad t \leq T. \tag{1}$$

It is implicit here that there are no dividends paid by the securities during the interval $[0, T)$, and that X_T is the vector of cum-dividend security prices at time T. We later extend the model to treat the case of intermediate dividends.

If there is some process r with the property that $\int_0^T |r_t| \, dt$ is finite almost surely and, for some security with price process β we have

$$\beta_t = \beta_0 \exp \left(\int_0^t r_s \, ds \right), \qquad t \in [0, T], \tag{2}$$

then we call r the *short-rate process*. In this case, $d\beta_t = r_t \beta_t \, dt$, allowing us to view r_t as the riskless short-term continuously compounding rate of interest, in an instantaneous sense, and to view β_t as the market value of a bank account that is continually reinvested at the interest rate r.

A self-financing strategy θ is an *arbitrage* if $\theta_0 \cdot X_0 < 0$ and $\theta_T \cdot X_T \geq 0$, or $\theta_0 \cdot X_0 \leq 0$ and $\theta_T \cdot X_T > 0$. Our main goal in this chapter is to characterize the properties of a price process X that admits no arbitrage.

B. Numeraire Invariance

It is often convenient to renormalize all security prices, sometimes relative to a particular price process. This section shows that such a renormalization has essentially no economic effects. A *deflator* is a strictly positive Ito process. We can deflate the previously given security price process X by a deflator Y to get the new price process X^Y defined by $X_t^Y = X_t Y_t$.

Numeraire Invariance Theorem. *Suppose Y is a deflator. Then a trading strategy θ is self-financing with respect to X if and only if θ is self-financing with respect to X^Y.*

Proof: Let $W_t = \theta_0 \cdot X_0 + \int_0^t \theta_s \, dX_s$, $t \in [0, T]$. Let W^Y be the process defined by $W_t^Y = W_t Y_t$. Since W and Y are Ito processes, Ito's Lemma implies, letting σ_X, σ_W, and σ_Y denote the respective diffusions of X, W, and Y, that

$$dW_t^Y = Y_t\, dW_t + W_t\, dY_t + \sigma_W(t) \cdot \sigma_Y(t)\, dt$$

$$= Y_t\theta_t\, dX_t + (\theta_t \cdot X_t)\, dY_t + [\theta_t^\top \sigma_X(t)]\sigma_Y(t)\, dt$$

$$= \theta_t \cdot [Y_t\, dX_t + X_t\, dY_t + \sigma_X(t)\sigma_Y(t)\, dt]$$

$$= \theta_t\, dX_t^Y.$$

Thus, $\theta_t \cdot X_t^Y = \theta_0 \cdot X_0^Y + \int_0^t \theta_s\, dX_s^Y$ if and only if $\theta_t \cdot X_t = \theta_0 \cdot X_0 + \int_0^t \theta_s\, dX_s$, completing the proof. ∎

Corollary. *Suppose Y is a deflator. A trading strategy is an arbitrage with respect to X if and only if it is an arbitrage with respect to the deflated price process X^Y.*

Proof: This is immediate from the Numeraire Invariance Theorem, the strict positivity of Y, and the definition of an arbitrage. ∎

C. Doubling Strategies and State-Price Deflators

Paralleling the terminology of Section 2C, a *state-price deflator* is a deflator π with the property that the deflated price process X^π is a martingale. We shall eventually see that as in Chapter 2 (and under some regularity), there is a state-price deflator if and only if there is no arbitrage. First, however, we need to establish some technical restrictions on trading strategies, as the following example shows.

Suppose we take B to be a single Brownian motion $(d = 1)$ and take the price process $X = (S, \beta)$, where $\beta_t = 1$ for all t and $dS_t = S_t\, dB_t$, with $S_0 = 1$. Even though X is a martingale before deflation and S is a log-normal process as typically used in the Black-Scholes option pricing model, we are able to construct an arbitrage that produces any desired constant payoff $\alpha > 0$ at T with no initial investment. For this, consider the stopping time

$$\tau = \inf\left\{ t : \int_0^t (T - s)^{-1/2}\, dB_s = \alpha \right\}.$$

A source cited in the Notes shows that $0 < \tau < T$ almost surely. This is not surprising given the rate at which $(T - t)^{-1/2}$ "explodes" as t approaches T.

Now consider the trading strategy θ defined by $\theta_t = (a_t, b_t)$, where

$$
a_t = \frac{1}{S_t\sqrt{T-t}}, \qquad t \leq \tau
$$

$$
\qquad = 0, \qquad t > \tau, \tag{3}
$$

and

$$
b_t = -a_t S_t + \int_0^t a_u \, dS_u. \tag{4}
$$

In effect, θ places a larger and larger "bet" on the risky asset as T approaches. It is immediate from (1) and (4) that θ is a self-financing trading strategy. It is also clear that $\theta_0 \cdot X_0 = 0$ and that $\theta_T \cdot X_T = \alpha$ almost surely. Thus θ is indeed an arbitrage, despite the natural assumptions on security prices. Some technical restrictions on trading strategies must be added if we are to expect some solid relationship between the existence of a state-price deflator and the absence of arbitrage.

For intuition, one may think of an analogy between the above example and a series of bets on fair and independent coin tosses at times $1/2$, $3/4$, $7/8$, and so on. Suppose one's goal is to earn a riskless profit of α by time 1, where α is some arbitrarily large number. One can bet α on heads for the first coin toss at time $1/2$. If the first toss comes up heads, one stops. Otherwise, one owes α to one's opponent. A bet of 2α on heads for the second toss at time $3/4$ produces the desired profit if heads comes up at that time. In that case, one stops. Otherwise, one is down 3α and bets 4α on the third toss, and so on. Since there is an infinite number of potential tosses, one will eventually stop with a riskless profit of α (almost surely), because the probability of losing on every one of an infinite number of tosses is $(1/2) \cdot (1/2) \cdot (1/2) \cdots = 0$. This is a classic "doubling strategy" that can be ruled out either by a technical limitation, such as limiting the total number of coin tosses, or by a credit restriction limiting the total amount that one is allowed to owe one's opponent.

For the case of continuous-time trading strategies, we will eliminate the possibility of such "doubling strategies" as (3)–(4) by either of two approaches. One approach requires some extra integrability condition on θ, the other requires a credit constraint, limiting the extent to which the market value $\theta_t \cdot X_t$ of the portfolio may become negative. Given a state-price deflator π, the extra integrability condition is that $\theta \in \mathcal{H}^2(X^\pi)$, as defined in Section 5I. The credit constraint is that $\theta_t \cdot X_t^\pi$, the deflated market value of the trading strategy, is bounded below, in that there is some constant k with $\theta_t \cdot X_t^\pi \geq k$ for all t almost surely. We let $\underline{\Theta}(X^\pi)$ denote the space of such credit-constrained trading strategies. In the above example (3)–(4) of an arbitrage, $\pi \equiv 1$ defines a state-price deflator since X is itself a martingale, and the trading strategy θ defined by (3)–(4) is neither in $\mathcal{H}^2(X)$ nor in $\Theta(X)$.

Proposition. *For any state-price deflator π, there is no arbitrage in $\mathcal{H}^2(X^\pi)$ or in $\Theta(X^\pi)$.*

Proof: Suppose π is a state-price deflator. Let θ be any self-financing trading strategy.

(a) Suppose θ is in $\mathcal{H}^2(X^\pi)$. Since X^π is a martingale, Proposition 5B implies that $E\left(\int_0^T \theta_t \, dX_t^\pi\right) = 0$. By numeraire invariance, θ is self-financing with respect to X^π, and we have

$$\theta_0 \cdot X_0^\pi = E\left(\theta_T \cdot X_T^\pi - \int_0^T \theta_t \, dX_t^\pi\right) = E\left(\theta_T \cdot X_T^\pi\right).$$

If $\theta_T \cdot X_T^\pi \geq 0$, then $\theta_0 \cdot X_0^\pi \geq 0$. Likewise, if $\theta_T \cdot X_T^\pi > 0$, then $\theta_0 \cdot X_0^\pi > 0$. It follows that θ cannot be an arbitrage for X^π. The Corollary to Theorem 6B implies that θ is not an arbitrage for X.

(b) Suppose θ is in $\Theta(X^\pi)$. Since X^π is a martingale, $\int \theta \, dX^\pi$ is a local martingale (as defined in Appendix D). By the Numeraire Invariance Theorem, since θ is self-financing with respect to X, θ is also self-financing with respect to X^π. From this and the self-financing condition (1), we see that the deflated wealth process W, defined by $W_t = \theta_t \cdot X_t^\pi$, is a local martingale. Since $\theta \in \Theta(X^\pi)$, we know that W is also bounded below. Since a local martingale that is bounded below is a supermartingale (see Appendix D), we know that $E(W_T) \leq W_0$. From this, if $\theta_T \cdot X_T > 0$, then $W_T > 0$, so $W_0 > 0$ and thus $\theta_0 \cdot X_0 > 0$. Likewise, if $\theta_T \cdot X_T \geq 0$, then $W_T \geq 0$, so $W_0 \geq 0$ and thus $\theta_0 \cdot X_0 \geq 0$. This implies that θ is not an arbitrage. ∎

D. State-Price Restrictions on Expected Rates of Return

Suppose that π is a state-price deflator for X, and consider an arbitrary security with price process S. Since a state-price deflator is an Ito process, we can write

$$d\pi_t = \mu_\pi(t) \, dt + \sigma_\pi(t) \, dB_t$$

for appropriate μ_π and σ_π. Since S is an Ito process, we can also write $dS_t = \mu_S(t) \, dt + \sigma_S(t) \, dB_t$ for some μ_S and σ_S. Since S^π is a martingale, its drift is zero. It follows from Ito's Lemma that almost everywhere,

$$0 = \mu_\pi(t)S_t + \mu_S(t)\pi_t + \sigma_S(t) \cdot \sigma_\pi(t).$$

We suppose that S is a strictly positive process, and can therefore rearrange to get

$$\frac{\mu_S(t)}{S_t} = \frac{-\mu_\pi(t)}{\pi_t} - \frac{\sigma_S(t) \cdot \sigma_\pi(t)}{\pi_t S_t}. \tag{5}$$

The *cumulative-return process* of this security is the Ito process R defined by $R_0 = 0$ and

$$dR_t = \mu_R(t)\,dt + \sigma_R(t)\,dB_t \equiv \frac{\mu_S(t)}{S_t}\,dt + \frac{\sigma_S(t)}{S_t}\,dB_t.$$

We can now write $dS_t = S_t\,dR_t$. Looking back at equations (5.3) and (5.4), μ_R may be viewed as the conditional expected rate of return, and $\sigma_R(t) \cdot \sigma_R(t)$ as the rate of change in the conditional variance of the return. We re-express (5) as

$$\mu_R(t) - \widehat{r}_t = -\frac{1}{\pi_t}\sigma_R(t) \cdot \sigma_\pi(t), \tag{6}$$

where $\widehat{r}_t = -\mu_\pi(t)/\pi_t$. In the sense of equation (5.33), $\sigma_R(t) \cdot \sigma_\pi(t)$ is a notion of "instantaneous covariance" of the increments of R and π. Thus (6) is reminiscent of the results of Section 1F. If $\sigma_R(t) = 0$, then $\mu_R(t) = \widehat{r}_t$, so the short-term riskless rate process, if there is one, must be $\widehat{r}$. In sum, (6) implies a sense in which excess expected rates of return are proportional to the "instantaneous" conditional covariance between returns and state prices. The constant of proportionality, $-1/\pi_t$, does not depend on the security. This interpretation is a bit loose, but (6) itself is unambiguous.

We have been unnecessarily restrictive in deriving (6) only for a particular security. The same formula applies in principle to the return on an arbitrary self-financing trading strategy θ. In order to define this return, let W^θ denote the associated *market-value process*, defined by $W_t^\theta = \theta_t \cdot X_t$. If one can define an Ito process R^θ by

$$R_t^\theta = \int_0^t \frac{1}{W_s^\theta}\,dW_s^\theta, \qquad t \in [0, T],$$

then R^θ represents the cumulative-return process for θ. In this case, it can be verified as an exercise that the drift μ_θ and diffusion σ_θ of R^θ satisfy the return restriction extending (6), given by

$$\mu_\theta(t) - \widehat{r}_t = -\frac{1}{\pi_t}\sigma_\theta(t) \cdot \sigma_\pi(t).$$

E. State-Price Beta Models

Continuing with the setup of the previous section, we can always find adapted processes φ and ϵ valued in $\mathbb{R}^N$ and $\mathbb{R}^d$ respectively such that

$$\sigma_\pi(t) = \sigma_X(t)^\top \varphi_t + \epsilon_t \quad \text{and} \quad \sigma_X(t)\epsilon_t = 0, \qquad t \in [0, T], \qquad (7)$$

where σ_X is the $\mathbb{R}^{N \times d}$-valued diffusion of the price process X. For each (ω, t) in $\Omega \times [0, T]$, the vector $\sigma_X(\omega, t)^\top \varphi(\omega, t)$ is the orthogonal projection in $\mathbb{R}^N$ of $\sigma_\pi(\omega, t)$ onto the span of the rows of the matrix $\sigma_X(\omega, t)$. Suppose $\theta = (\theta^1, \dots, \theta^N)$ is a self-financing trading strategy with $\sigma_X^\top \theta = \sigma_X^\top \varphi$. (For example, if $X_t^1 = \exp(\int_0^t r_s \, ds)$ for a short-rate process r, we can construct θ by letting $\theta_t^j = \varphi_t^j$, $j > 1$, and by choosing θ^1 so that the self-financing condition is met.) The market-value process W^θ of θ is an Ito process since θ is self-financing. If W^θ is also strictly positive, we can define the associated return process $R^* \equiv R^\theta$ by

$$dR_t^* = \frac{1}{W_t^\theta} \, dW_t^\theta; \qquad R_0^* = 0.$$

Since the diffusion of W^θ is $\sigma_X^\top \varphi$, the diffusion of R^* is $\sigma^* \equiv \sigma_X^\top \varphi / W^\theta$. For an arbitrary Ito return process R, (6) implies that

$$\mu_R(t) - \widehat{r}_t = -\frac{1}{\pi_t} \sigma_R(t) \cdot \sigma_\pi(t)$$

$$= -\frac{1}{\pi_t} \sigma_R(t) \cdot [\sigma_X(t)^\top \varphi_t + \epsilon_t]$$

$$= -\frac{W_t^\theta}{\pi_t} \sigma_R(t) \cdot \sigma_t^*,$$

using the fact that $\sigma_R(t)$ is (in each state ω) a linear combination of the rows of $\sigma_X(t)$. This in turn implies that $\sigma_R(t) \cdot \epsilon_t = 0$. In particular, for the return process R^*, we have

$$\mu_t^* - \widehat{r}_t = \frac{-W_t^\theta}{\pi_t} \sigma_t^* \cdot \sigma_t^*,$$

where μ^* is the drift (expected rate of return) of R^*. Substituting back into (6) the resulting expression for W_t^θ / π_t leaves the *state-price beta model of returns* given by

$$\mu_R(t) - \widehat{r}_t = \beta_R(t) \, (\mu_t^* - r_t), \qquad (8)$$

where

$$\beta_R(t) = \frac{\sigma_R(t) \cdot \sigma_t^*}{\sigma_t^* \cdot \sigma_t^*}.$$

In the "instantaneous sense" in which $\sigma_t^* \cdot \sigma_t^*$ stands for the conditional variance for dR_t^* and $\sigma_R(t) \cdot \sigma_t^*$ stands for the conditional covariance between dR_t and dR_t^*, we can view (8) as the continuous-time analogue to the state-price beta models of Section 1F and Exercise 2.6(C). Likewise, we can loosely think of R^* as a return process having maximal conditional correlation with the state-price deflator π.

F. Equivalent Martingale Measures

A probability measure Q on $(\Omega, \mathcal{F})$ is said to be *equivalent* to P provided, for any event A, we have $Q(A) > 0$ if and only if $P(A) > 0$. An equivalent probability measure Q is an *equivalent martingale measure* for X if X is a martingale with respect to Q, and if the Radon-Nikodym derivative dQ/dP (defined in Appendix C) has finite variance.

In the finite-state setting of Chapter 2, it was shown that the existence of a state-price deflator is equivalent to the existence of an equivalent martingale measure (after some deflation). Later in this chapter, technical conditions will be given that sustain that equivalence in this continuous-time setting. Aside from offering a conceptual simplification of some asset-pricing and investment problems, the use of equivalent martingale measures is justified by the large body of useful properties of martingales that are known.

First, we establish the sufficiency of an equivalent martingale measure for the absence of arbitrage. The last section of this chapter gives a result that is almost a converse, supplying conditions under which the absence of arbitrage implies the existence of an equivalent martingale measure. Aside from technical issues, the arguments are the same as those used to show this equivalence in Chapter 2. As in Section C, we need to apply an integrability condition or a credit constraint to trading strategies.

Theorem. *If the price process X admits an equivalent martingale measure, then there is no arbitrage in $\mathcal{H}^2(X)$ or in $\Theta(X)$.*

Proof: The proof is quite similar to that of Proposition 6C. Let Q be an equivalent martingale measure. Let θ be any self-financing trading strategy.

We first consider the case in which θ is bounded. The fact that X is a martingale under Q implies that $E^Q(\int_0^T \theta_t \, dX_t) = 0$. The self-financing condition (1) therefore implies that

$$\theta_0 \cdot X_0 = E^Q\left(\theta_T \cdot X_T - \int_0^T \theta_t \, dX_t\right) = E^Q(\theta_T X_T).$$

Thus, if $\theta_T \cdot X_T \geq 0$, then $\theta_0 \cdot X_0 \geq 0$. Likewise, if $\theta_T \cdot X_T > 0$, then $\theta_0 \cdot X_0 > 0$. An arbitrage is therefore impossible using bounded trading strategies.

For the case of any self-financing trading strategy $\theta \in \mathcal{H}^2(X)$, additional technical arguments are needed to show that $E^Q(\int_0^T \theta_t \, dX_t) = 0$. Since X is an Ito process, we can write $dX_t = \mu_t \, dt + \sigma_t \, dB_t$ for appropriate μ and σ. By the Diffusion Invariance Principle (Appendix D), there is a standard Brownian motion $\hat{B}$ in $\mathbb{R}^d$ under Q such that $dX_t = \sigma_t \, d\hat{B}_t$. Let $Y = \int_0^T \|\theta_t \sigma_t\|^2 \, dt$. Since θ is in $\mathcal{H}^2(X)$, Y has finite expectation under P. Since the product of two random variables of finite variance is of finite expectation, $\frac{dQ}{dP} \sqrt{Y}$ is also of finite expectation under P. Thus, $E^Q(\sqrt{Y}) < \infty$. Since $dX_t = \sigma_t \, d\hat{B}_t$, this implies by Proposition 5B that $\int \theta_t \, dX_t$ is a Q-martingale, so $E^Q(\int_0^T \theta_t \, dX_t) = 0$. The remainder of the proof for this case is now covered by the arguments used for bounded θ.

For the case of $\theta \in \underline{\Theta}(X)$, the arguments used in the proof of Proposition C imply that the wealth process W, defined by $W_t = \theta_t \cdot X_t$, is a supermartingale under Q, so that $E^Q(\theta_T \cdot X_T) \leq \theta_0 \cdot X_0$, implying that θ cannot be an arbitrage. ∎

In most cases, we apply the theorem via the following result, which follows from the corollary to the Numeraire Invariance Theorem in Section 6B.

Corollary. *If there is a deflator Y such that the deflated price process X^Y admits an equivalent martingale measure, then there is no arbitrage in $\mathcal{H}^2(X^Y)$ or $\underline{\Theta}(X^Y)$.*

If there is a short rate process r, it is typical in applications to take the deflator Y defined by $Y_t = \exp\left(-\int_0^t r_s \, ds\right)$. If r is bounded, then we have $\mathcal{H}^2(X^Y) = \mathcal{H}^2(X)$ and $\underline{\Theta}(X^Y) = \underline{\Theta}(X)$, so the previous result can be stated in a more natural form.

G. Girsanov's Theorem and Equivalent Martingale Measures

We now look for convenient conditions on X supporting the existence of an equivalent martingale measure, and conditions for the uniqueness of such a measure. Girsanov's Theorem (Appendix D) can be applied, as follows.

Since X is an Ito process, we can write $dX_t = \mu_t \, dt + \sigma_t \, dB_t$ and consider the linear equations

$$\sigma_t \eta_t = \mu_t, \qquad t \in [0, T], \tag{9}$$

to be solved for an $\mathbb{R}^d$-valued process η with components in $\mathcal{L}^2$. If such a solution to (9) exists, we say that X is *reducible*. We can view a solution η to (9) as providing a proportional relationship between mean rates of change of prices (μ) and the amounts (σ) of "risk" in price changes stemming from each Brownian motion. For this reason, η is sometimes called a *market-price-of-risk process*. This term is actually more frequently applied after normalization by some *numeraire deflator*, a deflator that is the reciprocal of the price process of one of the securities. This is technically convenient since one of the securities has a price that is always 1 after such a deflation. If there is a short rate process r, a typical numeraire deflator is given by Y, where $Y_t = \exp\left(-\int_0^t r_s \, ds\right)$.

If there is no market price of risk, one may guess that something is "wrong," as the following result confirms.

Lemma. *Suppose, for some numeraire deflator Y, that X^Y is not reducible. Then there are arbitrages in both $\underline{\Theta}(X^Y)$ and $\mathcal{H}^2(X^Y)$. Moreoever, there is no equivalent martingale measure for X^Y.*

Proof: Some of the details of the following proof are left to the reader as an exercise.

Suppose X^Y is not reducible, and has drift process μ^Y and diffusion σ^Y. Then, as a matter of linear algebra, there exists a process θ taking values that are row vectors in $\mathbb{R}^N$ such that $\theta\sigma^Y \equiv 0$ and $\theta\mu^Y \neq 0$. By replacing $\theta(\omega, t)$ with zero for any (ω, t) such that $\theta(\omega, t)\mu^Y(\omega, t) < 0$, we can arrange to have $\theta\mu^Y > 0$. (This works provided the resulting process θ is not identically zero; in that case the same procedure applied to $-\theta$ works.) These properties for θ are preserved after multiplication by any strictly positive adapted scaling process, so we can assume without loss of generality that θ is in $\mathcal{H}^2(X^Y)$. It follows that the process θ is a trading strategy in $\mathcal{H}^2(X^Y)$ whose wealth process W, defined by $W_t = \theta_t \cdot X_t^Y$, is increasing and not constant. In particular, θ is in $\underline{\Theta}(X^Y)$. Finally, since the numeraire security associated with the deflator has a price that is identically equal to 1 after deflation, we can also choose the trading strategy for this particular security so that in addition to the above properties, θ is self-financing with $\theta_0 \cdot X_0^Y = 0$. It follows that θ is an arbitrage for X^Y, and therefore for X.

If X^Y is not reducible, then Girsanov's Theorem implies that there cannot be an equivalent martingale measure for X^Y. ∎

Thus, the existence of a market-price-of-risk process is effectively a necessary condition for the absence of arbitrage. If $\sigma(\omega, t)$ is of rank less than d, there are multiple solutions $\eta(\omega, t)$ to (9). There may, therefore, be more than one market-price-of-risk process. If X is reducible, however, we can single out the solution η^X to (9), defined as follows. Let $\hat{\sigma}_t$ and $\hat{\mu}_t$ be obtained, respectively, by eliminating (ω by ω) as many linearly dependent rows from

σ_t as possible and by eliminating the corresponding elements of μ_t. Regardless of how this is done, if X is reducible, then a particular solution η^X to (9) is uniquely defined by

$$\eta_t^X = \hat{\sigma}_t^\top \left(\hat{\sigma}_t \hat{\sigma}_t^\top \right)^{-1} \hat{\mu}_t.$$

If X is reducible, let $\nu(X) = \int_0^T \eta_t^X \cdot \eta_t^X \, dt/2$, and let

$$\xi(X) = \exp\left[-\int_0^T \eta_t^X \, dB_t - \nu(X) \right]. \tag{10}$$

If X is reducible, $\exp[\nu(X)]$ has a finite expectation, and $\xi(X)$ has finite variance, we say that X is L^2-*reducible*. All of this sets up L^2-reducibility as a convenient condition for the existence of an equivalent martingale measure. For example, if X is reducible and η^X is bounded, then X is L^2-reducible.

Theorem. *If X is L^2-reducible, then there is an equivalent martingale measure for X, and there is no arbitrage.*

Proof: If X is L^2-reducible, then Girsanov's Theorem (Appendix D) implies that Q is an equivalent martingale measure when defined by $dQ/dP = \xi(X)$. The lack of arbitrage follows from the theorem in Section 6F. ∎

　　Putting this result together with the previous lemma, we see that reducibility is necessary and, coupled with the technical integrability conditions for L^2-reducibility, sufficient for the absence of arbitrage. Likewise, reducibility is necessary and, together with these same technical conditions, sufficient for the existence of an equivalent martingale measure.

　　For uniqueness of equivalent martingale measures, we can use the fact that for any such measure Q, Girsanov's Theorem implies that we must have $\frac{dQ}{dP} = \xi(X)$, where $\xi(X)$ is given by (10) for some solution η^X of (9). If $\sigma_t(\omega)$ is of maximal rank d, however, there can be at most one solution $\eta(\omega, t)$ to (9) in state ω. This maximal rank condition is equivalent to the condition that the span of the rows of $\sigma(\omega, t)$ is all of $\mathbb{R}^d$, which is reminiscent of the uniqueness condition for equivalent martingale measures found in Chapter 2.

Proposition. *If $\text{rank}(\sigma) = d$ almost everywhere, then there is at most one equivalent martingale measure.*

H. Black-Scholes, One More Time

Suppose the given security-price process is $X = (\beta, S^1, \ldots, S^{N-1})$, where

$$dS_t = \mu_t \, dt + \sigma_t \, dB_t$$

and

$$d\beta_t = r_t \beta_t \, dt; \qquad \beta_0 > 0,$$

where μ, σ, and r are adapted processes (valued in $\mathbb{R}^{N-1}$, $\mathbb{R}^{(N-1) \times d}$, and $\mathbb{R}$ respectively). If the short-rate process r is bounded, then β^{-1} is a convenient numeraire deflator. Let $Z_t = S_t / \beta_t$, $t \in [0, T]$. By Ito's Lemma,

$$dZ_t = \left(-r_t Z_t + \frac{\mu_t}{\beta_t} \right) dt + \frac{\sigma_t}{\beta_t} \, dB_t.$$

In order to apply Theorem 6G to the deflated price process $\hat{X} = (1, Z)$, one needs to check that Z is L^2-reducible. Given this, there would be an equivalent martingale measure Q and no arbitrage. Suppose, for the moment, that this is the case. By the Diffusion Invariance result of Appendix D, there is a standard Brownian motion $\hat{B}$ in $\mathbb{R}^d$ under Q such that

$$dZ_t = \frac{\sigma_t}{\beta_t} \, d\hat{B}_t.$$

Since $S_t = \beta_t Z_t$, $t \in [0, T]$, another application of Ito's Lemma yields

$$dS_t = r_t \, S_t \, dt + \sigma_t \, d\hat{B}_t. \tag{11}$$

Equation (11) is an important intermediate result for arbitrage-free asset pricing, giving an explicit expression for security prices under a probability measure Q with the property that the "discounted" price process S/β is a martingale. For example, this leads to an easy recovery of the Black-Scholes formula, for suppose that the second security is a call option on the first, so that $S_T^2 = (S_T^1 - K)^+$, for expiration at time T with some given exercise price K. Since S^2/β is by assumption a martingale under Q, the option-price process S^2 is given by

$$S_t^2 = \beta_t E_t^Q \left(\frac{S_T^2}{\beta_T} \right) = E_t^Q \left[\exp \left(-\int_t^T r_s \, ds \right) (S_T^1 - K)^+ \right]. \tag{12}$$

The reader is asked to verify as an exercise that this is the Black-Scholes formula for the case of $d = 1$, $N = 3$, $S_0^1 > 0$, and with constants $\bar{r}$ and

$\overline{\sigma}$ such that for all t, $r_t = \overline{r}$ and $\sigma_t^1 = \overline{\sigma} S_t^1$. Indeed, in this case, Z is L^2-reducible, an exercise, so the assumption of an equivalent martingale measure is justified. To be more precise, it is sufficient for the absence of arbitrage that the option-price process is given by (12). Necessity of the Black-Scholes formula for the absence of arbitrage is formally addressed in the next section. We can already see, however, that the expectation in (12) defining the Black-Scholes formula does not depend on which equivalent martingale measure Q one chooses, so one should expect that the Black-Scholes formula (12) is also necessary for the absence of arbitrage. If (12) is not satisfied, for instance, there cannot be an equivalent martingale measure for S/β. Unfortunately, and for purely technical reasons, this is not enough to imply directly the necessity of (12) for the absence of arbitrage, since we do not have a precise equivalence between the absence of arbitrage and the existence of equivalent martingale measures. In the next section, other methods will be used to show necessity.

In the Black-Scholes setting, we have at most one equivalent martingale measure since $\sigma^1 = \overline{\sigma} S$, being strictly positive almost everywhere, implies that σ is of maximal rank $d = 1$ almost everywhere. Thus, from the proposition of the previous section, there is exactly one equivalent martingale measure.

The detailed calculations of Girsanov's Theorem appear nowhere in the actual solution (11) for arbitrage-free security prices, which can be given by inspection in terms of σ and r only. The results extend to the case of an infinite horizon under technical conditions given in sources cited in the Notes.

I. Complete Markets and Redundant Security Prices

In this setting, *complete markets* means that any random variable Y with finite variance can be obtained as the terminal value $\theta_T \cdot X_T$ of some self-financing trading strategy θ. For this section, let the price process X be (β, S) as in Section 6H, for a bounded short-rate process r. Section 6H gave sufficient conditions for the absence of arbitrage in the Black-Scholes setting. This section gives necessary conditions based on the completeness of markets in the Black-Scholes model. First, we provide a spanning condition for complete markets in the presence of an equivalent martingale measure. The proof is based on the Martingale Representation Theorem, shown in Appendix D, which states that for any martingale M there is some η in $\mathcal{L}(B)$ such that for all t we have $M_t = M_0 + \int_0^t \eta_s \, dB_s$. In effect, any martingale can be represented as a stochastic integral with respect to the Brownian motion B that generates the underlying information filtration.

Proposition. *Suppose there is an equivalent martingale measure for the deflated price process S/β. Markets are complete if and only if $\mathrm{rank}(\sigma) = d$ almost everywhere.*

Proof: Suppose that $\mathrm{rank}(\sigma) = d$ almost everywhere. Let Y be an arbitrary random variable with finite variance. Let $Z = S/\beta$ as in Section 6H, let Q be an equivalent martingale measure for Z, and let $\hat{B}$ be a standard Brownian motion in $\mathbb{R}^d$ under Q satisfying (11). By Girsanov's Theorem of Appendix D, $\hat{B}$ has the martingale representation property, implying that there is some η in $\mathcal{L}(\hat{B})$ such that $Y/\beta_T = E^Q(Y/\beta_T) + \int_0^T \eta_t \, d\hat{B}_t$. By the rank assumption on σ, there are some adapted processes $\theta^1, \ldots, \theta^{N-1}$ solving

$$(\theta_t^1, \ldots, \theta_t^{N-1})\sigma_t = \beta_t \eta_t^\top, \qquad t \in [0, T]. \tag{13}$$

Let θ^0 be defined by

$$\theta_t^0 = E^Q\left(\frac{Y}{\beta_T}\right) + \sum_{i=1}^{N-1}\left(\int_0^t \theta_s^i \, dZ_s^i - \theta_t^i Z_t^i\right).$$

Then a simple calculation shows that $\theta = (\theta^0, \ldots, \theta^{N-1})$ is self-financing with respect to the price process $(1, Z)$ and that $\theta_T \cdot (1, Z_T) = Y/\beta_T$. By the Numeraire Invariance Theorem, taking β as a deflator, θ is also self-financing with respect to (β, S) and $\theta_T \cdot (\beta_T, S_T) = Y$, proving the completeness of markets.

Conversely, suppose that it is not true that $\mathrm{rank}(\sigma) = d$ almost everywhere. We will show that markets are not complete. By the rank assumption on σ, there is some bounded $\eta \in \mathcal{L}(\hat{B})$ with the property that there is no solution $\theta^1, \ldots, \theta^{N-1}$ to (13). It is then easy to see that there is no trading strategy θ that is self-financing with respect to $(1, Z)$ such that $\theta_T \cdot (1, Z_T) = \int_0^T \eta_t \, d\hat{B}_t$. By the Numeraire Invariance Theorem, there is no trading strategy θ self-financing with respect to (β, S) with $\theta_T \cdot (\beta_T, S_T) = \beta_T \int_0^T \eta_t \, d\hat{B}_t$ (which can be taken to have finite variance because, without loss of generality, η can be rescaled by any bounded strictly positive adapted process). ∎

We return to the Black-Scholes example of Section 6H, with $N = 2$, $d = 1$, $S_0^1 > 0$, and assume that for all t, we have $\sigma_t^1 = \bar{\sigma} S_t^1$ and $r_t = \bar{r}$, for constants $\bar{\sigma}$ and $\bar{r}$. Since $\mathrm{rank}(\sigma^1) = d$ almost everywhere, the existence of an equivalent martingale measure implies that there is no arbitrage and that markets are complete, even if we restrict trading to the two securities ("bond and stock") with price process (β, S^1). The construction in the last proof implies that given the option payoff $(S_T^1 - K)^+$, there is a self-financing trading strategy (θ^0, θ^1) whose value at any time t is

$$Y_t \equiv E_t^Q[e^{-\bar{r}(T-t)}(S_T^1 - K)^+].$$

In Section 6H, we showed that $S^2 = Y$ is sufficient for the absence of arbitrage with respect to (β, S^1, S^2), where S^2 is the call-option price process. Now we show that $S^2 = Y$ is also necessary for the absence of arbitrage. (This was already shown, in effect, in Chapter 5, but the following argument leads to a more general theorem.) Suppose, to set up a contradiction, that $S^2 \neq Y$. Then there is some constant $\epsilon > 0$ such that at least one of the events A^+ or A^- has strictly positive probability, with A^+ denoting the event that $S^2_t - Y_t \geq \epsilon$ for some t in $[0, T]$, and A^- denoting the event that $Y_t - S^2_t \geq \epsilon$ for some t in $[0, T]$. Without loss of generality, suppose A^+ has strictly positive probability, and let $\tau = \inf\{t : S^2_t - Y_t \geq \epsilon\}$, a stopping time that is valued in $[0, T]$ with strictly positive probability. Let φ be the trading strategy defined by $\varphi_t = 0$, $t < \tau$, and $\varphi_t = (\theta^0_t + e^{\bar{r}(t-\tau)}\epsilon, \theta^1_t, -1)$, $t \geq \tau$, where (θ^0, θ^1) is the option-replicating strategy described above. It can be checked that φ is self-financing and that $\varphi_T \cdot (\beta_T, S^1_T, S^2_T) > 0$, implying that φ is an arbitrage.

By generalizing the above argument, one can prove the following result concerning a *redundant security* given (β, S), a security with price process Y such that there exists a self-financing trading strategy θ in $\mathcal{H}^2(\beta, S)$ with terminal value $\theta_T \cdot (\beta_T, S_T) = Y_T$. Complete markets implies that any security (with finite-variance price process) is redundant.

Theorem. *Suppose S/β admits an equivalent martingale measure Q. Given (β, S), consider a redundant security with price process Y. Then $(X, Y) \equiv (\beta, S^1, \ldots, S^{N-1}, Y)$ admits no arbitrage in $\mathcal{H}^2(X, Y)$ if and only if Y/β is a Q-martingale.*

Proof: If Y/β is a Q-martingale, then Q is an equivalent martingale measure for (X, Y), implying no arbitrage in $\mathcal{H}^2(X, Y)$ by Theorem F.

Conversely, suppose Y/β is not a Q-martingale. The arguments used for the preceding Black-Scholes example imply the existence of an arbitrage in $\mathcal{H}^2(X, Y)$. ∎

In the definition of a redundant security, one could have as easily substituted the credit-constrained class $\underline{\Theta}(X, Y)$ of trading strategies for $\mathcal{H}^2(X, Y)$, allowing a like substitution in the statement of the theorem.

J. State Prices and Equivalent Martingale Measures

We now investigate the relationship between equivalent martingale measures and state-price deflators. They turn out to be effectively the same concept. We take as given the setup of Section 6A, including a price process X for N securities. Suppose that Q is an equivalent martingale measure after deflation by Y, where $Y_t = \exp(-\int_0^t r_s \, ds)$ for a bounded short-rate process r. The *density process* ξ for Q is the martingale defined by

$$\xi_t = E_t \left(\frac{dQ}{dP} \right), \qquad t \in [0, T],$$

where $\frac{dQ}{dP}$ is the Radon-Nikodym derivative of Q with respect to P. As stated in Appendix C, for any times t and $s > t$, and any $\mathcal{F}_s$-measurable random variable W such that $E^Q(|W|) < \infty$,

$$E_t^Q(W) = \frac{E_t(\xi_s W)}{\xi_t}, \qquad t \in [0, T]. \tag{14}$$

We will show that a state-price deflator π is given by $\pi_t = Y_t \xi_t$. Conversely, given a state-price deflator π with $\mathrm{var}(\pi_T) < \infty$, we will show that an equivalent martingale measure is given by defining its density process ξ according to

$$\xi_t = \exp \left(\int_0^t r_s \, ds \right) \frac{\pi_t}{\pi_0}, \qquad t \in [0, T]. \tag{15}$$

In order to verify this relationship between state-price deflators and equivalent martingale measures, suppose Q is an equivalent martingale measure for X^Y with density process ξ, and let $\pi_t = \xi_t Y_t$. Then, for any times t and $s > t$, using (14),

$$E_t(\pi_s X_s) = E_t(\xi_s X_s^Y) = \xi_t E_t^Q(X_s^Y) = \xi_t X_t^Y = \pi_t X_t. \tag{16}$$

This shows that X^π is a martingale, so π is a state-price deflator. The same calculations in reverse show the converse. The general equivalence between state-price deflators and equivalent martingale measures was shown in the simpler setting of Chapter 2 without technical qualification. An exercise further pursues the equivalence in this setting.

K. Arbitrage Pricing with Dividends

Sections K–M extend the basic approach to securities with dividends paid during $[0, T]$. Consider an Ito process D for the *cumulative dividend* of a security. This means that the cumulative total amount of dividends paid by the security until time t is D_t. For example, if $D_t = \int_0^t \delta_s \, ds$, then δ represents the *dividend-rate process*, as treated in Exercises 5.7, 5.8, and 5.9. Given a cumulative-dividend process D and the associated security-price process X, the *gain process* $G = X + D$ measures the total (capital plus dividend) gain generated by holding the security. A trading strategy is now defined to be a process θ in $\mathcal{L}(G)$, allowing one to define the stochastic integral $\int \theta \, dG$

representing the total gain generated by θ. By the linearity of stochastic integrals, if $\int \theta \, dX$ and $\int \theta \, dD$ are well defined, then $\int \theta dG = \int \theta \, dX + \int \theta \, dD$, once again the sum of capital gains and dividend gains.

Suppose we are given N securities defined by the price process $X = (X^1, \ldots, X^N)$ and cumulative-dividend process $D = (D^1, \ldots, D^N)$, with the associated gain process $G = X + D$. We assume, for each j, that X^j and D^j are finite-variance Ito processes. A trading strategy θ is *self-financing*, extending our earlier definition, if

$$\theta_t \cdot X_t = \theta_0 \cdot X_0 + \int_0^t \theta_s \, dG_s, \qquad t \in [0, T].$$

As before, an *arbitrage* is a self-financing trading strategy θ with $\theta_0 \cdot X_0 \leq 0$ and $\theta_T \cdot X_T > 0$, or with $\theta_0 \cdot X_0 < 0$ and $\theta_T \cdot X_T \geq 0$.

We can extend our earlier results characterizing security prices in the absence of arbitrage. An equivalent martingale measure for the dividend-price pair (D, X) is defined as an equivalent probability measure Q under which $G = X + D$ is a martingale, and such that dQ/dP has finite variance. The existence of an equivalent martingale measure implies, by the same arguments as those given in the proof of Theorem 6F, that there is no arbitrage in $\mathcal{H}^2(G)$ or in $\underline{\Theta}(X)$.

Given a trading strategy θ, if there is an Ito process D^θ such that

$$D_t^\theta = \theta_0 \cdot X_0 + \int_0^t \theta_s \, dG_s - \theta_t \cdot X_t, \qquad t \in [0, T],$$

then we say that D^θ is the cumulative dividend process *generated* by θ. Suppose there exists an equivalent martingale measure Q for (D, X), and consider an additional security defined by the cumulative dividend process H and price process V; both H and V are assumed to be Ito processes of finite variance. Suppose that the additional security is *redundant*, in that there exists some trading strategy θ in $\mathcal{H}^2(G)$ such that $D^\theta = H$ and $\theta_T \cdot X_T = V_T$. The absence of arbitrage involving all $N + 1$ securities implies that for all t, we have $V_t = \theta_t \cdot X_t$ almost surely. From this, the gain process $V + H$ of the redundant security is also a martingale under Q. The proof is a simple extension of that of Theorem 6I.

Under an equivalent martingale measure Q for (D, X), we have, for any time $t \in [0, T]$,

$$X_t + D_t = G_t = E_t^Q(G_T) = E_t^Q(X_T + D_T),$$

which implies that $X_t = E_t^Q(X_T + D_T - D_t)$. For example, if D is defined by $D_t = \int_0^t \delta_s \, ds$, then

$$X_t = E_t^Q \left(X_T + \int_t^T \delta_s \, ds \right). \tag{17}$$

Given the dividend-price pair (D, X), there should be no economic effect, in principle, from a change of numeraire given by a deflator Y. We can write $dY_t = \mu_Y(t) \, dt + \sigma_Y(t) \, dB_t$ for appropriate μ_Y and σ_Y, and $dD_t = \mu_D(t) \, dt + \sigma_D(t) \, dB_t$ for appropriate μ_D and σ_D. The *deflated cumulative dividend process* D^Y is defined by $dD_t^Y = Y_t \, dD_t + \sigma_D(t) \cdot \sigma_Y(t) \, dt$. The *deflated gain process* G^Y is defined by $G_t^Y = D_t^Y + S_t Y_t$. If the dividend process D^θ generated by θ with respect to (D, X) is an Ito process, then its deflated version is the dividend process generated by θ with respect to (X^Y, D^Y), a form of numeraire invariance. This can be shown as an exercise.

The term "$\sigma_D(t) \cdot \sigma_Y(t) \, dt$" in the definition of dD_t^Y might seem puzzling at first. This term is in fact dictated by numeraire invariance. In all applications that appear in this book, however, we have either $\sigma_D = 0$ or $\sigma_Y = 0$, implying the more "obvious" definition $dD_t^Y = Y_t \, dD_t$, which can be intuitively treated as the dividend "increment" dD_t deflated by Y_t.

Suppose that $X = (\beta, S)$, with $S = (S^1, \ldots, S^{N-1})$ and

$$\beta_t = \beta_0 \exp \left(\int_0^t r_s \, ds \right); \qquad \beta_0 > 0,$$

where r is a bounded short-rate process. Consider the deflator Y defined by $Y_t = \beta_t^{-1}$. If, after deflation by Y, there is an equivalent martingale measure Q, then (17) implies the convenient pricing formula

$$S_t = E_t^Q \left[\exp \left(\int_t^T -r_u \, du \right) S_T + \int_t^T \exp \left(\int_t^s -r_u \, du \right) dD_s \right]. \tag{18}$$

Proposition 6I and Theorem 6I extend in the obvious way to this setting.

L. Lumpy Dividends and the Term Structure

By means going beyond the scope of this book, one can extend (18) to the case of finite-variance cumulative-dividend process of the form $D = Z + V - W$, for an Ito process Z and increasing adapted processes V and W that are right continuous. By *increasing*, we mean that $V_s \geq V_t$ whenever $s \geq t$. By *right continuous*, we mean that for any t, $\lim_{s \downarrow t} V_s = V_t$. The *jump* ΔV_t of V at time t, as depicted in Figure 6.1, is defined by $\Delta V_t = V_t - V_{t-}$,

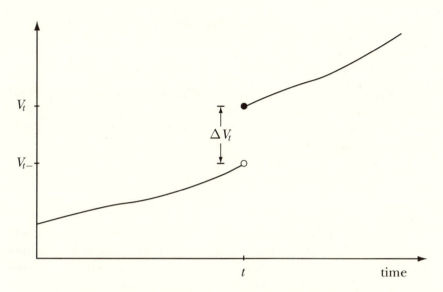

Figure 6.1. *A Right-Continuous Increasing Sample Path*

where $V_{t-} \equiv \lim_{s \uparrow \uparrow t} V_s$ denotes the left limit. By convention, $V_{0-} = V_0 = 0$. The jump $\Delta D_t \equiv D_t - D_{t-}$ of the total dividend process D represents the lump-sum dividend paid at time t.

Each of the above implications of the absence of arbitrage for security prices has a natural extension to this case of "lumpy" dividends. In particular, (18) applies as stated, with $\int \theta \, dD$ defined by $\int \theta \, dZ + \int \theta \, dV - \int \theta \, dW$ whenever all three integrals are well defined, the first as a stochastic integral and latter two as *Stieltjes integrals*. A reader unfamiliar with the Stieltjes integral may consult sources given in the Notes. Happily, the stochastic integral and the Stieltjes integral coincide whenever both are well defined. In this book, we only consider applications that involve two trivial examples of the Stieltjes integral $\int \theta \, dV$.

(a) For the first example of a Stieltjes integral, we let $V = \int \delta_t \, dt$ for some δ in $\mathcal{L}^1$, in which case $\int_0^t \theta_s \, dV_s = \int_0^t \theta_s \delta_s \, ds$.

(b) In the second case, for some stopping time τ, we have $V_t = 0$, $t < \tau$, and $V_t = v$, $t \geq \tau$, where $v = \Delta V_\tau$ is the jump of V at time τ. For this second case, we have $\int_0^t \theta_s \, dV_s = 0$, $t < \tau$, and $\int_0^t \theta_s \, dV_s = \theta_\tau \Delta V_\tau$, $t \geq \tau$, which is natural for our purposes.

Because of the possibility of jumps in dividends, it is now necessary to take an explicit stance on whether security prices will be measured *ex dividend* or *cum dividend*. We opt for the former convention, which means that for a dividend-price pair (D, X), a trading strategy θ is self-financing if

$$\theta_t \cdot (X_t + \Delta D_t) = \theta_0 \cdot X_0 + \int_0^t \theta_s \, dG_s, \qquad t \in [0, T].$$

With this, an *arbitrage* is defined as self-financing trading strategy θ with $\theta_0 \cdot X_0 \leq 0$ and $\theta_T \cdot (X_T + \Delta D_T) > 0$, or with $\theta_0 \cdot X_0 < 0$ and $\theta_T \cdot (X_T + \Delta D_T) \geq 0$.

Extending our earlier definition to allow for lumpy dividends, a trading strategy θ finances a dividend process D^θ if

$$\theta_t \cdot (X_t + \Delta D_t) = \theta_0 \cdot X_0 + \int_0^t \theta_s \, dG_s - D_{t-}^\theta, \qquad t \in [0, T],$$

with $\Delta D_T^\theta = \theta_T \cdot (X_T + \Delta D_T)$.

With these new definitions in place, the *term structure* can be characterized from (18) as follows. Given a bounded short-rate process r, suppose that Q is an equivalent martingale measure after deflation by Y, where $Y_t = \exp(-\int_0^t r_s \, ds)$. A unit zero-coupon riskless bond maturing at time τ is defined by the cumulative-dividend process H with $H_s = 0$, $s < \tau$, and $H_s = 1$, $s \geq \tau$. Since $dH_s = 0$ for $s \neq \tau$, and since $\Delta H_\tau = 1$, we know from case (b) above of the Stieltjes integral that

$$\int_t^T \exp\left(\int_t^s -r_u \, du\right) dH_s = \exp\left(\int_t^\tau -r_u \, du\right).$$

Then (18) implies that the price at time t of a unit zero-coupon riskless bond maturing at time $\tau > t$ is given by

$$\Lambda_{t,\tau} = E_t^Q \left[\exp\left(\int_t^\tau -r_u \, du\right)\right]. \tag{19}$$

The solution for the term structure given by (19) is based on the implicit assumption that the price of a bond after its maturity date is zero. This is also consistent with our earlier analysis of option prices, where we have implicitly equated the terminal cum-dividend price of an option with its terminal dividend payment. For example, with an option expiring at T on a price process S with exercise price K, we set the terminal option price at its expiration value $(S_T - K)^+$. This seems innocuous. Had we actually allowed for the possibility that the terminal cum-dividend option price might be something other than $(S_T - K)^+$, however, we would have needed a more complicated model and further analysis to conclude from the absence of arbitrage that the $(S_T - K)^+$ is indeed the cum-dividend expiration value. This issue of terminal security prices is further pursued in a source cited in the Notes.

M. Equivalent Martingale Measures Implied by No Arbitrage

So far, we have exploited the existence of an equivalent martingale measure as a sufficient condition for the absence of arbitrage. Now we turn to the converse issue: Does the absence of arbitrage imply the existence of an equivalent martingale measure? In the finite-dimensional setting of Chapter 2, we know that the answer is always: "After a change of numeraire, yes." Only technicalities stand between this finite-dimensional equivalence and the infinite-dimensional case we face here. Because of these technicalities, the remainder of the chapter is somewhat advanced and can be skipped on a first reading.

Given a dividend-price pair (D, X), with associated gain process G, let Θ denote the space of self-financing trading strategies in $\mathcal{H}^2(G)$. The *marketed subspace* is

$$M = \{\theta_T \cdot (X_T + \Delta D_T) : \theta \in \Theta\}.$$

Suppose there is no arbitrage in Θ. Then, for each $Z = \theta_T \cdot (X_T + \Delta D_T)$ with θ in Θ, let $\psi(Z) = \theta_0 \cdot X_0$ denote the unique initial investment required to obtain the payoff Z. We know that this function $\psi : M \to \mathbb{R}$ is well defined since, if there are two trading strategies θ and φ in Θ with $\theta_T \cdot (X_T + \Delta D_T) = \varphi_T \cdot (X_T + \Delta D_T)$ and $\theta_0 \cdot X_0 > \varphi_0 \cdot X_0$, then $\varphi - \theta$ is an arbitrage. The function ψ is linear since stochastic integration is linear. Finally, again from the absence of arbitrage, ψ is strictly increasing, meaning that $\psi(Z) > \psi(Z')$ whenever $Z > Z'$. Let $L^2(P)$ denote the space of random variables with finite variance. The marketed subspace M is a subset of $L^2(P)$ because all trading strategies are in $\mathcal{H}^2(G)$. Moreover, M is a *linear subspace*, in this sense: Whenever $Z = \theta_T \cdot (X_T + \Delta D_T)$ and $W = \varphi_T \cdot (X_T + \Delta D_T)$ are in M, $aZ + bW$ is also in M for any constants a and b, since $a\theta + b\varphi$ is a self-financing strategy (from the linearity of stochastic integration).

We adopt the usual *mean-square norm* for $L^2(P)$, defined by $\|Z\| \equiv [E(Z^2)]^{1/2}$. We say that a sequence $\{Z_n\}$ in $L^2(P)$ converges to Z, denoted $Z_n \to Z$, if $\| Z_n - Z \| \to 0$. For example, we say that $\psi : M \to \mathbb{R}$ is *continuous* if $\psi(Z_n) \to \psi(Z)$ whenever $Z^n \to Z$.

There seems no obvious method to deduce the existence of an equivalent martingale measure directly from the absence of arbitrage. We can resort, however, to the notion of an *approximate arbitrage*, a sequence $\{Z_n\}$ in M, with $\psi(Z_n) \leq 0$ for all n, such that there exists some sequence $\{Z_n'\}$ in $L^2(P)$ with $Z_n' \to Z' > 0$ and $Z_n' \leq Z_n$ for all n. The idea is that no Z_n has positive market value, yet Z_n is larger than Z_n', which in turns converges to a positive, nonzero, random value. For example, suppose θ is an arbitrage in Θ with $\theta_T \cdot X_T > 0$. Then the sequence $\{Z_n\}$ defined by $Z_n = \theta_T \cdot X_T$ for all

n is an approximate arbitrage. (Just take $Z'_n = \theta_T \cdot X_T$ for all n.) Provided there is a bounded short rate process, or under other weak assumptions, the absence of approximate arbitrage is indeed a stronger assumption than the absence of arbitrage in Θ, and the difference is only important (for technical reasons) in this infinite-dimensional setting. If we strengthen the assumption of no arbitrage in $\mathcal{H}^2(G)$ to the assumption of no approximate arbitrage, we can recover the existence of an equivalent martingale measure.

In order to simplify the statement and proof of the main result for this section, we revert to the setting of Section 6A, in which prices are implicitly measured cum dividend, and in which $D_t = 0$ for $t < T$. The case of general dividends can be handled with minor alterations as an exercise.

Proposition. *Suppose $X^1 \equiv 1$. Then there is no approximate arbitrage if and only if there is an equivalent martingale measure for X.*

Proof: Suppose there is no approximate arbitrage. Then there is no arbitrage, and the pricing functional $\psi : M \to \mathbb{R}$ is well defined, linear, and strictly increasing. By a technical result cited in the Notes, ψ can be extended to a strictly increasing continuous linear functional $\Psi : L^2(P) \to \mathbb{R}$. By "extension," we mean that for any Z in M, $\Psi(Z) = \psi(Z)$. Since Ψ is continuous and linear, the Riesz Representation Theorem for $L^2(P)$ (Exercise 6.8) implies that there is a unique π in $L^2(P)$ such that

$$\Psi(Z) = E(\pi Z), \qquad Z \in L^2(P).$$

Since $X^1 \equiv 1$, we have $E(\pi X_T^1) = X_0^1 = 1$, so $E(\pi) = 1$. Let Q be the probability measure defined by $dQ/dP = \pi$. Since Ψ is strictly increasing, $\pi \gg 0$, so Q is equivalent to P.

Obviously X^1 is a martingale. To show that X^i is a Q-martingale for each $i > 1$, let τ be an arbitrary stopping time valued in $[0, T]$, and let θ be the trading strategy defined by

(a) $\theta^j = 0, j \neq i, j \neq 1$;
(b) $\theta_t^i = 1, t \leq \tau; \theta_t^i = 0, t > \tau$;
(c) $\theta_t^1 = 0, t \leq \tau; \theta_t^1 = X_\tau^i, t > \tau$.

It is easily seen that $\theta \in \Theta$ and that $\theta_T \cdot X_T = X_\tau^i$, with initial investment $X_0^i = \psi(X_\tau^i) = E(\pi X_\tau^i) = E^Q(X_\tau^i)$. This characterizes X^i as a Q-martingale. Thus, since dQ/dP is of finite variance, Q is an equivalent martingale measure for X.

Conversely, if there is an equivalent martingale measure Q, then there is no arbitrage by Theorem 6F, and the linear functional $\Psi : L^2(P) \to \mathbb{R}$

defined by $\Psi(Z) = E^Q(Z)$ is an extension of the pricing functional ψ. Suppose, for purposes of contradiction, that $\{Z_n\}$ is an approximate arbitrage. Then there is some sequence $\{Z'_n\}$ in $L^2(P)$ such that $\Psi(Z'_n) \leq \Psi(Z_n) \leq 0$ and $\Psi(Z'_n)$ converges to a strictly positive number. This is impossible, so there is no approximate arbitrage. ∎

Corollary. *Suppose there is a bounded short-rate process r. Then there is no approximate arbitrage for X if and only if there an equivalent martingale measure for the deflated price process X^Y, where $Y_t = \exp(-\int_0^t r_s\, ds)$.*

Proof: After deflation by Y, one of the securities has a price identically equal to 1. Since r is bounded, a trading strategy θ is an approximate arbitrage for X if and only if it is an approximate arbitrage for X^Y. The Theorem then applies. ∎

Exercises

6.1 Provide the details left out of the proof provided for Lemma 6G.

6.2 Verify relation (11).

6.3 Consider the case given in Section 6H of $d = 1$, $N = 3$, $S_0^1 > 0$, and with constants $\bar{r}$ and $\bar{\sigma}$ such that for all t, $r_t = \bar{r}$ and $\sigma_t^1 = \bar{\sigma}\, S_t^1$. Assume that $\mu_t^1/S_t^1 - \bar{r} \geq k > 0$, where k is a fixed constant. For the option-price process S^2 given by (12), show that $Z = (S^1/\beta, S^2/\beta)$ is L^2-reducible, justifying the assumption of an equivalent martingale measure and the absence of arbitrage.

6.4 Show, in the context of the previous exercise, that (12) defines the Black-Scholes option-pricing formula.

6.5 Prove Theorem 6I.

6.6 Suppose that the return process R^θ for a self-financing trading strategy θ is well defined as an Ito process, as at the end of Section 6D. Show, as claimed there, that R^θ satisfies the state-price restriction (6).

6.7 Extend the arguments of Section 6I to the case of intermediate dividends, as follows. First, consider a particular security with a dividend-rate process δ in $\mathcal{H}^2$. The cumulative-dividend process H is thus defined by $H = \int_0^t \delta_s\, ds$, $t \in [0, T]$. Suppose that the security's price process V satisfies $V_T = 0$. Suppose that Q is an equivalent martingale measure with density ξ.

Let π be defined by $\pi_0 = 1$ and (15). The fact that $H^Y + V^Y$ is a Q-martingale is equivalent to

$$V_t = \frac{1}{Y_t} E_t^Q \left(\int_t^T Y_s \delta_s \, ds \right), \qquad t \in [0, T].$$

(A) From the definition of ξ, Fubini's Theorem, the law of iterated expectations, and the fact that ξ is a martingale, show each of the equalities

$$V_t = \frac{1}{\xi_t Y_t} E_t \left(\xi_T \int_t^T Y_s \delta_s \, ds \right)$$

$$= \frac{1}{\xi_t Y_t} E_t \left(\int_t^T \xi_T Y_s \delta_s \, ds \right)$$

$$= \frac{1}{\xi_t Y_t} \int_t^T E_t(\xi_T Y_s \delta_s) \, ds$$

$$= \frac{1}{\xi_t Y_t} \int_t^T E_t[E_s(\xi_T Y_s \delta_s)] \, ds$$

$$= \frac{1}{\xi_t Y_t} \int_t^T E_t(\xi_s Y_s \delta_s) \, ds$$

$$= \frac{1}{\xi_t Y_t} E_t \left(\int_t^T \xi_s Y_s \delta_s \, ds \right)$$

$$= \frac{1}{\pi_t} E_t \left(\int_t^T \pi_s \delta_s \, ds \right).$$

This calculation shows that $H^\pi + V^\pi$ is a martingale, consistent with the definition of π as a state-price deflator. Reversing the calculations shows that if π is a state-price deflator and $\text{var}(\pi_T) < \infty$, then $H^Y + V^Y$ is a Q-martingale, where Q is the probability measure defined by its density process ξ from (15).

(B) Extend to the case of V_T not necessarily zero. That is, suppose Q is an equivalent probability measure whose density process ξ is of finite variance. Show that $V^Y + H^Y$ is a Q-martingale if and only if $V^\pi + H^\pi$ is a P-martingale.

(C) Extend to the case of a cumulative-dividend process H that is a bounded Ito process. (Although beyond the scope of this book, an extension of Ito's Lemma applying to general dividend processes that are not necessarily Ito processes shows that one need not assume that H is an Ito process.)

6.8 Extend Exercise 6.5 to allow for cumulative-dividend processes, as follows. Recall that the cumulative-dividend process D^θ generated by a trading strategy θ is defined by $\Delta D_T = W_T^\theta$ and $W_t^\theta = W_0^\theta + \int_0^t \theta_s \, dG_s - D_{t-}^\theta$, where $W_t^\theta = \theta_t \cdot (X_t + \Delta D_t)$ and G is the gain process of the given securities. Let G^θ denote the gain process generated by θ, defined by $G_t^\theta = W_t^\theta + D_t^\theta$. Assuming that an Ito return process R^θ for θ is well defined by $dR_t^\theta = (W_t^\theta)^{-1} \, dG_t^\theta$, show that R^θ satisfies the return restriction (6).

6.9 Prove the Riesz Representation Theorem for $L^2(P)$, as follows. For any continuous linear functional $F : L^2(P) \to \mathbb{R}$, there is a unique π in $L^2(P)$ such that $F(x) = E(\pi x)$ for all x in $L^2(P)$. Hint: Follow the hint given for Exercise 1.17.

6.10 Extend the proof of Theorem 6M to allow for general dividend processes. Add technical conditions as necessary.

6.11 In the proof of Proposition 6I, show the following. We may also take Y to be any Q-integrable random variable. In either case, the "discounted value process" V, defined by $V_t = \exp(-\int_0^t r_s \, ds)\theta_t \cdot (\beta_t, S_t)$, is a Q-martingale.

Notes

The basic approach of this chapter is from Harrison and Kreps (1979) and Harrison and Pliska (1981), who coined most of the terms and developed most of the techniques and basic results. Huang (1985a,b) generalized the basic theory. The development here differs in some minor ways.

The notion of a doubling strategy, as described here in terms of coin tosses, appears in Harrison and Kreps (1979). The actual continuous-time "doubling" strategy (3)–(4), and proof that the associated stopping time τ is valued in $(0, T)$, is from Karatzas (1993), as is a version of Lemma 6G. The relevance of the credit-constrained class of trading strategies $\underline{\Theta}(X)$, and results such as Proposition 6C, originates with Dybvig and Huang (1988). Hindy (1995) explores further the implications of a nonnegative wealth constraint.

Banz and Miller (1978) and Breeden and Litzenberger (1978) explore the ability to deduce state prices from the valuation of derivative securities. Huang and Pagès (1992) give an extension to the case of an infinite-time horizon. The Stieltjes integral, mentioned in Section 6L, can be found in an analysis text such as Royden (1968).

In order to see a sense in which the absence of arbitrage implies that terminal ex-dividend prices are zero, see Ōhashi (1991). This issue is especially delicate in non-Brownian information settings, since the event that

$X_T^n > 0$, in some informational sense not explored here, can be suddenly revealed at time T, and therefore be impossible to exploit with a simultaneous trade. For further discussion of the terminal arbitrage issue, see Ōhashi (1991).

The main technical result used in Section 6M, on the extension of positive linear functionals, is inspired by Kreps (1981), and can be found specifically in Clark (1993). Related results can be found in Harrison and Kreps (1979), Kreps (1981), Duffie and Huang (1986), Stricker (1990), Ansel and Stricker (1992, 1994), El Karoui and Quenez (1993), Delbaen (1992), Delbaen and Schachermayer (1992, 1993, 1994a,b,c,d), Schachermayer (1992, 1994), Schweizer (1992), Kusuoka (1992a), Lakner (1993a,b), Dalang, Morton, and Willinger (1990), Kabanov and Kramkov (1993, 1995), Levental and Skorohod (1994), and Rogers (1993a).

Further references are found in Duffie (1988b). Most of the results in this chapter extend to an abstract filtration, not necessarily generated by Brownian motion. On market completeness under a change of measure in the abstract case, see Duffie (1985).

On the relationship between complete markets and equivalent martingale measures, see Artzner (1995), Artzner and Heath (1990), Jarrow and Madan (1991), Müller (1985), and Stricker (1984).

For various notions of counterexamples to the existence of an equivalent martingale measure in the absence of arbitrage, see Stricker (1990), Back and Pliska (1991), Delbaen and Schachermayer (1992), Schachermayer (1993), and Levental and Skorohod (1994). The notion of an approximate arbitrage is a slight variation on the notion of a *free lunch*, introduced by Kreps (1981).

Carr and Jarrow (1990) show a connection between *local time* and the Black-Scholes model. See, also, Bick (1993). Delbaen, Monat, Schachermayer, Schweizer, and Stricker (1994), Monat and Stricker (1993a,b), provide conditions for closedness of the marketed space of contingent claims, a property used in the last section.

Analogues to some of the results in Chapter 5 or in this chapter for the case of market imperfections such as portfolio constraints or transactions costs are provided by Avellaneda and Parás (1994), Bergman (1991), Boyle and Vorst (1992), Constantinides (1993), Cvitanić and Karatzas (1993), Davis and Clark (1993), Davis and Panas (1991), Davis, Panas, and Zariphopoulou (1993), Edirisinghe, Naik, and Uppal (1991), Grannan and Swindle (1992), Henrotte (1991), Jouini and Kallal (1991, 1993a), Karatzas and Kou (1994), Korn (1992), Kusuoka (1992b, 1993), Leland (1985), Luttmer (1991), Soner, Shreve, and Cvitanić (1994), and Whalley and

Wilmott (1994). Many of these results are asymptotic, for "small" proportional transactions costs. Additional implications of transactions costs and portfolio constraints for optimal portfolio and consumption choice are cited in the Notes of Chapter 9.

An application to international markets is given by Delbaen and Shirakawa (1994). General treatments of some of the issues covered in this chapter can be found in Babbs and Selby (1993), Back and Pliska (1991), Christensen (1987), Christensen (1991), Conze and Viswanathan (1991a), Dothan (1990), Geman, El Karoui, and Rochet (1991), Jarrow and Madan (1994), Jouini and Kallal (1991), Karatzas (1993), Müller (1985), and Rady (1993).

7

Term-Structure Models

THIS CHAPTER REVIEWS models of the term structure of interest rates that are used for the pricing and hedging of *fixed-income securities*, those whose future payoffs are contingent on future interest rates. Term-structure modeling is one of the major success stories in the application of financial models to everyday business problems, ranging from managing the risk of a bond portfolio to the design and pricing of collateralized mortgage obligations.

Included in this chapter are such standard examples as the Merton, Ho-Lee, Dothan, Brennan-Schwartz, Vasicek, Black-Derman-Toy, Black-Karasinski, and Cox-Ingersoll-Ross models, and variations of these "single-factor" term-structure models, so named because they treat the entire term structure of interest rates at any time as a function of a single state variable, the short rate of interest. We will also review multifactor models, including multifactor extensions of the Cox-Ingersoll-Ross model.

All of the named single-factor and multifactor models can be viewed in terms of marginal forward rates rather than directly in terms of interest rates, within the Heath-Jarrow-Morton (HJM) term-structure framework. In the HJM model, the "state variable" on which the future evolution of the yield curve depends is the entire current yield curve, rather than a finite-dimensional state vector. The HJM forward-rate-based class of models is reviewed at the end of the chapter.

An important class of bonds conveys the right to "prepay," that is, the right of the borrower to cancel the bond during certain time windows by paying the remaining principle to the owner of the bond. This call option conveyed to the borrower is often exercised for reasons only partly related to the "optimal exercise" motives described in Chapter 2 (and to be described in a continuous-time setting in Chapter 8). The resulting valuation problem is correspondingly more involved, and receives separate, but unfortunately brief, treatment in this chapter.

Numerical tractability is essential for practical applications. The "calibration" of model parameters and the pricing of term-structure derivatives are typically done by such numerical methods as "binomial trees" (Chapter 3), Monte-Carlo simulation (Chapter 11), and finite-difference solution of PDEs (Chapter 11).

This chapter does not make direct use of the pricing theory developed in Chapter 6 beyond the basic idea of an equivalent martingale measure, which can therefore be treated as a "black box" for those readers who are not familiar with Chapter 6. One need only remember that with probabilities assigned by an equivalent martingale measure, the expected rate of return on any security is the short rate of interest. Since the existence of an equivalent martingale measure is, under purely technical conditions, equivalent to the absence of arbitrage, we find it safe and convenient to work almost from the outset under an assumed equivalent martingale measure. Sufficient conditions for an equivalent martingale measure are reviewed at the end of Chapter 6. An equilibrium example is given in Chapter 10.

A. The Term Structure

We fix a Standard Brownian Motion $B = (B^1, \ldots, B^d)$ in $\mathbb{R}^d$, for some dimension $d \geq 1$, restricted to some time interval $[0, T]$, on a given probability space $(\Omega, \mathcal{F}, P)$. We also fix the standard filtration $\mathbb{F} = \{\mathcal{F}_t : 0 \leq t \leq T\}$ of B, as defined in Section 5I. This establishes the structure of information for all of our interest rate models.

We take as given an adapted short-rate process r with $\int_0^T |r_t|\, dt < \infty$. Conceptually, r_t is the continually compounding rate of interest on riskless securities at time t. This is formalized by taking $\exp\left(\int_t^s r_u\, du\right)$ to be the market value at time s of an investment made at time t of 1 unit of account, continually reinvested at the short rate between t and s.

Consider a *zero-coupon bond* maturing at some future time $s > t$. By definition, the bond pays no dividends before time s, and offers a fixed lump-sum payment at time s that we can take without loss of generality to be 1 unit of account. Although it is not always essential to do so, we will assume throughout the chapter that such a bond exists for each maturity date s. One of our main preoccupations in this chapter is characterizing the price $\Lambda_{t,s}$ at time t of the s-maturity bond.

In the absence of arbitrage, purely technical conditions reviewed in Chapter 6 are required for the existence of an equivalent martingale measure. Such a probability measure Q has the property that any security with a finite-variance payoff of Z at time s has a price, at any time $t \le s$, of

$$E_t^Q \left[\exp \left(\int_t^s -r_u \, du \right) Z \right], \tag{1}$$

where E_t^Q denotes $\mathcal{F}_t$-conditional expectation under Q. (A review of Theorem 2G justifies the easy finite-dimensional version of (1).) In particular, taking $Z = 1$ in (1), the price at time t of the zero-coupon bond maturing at s is

$$\Lambda_{t,s} \equiv E_t^Q \left[\exp \left(\int_t^s -r_u \, du \right) \right]. \tag{2}$$

The doubly indexed process Λ is sometimes known as the *discount function*, or more loosely as the *term structure of interest rates*. The term structure is often expressed in terms of the *yield curve*. The *continuously compounding yield* $y_{t,\tau}$ on a zero-coupon bond maturing at time $t + \tau$ is defined by

$$y_{t,\tau} = -\frac{\log(\Lambda_{t,t+\tau})}{\tau}.$$

The term structure can also be represented in terms of forward interest rates, as explained in Section L.

In this chapter, we will be developing alternative models of the behavior of the short rate r under an equivalent martingale measure Q. In each case, r is modeled in terms of the standard Brownian motion $\widehat{B}$ in $\mathbb{R}^d$ under Q that is obtained from B via Girsanov's Theorem (Appendix D). The Notes cite more general models. We will characterize the term structure and the pricing of term-structure derivatives, securities whose payoffs depend on the term structure.

B. One-Factor Term-Structure Models

We begin with *one-factor term-structure models*, by which we mean models of the short rate r given by an SDE of the form

$$dr_t = \mu(r_t, t) \, dt + \sigma(r_t, t) \, d\widehat{B}_t, \tag{3}$$

where $\mu : \mathbb{R} \times [0, T] \to \mathbb{R}$ and $\sigma : \mathbb{R} \times [0, T] \to \mathbb{R}^d$ satisfy technical conditions guaranteeing the existence of a solution to (3) such that for all t and $s \ge t$, the price $\Lambda_{t,s}$ of the zero-coupon bond maturing at s is finite and well defined by (2). Without loss of generality for our purposes, we take $d = 1$ to simplify the notation, until further notice.

The one-factor models are so named because the Markov property of the solution r to (3) implies from (2) that the short rate is the only state variable, or "factor," on which the current yield curve depends. That is, for all t and $s \geq t$, we can write $\Lambda_{t,s} = F(t, s, r_t)$, for some fixed $F : [0, T] \times [0, T] \times \mathbb{R} \to \mathbb{R}$.

Table 7.1 shows most of the parametric examples of one-factor models appearing in the literature, with their conventional names. Each of these models is a special case of the SDE

$$dr_t = [\alpha_1(t) + \alpha_2(t)r_t + \alpha_3(t)r_t \log(r_t)] \, dt + [\beta_1(t) + \beta_2(t)r_t]^\nu \, d\widehat{B}_t,$$

for continuous functions $\alpha_1, \alpha_2, \alpha_3, \beta_1,$ and β_2 on $[0, T]$ into $\mathbb{R}$, and for some exponent $\nu \in [0.5, 1.5]$. Coefficient restrictions, and restrictions on the space of possible short rates, are needed for the existence and uniqueness of solutions. For each model, Table 7.1 shows the associated exponent ν, and uses the symbol "•" to indicate those coefficients that appear in nonzero form.

In most cases, the original versions of these models had constant coefficients, and were only later extended to allow $\alpha_i(t)$ and $\beta_i(t)$ to depend on t, for practical reasons described in Section 11M. For example, with time-varying coefficients, the *Merton model* of the term structure is often called the *Ho-Lee model*.

A popular special case of the *Black-Karasinski model* is the *Black-Derman-Toy model*, defined in Exercise 7.2. References to the literature are given in the Notes.

Each of these single-factor models has its own desirable properties, some of which will be reviewed below. It tends to depend on the application which of these, if any, is used in practice. The Notes cite some of the empirical evidence regarding these single-factor models.

For essentially any single-factor model, the term structure can be computed (numerically, if not explicitly) by taking advantage of the Feynman-Kac relationship between PDEs and SDEs given in Appendix E. Fixing for convenience the maturity date T, the Feynman-Kac approach implies from (2), under technical conditions on μ and σ, that for all t,

$$\Lambda_{t,T} = f(r_t, t), \tag{4}$$

where $f \in C^{2,1}(\mathbb{R} \times [0, T))$ solves the PDE

$$\mathcal{D}f(x, t) - xf(x, t) = 0, \qquad (x, t) \in \mathbb{R} \times [0, T), \tag{5}$$

Table 7.1. *Common Single-Factor Model Parameters*

Model	α_1	α_2	α_3	β_1	β_2	ν
Cox-Ingersoll-Ross	•	•			•	0.5
Pearson-Sun	•	•		•	•	0.5
Dothan					•	1.0
Brennan-Schwartz	•	•			•	1.0
Merton (Ho-Lee)	•			•		1.0
Vasicek	•	•		•		1.0
Black-Karasinski		•	•		•	1.0
Constantinides-Ingersoll					•	1.5

with boundary condition

$$f(x, T) = 1, \qquad x \in \mathbb{R}, \tag{6}$$

where

$$\mathcal{D}f(x, t) = f_t(x, t) + f_x(x, t)\mu(x, t) + \frac{1}{2}f_{xx}(x, t)\sigma(x, t)^2.$$

According to the results in Appendix E, in order for (4)–(5)–(6) to be consistent, it is enough that r is nonnegative and that μ and σ satisfy Lipschitz conditions in x and have derivatives μ_x, σ_x, μ_{xx}, and σ_{xx} that are continuous and satisfy growth conditions in x. These conditions are not necessary and can be weakened. We note that the Lipschitz condition is violated for several of the examples considered in Table 7.1, which must be treated on a case-by-case basis.

The PDE (5)–(6) can be quickly solved using numerical algorithms described in Chapter 11. If μ and σ do not depend on t, then we can also view $f(r_0, t)$ as the bond price $\Lambda_{0,T-t}$, so that a single function f describes the entire term structure at any time.

C. The Gaussian Single-Factor Models

A subset of the models considered in Table 7.1, those with $\alpha_3 = \beta_2 = 0$, are *Gaussian*, in that the short rates $\{r(t_1), \ldots, r(t_k)\}$ at any finite set $\{t_1, \ldots, t_k\}$ of times have a joint normal distribution under Q. This follows from the properties of linear stochastic differential equations reviewed in Appendix E. Special cases are the Merton (often called "Ho-Lee") and Vasicek models.

In the Gaussian case, we can view a negative coefficient function α_2 as a *mean-reversion* parameter, in that a higher short rate generates a lower drift, and vice versa. Empirically speaking, mean reversion is widely believed to be a useful attribute to include in single-factor short-rate models.

For the Gaussian model, we can show that bond-price processes are log-normal by defining a new process y satisfying $dy_t = -r_t \, dt$. Since (r, y) is the solution of a two-dimensional linear stochastic differential equation, in the sense of Appendix E, for any t and $s \geq t$, the random variable $y_s - y_t = -\int_t^s r_u \, du$ is normally distributed. Under Q, the mean m and variance v of $-\int_t^s r_u \, du$, conditional on $\mathcal{F}_t$, are easily computed in terms of r_t, α_1, α_2, and β_1, and we have

$$
\begin{aligned}
\Lambda_{t,s} &= E_t^Q \left[\exp \left(-\int_t^s r_u \, du \right) \right] \\
&= \exp \left(m + \frac{v}{2} \right) \\
&= \exp[a(t, s) r_t + b(t, s)],
\end{aligned}
$$

for some coefficients $a(t, s)$ and $b(t, s)$ that depend only on t and s, and whose calculation is left as a part of an exercise. Since r_t is normally distributed under Q, this means that any zero-coupon bond price is log-normally distributed under Q. Using this property, a further exercise requests explicit computation of bond-option prices in this setting, along the lines of the original Black-Scholes formula. Aside from the simplicity of the Gaussian model, this explicit computation is one of its main advantages in applications.

An undesirable feature of the Gaussian model is that it implies (for β_1 everywhere nonzero) that the short rate and yields on bonds of any maturity are negative with positive probability at any future date. While negative interest rates are quite plausible when expressed in "real" (consumption numeraire) terms, it is common in practice to express term structures in nominal terms, relative to the price of money. In nominal terms, negative bond yields imply a kind of arbitrage. In order to describe this arbitrage, we can formally view *money* as a security with no dividends whose price process is identically equal to 1. If a particular zero-coupon bond were to offer a negative yield, consider a short position in the bond and a long position of an equal number of units of money, both held to the maturity of the bond. With a negative bond yield, the initial bond price is larger than 1, implying that this position is an arbitrage. Of course, the proposed alternative of everywhere positive interest rates, along with money, implies that the opposite strategy is an arbitrage if money can be freely shorted. One normally assumes that money is a special kind of security that cannot be shorted. (Indeed, the fact that money has a strictly positive price despite having no dividends means that shorting money is itself a kind of arbitrage.) To address properly the role of money in supporting nonnegative interest rates would therefore require a rather wide detour into monetary theory. It may suffice for our purposes to point out that money conveys certain special advantages, for example the ability to undertake certain types of transactions with reduced transactions costs, which would imply a fee in equilibrium for the shorting of money. Let us merely leave this issue with the sense that allowing negative interest rates is not necessarily "wrong," but is somewhat undesirable.

Gaussian short-rate models are nevertheless useful, and frequently used, since the probability of negative interest rates within a reasonably short time, with reasonable choices for the coefficient functions, is relatively small. Since any model is only an approximation, there may, therefore, be applications for which it is worth the trouble of having negative interest rates if the tractability that is offered in return is sufficiently great.

D. The Cox-Ingersoll-Ross Model

One of the best-known single-factor term-structure models is the *Cox-Ingersoll-Ross* (CIR) model indicated in Table 7.1. For constant coefficient functions α_1, α_2, and β_2, the CIR drift and diffusion functions, μ and σ, may be written in the form

$$\mu(x, t) = A(\bar{x} - x); \qquad \sigma(x, t) = C\sqrt{x}, \qquad x \geq 0, \qquad (7)$$

for constants A, $\bar{x}$, and C. Provided A and $\bar{x}$ are positive, there is a nonnegative solution to the SDE (3), based on a source cited in the Notes. (Obviously, nonnegativity is important, if only for the fact of the square root in the diffusion). Of course, we assume that $r_0 \geq 0$, and treat (5)–(6) as applying only to a short rate x in $[0, \infty)$. Some of the properties of this model are discussed in Section 10I, where the coefficients A, $\bar{x}$, and C are calculated in a general equilibrium setting in terms of the utility function and endowment of a representative agent. For the CIR model, it can be verified by direct computation of the derivatives that the solution for the term-structure PDE (5)–(6) is given by

$$f(x, t) = H_1(T - t) \exp\left[-H_2(T - t)x\right], \qquad (8)$$

where

$$H_1(t) = \left[\frac{2\gamma e^{(\gamma+A)t/2}}{(\gamma + A)(e^{\gamma t} - 1) + 2\gamma} \right]^{2A\bar{x}/C^2} \tag{9}$$

$$H_2(t) = \frac{2(e^{\gamma t} - 1)}{(\gamma + A)(e^{\gamma t} - 1) + 2\gamma}, \tag{10}$$

for $\gamma = (A^2 + 2C^2)^{1/2}$. The CIR term structure is thus

$$\Lambda_{t,s} = H_1(s - t) \exp[-H_2(s - t)r_t].$$

In practical applications, the coefficients A, $\bar{x}$, and C of the model are allowed to depend on time, as indicated in Table 7.1. Section J provides a multivariate extension of the CIR model.

E. The Affine Single-Factor Models

The Gaussian and Cox-Ingersoll-Ross models are special cases of single-factor models with the property that the solution f of the term-structure PDE (5)–(6) is given by

$$f(x, t) = \exp\left[a(T - t) + b(T - t)x\right], \tag{11}$$

for some a and b that are continuously differentiable.

Since, for all t, the yield $-\log[f(x, t)]/(T - t)$ obtained from (11) is affine in x, we call (11) an *affine term-structure model*. (A function $H : \mathbb{R} \to \mathbb{R}$ is *affine* if there are constants α and β such that for all x, $H(x) = \alpha + \beta x$.) For example, from (8), the CIR model is an affine term-structure model with $a(t) = \log[H_1(t)]$ and $b(t) = -H_2(t)$.

Given an affine term-structure model, we can deduce from the PDE (5) some of the properties of the drift and diffusion functions, μ and σ, that underly it. Specifically, substituting (11) into (5) leaves, for each $(x, t) \in \mathbb{R} \times [0, T)$, the key relationship

$$b(T - t)\mu(x, t) = [1 + b'(T - t)]x + a'(T - t) - \frac{1}{2}b^2(T - t)\sigma^2(x, t). \tag{12}$$

Suppose, for simplicity, that μ and σ do not depend on t. Applying (12) at two possible choices of maturity $T - t$, say τ_1 and τ_2, we have two linear equations in the two unknowns $\mu(x)$ and $\sigma^2(x)$:

$$A(\tau_1, \tau_2) \begin{pmatrix} \mu(x) \\ \sigma^2(x) \end{pmatrix} = \begin{pmatrix} a'(\tau_1) + [1 + b'(\tau_1)]x \\ a'(\tau_2) + [1 + b'(\tau_2)]x \end{pmatrix}, \tag{13}$$

where

$$A(\tau_1, \tau_2) = \begin{pmatrix} b(\tau_1) & b^2(\tau_1)/2 \\ b(\tau_2) & b^2(\tau_2)/2 \end{pmatrix}.$$

Except at maturities τ_1 and τ_2 chosen so that $A(\tau_1, \tau_2)$ is singular, we can conclude from (13) that μ and σ^2 must themselves be affine in x.

Going the other way, suppose that μ and σ^2 are affine in x, in that

$$\mu(x, t) = \alpha_1(t) + \alpha_2(t)x; \qquad \sigma^2(x, t) = \beta_1(t) + \beta_2(t)x.$$

Then we can recover an affine term-structure model by showing that the solution to (5)–(6) is of the affine form (11). Such a solution applies if there exists (a, b) solving (12). The terms proportional to x in (12) must sum to zero, for otherwise we could vary x and contradict (12). This supplies us with an ordinary differential equation (ODE) for b:

$$b'(\tau) = \alpha_2(\tau)b(\tau) + \frac{1}{2}\beta_2(\tau)b^2(\tau) - 1; \qquad b(0) = 0, \tag{14}$$

whose boundary condition $b(0) = 0$ is dictated by (6) and (11). Likewise, the "intercept" term in (12), that is not dependent on x, must also be zero. Having solved for b from (14), this gives us another ODE for a:

$$a'(\tau) = \alpha_1 b(\tau) + \frac{1}{2}\beta_1 b^2(\tau); \qquad a(0) = 0. \tag{15}$$

Again, the boundary condition $a(0) = 0$ is from (6) and (11). The combined ODE (14)–(15) is a form of what is known as a *Ricatti equation*. Solutions are finite given technical conditions on α_2 and β_2.

Thus, technicalities aside, μ and σ^2 are affine in x if and only if the term structure is itself affine in x. Numerical solutions of (14)–(15), for example by discretization methods such as Runge-Kutta, are easy and given in a source cited in the Notes. The special cases associated with the Gaussian model and the constant-coefficient CIR model have explicit solutions.

We have shown, basically, that affine term-structure models are easily classified and solved. This idea is further pursued in a multifactor setting in Section I and in sources cited in the Notes.

From the above characterization, we know that the "affine class" of term-structure models includes those shown in Table 7.1 with $\alpha_3 = 0$ and $\nu = 0.5$, including

(a) The *Vasicek model*, for which $\beta_2 = 0$.
(b) The *Cox-Ingersoll-Ross model*, for which $\beta_1 = 0$.

(c) The *Merton (Ho-Lee)* model, for which $\alpha_2 = \beta_2 = 0$.

(d) The *Pearson-Sun model*.

For affine models with $\beta_2 \neq 0$, existence of a solution to the SDE (3) requires coefficients with

$$\alpha_1(t) - \alpha_2(t)\frac{\beta_1(t)}{\beta_2(t)} \geq 0, \qquad t \in [0, T]. \tag{16}$$

This condition guarantees the existence of a solution r to the SDE (3) with $r(t) \geq -\beta_1(t)/\beta_2(t)$ for all t.

F. Term-Structure Derivatives

We return to the general one-factor model (3) and consider one of its most important applications, the pricing of derivative securities. Suppose a derivative has payoffs defined in terms of measurable real-valued functions h and g on $\mathbb{R} \times [0, T]$, specifying the dividend rate $h(r_t, t)$ at any time t in $[0, T]$, and the terminal payoff $g(r_\tau, \tau)$ at some particular time $\tau \leq T$. By the definition of an equivalent martingale measure, the price at time t for such a security is

$$F(r_t, t) \equiv E_t^Q \left[\int_t^\tau \varphi_{t,s} h(r_s, s) \, ds + \varphi_{t,\tau} g(r_\tau, \tau) \right],$$

where $\varphi_{t,s} = \exp\left(-\int_t^s r_v \, dv\right)$. The Feynman-Kac PDE results of Appendix E give technical conditions on μ, σ, h, and g under which F solves the PDE

$$\mathcal{D}F(x, t) - xF(x, t) + h(x, t) = 0, \qquad (x, t) \in \mathbb{R} \times [0, \tau), \tag{17}$$

with boundary condition

$$F(x, \tau) = g(x, \tau), \qquad x \in \mathbb{R}, \tag{18}$$

where

$$\mathcal{D}F(x, t) = F_t(x, t) + F_x(x, t)\mu(x, t) + \frac{1}{2}F_{xx}(x, t)\sigma(x, t)^2.$$

Some examples follow, abstracting from many institutional details.

(a) Consider a European option on a zero-coupon bond maturing at time T. The call-option value, with exercise price K and expiration date

$\tau < T$, is given by the solution F to (17)–(18), with $h = 0$ and $g(x, \tau) = [f(x, \tau) - K]^+$, where f solves (5)–(6).

(b) An *interest-rate swap* can be idealized as a contract paying the dividend rate $h(r_t, t) = r_t - r^*$, where r^* is a fixed interest rate agreed upon at time zero. An exercise shows that the value of the swap at time t is merely $v_t = 1 - \Lambda_{t,\tau} - r^* \int_t^T \Lambda_{t,s}\,ds$. The swap is *at the money* if $v_t = 0$, which estabishes the current *swap rate* at $r_t^* \equiv (1 - \Lambda_{t,\tau}) / \int_t^T \Lambda_{t,s}\,ds$.

(c) A *cap* is a loan at a variable interest rate that is capped at some level $\bar{r}$. Per unit of the principal amount of the loan, the value of the cap is given by (17)–(18) with, in the idealized case, $h(r_t, t) = \min(r_t, \bar{r})$ and $g(r_\tau, \tau) = 1$. The terminology varies, and some treat the cap instead as a claim to the dividend rate $(r_t - \bar{r})^+$.

(d) A *floor* is defined symmetrically with a cap, replacing the capped variable rate $\min(r_t, \bar{r})$ with a "floored" rate $h(r_t, t) = \max(r_t, \underline{r})$, for some floor rate $\underline{r}$. A *collar*, that is, a loan with a capped and floored variable rate, can also be valued in the obvious way.

(e) A *yield-curve option* is defined by $h \equiv 0$ and, for the case of a call at strike K and expiration time τ, the terminal payoff $g(r_\tau, \tau) = (Y_n(r_\tau, \tau) - K)^+$, where $Y_n(r_\tau, \tau)$ is the yield at time τ on some particular n-period bond that is an industry benchmark for the term structure. Since a yield is not the price of anything in particular, this is not literally an option to buy anything, but rather is a contingent claim that allows one to speculate or hedge based on the level of the yield in question. The notion of a yield-curve option has been extended to that of a *slope-of-the-yield-curve option*, for which $g(r_\tau, \tau) = [S_{m,n}(r_\tau, \tau) - K]^+$, where

$$S_{m,n}(r_\tau, \tau) = \frac{Y_n(r_\tau, \tau) - Y_m(r_\tau, \tau)}{n - m}$$

defines the slope of the yield curve between two different times to maturity, m and $n > m$.

In each of the above cases, practical considerations cause variations. For instance, the dividend payments that we have modeled at a rate $h(r_t, t)$ are usually paid periodically (say monthly or quarterly) in lump-sum amounts. Such an instrument can be treated as a portfolio of different derivative securities, consisting of a security paying a lump sum $g_1(r_{\tau(1)})$ at the first dividend date $\tau(1)$, a security paying a lump sum $g_2(r_{\tau(2)})$ at the second dividend date $\tau(2)$, and so on. The value of a portfolio is of course the sum of the values of its constituent securities. A special case is a coupon bond, for which g_i is constant for all i. Another practical consideration is that for swaps, caps, floors, and other such securities, the relevant variable interest rate is not literally the short rate r_t, but rather the current yield, y_t on some particular short-term bond. We can often write $y_t = Y(r_t, t)$ for some suitable function Y, in which case the same approach applies. There are typically lags between the dates at which payments are calculated, based on current interest rates, and the dates on which the payments are actually made. This can also be accommodated. Yield-curve options are usually based on the bond-equivalent yields of coupon bonds.

Path-dependent derivative securities, such as mortgage-backed securities, sometimes call for additional state variables, as explained in Section K. Some interest-rate derivative securities are based on the yields of bonds that are subject to some risk of default, in which case the approach must be modified by accounting for default risk. Sources are cited in the Notes.

There are relatively few cases of practical interest for which the PDE (17)–(18) can be solved explicitly. Chapter 11 reviews a number of numerical solution techniques.

G. Hedging

The term *hedging* has different meanings in different contexts. For our narrow purposes here, we will take it to mean the construction of a trading strategy involving certain securities that replicates the value of another "target" security. By virtue of such a replication, one can offset the risk of the target security completely by selling the replicating strategy. In practice, of course, this is unrealistic for it usually assumes both that the underlying valuation model is correct and that the necessary hedging strategy can be executed precisely and without transactions costs. This replication approach to hedging has nevertheless been shown to be useful in applications.

To start with a simple case, consider the single-factor model (3) and suppose that the security to be hedged is defined by the payoff $g(r_\tau, \tau)$ at time $\tau \leq T$. As shown earlier, the price process V for this security is, under technical regularity conditions, given by $V_t = F(r_t, t)$, for some function F solving the PDE (17)–(18).

For hedging purposes, consider another security, similarly defined, and with a market value at time t given by $U_t = \Phi(r_t, t)$, for some $\Phi \in C^{2,1}(\mathbb{R} \times [0, T))$ satisfying (17). We are interested in computing the trading strategy θ to be adopted for the hedge security. Thinking of θ_t as a fixed position, the total market value $F(r_t, t) + \theta_t \Phi(r_t, t)$ of the hedged position has a derivative (or "sensitivity") with respect to the short rate of $F_x(r_t, t) + \theta_t \Phi_x(r_t, t)$. Since the only source of risk in this single-factor setting is the short rate r, an intuitive choice for θ_t is one that equates this derivative to zero, or

$$\theta_t = -\frac{F_x(r_t, t)}{\Phi_x(r_t, t)}, \qquad t \in [0, T],$$

assuming that Φ_x is everywhere nonzero.

In order to show that this intuitive position is in fact appropriate, we augment the position θ_t in the hedging asset with deposits of Z_t at the short rate at time t. The total market value process W would then satisfy

$$dW_t = dV_t + \theta_t \, dU_t + Z_t r_t \, dt.$$

From Ito's Lemma,

$$\begin{aligned}
dW_t = \mathcal{D}F(r_t, t) \, dt &+ F_x(r_t, t) \, dr_t \\
&+ \theta_t[\mathcal{D}\Phi(r_t, t) \, dt + \Phi_x(r_t, t) \, dr_t] + Z_t r_t \, dt.
\end{aligned}$$

From (17), assuming zero dividend rates for simplicity, we have $\mathcal{D}F(x, t) = xF(x, t)$ and $\mathcal{D}\Phi(x, t) = x\Phi(x, t)$ for all x and t. Thus, once one applies the specified hedge position $\theta_t = -F_x(r_t, t)/\Phi_x(r_t, t)$, we have

$$dW_t = r_t[F(r_t, t) + \theta_t \Phi(r_t, t) + Z_t] \, dt.$$

In order for the market value W of the hedged position to remain constant, we can therefore let

$$Z_t = -F(r_t, t) - \theta_t \Phi(r_t, t).$$

The total initial cost of the hedge is then

$$\theta_0 \Phi(r_0, 0) + Z_0 = -F(r_0, 0),$$

as one would expect from the fact that the trading strategy (θ, Z) in the hedging asset and short-term deposits merely replicates $-F(r_T, T)$. This hedging strategy (θ, Z) is self-financing, in the sense of Chapters 5 and 6, a fact left as an exercise for the reader.

The restrictiveness of a single-factor model is apparent from its implication, just shown, that essentially any derivative (or bond) can be used to hedge any other perfectly.

H. Green's Function and the Term Structure

Based on the results of Appendix E, under technical conditions we can also express the solution F of the PDE (17)–(18) for the value of a derivative term-structure security in the form

$$F(x, t) = \int_t^\tau \int_{-\infty}^{+\infty} G(x, t, y, s) h(y, s) \, dy \, ds$$

$$+ \int_{-\infty}^{+\infty} G(x, t, y, \tau) g(y, \tau) \, dy, \tag{19}$$

where G is the *fundamental solution* of the PDE (17). One sometimes calls G the *Green's function* associated with (17). From (19), for any time $s > t$ and any interval $[y(1), y(2)]$,

$$\int_{y(1)}^{y(2)} G(x, t, y, s) \, dy$$

is the price at time t, given the current short rate $r_t = x$, of a security that pays one unit of account at time s in the event that r_s is in $[y(1), y(2)]$. For example, the current price $\Lambda_{t,s}$ of the zero-coupon bond maturing at s is given by $\int_{-\infty}^{+\infty} G(r_t, t, y, s) \, dy$.

One can compute the Green's function G by solving a PDE that is "dual" to (5)–(6), in the following sense. As explained in Appendix E, under technical conditions, for each (x, t) in $\mathbb{R} \times [0, T)$, a function $\psi \in C^{2,1}(\mathbb{R} \times (0, T])$ is defined by $\psi(y, s) = G(x, t, y, s)$, and solves the *forward Kolmogorov equation* (also known as the *Fokker-Planck equation*):

$$\mathcal{D}^* \psi(y, s) - y \psi(y, s) = 0,$$

where

$$\mathcal{D}^* \psi(y, s) = -\psi_t(y, s) - \frac{\partial}{\partial y} [\psi(y, s) \mu(y, s)] + \frac{1}{2} \frac{\partial^2}{\partial y^2} [\psi(y, s) \sigma(y, s)^2]. \tag{20}$$

The "intuitive" boundary condition for (20) is obtained from the role of G in pricing securities. Imagine that the current short rate is x and time is t, and consider an instrument that pays one unit of account immediately, if and only if the current short rate is some number y. Presumably this contingent claim is valued at 1 unit of account if $x = y$, and otherwise has no value. From continuity in s, one can thus think of $\psi(\cdot, s)$ as the density at time s of a measure on $\mathbb{R}$ that converges as $s \downarrow t$ to a probability measure ν with $\nu(\{x\}) = 1$, sometimes called the *dirac measure* at x. Although this initial boundary condition on ψ can be made more precise, we leave that to sources cited in Appendix E. The implementation of this boundary condition for a numerical solution of (20) is spelled out in Chapter 11.

Given G, the derivative asset price function F is more easily computed by numerically integrating (19) than from a direct numerical attack on the PDE (17)–(18). Thus, given a sufficient number of derivative securities whose prices must be computed, it may be worth the effort to compute G. Numerical methods for calculating F and G are indicated in Chapter 11.

A lengthy argument given by a source cited in the Notes shows that the fundamental solution G^* of the Cox-Ingersoll-Ross model (7) is given explicitly in terms of the parameters A, $\bar{x}$, and C by

$$G^*(x, 0, y, t) = \frac{\alpha(t) I_q \left(\alpha(t) \sqrt{xye^{-\gamma t}} \right)}{\exp \left[\alpha(t)(y + xe^{-\gamma t}) - \eta(x + A\bar{x}t - y) \right]} \left(\frac{e^{\gamma t}y}{x} \right)^{q/2},$$

where $\gamma = (A^2 + 2C^2)^{1/2}$, $\eta = (A - \gamma)/C^2$,

$$\alpha(t) = \frac{2\gamma}{C^2(1 - e^{-\gamma t})}, \qquad q = \frac{2A\bar{x}}{C^2} - 1,$$

and I_q is the modified Bessel function of the first kind of order q. The same source gives explicit solutions for the Green's functions of other models. For time-independent μ and σ, as with the CIR model, $G(x, t, y, s) = G(x, 0, y, s - t)$.

I. Multifactor Models

The one-factor model (3) for the short rate is limiting. Even a casual review of the empirical properties of the term structure, some of which can be found in papers cited in the Notes, shows the potential value of a *multifactor term-structure model*. While terminology varies from place to place, by a "multi-factor" model, we mean a model in which the short rate is of the form $r_t = R(X_t, t)$, $t \geq 0$, where X is an Ito process in $\mathbb{R}^d$ solving a stochastic differential equation of the form

$$dX_t = \mu(X_t, t)\, dt + \sigma(X_t, t)\, d\widehat{B}_t, \tag{21}$$

where the given functions R, μ, and σ on $\mathbb{R}^d \times [0, \infty)$ into $\mathbb{R}$, $\mathbb{R}^d$, and $\mathbb{R}^{d \times d}$, respectively, satisfy enough technical regularity to guarantee that (21) has a unique solution and that the term structure (2) is well defined. (Sufficient conditions are given in Appendix E.)

Thus, for a multifactor model, the current short rate depends on the current values of certain "state variables" whose interpretation is left open for the time being. For example, in an equilibrium model such as later considered in Chapter 10, the state vector X_t could be exogenously specified "shocks" to aggregate consumption or production technologies. In many examples, one of the component processes $X^1, \ldots, X^d$, say X^1, is itself the short-rate process r. In some examples, other component processes are explictly related to price levels, inflation rates, the yields of bonds, or the diffusion coefficient of the short-rate process. The last of these are often called *stochastic volatility models.*

A derivative security is, in this setting, given by some real-valued dividend rate function h and terminal payment function g on $\mathbb{R}^d \times [0, \tau]$, for some maturity date $\tau \leq T$. By the definition of an equivalent martingale measure, the associated arbitrage-free derivative security value is given by

$$F(X_t, t) = E_t^Q \left[\int_t^\tau \varphi_{t,s} h(X_s, s) \, ds + \varphi_{t,\tau} g(X_\tau, \tau) \right],$$

where $\varphi_{t,s} = \exp\left(-\int_t^s r_v \, dv\right)$. Extending (17)–(18), under technical conditions given in Appendix E, we have the PDE characterization

$$\mathcal{D}F(x, t) - R(x, t)F(x, t) + h(x, t) = 0, \qquad (x, t) \in \mathbb{R} \times [0, \tau), \qquad (22)$$

with boundary condition

$$F(x, \tau) = g(x, \tau), \qquad x \in \mathbb{R}, \qquad (23)$$

where

$$\mathcal{D}F(x, t) = F_t(x, t) + F_x(x, t)\mu(x, t) + \frac{1}{2}\text{tr}\left[\sigma(x, t)\sigma(x, t)^\top F_{xx}(x, t)\right].$$

Under technical conditions, we can also express the solution F, as in (19), in terms of the fundamental solution G of the PDE (22), as discussed in Appendix E. Also, barring singularities, hedging calculations are done as a straightforward multivariate extension of those shown in Section G.

J. The Multifactor CIR Term-Structure Model

An example of a multifactor model is one in which the i-th factor, for each $i \in \{1, \ldots, d\}$, is the solution of a CIR stochastic differential equation of the form

$$dX_{it} = A_i(\overline{x}_i - X_{it}) \, dt + C_i\sqrt{X_{it}} \, d\widehat{B}_t^i; \qquad X_{i0} > 0,$$

where A_i, $\bar{x}_i$, and C_i are positive constants, analogous to A, $\bar{x}$, and C in (7). We can then take $r_t = R(X_t, t) \equiv \sum_{i=1}^{d} X_{it}$, generating what is known as the *multifactor CIR model*. As a sum of positive processes, r is positive. What follows would change only slightly if one added a constant, or allowed r to be a general linear combination of the factors. More radical extensions of the multifactor CIR model are found in sources cited in the notes.

It can be shown, based on the fact that $\widehat{B}^i$ and $\widehat{B}^j$ are independent under Q for $i \neq j$, that the "factor" processes $X^1, \ldots, X^d$ are also independent under Q. With this, we have

$$
\begin{aligned}
\Lambda_{t,s} &= E_t^Q \left[\exp \left(-\int_t^s r_u \, du \right) \right] \\
&= E_t^Q \left[\exp \left(-\int_t^s \left(\sum_{i=1}^d X_{iu} \right) du \right) \right] \\
&= E_t^Q \left[\exp \left(-\sum_{i=1}^d \int_t^s X_{iu} \, du \right) \right] \\
&= E_t^Q \left[\Pi_{i=1}^d \exp \left(-\int_t^s X_{iu} \, du \right) \right] \\
&= \prod_{i=1}^d E_t^Q \left[\exp \left(-\int_t^s X_{iu} \, du \right) \right] \\
&= \prod_{i=1}^d H_{1i}(s-t) \exp \left[-H_{2i}(s-t) X_{it} \right] \\
&= \exp[-h(s-t) - H_2(s-t) \cdot X_t],
\end{aligned} \tag{24}
$$

where

$$
h(s-t) = -\sum_i \log[H_{1i}(s-t)]; \qquad H_2(t) = (H_{21}(t), \ldots, H_{2d}(t))
$$

for functions H_{1i} and H_{2i} that are defined analogously with (9)–(10) in terms of the coefficients A_i, $\bar{x}_i$, and C_i.

Given any choice for the factors $X_{1t}, \ldots, X_{dt}$, we can almost always make a change of variables under which the state vector is made up of bond yields of various fixed maturities $\tau(1), \ldots, \tau(d)$. That is, consider the Ito process Y in $\mathbb{R}^d$ defined by

$$
Y_{it} = -\frac{\log(\Lambda_{t,t+\tau(i)})}{\tau(i)} = \frac{1}{\tau(i)} \left[h(\tau(i)) + H_2(\tau(i)) \cdot X_t \right]. \tag{25}
$$

For almost every choice of the underlying coefficient vector

$$(A_1, \ldots, A_d, \overline{x}_1, \ldots, \overline{x}_d, C_1, \ldots, C_d, \tau(1), \ldots, \tau(d)) \in \mathbb{R}_{++}^{4d},$$

a nonsingular $d \times d$ matrix Γ is defined by $\Gamma_{ij} = H_{2j}(\tau(i))/\tau(i)$. With this,

$$Y_t = \overline{h} + \Gamma X_t,$$

where $\overline{h}_i = h(\tau(i))/\tau(i)$, and we can write

$$dY_t = \Gamma \, dX_t = (aY_t + b) \, dt + \Sigma(Y_t) \, d\widehat{B}_t, \tag{26}$$

where the matrix a and vector b are defined in the obvious way, and where

$$\Sigma(y)_{ij} = \Gamma_{ij} C_i \sqrt{\Gamma_i^{-1}(y - \overline{h})}, \tag{27}$$

with Γ_i^{-1} denoting the i-th row of Γ^{-1}. The short-rate process, moreover, can be reexpressed as

$$r_t = \gamma(Y_t - \overline{h}), \tag{28}$$

where $\gamma = \sum_i \Gamma_i^{-1}$. The yield curve can be reexpressed in terms of Y_t since, from (24),

$$\Lambda_{t,s} = \exp\left[-h(s - t) - H_2(s - t)^\top \Gamma^{-1} Y_t\right].$$

One could call (26)–(28) a *yield-factor model*, in that it represents the short rate and yield curve in terms of factors that can be identified as the yields of bonds of fixed maturities, and which moreover are the solution of a stochastic differential equation under an equivalent martingale measure. The Notes cite a general class of yield-factor models that includes this example as a special case. Another special case is a multivariate version of the Gaussian model. As with any Gaussian model for the short-rate process, zero-coupon bond price processes are log-normally distributed, and bond option prices may be computed explicitly as a variant of the Black-Scholes formula.

K. Mortgage-Backed Securities

This section briefly reviews the modeling of bonds whose outstanding principle may be continually reduced at a random rate. This typically creates "path dependencies" or, at least, the need to keep track of additional state variables upon which the payments of derivative securities may depend. Important examples include *mortgage-backed securities* (MBS), a class of securities based on home mortgages. For MBS, the reduction in principle is caused by the prepayment of mortgages by homeowners.

We will begin with the case of a *sinking-fund bond*, which one can think of as an idealized mortgage bond. At origination, a sinking-fund bond is defined in terms of a *coupon rate*, a scheduled maturity date, and an initial principle. For each time t before maturity, there is an associated *scheduled principle*, which can be calculated by breaking each of the scheduled payments on the bond into two pieces: an "interest" payment, and a "reduction of principle." In order to simplify notation, we will take the scheduled payments on a given bond with maturity T and coupon rate ρ to be made continually at a constant rate of h. The scheduled principle p_t remaining at time t, per dollar of original principle, is therefore the solution of the ordinary differential equation

$$\frac{dp_t}{dt} = \rho p_t - h, \tag{29}$$

for given initial principle $p_0 > 0$. The scheduled payment rate h is chosen so that the scheduled principle p_T remaining at the maturity date T is zero. Since the unique solution of (29) is

$$p_t = \left(p_0 - \frac{h}{\rho} \right) e^{\rho t} + \frac{h}{\rho}, \tag{30}$$

we have

$$h = \frac{\rho p_0 e^{\rho T}}{e^{\rho T} - 1}. \tag{31}$$

Home mortgages are prepayable sinking-fund bonds, meaning that the borrower has the option to discontinue payments at any time (or subject to certain restrictions) by making a lump-sum payment of the remaining principle to the owner of the bond. Because of the importance and size of the market for mortgage-backed securities, the prepayment option accorded homeowners is the subject of much scrutiny. To this point, however, practical prepayment modelers have shied away from the American-option style of analysis considered elsewhere in this book, and have instead used empirically estimated models of prepayment behavior. We will describe this only briefly in what follows.

Indeed, because of the limited space that we can devote to this problem, we will focus on the simpler case of a sinking-fund bond that has unscheduled amortization according to some exogenously specified index. That is, we simply assume that there is some given process φ describing the fractional rate at which the remaining principle of the given bond is reduced, above and beyond the scheduled rate. We always take the *unscheduled amortization rate process* φ to be adapted, with $\int_0^T \varphi_t \, dt$ well defined. (For certain applications, one could allow φ to take negative values.) The ratio κ_t of actual to scheduled principle remaining at time t is given by the solution of the ordinary differential equation

$$\frac{d\kappa_t}{dt} = -\varphi_t \kappa_t; \qquad \kappa_0 = 1. \tag{32}$$

This solution is

$$\kappa_t = \exp\left(-\int_0^t \varphi_s \, ds\right).$$

The rate of principle payments at time t, both scheduled and unscheduled, is then given by

$$\Psi_t = \kappa_t(h - \rho p_t) + \varphi_t \kappa_t p_t. \tag{33}$$

The rate of interest payments at time t is $\rho \kappa_t p_t$.

   This approach will allow us to treat, by approximation, the modeling of a *mortgage pool*, a single security that lays claim to all of the payments of a set of specified individual mortgages. (Individual mortgages are often aggregated for trading purposes into such pools.) If a pool is sufficiently large and heterogeneous in its prepayment behavior, the fraction prepaid on any one date is small, and for rough modeling purposes one could treat the whole pool as a single bond and assume that prepayments are made continually at rate φ, treated as an unscheduled amortization rate processs.

   The accounting distinction between principle and interest payments is sometimes important because of the popularity of mortgage-based derivatives, such as *collateralized mortgage obligations* (CMOs), whose cash flows at any time t are often contractually based on interest and principle payments, separately. A particular CMO might, for instance, pay the first half of all principle payments, as they occur. This instrument would pay dividends at the rate Ψ_t defined above, until the stopping time

$$\tau = \inf\{t : \int_0^t \Psi_s \, ds = 0.5 p_0\}.$$

Using the definition of an equivalent martingale measure Q, the market value at time t of this CMO would be

$$E_t^Q\left[\int_t^\tau \exp\left(-\int_t^s r_u \, du\right) \Psi_s \, ds\right].$$

It may be difficult to exploit the PDE approach of earlier sections to compute a price of this form, as this would involve a representation of Ψ_t in terms of state variables that capture the information necessary to compute $\kappa_t, \varphi_t,$ and r_t. Indeed, φ_t itself could depend on several additional state variables. As the dimension of the state vector grows large, the PDE approach becomes computationally inefficient relative to, for example, Monte Carlo simulation, a topic considered in Chapter 11.

The average rate of prepayment of homeowners tends to be higher, empirically speaking, when interest rates are low relative to the coupon rate, since this situation gives the homeowner the opportunity to prepay a high-coupon mortgage and initiate a new mortgage at a lower coupon rate. A homeowner may not always take advantage of such opportunities for various reasons, including transactions costs and credit constraints. Conversely, a homeowner may actually prepay out of a low rate mortgage into a high rate mortgage for many reasons, including the need to sell one's home in order to move to another location.

One possible index of the incentive to prepay a mortgage is the amount by which the short rate r_t is below some given interest rate level $\underline{r}$. The cumulative version,

$$b_t \equiv \int_0^t (\underline{r} - r_s)^+ \, ds,$$

also tends to be an important explanatory variable for mortgage prepayment rates, empirically speaking. Here, b_t is a simple example of what is often called a *burnout* factor. The greater the burnout, the more likely it is that homeowners with a high propensity to prepay (due, say, to low transactions costs for prepayment) have already prepaid and left the pool. Thus a higher burnout index, other factors remaining constant, implies lower than average expected future prepayment rates.

Accuracy in the valuation of MBS is often achieved by estimating unscheduled prepayment rates as a function of various interest rate levels, burnout factors, and other explanatory variables, such as seasonality, geography, tax variables, and so on. The reader should merely take away the impression that prepayment rate models are estimated in order to value mortgage-backed securities, and that the econometric models used for this task are normally imperfect and complex.

The valuation and hedging of mortgage-backed securities is an important and challenging application of term-structure models whose richness far exceeds anything that could be offered in such a brief overview as this.

L. The Heath-Jarrow-Morton Model of Forward Rates

In modeling the term structure, we have so far taken as the primitive a model of the short rate process of the form $r_t = R(X_t, t)$, where (under some equivalent martingale measure) X solves a given stochastic differential equation. In the one-factor case, one usually takes $r_t = X_t$. This approach has the advantage of a finite-dimensional "state-space." For example, with this state-space approach one can compute certain derivative prices by solving PDEs.

An alternative approach is to take the entire yield curve as a state variable. This is the essence of the Heath-Jarrow-Morton (HJM) model. The remainder of this section is a summary of the basic elements of the HJM model. Exercises provide further details.

The forward price at time t of a zero-coupon bond for delivery at time $\tau \geq t$ with maturity at time $s \geq \tau$ is (in the absence of arbitrage) given by $\Lambda_{t,s}/\Lambda_{t,\tau}$, the ratio of zero-coupon bond prices at maturity and delivery, respectively. Proof of this is left as an exercise. The associated *forward rate* is defined by

$$\Phi_{t,\tau,s} \equiv \frac{\log(\Lambda_{t,\tau}) - \log(\Lambda_{t,s})}{s - \tau}, \tag{34}$$

which can be viewed as the continuously compounding yield of the bond bought forward. The *instantaneous forward rate*, when it exists, is defined for each time t and forward delivery date $\tau \geq t$, by

$$f(t, \tau) = \lim_{s \downarrow \tau} \Phi_{t,\tau,s}. \tag{35}$$

Thus, the instantaneous forward-rate process f exists if and only if, for all t, the discount $\Lambda_{t,s}$ is differentiable with respect to s.

A convenient fact is that the price at time t of a zero-coupon bond maturing at s can be computed as

$$\Lambda_{t,s} = \exp\left(-\int_t^s f(t, u)\, du\right), \tag{36}$$

so the term structure can be recovered from the instantaneous forward rates, and vice versa.

Given a stochastic model f of forward rates, we will assume that $r_t = f(t, t)$ defines the short rate process r. This means that we will treat r_t as the limit of bond yields as maturity goes to zero. Justification of this assumption can be given under technical conditions cited in the Notes.

The *HJM model of forward rates*, for each fixed maturity s, is given by

$$f(t, s) = f(0, s) + \int_0^t \mu(u, s)\, du + \int_0^t \sigma(u, s)\, d\widehat{B}_u, \qquad t \leq s, \tag{37}$$

where $\{\mu(t, s) : 0 \le t \le s\}$ and $\{\sigma(t, s) : 0 \le t \le s\}$ are adapted processes valued in $\mathbb{R}$ and $\mathbb{R}^d$ respectively such that (37) is well defined as an Ito process. We may think of μ and σ as measurable functions on $\mathcal{T} \times \Omega$, where $\mathcal{T} = \{(t, s) \in \mathbb{R}_+^2 : t \le s\}$. Here, $\widehat{B}$ is the standard Brownian motion in $\mathbb{R}^d$ under an equivalent martingale measure Q that arises in an application of Girsanov's Theorem.

It turns out that there is an important consistency relationship between μ and σ. Under purely technical conditions, it must be the case that

$$\mu(t, s) = \sigma(t, s) \int_t^s \sigma(t, u)^\top \, du. \tag{38}$$

We will delay a demonstration of this fact to the end of the section. For now, let us point out that knowledge of the forward-rate "volatility" process σ, alone, is enough for the computation of all prices. That is, given (38), we can use the definition $r_t = f(t, t)$ of the short rate to obtain

$$r_t = f(0, t) + \int_0^t \sigma(v, t) \int_v^t \sigma(v, u)^\top \, du \, dv + \int_0^t \sigma(v, t) \, d\widehat{B}_v. \tag{39}$$

We can see that if σ is everywhere zero, the spot and forward rates must coincide, as one would expect from the absence of arbitrage in a deterministic bond market!

Given (39), we can price any security from the basic formula (1). Aside from Gaussian special cases such as that studied in Exercise 7.7, most valuation work in the HJM setting is done numerically. Barring special cases cited in the Notes, there is no finite set of state variables for the model, so PDE-based computational methods cannot be used. Instead, one can build an analogous model in discrete time with a finite number of states, and compute prices from "first principles." For the discrete model, the expectation analogous to (1) is obtained by constructing all sample paths for r from the discretization of (39), and by computing the probability (under Q) of each. Sources given in the Notes provide details.

It remains to confirm the key relationship (38) between the drifts and diffusions of forward rates. Consider the Q-martingale M defined, for fixed maturity s, by

$$\begin{aligned} M_t &= E_t^Q \left[\exp\left(-\int_0^s r_u \, du \right) \right] \\ &= \exp\left(-\int_0^t r_u \, du \right) \Lambda_{t,s} \\ &= M_0 \, e^{J(t)}, \end{aligned} \tag{40}$$

where, using (36),

$$J_t = -\log M_0 - \int_0^t r_u \, du - \int_t^s f(t, u) \, du. \tag{41}$$

By the martingale representation corollary of Girsanov's Theorem (Appendix D), since M is a Q-martingale, it can also be represented in the form

$$M_t = M_0 + \int_0^t \eta_s(u) \, d\widehat{B}_u, \tag{42}$$

for some $\mathbb{R}^d$-valued process η_s in $\mathcal{L}(\widehat{B})$. (Note the dependence, indicated by a subscript, of the entire process η_s on the maturity date s.) Since M is strictly positive, we can use Ito's Lemma to reexpress (42) as

$$M_t = M_0 e^{K(t)}, \tag{43}$$

where

$$K_t = \int_0^t H(u, s) \, d\widehat{B}_u - \frac{1}{2} \int_0^t H(u, s) \cdot H(u, s) \, du. \tag{44}$$

for $H(u, s) = \eta_s(u)/M_u$. From (40) and (43), we have $J = K$.

In order to continue, we need to express J as an Ito process. Specifically, we want to compute its drift and diffusion. Using the unique decomposition property of Ito processes (Appendix D), this will allow us to match the drift and diffusion of J with those of K, respectively, and thereby produce the desired relation (38).

The term $\int_t^s f(t, u) \, du$ in (41) may be viewed as an integral (an "infinite sum," over u) of Ito processes. Since the diffusion of a finite sum of Ito processes is the sum of the individual diffusions (a basic linearity property spelled out in Chapter 5), one can expect the same linearity to apply for an infinite sum of Ito processes, at least under technical regularity. In that case, since the diffusion of $f(t, u)$ is $\sigma(t, u)$, the diffusion of J is merely $\int_t^s \sigma(t, u) \, du$. (This is known as *Fubini's Theorem* for stochastic integrals; sufficient technical conditions are cited in the Notes.) Matching this with the diffusion $H(t, s)$ of K, we have

$$H(t, s) = \int_t^s \sigma(t, u) \, du. \tag{45}$$

Likewise, from (41), and assuming enough technical regularity to express the drift of $\int_t^s f(t, u) \, du$ as the integral (sum over u) of the drifts of $f(t, u)$, the drifts of J and K are then equated at

$$-\frac{1}{2} H(t, s) \cdot H(t, s) = -r_t - \int_t^s \mu(t, u) \, du. \tag{46}$$

Given (45) and (46), partial derivatives with respect to s are well defined throughout, and leave us with, respectively,

$$\frac{\partial H(t, s)}{\partial s} = \sigma(t, s)^\top \tag{47}$$

and

$$H(t, s)\frac{\partial H(t, s)}{\partial s} = \mu(t, s). \tag{48}$$

Finally, combining (45), (47), and (48) gives us the basic result (38), as desired. The technical conditions under which the above calculations are justified are cited in the Notes.

Exercises

7.1 Verify, for the CIR term-structure model specified by (7), that the bond price formula (8) satisfies the PDE (5)–(6).

7.2 The *Black-Derman-Toy model* is normally expressed in the form

$$r_t = U(t) \exp[\gamma(t)\widehat{B}(t)], \tag{49}$$

for some functions U and γ in $C^1(\mathbb{R}_+)$. Find conditions on α_2, α_3, and β_2 under which the parameterization for the Black-Karasinski model shown in Table 7.1 specializes to the Black-Derman-Toy model (49).

7.3 For the Vasicek model, as specified in Table 7.1, show that

$$\Lambda_{t,s} = \exp[a(t, s)r_t + b(t, s)],$$

and show how to compute the coefficients $a(t, s)$ and $b(t, s)$ in terms of the functions α_1, α_2, and β_1. Hint: Use the expressions given in Appendix E for the mean and variance of the solution of a linear stochastic differential equation.

7.4 For the Vasicek model, compute the price at time zero of a zero-coupon bond call option. The underlying bond matures at time s. The option is European, struck at $K \in (0, 1)$, and expiring at τ. That is, compute the price of a derivative that pays $(\Lambda_{\tau,s} - K)^+$ at time τ. Hint: Normalize the price of all securities by the price of the zero-coupon bond maturing at time τ. Relative to this numeraire, the short rate is zero and the payoff of the option is unaffected since $\Lambda_{\tau,\tau} = 1$. Use Ito's Lemma and the solution to the previous exercise to write a stochastic differential expression for the normalized bond price $p_t \equiv \Lambda_{t,s}/\Lambda_{t,\tau}$, $t \leq \tau$. As such, p is a "log-normal" process. Now apply the approach taken in Chapter 5 or Chapter 6. Express the solution for the bond option price in the form of the Black-Scholes option-pricing formula, replacing the usual arguments with new expressions based on α_1, α_2, and β_1. Do not forget to renormalize to the original numeraire! This exercise is extended below to the Heath-Jarrow-Morton setting.

7.5 Show, as claimed in Section 7L, that in the absence of arbitrage the forward price at time t for delivery at time τ of a zero-coupon bond maturing at time $s > \tau$ is given by $\Lambda_{t,s}/\Lambda_{t,\tau}$. Show that if the short-rate process r is non-negative then the forward interest rates defined by (34) and instantaneous forward rates defined by (35) are nonnegative. Finally, show (36).

7.6 Let $\lambda_{t,\tau,s}$ denote the forward price at time t for delivery at time τ of one zero-coupon bond maturing at time s. Now consider the forward price F_t at time t for delivery at time s of a security with price process S and deterministic dividend rate process δ. Show, assuming integrability as needed, that the absence of arbitrage implies that

$$F_t = \frac{S_t}{\Lambda_{t,s}} - \int_t^s \lambda_{t,\tau,s}^{-1} \delta_\tau \, d\tau.$$

Do not assume the existence of an equivalent martingale measure.

7.7 Consider the Gaussian forward-rate model, defined by taking the HJM model of Section 7L with coefficients $\mu(t, s)$ and $\sigma(t, s)$ of (37) that are deterministic and differentiable with respect to s. Let $d = 1$ for simplicity.

Calculate the arbitrage-free price at time t of a European call option on a unit zero-coupon bond maturing at time s, with strike price K and expiration date τ, with $t < \tau < s$. To be specific, the option has payoff $(\Lambda_{\tau,s} - K)^+$ at time τ. Hint: Consider the deflator defined by normalizing prices relative to the price $\Lambda_{t,\tau}$ of the pure discount bond maturing at τ. With this deflation, compute an equivalent martingale measure $P(\tau)$ and the stochastic differential equation under $P(\tau)$ for the deflated bond-price process Z defined by $Z_t = \Lambda_{t,s}/\Lambda_{t,\tau}$, $t \leq \tau$ and $Z_t = \Lambda_{t,s}$, $t > \tau$. Show that Z_τ is log-normally distributed under $P(\tau)$. Using the fact that $\Lambda_{\tau,\tau} = 1$, show that the relevant option price is $\Lambda_{t,\tau} E_t^{P(\tau)}[(\Lambda_{\tau,s} - K)^+]$. An explicit solution is then obtained by exploiting the Black-Scholes option-pricing formula. Under $P(\tau)$, conditioning on $\mathcal{F}_t$, one needs to compute the variance of $\log \Lambda_{\tau,s}$, which is normally distributed.

7.8 Consider a setting in which there exists an equivalent martingale measure Q. Under Q, the short-rate process r satisfies the SDE $dr_t = a(t) \, dt + b(t) \, d\widehat{B}_t$, for continuous functions a and b of time alone, where $\widehat{B} = (\widehat{B}^1, \widehat{B}^2)$ is a standard Brownian motion in $\mathbb{R}^2$ under Q, and b is therefore valued in $\mathbb{R}^2$.

(A) For a given maturity T_1, show that the price process U of a zero-coupon bond maturing at T_1 satisfies $dU_t = r_t U_t \, dt + U(t)v(t) \, d\widehat{B}_t$, $t < T_1$, and compute $v(t)$ explicitly in terms of a and b. Hint: Use the fact that $\int_0^{T_1} r_t \, dt$ is normally distributed under Q.

(B) Consider a firm whose total market value process V, under the equivalent martingale measure Q, solves the SDE $dV_t = r_t V_t \, dt + V_t \sigma_V \, dB_t$, $V_0 > 0$, where $\sigma_V \in \mathbb{R}^2$. (The form of the drift, $r_t V_t$, is of course dicated by the definition of an equivalent martingale measure.) The firm has issued K bonds maturing at T_1, each promising to pay 1 unit of account at maturity unless the value V_T of the firm is not large enough to cover the debt, in which case the bonds share the value of the firm on a pro rata basis, meaning a default payment of V_T/K to each bond holder. Letting Z_0 denote the price of a bond at time zero, compute explicitly the *default risk premium* $U_0 - Z_0$, showing it to be of the form of a Black-Scholes put option price with explicitly stated coefficients. Hint: Take U as a deflator. Relative to this deflator, the short rate is zero and the market-value process $W = V/U$ of the firm has a diffusion of the form $W_t \sigma_W(t)$, where σ_W is a function of time alone that can be written in terms of $v(t)$ and σ_V. An application of Girsanov's Theorem (or merely a careful inspection of the basis of the Black-Scholes formula) then gives the result.

7.9 Verify the market value of a fixed-for-floating swap, v_t, asserted in Section 7F, example (b). Hint: A *floating-rate note* is a security that pays a dividend rate given by the short rate r itself, until some maturity τ, and then pays one unit of account. Show, in the absence of arbitrage, that the market value of a floating-rate note is always 1.

7.10 In the context of the HJM model with forward-rate process f, consider a bond issued at time t that pays a dividend process $\{\delta_s : t \le s \le \tau\}$ until some maturity date τ, at which time it pays 1 unit of account. Suppose that, for all s, we have $\delta_s = f(t, s)$. Show that, barring arbitrage, the price at time t of this bond is 1.

7.11 Show that the hedging strategy (θ, Z) defined in Section 7G is indeed self-financing, in the sense of Chapter 6.

7.12 We can derive the equivalent martingale measure Q for the HJM model as follows, at the same time obtaining conditions under which an arbitrage-free instantaneous forward-rate model f is defined in terms of the Brownian motion B under the original measure P, for each fixed maturity s, by

$$f(t, s) = f(0, s) + \int_0^t \alpha(u, s)\, du + \int_0^t \sigma(u, s)\, dB_u, \qquad t \le s. \qquad (50)$$

Here, $\{\alpha(t, s) : 0 \le t \le s\}$ and $\{\sigma(t, s) : 0 \le t \le s\}$ are adapted processes valued in $\mathbb{R}$ and $\mathbb{R}^d$ respectively such that (50) is well defined as an Ito process. This proceeds as follows.

(A) For each fixed s, suppose an $\mathbb{R}^d$-valued process a^s and a real-valued process b^s are well defined by

$$a_t^s = -\int_t^s \sigma(t, v)\, dv; \qquad b_t^s = \frac{\|a_t^s\|^2}{2} - \int_t^s \alpha(t, v)\, dv, \qquad t \le s. \qquad (51)$$

Show, under additional technical conditions, that for each fixed s,

$$\Lambda_{t,s} = \Lambda_{0,s} + \int_0^t \Lambda_{u,s}(r_u + b_u^s)\, du + \int_0^t \Lambda_{u,s}\, a_u^s\, dB_u, \qquad 0 \le t \le s. \qquad (52)$$

Now, taking an arbitrary set $\{s(1), \ldots, s(d)\}$ of d different maturities, consider the deflated bond price processes $Z^1, \ldots, Z^d$, defined by

$$Z_t^i = \exp\left(-\int_0^t r_u\, du\right) \Lambda_{t,s(i)}, \qquad t \le s(i). \qquad (53)$$

For the absence of arbitrage involving these d bonds until time $S \equiv \min\{s(i) : 1 \le i \le d\}$, Chapter 6 shows that it suffices, and in a sense is almost necessary, that there exists an equivalent martingale measure Q for $Z = (Z^1, \ldots, Z^d)$. For this, it is sufficient that Z is L^2-reducible, in the sense of Section 6G. The question of L^2-reducibility hinges on the drift and diffusion processes of Z. For the remainder of the exercise, we restrict ourselves to the time interval $[0, S]$.

(B) Show that for all i,

$$dZ_t^i = Z_t^i b_t^{s(i)}\, dt + Z_t^i a_t^{s(i)}\, dB_t, \qquad t \in [0, S]. \qquad (54)$$

For each $t \leq S$, let A_t be the $d \times d$ matrix whose (i, j)-element is the j-th element of the vector $a_t^{s(i)}$, and let λ_t be the vector in $\mathbb{R}^d$ whose i-th element is $b_t^{s(i)}$. We can then consider the system of linear equations

$$A_t \eta_t = \lambda_t, \qquad t \in [0, S], \tag{55}$$

to be solved for an $\mathbb{R}^d$-valued process η in $\mathcal{L}^2$. Assuming such a solution η to (55) exists, and letting $\nu(Z) = \int_0^S \eta_t \cdot \eta_t \, dt/2$ and $\xi(Z) = \exp[\int_0^S -\eta_t \, dB_t - \nu(Z)]$, Proposition 6G implies that α and σ are consistent with the absence of arbitrage, and that there exists an equivalent martingale measure for Z that is denoted $Q(S)$, provided $\exp[\nu(Z)]$ has finite expectation and $\xi(Z)$ has finite variance. In this case, we can let

$$\frac{dQ(S)}{dP} = \xi(Z). \tag{56}$$

Provided A_t is nonsingular almost everywhere, $Q(S)$ is uniquely defined. Of course, S is arbitrary. A sufficient set of technical conditions for each of the above steps is cited in the Notes.

(C) Suppose A_t is everywhere nonsingular. Using Girsanov's Theorem of Appendix D, show that

$$f(t, s) = f(0, s) + \int_0^t [\alpha(u, s) - \sigma(u, s)\eta_u] \, du + \int_0^t \sigma(u, s) \, d\widehat{B}_u, \tag{57}$$

$$t \leq s,$$

where $\widehat{B}$.

(D) Show that (57) and (38) are consistent.

7.13 Consider the single-factor model with $dr_t = qr_t^{3/2} \, d\widehat{B}_t$, where $\widehat{B}$ is a standard Brownian motion under an equivalent martingale measure Q. A *consol* is a claim to a constant dividend rate process, say 1, perpetually. The market value of the consol at time t, if well defined, is therefore

$$V(r_t) = E\left[\int_t^\infty \exp\left(-\int_t^s r_u \, du\right) du \,\middle|\, r_t\right].$$

Give technical conditions on q under which V is well defined, and show that $V(r_t) = A/r_t$. Compute the coefficient A.

7.14   (Foreign Bond Derivatives)   Suppose you are to price a foreign bond option. The underlying zero-coupon bond pays one unit of foreign currency at some maturity date T, and has a dollar price process of S. With an expiration date for the option of τ and a strike price of K, the bond option pays $(S_\tau - K)^+$ dollars at time τ. Our job is to obtain the bond option-price process C.

The foreign currency price process, say U_t, is given. The foreign currency is defined as a security having a continuous dividend process of $U_t R_t$, where R is the foreign short-rate process. The exchange-rate process U is assumed to be a strictly positive Ito process of the form

$$dU_t = \alpha_t U_t \, dt + U_t \beta_t \, dB_t,$$

where α, a real-valued adapted process, and β, an $\mathbb{R}^d$-valued adapted process, are both bounded.

Foreign interest rates are given by a forward-rate process F, as in the HJM setting. That is, the price of the given zero-coupon foreign bond at time t, in units of foreign currency, is $\exp\left(\int_t^T -F(t, u) \, du\right)$, and we have $R_t = F(t, t)$. It follows that the bond-price process in dollars is given by

$$S_t = U_t \exp\left(\int_t^T -F(t, u) \, du\right),$$

and that the price of the bond option, in dollars, is

$$C_t = E_t^Q\left[\exp\left(\int_t^\tau -r_u \, du\right)(S_\tau - K)^+\right], \tag{58}$$

where r is the dollar short-rate process and Q is an equivalent martingale measure. In general we assume that the vector X of security-price processes (in dollars) for all available securities is such that $\exp\left(\int_0^t -r_u \, du\right) X_t$ defines a Q-martingale, consistent with the definition of Q as an equivalent martingale measure. It is assumed that for each t and $s \geq t$,

$$F(t, s) = F(0, s) + \int_0^t a(u, s) \, du + \int_0^t b(u, s) \, d\widehat{B}_u,$$

where $\widehat{B}$ is a standard Brownian motion in $\mathbb{R}^d$ under Q, and where the s-dependent drift process $a(\,\cdot\,, s) : \Omega \times [0, T] \to \mathbb{R}$ and the s-dependent diffusion process $b(\,\cdot\,, s) : \Omega \times [0, T] \to \mathbb{R}^d$ are assumed to satisfy sufficient regularity conditions for Q to indeed be an equivalent martingale measure and for foreign bond price processes to be well defined.

(A) Demonstrate the "risk-neutral" drift restriction on the foreign forward-rate process F given by $a(t, s) = b(t, s) \cdot \left[\int_t^s b(u, s) \, du - \beta_t \right]$.

(B) Suppose the domestic forward-rate process f is also of the HJM form. That is, we have $r_t = f(t, t)$, where

$$f(t, s) = f(0, s) + \int_0^t \mu(u, s) \, du + \int_0^t \sigma(u, s) \, d\widehat{B}_u, \qquad (59)$$

and where the s-dependent drift process $\mu(\cdot, s) : \Omega \times [0, T] \to \mathbb{R}$ and the s-dependent diffusion process $\sigma(\cdot, s) : \Omega \times [0, T] \to \mathbb{R}^d$ are assumed to satisfy regularity conditions analogous to a and b, respectively. Suppose the coefficient processes β, b, and σ are all deterministic. Derive a relatively explicit expression for the foreign bond-option price.

(C) An *international yield spread option* is a derivative security that promises a dollar payoff that depends on the difference $\delta = F - f$ between the foreign and domestic forward-rate curves. For various reasons, it has been proposed to develop a model directly for the *spread curve* δ. We will have (59) and

$$\delta(t, s) = \delta(0, s) + \int_0^t m(u, s) \, du + \int_0^t v(u, s) \, d\widehat{B}_u, \qquad (60)$$

where the s-dependent drift process $m(\cdot, s) : \Omega \times [0, T] \to \mathbb{R}$ and the s-dependent diffusion process $v(\cdot, s) : \Omega \times [0, T] \to \mathbb{R}^d$ are assumed to satisfy regularity conditions analogous to a and b, respectively. Develop the drift restriction on δ. That is, obtain an expression for m that does not explicitly involve a and b. Do not assume deterministic coefficient processes β, σ, and v.

Notes

We have taken the zero-coupon yield curve throughout as though it can be directly observed in the marketplace. In fact, it is normal practice in the finance industry to estimate the current zero-coupon yield curve (or forward rates) from the prices of both zero-coupon and coupon bonds. Such curve-fitting methods as nonlinear least squares or splines of several varieties are used for this purpose. See, for example, Coleman, Fisher, and Ibbotson (1992), Diament (1993), Fisher, Nychka, and Zervos (1994), and Svensson and Dahlquist (1993).

The Gaussian short-rate model appears in Merton (1974), who orig-inated much of the approach taken in this chapter. Pye (1966) has an early precursor of modern term-structure modeling. Ho and Lee (1986) extended the model and developed the idea of calibration of the model to the current yield curve. Option evaluation and other applications of the Gaussian model is provided by Carverhill (1988), Jamshidian (1989a,b,d; 1991a, 1993b), and El Karoui and Rochet (1989). The calibration idea, reviewed in Chapter 11, has been further developed by Black, Derman, and Toy (1990), Hull and White (1990a, 1993), and Black and Karasin-ski (1991), among others. The Black-Derman-Toy model was shown in a discrete-time version in Exercise 3.12. Exercise 11.5 shows convergence of the discrete-time Black-Derman-Toy model, with appropriate parameters, to the continuous-time, "log-normal" model shown in Exercise 7.2. Prop-erties of the "log-normal" model are explored by Dothan (1978), Hogan (1993a), Miltersen, Sandmann, and Sondermann (1994), and Sandmann and Sondermann (1993).

The CIR term-structure model of Cox, Ingersoll, and Ross (1985a) was developed in a general equilibrium setting, as explained in Chapter 10. It was also developed as a primitive arbitrage-based term-structure model by Richard (1978). One can see that the associated CIR short-rate process exists from the results of Yamada and Watanabe (1971) reviewed in Appendix E. In order to apply their results, we can let $\sigma(x) = 0$ for $x < 0$. The nonnegativity of solutions is then implied by the fact that zero is a natural boundary, in the sense of Gihman and Skorohod (1972). Feller (1951) solved for the Laplace Transform of the distribution of the CIR interest rate r_t. The associated density was calculated by Yao, according to a footnote of Richard (1978). Further characterization is given in Cox, Ingersoll, and Ross (1985a), Cherubini (1993), Cherubini and Esposito (1992), Deelstra and Delbaen (1994a,b), Delbaen (1993), Jamshidian (1992, 1993a), and Rogers (1993b). Sun (1992) provides discrete-time model that converges with shrinking period length to the CIR model. Exercise 7.13 shows a variant of the CIR model that was developed by Cox, Ingersoll, and Ross (1980) and Richard (1994).

The pricing of mortgage-backed securities based on term-structure models is pursued by Jakobsen (1992), Stanton (1990), and Stanton and Wallace (1994), who also review some of the related literature. Richard and Roll (1989) present estimates of mortgage prepayment rate functions.

The idea that an affine term-structure model is typically associated with affine drift and squared diffusion is foreshadowed in Cox, Ingersoll, and Ross (1985a), and is explicit in Brown and Schaefer (1993). [See also Duffie

and Kan (1992).] Hull and White (1990a) solve for the coefficient functions
a and b along the lines of (14)–(15). Examples of the affine class listed in
Section 7F are based on Carverhill (1988), Chen (1994), Cox, Ingersoll,
and Ross (1985a), Dybvig (1988), Jamshidian (1989a,b,d, 1991a), Pearson
and Sun (1994), Selby and Strickland (1993), and Vasicek (1977). Pearson
and Sun (1994) refer to their model as the *translated CIR model*, for obvious
reasons. Empirical estimation of various forms of the affine model is pursued by Brown and Schaefer (1994), Chan, Karolyi, Longstaff, and Sanders
(1992), Chen and Scott (1992b, 1993a), Duan and Simonato (1993), Duffie
and Singleton (1995), Gibbons and Ramaswamy (1993), Heston (1989), de
Munnik (1992), Longstaff and Schwartz (1993), Pearson and Sun (1994),
Pennachi (1991), Rogers and Stummer (1994), and Stambaugh (1988).

Cherif, El Karoui, Myneni, and Viswanathan (1995), Constantinides
(1992), El Karoui, Myneni, and Viswanathan (1992), Jamshidian (1992,
1993a), and Rogers (1993b) characterize a model in which the short rate
is a linear-quadratic form in a multivariate Markov Gaussian process. This
model clearly overlaps with the general affine model, under a change of
variables, although the degree of overlap remains to be worked out in full.
Other term-structure models appearing in this chapter are from Courtadon
(1982).

Study of the term structure in terms of the Green's function associated
with the short-rate process is developed by Dash (1989), Beaglehole (1990),
Beaglehole and Tenney (1990), Büttler and Waldvogel (1994), Dai (1994),
and Jamshidian (1991c). The Green's function for the Dothan (log-normal)
short-rate model can be deduced from the form of Hogan's (1993a) solution
for what he calls the "conditional discounting function" for this model.

Affine multifactor term-structure models include those of Berardi and
Esposito (1994), Brown and Shafer (1993), Chen (1994), Cox, Ingersoll,
and Ross (1985a), Duffie and Kan (1992), Heston (1988b), Langetieg
(1980), Longstaff and Schwartz (1992a, 1993), and Selby and Strickland
(1993). Other multifactor models include those of Black, Derman, and
Kani (1992), Chan (1992), Kraus and Smith (1993), and Platten (1993).
The consol-rate multifactor model of Brennan and Schwartz (1979, 1980a,
1982) is further analyzed by Nelson and Schaefer (1983), Schaefer and
Schwartz (1984), Hogan (1993b), and Duffie, Ma, and Yong (1993).

The idea of using the instantaneous forward-rate process appears in
Richard (1978). The forward rate model of Heath, Jarrow, and Morton
(1992a) has been extensively treated in the case of Gaussian instantaneous
forward rates by Jamshidian (1989a,b,d, 1991a, 1993b), El Karoui and Rochet (1989), El Karoui, Lepage, Myneni, Roseau, and Viswanathan (1991a,

b), El Karoui and Lacoste (1992), Frachot (1993), Frachot, Janci, and Lacoste (1993), Frachot and Lesne (1993a,b,c), Miltersen (1994), and
de Munnik (1992). The illustration of the basic HJM drift restriction (38)
is based on Rogers (1993b). A quicker alternative derivation, based on an
assumption that bond price diffusions are differentiable with respect to maturity, is given by Hull (1993). The original derivation of (38) by Heath,
Jarrow, and Morton (1992a) is based on the approach in Exercise 7.12.
This exercise is useful as a means of establishing the relationship between
the behavior of forward rates under the original measure P and under the
equivalent martingale measure Q. Technical conditions justifying the calculations leading to (38) and the relationship $r_t = f(t, t)$ between the short
rate and forward rates are found in Carverhill (1994), Heath, Jarrow, and
Morton (1992a) and Miltersen (1990).

Exercise 7.7, on bond-option pricing in a Gaussian forward-rate setting,
is from several of the above papers on the HJM model. Heath, Jarrow, and
Morton (1992a) provide a model for forward rates in the form

$$f(t, s) = f(0, s) + \int_0^t \nu[u, s, f(u, s)] \, du$$

$$+ \int_0^t v[u, s, f(u, s)] \, d\widehat{B}_u, \qquad t \le s, \tag{61}$$

where $\nu : [0, T] \times [0, T] \times \mathbb{R} \to \mathbb{R}$ and $v : [0, T] \times [0, T] \times \mathbb{R} \to \mathbb{R}^d$ are
bounded and Lipschitz continuous. Under additional regularity, the solu-
tion for the forward-rate process is nonnegative. The HJM model has been
extended by Kennedy (1994) and Miltersen (1990). For related work and
computational methods in the HJM setting, see Babbs (1991), Carverhill
and Pang (1995), and Heath, Jarrow, and Morton (1990, 1992b). Musiela
(1994a) developed a version of the HJM model in which the forward-rate
curve is a Markov process. For related work, see Musiela and Sondermann
(1994). The technical problems with "log-normal" forward rates shown by
Heath, Jarrow, and Morton (1992a) is circumvented by Goldys, Musiela,
and Sondermann (1994), Miltersen, Sandmann, and Sondermann (1994),
Sandmann and Sondermann (1993), and Musiela (1994b). Markovian versions of the HJM model are presented by Au and Thurston (1993), Brace
and Musiela (1994a), Cheyette (1992), Li, Ritchken, and Sankarasubramanian (1993), Musiela (1994a), and Ritchken and Sankarasubramanian
(1992, 1993).

Exercise 7.8 on corporate bond pricing under Gaussian interest rates
is from Decamps and Rochet (1993). The literature on the valuation of
defaultable term-structure instruments in a setting like that of this chapter

begins essentially with Merton (1974). Recent contributions include those of Artzner and Delbaen (1990a, 1992, 1994), Cooper and Mello (1991, 1992), Duffie and Huang (1994), Duffie, Schroder, and Skiadas (1994), Duffie and Singleton (1994), Hull and White (1992, 1995), Jarrow, Lando, and Turnbull (1993), Jarrow and Turnbull (1991, 1992a, b), Lando (1993, 1994a,b), Leland (1993), Longstaff and Schwartz (1992b), Madan and Unal (1993), Nielsen, Saá-Requejo, and Santa-Clara (1993), and Ramaswamy and Sundaresan (1986).

For term-structure models in a foreign exchange setting, see Nielsen and Saá-Requejo (1992) and Saá-Requejo (1993). The exercise on pricing foreign bond options in the HJM setting is based on Amin and Jarrow (1993) and Amin and Bodurtha (1995). The explicit form of the drift restriction on the foreign forward rates appearing as a solution in this exercise seems to be new. Swap markets are analyzed by Baz and Pascutti (1994), Brace and Musiela (1994b), Carr (1993a), Duffie and Huang (1994), El Karoui and Geman (1991), and Sundaresan (1991). For institutional features of the swap markets, see Litzenberger (1992). For the valuation of caps, see, for example, Miltersen, Sandmann, and Sondermann (1994). On the valuation of other specific forms of term-structure derivatives, see Bajeux-Besnainou and Portait (1992), Brace and Musiela (1994b), Chen and Scott (1992a, 1993b), Cherubini and Esposito (1993), Chesney, Elliott, and Gibson (1993), Daher, Romano, and Zacklad (1992), Decamps and Rochet (1993), El Karoui, Lepage, Myneni, Roseau, and Viswanathan (1991a,b), and Turnbull (1993), Fleming and Whaley (1994) (wildcard options), Ingersoll (1977) (convertible bonds), Jamshidian (1993c; 1994) (diff swaps and quantos), Jarrow and Turnbull (1994), Jorgensen (1994b) (American bond options), Longstaff (1990) (yield options), and Turnbull (1994).

Cox, Ingersoll, and Ross (1981b), Duffie and Stanton (1988), and Grinblatt and Jegadeesh (1993) consider the relative pricing of futures and forwards. Apelfeld and Conze (1990) study the term structure under imperfect information using filtering theory, extending the work of Dothan and Feldman (1986).

Cox, Ingersoll, and Ross (1981a) and Cheng (1991) show what can go wrong if one begins with a model for the stochastic behavior of bond prices without first verifying conditions for the absence of arbitrage. See also Campbell (1986). Amin and Morton (1994) show how to estimate implied volatilities of interest rates from term-structure models. Theoretical arbitrage problems with the calibration approach, as often applied in practice, are explained by Backus, Foresi, and Zin (1994).

There is a growing literature on the econometric estimation of term-structure models. In addition to papers mentioned above, this includes the work of Ait-Sahalia (1992), Ball (1994), Ball and Torous (1994), Broze, Scaillet, and Zakoïan (1993), Buono, Gregory-Allen, and Yaari (1992), Chan, Karolyi, Longstaff, and Sanders (1992), Danesi, Garcia, Genon-Catalot, and Laurent (1993), Das (1993a,b), Duffee (1994), Fournie and Talay (1993), Gourieroux and Laurent (1994), Gourieroux and Scaillet (1994), Grinblatt and Jegadeesh (1993), Koedjik, Nissen, Schotman, and Wolff (1994), Litterman and Scheinkman (1988), and de Munnik (1992). For estimation in the HJM setting, see Frachot (1993), Frachot, Janci, and Lacoste (1993), Frachot and Lesne (1993a,b,c), Flesaker (1993), and Miltersen (1993).

Dybvig, Ingersoll, and Ross (1994) show that the asymptote of long-term interest rates, as maturity goes to infinity, defines a process that is nondecreasing in calendar time.

Further reading on arbitrage-free models of the term structure is found in Artzner and Delbaen (1990b), Babbs and Webber (1994), Back (1991b), Balduzzi (1994), Bossaerts (1990), Carverhill (1990, 1991), Heston (1988a, 1989), Hull and White (1993), Marsh (1994), Pederson and Shiu (1993), Pederson, Shiu, and Thorlacius (1989), Rogers (1993b), and Webber (1990, 1992). de Munnik (1992) is a good basic reference on many aspects of term-structure modeling.

For a Runge-Kutta method of numerically solving an ODE such as (14), see Press, Flannery, Teukolsky, and Vetterling (1993). Numerical methods for solving term-structure models and the pricing of derivative securities are described in Chapter 11. Exercise 14 is from Cox, Ingersoll, and Ross (1980).

Alternative approaches to modeling the term structure of interest rates are given by Backus and Zin (1994), Naik and Lee (1993), Kim (1992, 1993, 1994), and Zheng (1994). The implications of special repo rates for term-structure modeling are explored by Barone and Risa (1994) and Duffie (1993). Van Horne (1993) describes the general features of fixed-income security markets.

8
Derivative Assets

THIS CHAPTER APPLIES arbitrage-free pricing techniques from Chapter 6 to derivative securities that are not always easily treated by the direct PDE approach of Chapter 5. A derivative security is one whose cash flows are contingent on the prices of other securities, or on closely related indices. After summarizing the essential results from Chapter 6 for this purpose, we study the valuation of forwards, futures, American options, and certain exotic options. A final topic is the role of "stochastic volatility" in the pricing and hedging of derivatives.

A. Equivalent Martingale Measures in a Black Box

Skipping over the foundational theory developed in Chapter 6, this section reviews the properties of an equivalent martingale measure, a convenient "black-box" approach to derivative asset pricing in the absence of arbitrage. Once again, we fix a Standard Brownian motion $B = (B^1, \ldots, B^d)$ in $\mathbb{R}^d$ restricted to some time interval $[0, T]$, on a given probability space $(\Omega, \mathcal{F}, P)$. The standard filtration $\mathbb{F} = \{\mathcal{F}_t : 0 \leq t \leq T\}$ of B is as defined in Section 5I.

We take as given an adapted short-rate process r, with $\int_0^T |r_t| \, dt < \infty$ almost surely, and an Ito security price process S in $\mathbb{R}^N$ with

$$dS_t = \mu_t \, dt + \sigma_t \, dB_t,$$

for appropriate μ and σ. It was shown in Chapter 6 that aside from technical conditions, the absence of arbitrage is equivalent to the existence of a probability measure Q with special properties, called an equivalent martingale measure. For this chapter, we will use a narrow definition of equivalent martingale measures under which all expected rates of return are equivalent to the riskless rate r; a broader definition is given in Chapter 6. This means that under Q, there is a Standard Brownian Motion $\widehat{B}$ in $\mathbb{R}^d$ such that if the given securities pay no dividends before T, then

$$dS_t = r_t S_t \, dt + \sigma_t \, d\widehat{B}_t, \tag{1}$$

which repeats (6.6). After substituting this "risk-neutralizing" measure Q for P, one can thus treat every security as though its "instantaneous expected rate of return" is the short rate r.

More generally, suppose the securities with price process S are claims to a cumulative dividend process D. (That is, D_t is the vector of cumulative dividends paid by the N securities up through time t.) In this case, we have

$$S_t = E_t^Q \left[\exp \left(\int_t^T -r_s \, ds \right) S_T + \int_t^T \exp \left(\int_t^s -r_u \, du \right) dD_s \right], \tag{2}$$

which repeats (6.18). For example, suppose that $D_t = \int_0^t \delta_s \, ds$ for some dividend-rate process δ. Then (2) implies that

$$dS_t = (r_t S_t - \delta_t) \, dt + \sigma_t \, d\widehat{B}_t, \tag{3}$$

generalizing (1). For another example, consider a unit discount riskless bond maturing at some time s. The cumulative-dividend process, say H, of this security is characterized by $H_u = 0$ for $u < s$ and $H_u = 1$ for $u \geq s$. The price of this bond at any time $t < s$ is therefore determined by (2) as

$$\Lambda_{t,s} \equiv E_t^Q \left[\exp \left(-\int_t^s r_u \, du \right) \right].$$

This doubly indexed process Λ is sometimes known as the *discount function*, or more loosely as *term structure of interest rates*. Details are given in Chapter 7.

By the definition of an equivalent martingale measure given in Chapter 6, any random variable that has finite variance with respect to P has finite expectation with respect to Q. Moreover, for any such random variable Z,

$$E_t^Q(Z) = \frac{1}{\xi_t} E_t(\xi_T Z), \tag{4}$$

where

$$\xi_t = \exp \left(-\int_0^t \eta_s \, dB_s - \frac{1}{2} \int_0^t \eta_s \cdot \eta_s \, ds \right),$$

and where η is a market price of risk process, that is, an adapted process in $\mathbb{R}^d$ solving the family of linear equations

$$\sigma_t \eta_t = \mu_t - r_t S_t, \qquad t \in [0, T].$$

The remainder of this chapter applies these concepts to the calculation of derivative asset prices, going beyond the simple cases treated in Chapter 5.

B. Forward Prices

Sections 8B through 8D address the pricing of forward and futures contracts, which form an important class of derivatives. A discrete-time primer on this topic is given in Exercise 2.17. The forward contract is the simpler of these two closely related securities. Let W be an $\mathcal{F}_T$-measurable finite-variance random variable underlying the claim payable to a holder of the forward contract at its delivery date T. For example, with a forward contract for delivery of a foreign currency at time T, the random variable W is the market value at time T of the foreign currency. The forward-price process F is an Ito process defined by the fact that one forward contract at time t is a commitment to pay the net amount $F_t - W$ at time T, with no other cash flows at any time. In particular, the true price of a forward contract is zero.

We fix a bounded short-rate process r and an equivalent martingale measure Q. The dividend process H defined by the forward contract made at time t is given by $H_s = 0$, $s < T$, and $H_T = W - F_t$. Since the true price of a forward contract is zero, (2) implies that

$$0 = E_t^Q \left[\exp\left(-\int_t^T r_s \, ds\right)(W - F_t) \right].$$

Solving for the forward price,

$$F_t = \frac{E_t^Q \left[\exp\left(-\int_t^T r_s \, ds\right) W \right]}{E_t^Q \left[\exp\left(-\int_t^T r_s \, ds\right) \right]}.$$

If we assume that there exists at time t a zero-coupon riskless bond maturing at time T, then

$$F_t = \frac{1}{\Lambda_{t,T}} E_t^Q \left[\exp\left(-\int_t^T r_s \, ds\right) W \right]. \tag{5}$$

In any case, it can be verified as an exercise that the forward-price process F is indeed an Ito process.

If r and W are statistically independent with respect to Q, we have the simplified expression $F_t = E_t^Q(W)$, implying that the forward price is a Q-martingale. This would be true, for instance, if the short-rate process r is deterministic.

As an example, suppose that the forward contract is for delivery at time T of one unit of a particular security with price process S and dividend process D. In particular, $W = S_T$. We can obtain a more concrete representation of the forward price than (5), as follows. From (5) and (2),

$$F_t = \frac{1}{\Lambda_{t,T}} \left(S_t - E_t^Q \left[\int_t^T \exp\left(-\int_t^s r_u \, du \right) dD_s \right] \right). \tag{6}$$

If the short-rate process r is deterministic, we can simplify further to

$$F_t = \frac{S_t}{\Lambda_{t,T}} - E_t^Q \left[\int_t^T \exp\left(\int_s^T r_u \, du \right) dD_s \right]. \tag{7}$$

which is known as the *cost-of-carry formula* for forward prices.

For deterministic r and D, the cost-of-carry formula (7) can be recovered from a direct and simple arbitrage argument. As an alternative to buying a forward contract at time t, one could instead buy the underlying security at t and borrow the required cost S_t by selling riskless zero-coupon bonds maturing at T. If one lends out the dividends as they are received by buying riskless bonds maturing at T, the net payoff to this strategy at time T is the value S_T of the underlying security, less the maturity value $S_t/\Lambda_{t,T}$ of the bonds sold at t, plus the total maturity value $\int_t^T \Lambda_{s,T}^{-1} \, dD_s$ of all of the bonds purchased with the dividends received between t and T. The total is $S_T - S_t/\Lambda_{t,T} + \int_t^T \Lambda_{s,T}^{-1} \, dD_s$. The payoff of the forward contract is $S_T - F_t$. Since these two strategies have no payoffs except at T, and since both F_t and $S_t/\Lambda_{t,T} - \int_t^T \Lambda_{s,T}^{-1} \, dD_s$ are known at time t, there would be an arbitrage unless F_t and $S_t/\Lambda_{t,T} - \int_t^T \Lambda_{s,T}^{-1} \, dD_s$ are equal, consistent with (7).

We have put aside the issue of calculating the equivalent martingale measure Q. The simplest case is that in which the forward contract is redundant, for in this case, the equivalent martingale measure does not depend on the forward price. The forward contract is automatically redundant if the underlying asset is a security with deterministic dividends between the contract date t and the delivery date T, provided there is at time t a complete set of bonds maturing at all dates between t and T. In that case, the forward contract can be replicated by a strategy similar to that used to verify the cost-of-carry formula directly. Construction of the strategy is assigned as an exercise.

C. Futures Contracts and Continuous Resettlement

As with a forward contract, a futures contract with delivery date T is keyed to some delivery value W, which we take to be an $\mathcal{F}_T$-measurable random variable with finite variance. The contract is completely defined by a *futures-price process* Φ with the property that $\Phi_T = W$. As we shall see, the contract is literally a security whose price process is zero and whose cumulative dividend process is Φ. In other words, changes in the futures price are credited to the holder of the contract as they occur. See Exercise 2.17 for an explanation in discrete time.

This definition is an abstraction of the traditional notion of a futures contract, which calls for the holder of one contract at the delivery time T to accept delivery of some asset (whose spot market value is represented here by W) in return for simultaneous payment of the current futures price Φ_T. Likewise, the holder of -1 contract, also known as a *short position* of 1 contract, is traditionally obliged to make delivery of the same underlying assset in exchange for the current futures price Φ_T. This informally justifies the property $\Phi_T = W$ of the futures-price process Φ given in the definition above. Roughly speaking, if Φ_T is not equal to W (and if we continue to neglect transactions costs and other details), there is a *delivery arbitrage*. We won't explicitly define a delivery arbitrage since it only complicates the analysis of futures prices that follows. Informally, however, in the event that $W > \Phi_T$, one could buy at time T the deliverable asset for W, simultaneously sell one futures contract, and make immediate delivery for a profit of $W - \Phi_T$. Thus the potential of delivery arbitrage will naturally equate Φ_T with the delivery value W. This is sometimes known as the principle of *convergence*.

Many modern futures contracts have streamlined procedures that avoid the delivery process. For these, the only link that exists with the notion of delivery is that the terminal futures price Φ_T is contractually equated to some such variable W, which could be the price of some commodity or security, or even some abstract variable of general economic interest such as a price deflator. This procedure, finessing the actual delivery of some asset, is known as *cash settlement*. In any case, whether based on cash settlement or the absence of delivery arbitrage, we shall always take it by definition that the delivery futures price Φ_T is equal to the given delivery value W.

The institutional feature of futures markets that is central to our analysis of futures prices is *resettlement*, the process that generates daily or even more frequent payments to and from the holders of futures contracts based on changes in the futures price. As with the expression "forward price," the term "futures price" can be misleading in that the futures price Φ_t at time t is not the price of the contract at all. Instead, at each resettlement time t, an investor who has held $\bar{\theta}$ futures contracts since the last resettlement time, say s, receives the resettlement payment $\bar{\theta}(\Phi_t - \Phi_s)$, following the simplest resettlement recipe. More complicated resettlement arrangements often apply in practice. The continuous-time abstraction is to take the futures-price process Φ to be an Ito process and a *futures position process* to be some θ in $\mathcal{H}^2(\Phi)$ generating the resettlement gain $\int \theta \, d\Phi$ as a cumulative-dividend process. In particular, as we have already stated in its definition, the futures-price process Φ is itself, formally speaking, the cumulative dividend process associated with the contract. The true price process is zero, since (again ignoring some of the detailed institutional procedures), there is no payment against the contract due at the time a contract is bought or sold.

D. Arbitrage-Free Characterization of Futures Prices

The futures-price process Φ can now be characterized as follows. We suppose that the short-rate process r is bounded. For all t, let $Y_t = \exp\left(-\int_0^t r_s \, ds\right)$. Since Φ is strictly speaking the cumulative-dividend process associated with the futures contract and since the true-price process of the contract is zero, from (2) we see that

$$0 = E_t^Q \left(\int_t^T Y_s \, d\Phi_s \right), \qquad t \leq T,$$

from which it follows that the stochastic integral $\int Y \, d\Phi$ is a Q-martingale. Because r is bounded, there are constants $k_1 > 0$ and k_2 such that $k_1 \leq Y_t \leq k_2$ for all t. The process $\int Y \, d\Phi$ is therefore a Q-martingale if and only if Φ is also a Q-martingale. (This seems obvious; proof is assigned as an exercise.) Since $\Phi_T = W$, we have deduced a convenient representation for the futures-price process:

$$\Phi_t = E_t^Q(W), \qquad t \in [0, T]. \tag{8}$$

If r and W are statistically independent under Q, the futures-price process Φ given by (8) and the forward-price process F given by (5) are thus identical. In particular, if r is deterministic, the cost-of-carry formula (7) applies as well to futures prices.

As for how to calculate an equivalent martingale measure Q, it is most convenient if the futures contract is redundant, for then a suitable Q can be calculated directly from the other available securities. We shall work on this approach, originating with an article cited in the Notes, and fix for the remainder of the section an equivalent martingale measure Q. Aside from the case of complete markets, it is not obvious how to establish the redundancy of a futures contract since the futures-price process Φ is itself the cumulative-dividend process of the contract, so any argument might seem circular. Suppose, however, that there is a self-financing strategy (in securities other than the futures contract) whose value at the delivery date T is

$$Z_T = W \exp \left(\int_t^T r_s \, ds \right).$$

We will give an example of such a strategy shortly. From the definition of Q, the market value of this strategy at time t is $Z_t = E_t^Q(W)$. We claim that if Φ_t is not equal to Z_t, then there is an arbitrage. In order to show this, we will construct a trading strategy, involving only the futures contract and borrowing or lending at the short rate, such that the strategy pays off exactly Z_T at time T and requires the investment of Φ_t at time t. It will be clear from this that the absence of arbitrage equates Φ_t and Z_t. The strategy is constructed as follows. Let θ be the futures position process defined by $\theta_s = 0, s < t$, and $\theta_s = \exp \left(\int_t^s r_u \, du \right), s \geq t$. Let V_t be the amount invested at the short rate at time t, determined as follows. Let $V_s = 0, s < t$, and $V_t = \Phi_t$. After t, let all dividends generated by the futures position be invested at the short rate and "rolled over." That is, let

$$dV_s = r_s V_s \, ds + \theta_s \, d\Phi_s, \qquad s \in [t, T].$$

The total market value at any time $s \geq t$ of this self-financing strategy in futures and investment at the short rate is the amount V_s invested at the short rate, since the true price of the futures contract is zero. We can calculate by Ito's Lemma that

$$V_T = \Phi_T \exp \left(\int_t^T r_s \, ds \right) = W \exp \left(\int_t^T r_s \, ds \right) = Z_T, \tag{9}$$

which verifies the claim that the futures contract is redundant.

Summarizing, the futures-price process is uniquely defined by (8) provided there is a self-financing strategy with value $Z_T = W \exp \left(\int_t^T r_s \, ds \right)$ at the delivery date T. It remains to look for examples in which Z_T is indeed the value at time T of some self-financing strategy. That is the case, for instance, if the futures contract delivers a security that pays no dividends before T and if the short-rate process is deterministic. With this, the purchase of $\exp \left(\int_t^T r_s \, ds \right)$ units of the underlying security at time 0 would suffice. More general examples can easily be constructed.

There is one loose end to tidy up. The assumption that the futures-price process Φ is an Ito process played a role in our analysis, yet we have not confirmed that the solution (8) for Φ is actually an Ito process. This can be shown as an application of Girsanov's Theorem (Appendix D).

E. American Security Valuation

We now take the setup given in Section A assuming (1). Consider an American security defined by an adapted process U and an expiration time $\bar{\tau}$. The American security is a claim to the payoff U_τ at a stopping time $\tau \leq \bar{\tau}$ chosen by the holder of the security. Such a stopping time is an *exercise policy*. As with the discrete-time treatment in Chapter 2, our objective is to calculate the price process V of the American security. The classic example is the case of a put option on a stock in the Black-Scholes setting of log-normal stock prices and constant short rates. In that case, we have $U_t = (K - S_t)^+$, where K is the exercise price and S is a log-normal stock price process.

We suppose that our primitive security price process X, defined by $X_t = (S_t^1, \ldots, S_t^N, \beta_t)$, where $\beta_t = \exp\left(\int_0^t r_s \, ds\right)$, generates complete markets. This means that for any random variable Z of finite variance, there is a self-financing trading strategy θ with the property that $\theta_T \cdot X_T = Z$.

The absence of arbitrage and the completeness of markets imply, by Theorem 6I, that the American security with fixed exercise policy τ would also be priced by the equivalent martingale measure Q. That is, it would have the price process V^τ given by

$$V_t^\tau = E_t^Q \left(\varphi_{t,\tau} U_\tau \right),$$

where $\varphi_{t,\tau} \equiv \exp\left(\int_t^\tau -r_s \, ds\right)$. Following the approach taken in Section 2I, a *rational exercise policy* is a solution to the optimal stopping problem

$$V_0^* = \sup_{\tau \in \mathcal{T}(0)} V_0^\tau, \tag{10}$$

where $\mathcal{T}(t)$ denotes the set of stopping times valued in $[t, \bar{\tau}]$. This is the problem of maximizing the initial arbitrage-free value, over the set of candidate exercise policies.

We will cite technical regularity conditions under which there is a stopping time τ^* solving (10), and under which the absence of arbitrage implies that the American security must sell initially for V_0^*. If $V_0 < V_0^*$, then purchase of the American security for V_0, adoption of the rational exercise policy τ^*, and replication of the payoff $-U(\tau^*)$ at τ^* at an initial payoff of

V_0^*, together generate a net initial profit of $V_0^* - V_0 > 0$ and no further cash flow. This is an arbitrage.

In order to rule out the other possibility, that $V_0 > V_0^*$, we will exploit the notion of a *super-replicating trading strategy*, a self-financing trading strategy θ with the property that $\theta_t \cdot X_t \geq U_t$ for all t in $[0, \bar{\tau}]$.

We will prove the existence of super-replicating trading strategy θ with initial market value $\theta_0 \cdot X_0 = V_0^*$. If $V_0 > V_0^*$; then sale of the American security and adoption of a super-replicating strategy implies an initial profit of $V_0 - V_0^* > 0$ and the ability to cover the payment U_τ demanded by the holder of the American security at exercise with the market value $\theta_\tau \cdot X_\tau$ of the super-replicating strategy, regardless of the exercise policy τ used by the holder of the American security. This constitutes an arbitrage. Indeed, then, the unique arbitrage-free American security price would be given by (10). One should bear in mind that we have implicitly extended the definition of an arbitrage slightly in order to handle American securities.

American Regularity Conditions. *U is a nonnegative continuous process and $E(U_*^q)$ $< \infty$ for some $q > 2$, where $U_* = \sup_{t \in [0,T]} U_t$. The short-rate process r is bounded.*

The condition $E(U_*^q) < \infty$ is certainly satisfied for an American put option, whose payoff is bounded by the strike price. In the original Black-Scholes setting, U is also continuous and r is bounded (in fact, constant). The American regularity conditions are based on a source cited in the Notes, which includes a proof of the following result. The conditions in that source are somewhat different, but the same proof carries over once one shows that $E^Q(\sqrt{U_*}) < \infty$, which follows from the fact that $\sqrt{U_*}$ has finite variance under P and from the definition of Q as an equivalent martingale measure.

Let $\hat{U}$ be the process defined by $\hat{U}_t = \exp\left(\int_0^t -r_s \, ds\right) U_t$, and let W be the *Snell envelope* of $\hat{U}$ under Q, meaning that

$$W_t = \sup_{\tau \in \mathcal{T}(t)} E_t^Q(\hat{U}_\tau), \qquad t \leq \bar{\tau}.$$

We recall from Chapter 6 that θ is defined to be a trading strategy in $\underline{\Theta}(X)$ if there is a constant k such that $\theta_t \cdot X_t \geq k$ for all t. The existence of such a lower bound on market value is a kind of credit constraint that prevents a "pathological" variety of arbitrage, called "doubling strategies," reviewed in Section 6C.

Proposition. *Suppose the American regularity conditions are satisfied. There exists a super-replicating trading strategy θ in $\underline{\Theta}(X)$ with inital market value $\theta_0 \cdot X_0 = V_0^*$. A rational exercise policy is given by $\tau^0 = \inf\{t : W_t = \hat{U}_t\}$.*

Proof: Under the American Regularity Conditions, a source cited in the Notes shows that W is a continuous supermartingale under Q, and can therefore be decomposed in the form $W = Z - A$, where Z is a Q-martingale and A is an increasing process with $A_0 = 0$. From the completeness of markets and Exercise 6.11 there is a self-financing trading strategy θ with $\theta_T \cdot X_T = Z_{\overline{T}} \exp\left(\int_{\overline{T}}^T r_t\, dt\right)$ and the process H, defined by $H_t = \theta_t \cdot X_t \exp\left(\int_0^t -r_s\, ds\right)$, is a Q-martingale. Thus, since Z is also a Q-martingale,

$$
\begin{aligned}
\theta_t \cdot X_t &= \exp\left(\int_0^t r_s\, ds\right) E_t^Q\left[\exp\left(-\int_t^T r_s\, ds\right)\theta_T \cdot X_T\right] \\
&= \exp\left(\int_0^t r_s\, ds\right) E_t^Q(Z_{\overline{T}}) \\
&= \exp\left(\int_0^t r_s\, ds\right) Z_t \\
&= \exp\left(\int_0^t r_s\, ds\right)(W_t + A_t) \\
&\geq \exp\left(\int_0^t r_s\, ds\right) W_t \\
&\geq U_t, \qquad t \leq \overline{T},
\end{aligned}
\tag{11}
$$

using the facts that A_t is nonnegative, the definition of $\widehat{U}_t$, and the fact that $W_t \geq \widehat{U}_t$. Since $A_0 = 0$, the first equality in (11) implies that $\theta_0 \cdot X_0 = W_0 = V_0^*$. Because U is nonnegative, (11) implies that θ is in $\Theta(X)$, and is a super-replicating strategy for $(U, \overline{T})$. Because $A_0 = 0$, the first inequality in (11) is satisfied with equality for $t = 0$, implying that $\theta_0 \cdot X_0 = V_0^*$, as claimed.

By essentially the same argument shown in Chapter 2, τ^0 is a rational exercise policy. ∎

Thus the American regularity conditions are sufficient for V_0^* of (10) to be the arbitrage-free value of the American security. In the case of the Black-Scholes model, all of the American regularity conditions are satisfied for the American put with exercise price K, expiration at time T, constant short rate $\overline{r}$, constant stock volatility $\overline{\sigma}$, and initial stock price x. We can write the stock-price process S as the solution to

$$
dS_t = \overline{r} S_t\, dt + \overline{\sigma} S_t\, d\epsilon_t; \qquad S_0 = x,
\tag{12}
$$

where ϵ is a standard Brownian motion under Q. The arbitrage-free put price is therefore

$$V_0^* = h(x, T) \equiv \max_{\tau \in \mathcal{T}(0)} E^Q \left[e^{-\bar{r}\tau} (K - S_\tau)^+ \right]. \tag{13}$$

In Chapter 11 we review some numerical recipes for approximating this value.

By extending our arguments, we can handle an American security that promises a cumulative-dividend process H until exercised at a stopping time $\tau \leq \bar{\tau}$ for a final payoff of U_τ. The absence of arbitrage implies that the price process V^* of the American security $(H, U, \bar{\tau})$ is given by

$$V_t^* \equiv \sup_{\tau \in \mathcal{T}(t)} E_t^Q \left(\int_t^\tau \varphi_{t,s} \, dH_s + \varphi_{t,\tau} U_\tau \right), \qquad t < \tau,$$

whenever this problem for $t = 0$ is well defined and has a solution τ^*, the rational exercise policy.

F. Exercise and Continuation Regions for American Securities

We take the case of an American security $(U, \bar{\tau})$ with $U_t = g(Y_t, t)$, where $g : \mathbb{R}^K \times [0, T] \to \mathbb{R}$ is continuous and Y is an Ito process in $\mathbb{R}^K$ satisfying the SDE (under the equivalent martingale measure Q)

$$dY_t = a(Y_t) \, dt + b(Y_t) \, d\widehat{B}_t, \tag{14}$$

for continuous functions a and b satisfying Lipschitz conditions. For simplicity, we take the interest-rate process r to be zero, and later show that, aside from technicalities, this is without loss of generality. We adopt the American regularity conditions and again assume redundancy of the American security for any exercise policy. Starting at time t with initial condition $Y_t = y$ for (14), the arbitrage-free value is given by

$$h(y, t) \equiv \sup_{\tau \in \mathcal{T}(t)} E_t^Q \left[g(Y_\tau, \tau) \right]. \tag{15}$$

By inspection, $h \geq g$. From Proposition 8E, an optimal exercise policy is given by

$$\tau^0 = \inf\{t \in [0, T] : h(Y_t, t) = g(Y_t, t)\}. \tag{16}$$

By (16), $h(Y_t, t) > g(Y_t, t)$ for all $t < \tau^0$. Letting

$$\mathcal{E} = \{(y, t) \in \mathbb{R}^K \times [0, T] : h(y, t) = g(y, t)\}, \tag{17}$$

we can write $\tau^0 = \inf\{t : (Y_t, t) \in \mathcal{E}\}$, and safely call $\mathcal{E}$ the *exercise region*, and its complement

$$C = \{(y, t) \in \mathbb{R}^K \times [0, T) : h(y, t) > g(y, t)\}$$

the *continuation region.* In order to solve the optimal exercise problem, it is enough to break $\mathbb{R}^K \times [0, T]$ into these two sets. An optimal policy is then to exercise when in $\mathcal{E}$, and otherwise to wait. Typically, solving for the exercise region $\mathcal{E}$ is a formidable problem.

For a characterization of the solution in terms of the solution of a partial differential equation, suppose that h is sufficiently smooth for an application of Ito's Lemma. Letting $\mathcal{H}_t = h(Y_t, t)$, we have $d\mathcal{H}_t = \mathcal{D}h(Y_t, t)\, dt + h_y(Y_t, t)b(Y_t)\, d\widehat{B}_t$, where

$$\mathcal{D}h(y, t) = h_t(y, t) + h_y(y, t)a(y) + \frac{1}{2}\mathrm{tr}\left[h_{yy}(y, t)b(y)b(y)^\top\right].$$

For any initial conditions (y, t) and any stopping time $\tau \geq t$, we know from the definition of h that $E^Q[h(Y_\tau, \tau)] \leq h(y, t)$. From this, it is natural to conjecture that $\mathcal{D}h(y, t) \leq 0$ for all (y, t). Moreover, from the fact that M is a Q-martingale and $M_t = h(Y_t, t)$, $t < \tau^0$, it is easy to see that $\mathcal{D}h(y, t) = 0$ for all (y, t) in C. We summarize these conjectured necessary conditions on h, supressing the arguments (y, t) everywhere for brevity. On $\mathbb{R}^K \times [0, T)$

$$h \geq g, \qquad \mathcal{D}h \leq 0, \qquad (h - g)(\mathcal{D}h) = 0. \tag{18}$$

The last of these three conditions means that $\mathcal{D}h = 0$ wherever $h > g$, and conversely that $h = g$ wherever $\mathcal{D}h < 0$. Intuitively, this is a Bellman condition prescribing a policy of not exercising so long as the expected rate of change of the value function is not strictly negative. We also have the boundary condition

$$h(y, T) = g(y, T), \qquad y \in \mathbb{R}^K. \tag{19}$$

Under strong technical assumptions that can be found in sources cited in the Notes, it turns out that these necessary conditions (18)–(19) are also sufficient for h to be the value function. This characterization (18)–(19) of the value function lends itself to a finite-difference algorithm for numerical solution of the value function h.

In order to incorporate nonzero interest rates, suppose that the short-rate process r can be written in the form $r_t = \alpha(Y_t)$ for some bounded measurable $\alpha : \mathbb{R}^K \to \mathbb{R}$. Letting $\beta_t = \int_0^t r_s\, ds$, we have $d\beta_t = \alpha(Y_t)\beta_t\, dt$,

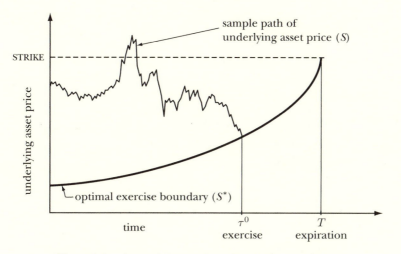

Figure 8.1. *Optimal Exercise Boundary for American Put*

so all of the above goes through, replacing the orginal Ito process Y in $\mathbb{R}^K$ with the augmented Ito process $\widehat{Y} = (Y, \beta)$ in $\mathbb{R}^{K+1}$, and replacing the original payoff function g with $\widehat{g}$, where $\widehat{g}[(Y_t, \beta_t), t] = g(Y_t, t)/\beta_t$. The variational inequality (18)–(19) for the value function h can then be written exactly as before, with the exception that $\mathcal{D}h(y, t)$ is replaced everywhere by $\mathcal{D}h(y, t) - \alpha(y)h(y, t)$. Likewise, time dependence in the functions a, b, and α can be accommodated by augmenting $\widehat{Y}$ with the trivial Ito process given by elapsed time.

For the special case of the American put with the standard log-normal set-up given by (12), a series of advances cited in the Notes has led to the following characterization of the solution. Since $Y = S$ is a nonnegative process, the continuation region $\mathcal{C}$ can be treated as a subset of $\mathbb{R}_+ \times [0, T)$. It turns out that there is an increasing continuously differentiable function $S^* : [0, T) \to \mathbb{R}$, called the *optimal exercise boundary*, such that $\mathcal{C} = \{(x, t) : x > S_t^*\}$. Letting, $S_T^* = K$, the optimal exercise policy τ^* is then to exercise when (and if) the stock price S "hits the optimal exercise boundary," as illustrated in Figure 8.1. That is, $\tau^0 = \inf\{t : S_t = S_t^*\}$.

Unfortunately, there is no explicit solution available for the optimal stopping boundary S^*. There are, however, numerical methods for estimating the value function h and exercise boundary S^*. One is the simple algorithm (3.23) for the "binomial" model, which as we see in Chapter 11 can be taken as an approximation of the Black-Scholes model. The other is a direct finite-difference numerical solution of the associated *partial differential inequality* (18)–(19), which in this case can be written, with the change of variables from stock price x to its logarithm $y = \log(x)$: On $\mathbb{R} \times [0, T)$

$$h(y, t) - (K - e^y)^+ \geq 0$$

$$\mathcal{D}h(y, t) - \bar{r}h(y, t) \leq 0 \tag{20}$$

$$[h(y, t) - (K - e^y)^+][\mathcal{D}h(y, t) - \bar{r}h(y, t)] = 0,$$

with boundary condition

$$h(y, T) = (K - e^y)^+, \qquad y \in \mathbb{R}, \tag{21}$$

where

$$\mathcal{D}h(y, t) = h_t(y, t) + \left(\bar{r} - \frac{\bar{\sigma}^2}{2} \right) h_y(y, t) + \frac{\bar{\sigma}^2}{2} h_{yy}(y, t). \tag{22}$$

Not all of the indicated derivatives of h may exist, but it turns out, from sources cited in the Notes, that there is no essential difficulty in treating (20)–(21) as written for computational purposes.

G. Lookback Options

Certain classes of derivative securities are said to be *path dependent*, in that the payoff of the derivative security at a given time depends on the path taken by the underlying asset price up until that time. An important and illustrative class of examples is given by *lookback options*.

Consider the case of a *sell-at-the-max option*, with exercise date T, a lookback option defined as follows. Let S be an Ito process defining the price of a security, and let r be a bounded adapted short rate process. For any times t and $s \geq t$, let $S^*_{t,s} = \max\{S_u : t \leq u \leq s\}$ denote the maximum level achieved by the security-price process between times t and s. This particular option offers the right to sell the stock at time T for $S^*_{0,T}$. Of course, $S^*_{0,T} \geq S_T$, so the option is always exercised for a payoff of $S^*_{0,T} - S_T$. Given an equivalent martingale measure Q, the market value of the option at time t is then by definition

$$V_t = E^Q_t \left[\exp \left(- \int_t^T r_s \, ds \right) (S^*_{0,T} - S_T) \right]. \tag{23}$$

For the case of a log-normal security-price process satisfying (12) and constant short interest rate $\bar{r}$, a closed-form solution can be obtained for the lookback-option price process V. We know that $S_t = S_0 \exp(\nu t + \overline{\sigma}\epsilon_t)$, where ϵ is a standard Brownian motion under Q and $\nu = \overline{r} - \sigma^2/2$. Thus

$$S_{0,T}^* = \max(S_{0,t}^*, S_{t,T}^*) \qquad (24)$$

$$= \max\left[S_{0,t}^*, S_t \exp(Z_{t,T})\right],$$

where

$$Z_{t,T} = \max_{u \in [t,T]} \nu(u-t) + \overline{\sigma}(\epsilon_u - \epsilon_t). \qquad (25)$$

The cumulative distribution function G_{T-t} of $Z_{t,T}$ is known, based on sources cited in the Notes, to be given by

$$G_\tau(z) = 1 - \Phi\left(\frac{z - \nu\tau}{\overline{\sigma}\sqrt{\tau}}\right) + e^{2\nu z/\overline{\sigma}^2} \Phi\left(\frac{-z - \nu\tau}{\overline{\sigma}\sqrt{\tau}}\right), \qquad z > 0, \qquad (26)$$

where Φ is the standard normal cumulative distribution function. Thus, from (24),

$$E_t^Q\left(S_{0,T}^*\right) = G_{T-t}(z^*)S_{0,t}^* + [1 - G_{T-t}(z^*)]S_t \int_{z^*}^\infty e^z G_{T-t}'(z)\, dz, \qquad (27)$$

where $z^* = \log(S_{0,t}^*) - \log(S_t)$.

Because there are no dividends, the payment of S_T at T has a market value at time t of S_t. From (23), we thus have

$$V_t = E_t^Q\left(e^{-\overline{r}(T-t)}S_{0,T}^*\right) - S_t.$$

After computing the integral in (27), we have the lookback sell-at-the-max put option price $V_t = p(S_t, S_{0,t}^*; T - t)$, where

$$p(x, y; \tau) = -x\Phi(-D) + e^{-\overline{r}\tau}y\,\Phi(-D + \overline{\sigma}\sqrt{\tau})$$

$$+ \frac{\overline{\sigma}^2}{2\overline{r}}e^{-\overline{r}\tau}x\left[-\left(\frac{x}{y}\right)^{-2\overline{r}/\overline{\sigma}^2}\Phi\left(D - \frac{2\overline{r}}{\overline{\sigma}}\sqrt{\tau}\right) + e^{\overline{r}\tau}\Phi(D)\right], \qquad (28)$$

where

$$D = \frac{1}{\overline{\sigma}\sqrt{\tau}}\left(\log\left(\frac{x}{y}\right) + \overline{r}\tau + \frac{1}{2}\overline{\sigma}^2\tau\right).$$

The analogous buy-at-the-min lookback price is also known in closed form. This is the derivative paying $S_T - S_{*,0,T}$ at time T, where

$$S_{*,t,s} = \min\{S_u : t \le u \le s\}.$$

A lookback option is often called *path dependent* because the payoff depends on the path taken by the underlying asset price. The many available varieties of path-dependent derivatives include

- *knock-outs*, whose payoff is zero if the underlying asset price touches a given boundary before expiration.
- *knock-ins*, whose payoff is zero unless the underlying asset price touches a given boundary before expiration.
- *barrier* derivatives, which payoff at the point in time at which a given process, usually the underlying asset price, touches some boundary.
- *asians*, whose payoff depends on the average over time of the sample path of the underlying asset price before expiration.

Path-dependent options are sometimes called *exotic options*, despite the fact that some are commonplace in the market. Exotic options include, however, a much wider variety of options that need not be path dependent. Some relevant sources are indicated in the Notes.

H. Stochastic Volatility

The Black-Scholes option-pricing formula, as we recall from Chapter 5, is of the form $C(x, K, \bar{r}, T, \bar{\sigma})$, for $C : \mathbb{R}^5_+ \to \mathbb{R}_+$, where x is the current underlying asset price, K is the exercise price, $\bar{r}$ is the short interest rate, T is the time to expiration, and $\bar{\sigma}$ is the volatility coefficient for the underlying asset. For each fixed $(x, K, \bar{r}, T)$, the map from $\bar{\sigma}$ to $C(x, K, \bar{r}, T, \bar{\sigma})$ is strictly increasing, and its range is unbounded. We may therefore invert and obtain the volatility from the option price. That is, we can define an *implied volatility* function $I : \mathbb{R}^5_+ \to \mathbb{R}_+$ by

$$c = C(x, K, \bar{r}, T, I(x, K, \bar{r}, T, c)),$$

for all sufficiently large $c \in \mathbb{R}_+$.

If c_1 is the Black-Scholes price of an option on a given asset at strike K_1 and expiration T_1, and c_2 is the Black-Scholes price of an option on the same asset at strike K_2 and expiration T_2, then the associated implied volatilities $I(x, K_1, \bar{r}, T_1, c_1)$ and $I(x, K_2, \bar{r}, T_2, c_2)$ must be identical if indeed the assumptions underlying the Black-Scholes formula apply literally, and in particular if the underlying asset-price process S satisfies (12). It has been widely noted, however, that actual market prices for European options on the same underlying asset have associated Black-Scholes implied volatilities that vary with both exercise price and expiration date. For example, in certain markets at certain times implied volatilities depend on strike prices

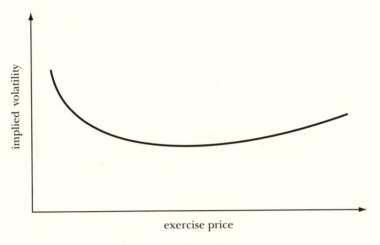

Figure 8.2.   *The Smile Curve*

in the convex manner illustrated in Figure 8.2, which is often termed a *smile curve*. Other forms of systematic deviation away from constant implied volatilities have been noted, both over time and across various derivatives at a point in time.

Two major lines of modeling address these systematic deviations from the assumptions underlying the Black-Scholes model. In both of these, the log-normal stock price model (12) is generalized by replacing the constant volatility parameter $\bar{\sigma}$ associated with the Black-Scholes model with a process V. That is, we can assume that the underlying asset price process S satisfies

$$dS_t = \mu_t S_t \, dt + S_t V_t \, c \, dB_t, \tag{29}$$

for some V in $\mathcal{L}^2$, some c in $\mathbb{R}^d$ of unit norm, and some μ in $\mathcal{L}^1$. As we shall see, the expected-rate-of-return process μ plays a small role. We will focus on the *volatility process V*.

In the first class of models, $V_t = v(S_t, t)$, for some function $v : \mathbb{R} \times [0, T] \to \mathbb{R}$ satisfying technical regularity conditions. In practical applications, the function v, or its discrete-time discrete-state analogue, is "calibrated" to the available option prices. This approach, sometimes referred to as the *implied-tree* model, is explored in literature cited in the Notes of this chapter and of Chapter 3.

In a second approach, the volatility process V and the underlying asset-price process S satisfy a stochastic differential equation of the form

$$dS_t = \bar{r}S_t\,dt + S_t V_t\,d\epsilon_t$$

(30)

$$dV_t = \alpha(V_t, t)\,dt + \gamma(V_t, t)\,d\zeta_t,$$

where ϵ and ζ are each standard Brownian motions under an equivalent martingale measure Q, and $\alpha : \mathbb{R} \times [0, T] \rightarrow \mathbb{R}$ and $\gamma : \mathbb{R} \times [0, T] \rightarrow \mathbb{R}$ are functions technically satisfying regularity conditions. The form of the equation for V involves some loss of generality in that V is *autonomous*, meaning that the drift α and diffusion γ of V depend at time t on V_t alone.

This setup (30) is often called a model of *stochastic volatility*, although the terminology varies from place to place, and one could view the implied-tree model, with $V_t = v(S_t, t)$, as one with stochastic volatility.

If ϵ and ζ are both processes of the form $c \cdot \widehat{B}$, for some constant vector c in $\mathbb{R}^d$, then (30) can be viewed as a stochastic differential equation, and we take the Feynman-Kac point of view illustrated in Chapter 5 to derive a partial differential equation to be solved for a function $f : \mathbb{R}_+ \times \mathbb{R} \times [0, T] \rightarrow \mathbb{R}$ that determines the option price at time t to be

$$f(S_t, V_t, t) = E_t^Q \left[e^{-\bar{r}(T-t)}(S_T - K)^+ \right].$$

Methods for solving such a PDE by discretization are cited in Chapter 11.

A special case of the stochastic volatility model that has often been applied in practice is one in which ϵ and ζ are in fact independently distributed under Q. This implies that the volatility process V is independently distributed (under Q) with ϵ. One can then more easily calculate the value an option (or another derivative) on the underlying asset by noting that conditional on the volatility process, the underlying asset price process is log-normal. That is, the distribution of $\log S_T$ conditional on the entire volatility process $\{V_t : t \in [0, T]\}$ is normal with standard deviation $\sigma(V)\sqrt{T}$, where

$$\sigma(V) = \frac{1}{\sqrt{T}} \left(\int_0^T V_t^2\,dt \right)^{1/2},$$

and with mean $\bar{r}T - \sigma(V)^2 T/2$. By the law of iterated expectations, the

European call option price, with expiration date T and strike K, is given by

$$\mathcal{C}(S_0, V_0, K, \bar{r}, T) = E^Q \left[e^{-\bar{r}T}(S_T - K)^+ \right]$$

$$= E^Q \left(E^Q \left[e^{-\bar{r}T}(S_T - K)^+ \mid \{V_t : t \in [0, T]\} \right] \right) \qquad (31)$$

$$= E^Q \left[C \left(S_0, K, \bar{r}, T, \sigma(V) \right) \right],$$

where $C(\cdot)$ as usual denotes the Black-Scholes formula. One could evaluate the option price (31) by several numerical methods. For example, one could independently (under Q) simulate sample paths $V^{(1)}, \ldots, V^{(n)}$ for V and calculate the average Black-Scholes price

$$\mathcal{C}_n = \frac{1}{n} \sum_{i=1}^{n} C(S_0, K, \bar{r}, T, \sigma(V^{(i)})).$$

The law of large numbers implies that $\mathcal{C}_n$ converges with n to the desired option price $\mathcal{C}(S_0, V_0, K, \bar{r}, T)$. Chapter 11 describes methods of simulating a discrete approximation of the sample path of V. Another method that has been considered is a numerical approximation of the expectation in (31), viewed as the integral

$$\int_0^\infty C(S_0, K, \bar{r}, T, v) \, dF(v), \qquad (32)$$

where F is the cumulative distribution function under Q of $\sigma(V)$. This integral can be approximated as a Taylor series around the mean of $\sigma(V)$, in terms of higher moments, using expressions for the moments of $\sigma(V)$ that can be obtained for special cases. By analysis of this approximation, sources indicated in the Notes have shown that the smile curve indicated in Figure 8.2 may arise naturally through stochastic volatility of this form.

As we know from Chapter 5, the implied-tree model has the property that an option can be replicated, and therefore hedged, by a self-financing trading strategy involving the underlying asset and funds invested at the short rate r. The stochastic volatility model does not generally have this property. Under regularity conditions, however, one can replicate a given option with a self-financing trading strategy involving the underlying asset, *a different option*, and funds invested at the riskless rate r. For example, in the case for which ϵ and ζ are independent, any European put or call option price is strictly monotonic increasing in the initial level V_0 of stochastic volatility. This follows from a standard comparison result for stochastic differential equations. Increasing the initial condition of a stochastic differential equation can, under mild regularity, increases the entire solution path.

Proposition. *Suppose α and γ are functions satisfying uniform Lipschitz and growth conditions, as described in Appendix E. Suppose V^a satisfies (30) with initial condition $V_0^a = a$, and V^b satisfies (30) with initial condition $V_0^b = b$. If $a \geq b$, then $V_t^a \geq V_t^b$ for all $t \in [0, T]$, almost surely. If $a > b$, then $\sigma(V^a) > \sigma(V^b)$ almost surely.*

A proof is cited in the Notes. Since the Black-Scholes formula is strictly increasing in the volatility parameter, it follows that $v \mapsto C(S_0, v, K, \bar{r}, T)$ is strictly increasing. By inverting, the volatility process V can therefore be represented in the form $V_t = \mathcal{V}(S_t, Y_t, t)$, where Y is the price of a given European call or put option. Assuming the smoothness that usually arises from the Feynman-Kac approach, it follows from Ito's Lemma that one can develop a stochastic differential equation (under Q) for the price process (S, Y). Given a second option, one can then proceed as in Chapter 5 to compute a self-financing trading strategy that replicates the second option.

Using a different method of proof cited in the Notes, it has been shown that one can replicate an option with positions in riskless borrowing or lending, the underlying asset, and a second option, *even if the Brownian motions ϵ and ζ are not independent,* provided some additional technical regularity conditions are added.

The literature on stochastic volatility and option pricing is often linked with the extensive body of available work on econometric models of *autoregressive conditional heteroskedasticity* (ARCH), and its extensions and variants, GARCH and EGARCH defined in sources cited in the Notes. It has been shown, for example, that typical discrete-time models of heteroskedasticity, including certain ARCH and EGARCH models, converge in a natural way with time periods of shrinking length to the continuous-time stochastic volatility model in which $v_t = \log V_t$ is well defined and satisfies the *Ornstein-Uhlenbeck* stochastic differential equation

$$dv_t = (a + bv_t)\,dt + c\,d\zeta_t, \tag{33}$$

where a, b, and c are coefficients that can be estimated from historical observations of the underlying asset-price process. As (33) is a linear stochastic differential equation, we know from Appendix E that its solution is a Gaussian process (under Q). One must bear in mind, especially for econometric applications, that our analysis has been under an equivalent martingale measure. In order to draw econometric implications, one may also wish to characterize the behavior of stochastic volatility under the original probability measure P. For example, one can adopt parametric assumptions regarding the market price of risk.

Attempts, cited in the Notes, have also been made to extend the econometric model to include observations on option prices in the data set used to estimate the parameters of the stochastic volatility process. In principal, use of options data should improve the econometric efficiency of the estimation, given the one-to-one relationship between v_t and a given option price at time t that follows from the proposition above.

Of course, one can combine the two approaches, "implied tree" and "stochastic volatility," in a model of the form

$$dS_t = \bar{r} S_t dt + S_t V_t \, d\epsilon_t$$

$$dV_t = \alpha(V_t, S_t, t) \, dt + \gamma(V_t, S_t, t) \, d\zeta_t. \tag{34}$$

Again, under regularity conditions, an option can be hedged with positions in riskless borrowing or lending, the underlying asset, and a different option.

Exercises

8.1 Show by use of Girsanov's Theorem that the futures-price process Φ defined by (8) is an Ito process (under the original measure P).

8.2 Verify (9) with Ito's Lemma.

8.3 Show, as claimed in Section D, that if Φ is an Ito process and Y is bounded and bounded away from zero, then $\int Y \, d\Phi$ is a martingale if and only if Φ is a martingale. Hint: Use the unique decomposition property of Ito processes.

8.4 Suppose there are three traded securities. Security 1 has the price process X given by $X_t = x \exp(\alpha t + \beta \cdot B_t)$, where $\alpha \in \mathbb{R}$, $\beta \in \mathbb{R}^2$, and B is a standard Brownian motion in $\mathbb{R}^2$. Security 2 has the price process Y given by $Y_t = y \exp(a + b \cdot B_t)$, where $a \in \mathbb{R}$, $b \in \mathbb{R}^2$. Security 3 has the price process e^{rt}, where r is a constant. None of the securities pay dividends during $[0, T]$. Consider a contract paying, at some time $T > 0$, either k units of security 1 or one unit of security 2, whichever is preferred by the owner of the contract at that time. Calculate the arbitrage-free price of that contract.

8.5 Consider the *rolling spot futures contract*, defined as follows. The contract promises to pay, continually, changes in the spot price S_t of the underlying asset as well as futures resettlement payments. That is, the rolling spot futures-price process associated with the contract, say U, contractually satisfies $U_T = S_T$, and the total gain for the contract between any two times t and $s \geq t$ is $G_s - G_t$, where $G_t = U_t + S_t$. Show that, given the existence of an equivalent martingale measure (which is essentially equivalent to no arbitrage), the rolling spot futures-price process is given by $U_t = 2F_t - S_t$, where F_t is the conventional futures price.

8.6 Compute the value of the buy-at-the-min lookback option defined in Section 8G under the same assumptions used to derive the price (27) of the sell-at-the-max option.

8.7 Consider an underlying asset price process S satisfying (12), the log-normal model, and a futures option on the asset. That is, we let f be the futures price for delivery of the underlying asset at time T, and consider a security that pays $(f_\tau - K)^+$ at some given time $\tau < T$. Compute the initial price of this futures option.

8.8 Suppose the short-rate process r is given by the Cox-Ingersoll-Ross model, defined in Section 7D. Compute the futures price and the forward price that would apply at time zero for delivery at time $\tau < T$ of a zero-coupon bond maturing at time T.

Notes

The relationship between forwards and futures in Sections 8B, 8C, and 8D was developed by Cox, Ingersoll, and Ross (1981b). The derivation given here for the martingale property (8) of futures prices is original, although the formula itself is due to Cox, Ingersoll, and Ross (1981b), as is the subsequent replication strategy. For additional work in this vein, see Bick (1994), Dezhbakhsh (1994), Duffie and Stanton (1988), and Myneni (1992b). An explicit Gaussian example is given by Jamshidian (1993b) and Jamshidian and Fein (1990). Grinblatt and Jegadeesh (1993) derived the futures prices for bonds in the setting of a Cox-Ingersoll-Ross model of the term structure. Grauer and Litzenberger (1979) give an example of the equilibrium determination of commodity forward prices. Carr (1989) provides option-valuation models for assets with stochastic dividends, in terms of the stochastic model for forward prices on the underlying asset. Carr and Chen (1993) treat the valuation of the *cheapest-to-deliver option* in Treasury Bond futures, sometimes called the *quality option*, and the associated problem of determining the futures price. For the related wildcard option, see Fleming and Whaley (1994). Bensoussan, Crouhy, and Galai (1992) treat the case of complex options.

Black (1976) showed how to extend the Black-Scholes option-pricing formula to the case of futures options. See, also, Bick (1988). Carr (1993a) and Hemler (1987) value the option to deliver various grades of the underlying asset against the futures contract. This problem is related to that of valuing compound options, and options on the maximum or minimum of several assets, which was solved (in the Black-Scholes setting) by Geske (1979), Johnson (1987), Margrabe (1978), Selby and Hodges (1987), and Stulz (1982). On put-call parity and symmetry, see Carr (1993b).

McKean (1965), Merton (1973b), Harrison and Kreps (1979), and Bensoussan (1984) did important early work on American option pricing. Proposition 8E is from Karatzas (1988), although his technical conditions are slightly different. Karatzas defines the *fair price* of an American security, which turns out to be equal to the arbitrage-free price when both exist, and also extends Merton's analysis of *perpetual options*, those with no expiration. Jaillet, Lamberton, and Lapeyre (1988, 1990) review the treatment of the optimal stopping valuation problem as a variational inequality, which can be written in the form (20)–(21). A decomposition of the American option in terms of an *early exercise premium* (19) was proposed in a collection of papers by Jamshidian (1989c), Jacka (1991), Kim (1990), and Carr, Jarrow, and Myneni (1992), working from McKean's (1965) formulation of the *free boundary problem*, sometimes called a *Stefan problem*. Van Moerbeke (1976) was the first to demonstrate, among other results, that the optimal stopping boundary S^* is continuously differentiable. In this regard, see also Ait Sahlia (1995). Jorgensen (1994a) and Myneni (1992a) survey this and other literature on American put option pricing in the Black-Scholes setting. Approximate solutions to the American option price are given by Allegretto, Barone-Adesi, and Elliott (1993), Broadie and Detemple (1993a), Carr (1994), Geske and Johnson (1984), Gandhi, Kooros, and Salkin (1993a), and Barone-Adesi and Elliott (1991) (who cite related literature). The behavior of the *optimal exercise boundary* near expiration is treated by Ait Sahlia (1995), Barles, Burdeau, Romano, and Samsoen (1993), Lamberton (1993), and Charretour, Elliott, Myneni, and Viswanathan (1992). Option pricing in a jump-diffusion setting was originated by Merton (1976), and more recently treated by Amin (1993a), Scott (1993), and Zhang (1994). Amaro de Matos (1993) gives a method-of-simulated-moments estimation technique for American options. Yu (1993) provides additional results on American option valuation. Broadie and Detemple (1993b, 1995) provide pricing for American capped call options, and for options on multiple assets.

Term-structure models such as those applied in Chapter 7 have been applied to commodity option valuation by Jamshidian (1991b, 1993b). The sell-at-the-max and buy-at-the-min lookback option valuation is from Goldman, Sosin, and Gatto (1979). The particular representation of the sell-at-the-max put formula (28) is copied from Conze and Viswanathan (1991b). The distribution of the maximum of a Brownian motion path between two dates, and related results on the distribution of first passage times, can be found in Chuang (1994), Dassios (1994), Harrison (1985), and Ricciardi and Sato (1988). For other lookback option valuation results, see Conze and Viswanathan (1991b), Duffie and Harrison (1993), and Shepp and Shiryaev (1993). The *asian option*, based on an arithmetic average of the underlying price process, is analyzed by Geman and Yor (1993), Oliveira (1994), Rogers and Shi (1994), and Yor (1991). Akahari (1993), Miura (1992), and Yor (1993) treat the related problem of *median-price options*.

The hedging of asian and lookback options is analysed by Kat (1993b). For hedging under leverage constraints, see Naik and Uppal (1992). For hedging with a "minimax" criterion, see Howe and Rustem (1994a,b).

Forms of *barrier options*, which are variously known as *knockouts, knockins, down-and-outs, up-and-ins, limited-risk options*, and *lock-in options* are covered by Carr and Ellis (1994), Conze and Viswanathan (1991b), Merton (1973b), and Yu (1993). On approximation methods for anlaysing path-dependent options, see Kind, Lipster, and Runggaldier (1991).

Beckers (1981) promoted the idea of using implied volatility, as measured by options prices. A generalized version of implied volatility is discussed by Bick and Reisman (1993). Cherian and Jarrow (1993) explore a related "rationality" issue. Option pricing with stochastic volatility was proposed as an answer to the "smile curve," and analyzed, by Hull and White (1987), Scott (1987, 1992a), and Wiggins (1987), and since has been addressed by Amin (1993b), Amin and Ng (1993), Ball and Roma (1994), Barles, Romano, and Touzi (1993), Duan (1995), Heston (1993), Hofmann, Platen, and Schweizer (1992), Lu and Yu (1993), Platen and Schweizer (1994), Renault and Touzi (1992a,b), and Touzi (1993, 1995). Renault and Touzi (1992b) consider the econometric use of option price data in this setting. Amin and Jarrow (1993) treat the problem of option valuation with stochastic interest rates, in a Heath-Jarrow-Morton setting. Melino and Turnbull (1990) illustrate an application to foreign exchange option pricing. Heynen and Kat (1993) and Heynen, Kemna, and Vorst (1994) provide formulas for prediction of volatility in a Markovian setting. Nelson

(1990, 1991, 1992) treats the convergence of ARCH, GARCH, and EGARCH models to stochastic volatility models of the style considered in Section 8H, as well as related issues. Bollerslev, Chou, and Kroner (1992) and Taylor (1994) survey applications in finance for ARCH and ARCH-related models, originated by Engle (1982). Harvey, Ruiz, and Shephard (1992), Harvey and Shephard (1993), and Lamoreux and Lastrapes (1993) present related econometric techniques and results. Hobson and Rogers (1993) describe a model for endogenous stochastic volatility. Proposition 8H can be deduced from results in Karatzas and Shreve (1988).

Derman and Kani (1994), Dupire (1992, 1994), and Rubinstein (1995) also construct implied-tree models of option pricing.

Nielsen and Saá-Requejo (1992) provide an example of a foreign exchange option-valuation model.

The hedging coefficients, "delta," "gamma," and so on, associated with derivative securities are studied by Carr (1991). On option pricing with transactions costs and constraints, see references cited in the Notes of Chapter 6. Johnson and Stulz (1987) and Rich (1993) deal with the impact of default risk on the Black-Scholes approach. Brennan and Schwarz (1980b) present a model for the valuation of convertible bonds.

General reviews of options, futures, or other derivative markets include those of Cox and Rubinstein (1985), Daigler (1993), Duffie (1989), Hull (1993), Jarrow and Rudd (1983), Rubinstein (1992), Siegel and Siegel (1990), and Stoll and Whaley (1993). For computational issues, see Chapter 11, or Wilmott, Dewynne, and Howison (1993). Dixit and Pindyck (1993) is a thorough treatment, with references, of the modeling of *real options*, which arise in the theory of production planning and capital budgeting under uncertainty.

The problem of valuing futures options, as considered in Exercise 8.7, was addressed and solved by Black (1976). The forward and futures prices for bonds in the Cox-Ingersoll-Ross model, addressed in Exercise 8.8, are found in Grinblatt (1994). A related problem, examined by Carr (1989), is the valuation of options when carrying costs are unknown. Gerber and Shiu (1994) describe a computational approach to option pricing based on the Escher transform.

9

Optimal Portfolio and Consumption Choice

THIS CHAPTER PRESENTS basic results on optimal portfolio and consumption choice, first using dynamic programming, then using general martingale and utility gradient methods. We begin with a review of the Hamilton-Jacobi-Bellman equation for stochastic control, and then apply it to Merton's problem of optimal consumption and portfolio choice in finite- and infinite-horizon settings. Then, exploiting the properties of equivalent martingale measures from Chapter 6, Merton's problem is solved once again in a non-Markovian setting. Finally, we turn to the general utility gradient approach from Chapter 2, and show that it coincides with the approach of equivalent martingale measures.

A. Stochastic Control

Dynamic programming in continuous time is often called *stochastic control* and uses the same basic ideas applied in the discrete-time setting of Chapter 3. The existence of well-behaved solutions in a continuous-time setting is a delicate matter, however, and we shall focus mainly on necessary conditions. This helps us to conjecture a solution that if correct, can often be easily validated.

Given is a standard Brownian motion $B = (B^1, \ldots, B^d)$ in $\mathbb{R}^d$ on a probability space $(\Omega, \mathcal{F}, P)$. We fix the standard filtration $\mathbb{F} = \{\mathcal{F}_t : t \geq 0\}$ of B and begin with the time horizon $[0, T]$ for some finite $T > 0$. The primitive objects of a stochastic control problem are

- a set $A \subset \mathbb{R}^m$ of *actions*;
- a set $\mathcal{Y} \subset \mathbb{R}^K$ of *states*;
- a set $\mathcal{C}$ of A-valued adapted processes, called *controls*;

- a *controlled drift function* $g : A \times \mathcal{Y} \to \mathbb{R}^K$;
- a *controlled diffusion function* $h : A \times \mathcal{Y} \to \mathbb{R}^{K \times d}$;
- a *running reward function* $f : A \times \mathcal{Y} \times [0, T] \to \mathbb{R}$;
- a *terminal reward function* $F : \mathcal{Y} \to \mathbb{R}$.

The set $\mathcal{Y}$ of states of the problem is not to be confused with the underlying set Ω of "states of the world." A control c in $\mathcal{C}$ is *admissible* given an initial state y in $\mathcal{Y}$ if there is a unique Ito process Y^c valued in $\mathcal{Y}$ with

$$dY_t^c = g(c_t, Y_t^c)\, dt + h(c_t, Y_t^c)\, dB_t; \qquad Y_0^c = y. \tag{1}$$

For this, there are of course technical conditions required of c, g, and h.

Let $\mathcal{C}_a(y)$ denote the set of admissible controls given initial state y. We assume that the primitives $(A, Y, \mathcal{C}, g, h, f, F)$ are such that given any initial state $y \in \mathcal{Y}$, the utility of any admissible control c is well defined as

$$V^c(y) = E\left[\int_0^T f(c_t, Y_t^c, t)\, dt + F(Y_T^c) \right],$$

which we allow to take the values $-\infty$ or $+\infty$. The value of an initial state y in $\mathcal{Y}$ is then

$$V(y) = \sup_{c \in \mathcal{C}_a(y)} V^c(y), \tag{2}$$

with $V(y) = -\infty$ if there is no admissible control given initial state y. If $V^c(y) = V(y)$, then c is an *optimal control* at y. (One may note that this forumulation allows for the possibility that an optimal control achieves infinite utility.)

One usually proceeds by conjecturing that $V(y) = J(y, 0)$ for some J in $C^{2,1}(\mathcal{Y} \times [0, T])$ that solves the Bellman equation:

$$\sup_{a \in A} \mathcal{D}^a J(y, t) + f(a, y, t) = 0, \qquad (y, t) \in (\mathcal{Y}, [0, T)), \tag{3}$$

where

$$\mathcal{D}^a J(y, t) = J_y(y, t) g(a, y) + J_t(y, t) + \frac{1}{2} \operatorname{tr}\left[h(a, y) h(a, y)^\top J_{yy}(y, t) \right],$$

with the boundary condition

$$J(y, T) = F(y), \qquad y \in \mathcal{Y}. \tag{4}$$

An intuitive justification of (3) is obtained from an analogous discrete-time, discrete-state, discrete-action setting, in which the Bellman equation would be something like

$$J(y, t) = \max_{a \in A} f(a, y, t) + E\left[J(Y^c_{t+1}, t+1) \mid Y^c_t = y,\ c_t = a \right],$$

where $f(a, y, t)$ is the running reward per unit of time. (The reader is invited to apply imagination liberally here. A complete development and rigorous justification of this analogy goes well beyond the goal of illustrating the idea. Sources that give such a justification are cited in the Notes.) For any given control process c, this discrete-time Bellman equation implies that

$$E_t\left[J(Y^c_{t+1}, t+1) - J(Y^c_t, t) \right] + f(c_t, Y^c_t, t) \le 0,$$

which for a model with intervals of length Δt may be rewritten

$$E_t\left[J(Y^c_{t+\Delta t}, t+\Delta t) - J(Y^c_t, t) \right] + f(c_t, Y^c_t, t)\Delta t \le 0.$$

Now, returning to the continuous-time setting, dividing the last equation by Δt, and taking limits as $\Delta t \to 0$ leaves, under technical conditions described in Chapter 5,

$$\frac{d}{ds} E_t\left[J(Y^c_s, s) \right] \Big|_{s=t+} = \mathcal{D}^{c(t)} J(Y^c_t, t) + f(c_t, Y^c_t, t) \le 0,$$

with equality if c_t attains the supremum in the discrete version of the Bellman equation. This leads, again only by this incomplete heuristic argument, to the Bellman equation (3).

The continuous-time Bellman equation (3) is often called the *Hamilton-Jacobi-Bellman* equation. One may think of $J(y, t)$ as the optimal utility remaining at time t in state y. Given a solution J to (3)–(4), suppose that a measurable function $C : \mathcal{Y} \times [0, T] \to A$ is defined so that for each (y, t), the action $C(y, t)$ solves (3). The intuitive idea is that if the time is t and the state is y, then the optimal action is $C(y, t)$. In order to verify the optimality in the original problem (2) of choosing actions in this manner, we need to turn this feedback form of control policy function C into a control in the sense of problem (2), that is, a process in the set $\mathcal{C}$. For this, suppose that there is a $\mathcal{Y}$-valued solution Y^* to the stochastic differential equation

$$dY^*_t = g[C(Y^*_t, t), Y^*_t]\, dt + h[C(Y^*_t, t), Y^*_t]\, dB_t; \qquad Y^*_0 = y.$$

Conditions on the primitives of the problem sufficient for the existence of a unique solution Y^* are difficult to formulate since C depends on J, which is not usually an explicit function. Sources indicated in the Notes address this existence issue. Given Y^*, we can define an admissible control c^* by $c_t^* = C(Y_t^*, t)$. We conjecture that c^* is an optimal control, and attempt to verify this conjecture as follows. Let $c \in \mathcal{C}_a(y)$ be an arbitrary admissible control. We want to show that $V^{c^*}(y) \geq V^c(y)$.

By (3),

$$\mathcal{D}^{c(t)} J(Y_t^c, t) + f(c_t, Y_t^c, t) \leq 0, \qquad t \in [0, T]. \tag{5}$$

By Ito's Lemma,

$$J(Y_T^c, T) = J(y, 0) + \int_0^T \mathcal{D}^{c(t)} J(Y_t^c, t) \, dt + \int_0^T \beta_t \, dB_t, \tag{6}$$

where $\beta_t = J_y(Y_t^c, t) h(c_t, Y_t^c)$, $t \in [0, T)$. Assuming that β is in $\mathcal{H}^1$ (which is usually verified on a problem-by-problem basis or circumvented by special tricks), we know from Proposition 5B that $E(\int_0^T \beta_t \, dB_t) = 0$. We can then take the expectation of each side of (6) and use the boundary condition (4) and inequality (5) to see that

$$V^c(y) = E\left[\int_0^T f(c_t, Y_t^c, t) \, dt + F(Y_T^c)\right] \leq J(y, 0). \tag{7}$$

The same calculation applies with $c = c^*$, except that "$\leq$" may be replaced everywhere with "$=$," implying that

$$J(y, 0) = V^{c^*}(y). \tag{8}$$

Then (7) and (8) imply that $V(y) = J(y, 0)$, and that c^* is indeed optimal.

This is only a sketch of the general approach, with several assumptions made along the way. These assumptions can be replaced by strong technical regularity conditions on the primitives $(A, \mathcal{Y}, \mathcal{C}, g, h, f, F)$, but the known general conditions are too restrictive for most applications in finance. Instead, one typically uses the Bellman equation (3)–(4) as a means of guessing an explicit solution that if correct, can often be validated by some variation of the above procedure. In some cases, the Bellman equation can also be used as the basis for a finite-difference numerical solution, as indicated in sources cited in Chapter 11.

B. Merton's Problem

We now apply the stochastic control approach to the solution of a "classic" optimal-consumption and investment problem in continuous time.

Suppose $X = (X^0, X^1, \ldots, X^N)$ is an Ito process in $\mathbb{R}^{N+1}$ for the prices of $N + 1$ securities. For each $i \geq 1$, we assume that

$$dX_t^i = \mu_i X_t^i \, dt + X_t^i \sigma^i \, dB_t; \qquad X_0 > 0, \qquad (9)$$

where σ^i is the i-th row of a matrix σ in $\mathbb{R}^{N \times d}$ with linearly independent rows, and where μ_i is a constant. (This implies, in particular, that each process X^i is a geometric Brownian motion of the sort used in the Black-Scholes model of option pricing.)

Given a constant short rate r, a riskless bond-price process X^0 is defined by

$$dX_t^0 = rX_t^0 \, dt; \qquad X_0^0 > 0. \qquad (10)$$

We assume, naturally, that $\mu_i > r$ for all i.

Utility is defined over the space D of *consumption* pairs (c, Z), where c is an adapted nonnegative consumption-rate process with $\int_0^T c_t \, dt < \infty$ almost surely and Z is an $\mathcal{F}_T$-measurable nonnegative random variable describing terminal consumption. Specifically, $U : D \to \mathbb{R}$ is defined by

$$U(c, Z) = E \left[\int_0^T u(c_t, t) \, dt + F(Z) \right], \qquad (11)$$

where

- $F : \mathbb{R}_+ \to \mathbb{R}$ is increasing and concave;
- $u : \mathbb{R}_+ \times [0, T] \to \mathbb{R}$ is continuous and, for each t in $[0, T]$, $u(\cdot, t) : \mathbb{R}_+ \to \mathbb{R}$ is increasing and concave, with $u(0, t) = 0$;
- F is strictly concave or, for each t in $[0, T]$, $u(\cdot, t)$ is strictly concave, or both.

A trading strategy is a process $\theta = (\theta^0, \ldots, \theta^N)$ in $\mathcal{L}(X)$. (As defined in Chapter 5, this means merely that the stochastic integral $\int \theta \, dX$ exists.) Given an initial wealth $w > 0$, we say that (c, Z, θ) is *budget feasible*, denoted $(c, Z, \theta) \in \Lambda(w)$, if (c, Z) is a consumption in D and $\theta \in \mathcal{L}(X)$ is trading strategy satisfying

$$\theta_t \cdot X_t = w + \int_0^t \theta_s \, dX_s - \int_0^t c_s \, ds \geq 0, \qquad t \in [0, T], \qquad (12)$$

and

$$\theta_T \cdot X_T = Z. \tag{13}$$

One may note the requirement in (12) that wealth is always nonnegative, which makes budget feasibility somewhat more restrictive than the usual notion of "financing" used in Chapters 5 and 6. We now have the problem, for each initial wealth w,

$$\sup_{(c,Z,\theta)\in\Lambda(w)} U(c, Z). \tag{14}$$

In order to convert this problem statement (14) into one that is more easily addressed within the stochastic control formulation set up in Section 9A, we represent trading strategies in terms of the fractions $\varphi^1, \ldots, \varphi^N$ of total wealth held in the "risky" securities, those with price processes $X^1, \ldots, X^N$, respectively. Since wealth is restricted to be nonnegative, this involves no loss of generality. That is, for a given trading strategy θ in the original sense, we can let

$$\varphi_t^n = \frac{\theta_t^n X_t^n}{\theta_t \cdot X_t}, \qquad \theta_t \cdot X_t \neq 0, \tag{15}$$

with $\varphi_t^n = 0$ if $\theta_t \cdot X_t = 0$.

Problem (14) is converted into a standard control problem of the variety in Section 9A by first defining a state process. Using portfolio fractions to define trading strategies allows one to leave the security prices $X^0, X^1, \ldots, X^N$ out of the definition of state process for the control problem. Instead, we can define a one-dimensional state process W for the investor's total wealth. As a notational convenience, we let $\lambda \in \mathbb{R}^N$ denote the vector in $\mathbb{R}^N$ with $\lambda_i = \mu_i - r$, the "excess expected rate of return" on security i. Given a consumption process c and an adapted process $\varphi = (\varphi^1, \ldots, \varphi^N)$ defining fractions of total wealth held in the risky securities, we can pose the question of existence of a nonnegative Ito process for wealth W satisfying

$$dW_t = [W_t(\varphi_t \cdot \lambda + r) - c_t] \, dt + W_t \varphi_t^\top \sigma \, dB_t; \qquad W_0 = w. \tag{16}$$

One may notice that in order for W to remain nonnegative, an admissible control (c, φ) has the property that $\varphi_t = 0$ and $W_t = c_t = 0$ for t larger than the stopping time $\inf\{s : W_s = 0\}$. Thus nonzero investment or consumption are ruled out once there is no remaining wealth.

The control problem associated with (14) is thus fixed by defining the primitives $(A, \mathcal{Y}, \mathcal{C}, g, h, f, F)$ as follows:

- $A = \mathbb{R}_+ \times \mathbb{R}^N$, with typical element $(\bar{c}, \bar{\varphi})$ representing the current consumption rate $\bar{c}$ and the fractions $\bar{\varphi}_1, \ldots, \bar{\varphi}_N$ of current wealth invested in the risky securities;
- $\mathcal{Y} = \mathbb{R}_+$, with typical element w representing current wealth;
- $\mathcal{C}$ is the set of adapted processes (c, φ) valued in $\mathbb{R}_+$ and $\mathbb{R}^N$, respectively, with $\int_0^T c_t \, dt < \infty$ almost surely and $\int_0^T \varphi_t \cdot \varphi_t \, dt < \infty$ almost surely;
- $g[(\bar{c}, \bar{\varphi}), w] = w\bar{\varphi} \cdot \lambda + rw - \bar{c}$;
- $h[(\bar{c}, \bar{\varphi}), w] = w\bar{\varphi}^\top \sigma$;
- $f[(\bar{c}, \bar{\varphi}), w, t] = u(\bar{c}, t)$, where u is as given by (11);
- $F(w)$ is as given by (11).

We recall that an admissible control given initial wealth w is a control (c, φ) in $\mathcal{C}$ for which there is a unique nonnegative Ito process W satisfying (16).

The control problem $(A, \mathcal{Y}, \mathcal{C}, g, h, f, F)$ is equivalent to the original problem (14). One shows this fact by verifying that (c, Z, θ) is in $\Lambda(w)$ if and only if the wealth process $\{W_t = \theta_t \cdot X_t : t \in [0, T]\}$ satisfies (16) and $W_T = Z$, where φ is defined from θ by (15).

Later in the chapter, other techniques are used to formulate the problem directly in terms of trading strategies. Although the formulation there will be slightly different on technical grounds, the solutions of the two formulations coincide. Still other formulations are given in sources cited in the Notes.

C. Solution to Merton's Problem

The Bellman equation (3) for Merton's problem is

$$\sup_{(\bar{c}, \bar{\varphi}) \in A} \mathcal{D}^{\bar{c}, \bar{\varphi}} J(w, t) + u(\bar{c}, t) = 0, \qquad w > 0, \tag{17}$$

where

$$\mathcal{D}^{\bar{c}, \bar{\varphi}} J(w, t) = J_w(w, t)(w\bar{\varphi} \cdot \lambda + rw - \bar{c}) + J_t(w, t) + \frac{w^2}{2} \bar{\varphi}^\top \sigma \sigma^\top \bar{\varphi} J_{ww}(w, t),$$

with the boundary condition

$$J(w, T) = F(w), \qquad w \geq 0. \tag{18}$$

For any t, one may think of $J(\,\cdot\,, t)$ as the investor's *indirect utility function for wealth* at time t. We note that

$$J(0, t) = \int_t^T u(0, s)\, ds + F(0), \qquad t \in [0, T],$$

from our remark regarding the nonnegativity of solutions to (16).

Assuming that for each t, $u(\,\cdot\,, t)$ is strictly concave and twice continuously differentiable on $(0, \infty)$, the first-order condition for interior optimal choice of $\overline{c}$ in (17) implies that

$$\overline{c} = C(w, t) \equiv I[J_w(w, t), t],$$

where $I(\,\cdot\,, t)$ inverts $u_c(\,\cdot\,, t)$, meaning that $I[u_c(x, t), t] = x$ for all x and t. We let $I = 0$ if $u = 0$. Assuming that the indirect utility function $J(\,\cdot\,, t)$ for wealth is strictly concave, the first-order condition for optimal choice of $\overline{\varphi}$ in (17) implies that

$$\overline{\varphi} = \Phi(w, t) \equiv \frac{-J_w(w, t)}{w J_{ww}(w, t)} (\sigma\sigma^\top)^{-1} \lambda. \tag{19}$$

We remark that the optimal portfolio fractions are given by a fixed vector $(\sigma\sigma^\top)^{-1}\lambda$ multiplied by the Arrow-Pratt measure of relative risk tolerance (reciprocal of relative risk aversion) of the indirect utility function $J(\,\cdot\,, t)$.

We focus for now on the special case of $u = 0$ and $F(w) = w^\alpha/\alpha$ for some *relative risk aversion coefficient* $\alpha \in (0, 1)$. This is often called a *hyperbolic absolute risk averse*, or *HARA*, utility. Since we take $u = 0$, only terminal consumption Z is optimally nonzero. An explicit value function J for this HARA utility example is conjectured as follows. Suppose Z is the optimal terminal consumption for initial wealth level 1. Now consider a new level w of initial wealth, for some fixed $w \in (0, \infty)$. One may see that wZ must be the associated optimal terminal consumption. Certainly, wZ can be obtained in a budget-feasible manner, for if $Z = \theta_T \cdot X_T$ can be obtained from initial wealth 1 with a trading strategy θ then, given the linearity of stochastic integrals, $w\theta$ is a budget-feasible strategy for initial wealth w, and we have $w\theta_T \cdot X_T = wZ$. If there were some alternative terminal consumption $\widehat{Z}$ that is budget feasible with initial wealth w and with

$$E\left(\frac{\widehat{Z}^\alpha}{\alpha}\right) > E\left[\frac{(wZ)^\alpha}{\alpha}\right], \tag{20}$$

then we would have a contradiction, as follows. First, dividing (20) through by w^α/α leaves

$$E\left[\left(\frac{\widehat{Z}}{w}\right)^\alpha\right] > E(Z^\alpha). \tag{21}$$

By the above reasoning, $\widehat{Z}/w$ can be financed with initial wealth 1, but then (21) contradicts the optimality of Z for initial wealth 1. Thus, as asserted, for any initial level of wealth w, the optimal terminal consumption is wZ. It follows that

$$J(w,0) = E\left[\frac{(wZ)^\alpha}{\alpha}\right] = \frac{w^\alpha}{\alpha}K,$$

where $K = E(Z^\alpha)$. Up to a constant K, which depends on all of the basic parameters $(\lambda, r, \sigma, \alpha, T)$ of the model, we have a reasonable conjecture for the initial indirect utility function $J(\cdot, 0)$. For $t \in (0, T)$, the optimal remaining utility can be conjectured in exactly the above manner, treating the problem as one with a time horizon of $T - t$ rather than T. We therefore conjecture that $J(w, t) = k(t)w^\alpha/\alpha$ for some function $k : [0, T] \to \mathbb{R}$. In order for J to be sufficiently differentiable for an application of Ito's Lemma, we conjecture that k is itself continuously differentiable.

With this conjecture for J in hand, we can solve (19) to get

$$\overline{\varphi} = \frac{(\sigma\sigma^\top)^{-1}\lambda}{1-\alpha}, \tag{22}$$

or fixed portfolio fractions. The total fraction of wealth invested in risky assets is therefore decreasing in the relative risk aversion coefficient α. Since $u = 0$, we have

$$\overline{c} = C(w, t) \equiv 0. \tag{23}$$

Based on the Bellman equation (17), we can substitute (22)–(23) into $\mathcal{D}^{\overline{c}, \overline{\varphi}}J(w, t) + u(\overline{c}, t) = 0$ for our conjectured solution for J to get the ordinary differential equation

$$k'(t) = -\epsilon k(t), \tag{24}$$

where

$$\epsilon = \frac{\alpha\lambda^\top(\sigma\sigma^\top)^{-1}\lambda}{2(1-\alpha)} + r\alpha, \tag{25}$$

with the boundary condition from (18):

$$k(T) = 1. \tag{26}$$

Solving (24)–(26), we have

$$k(t) = e^{\epsilon(T-t)}, \qquad t \in [0, T].$$

We have found that the function J defined by $J(w, t) = e^{\epsilon(T-t)}w^\alpha/\alpha$ solves the Bellman equation (17) and the boundary condition (18), so J is therefore a logical candidate for the value function.

We now verify this candidate for the value function, and also that the conjectured optimal control (c^*, φ^*), which is given by $c_t^* = 0$ and $\varphi_t^* = (\sigma\sigma^\top)^{-1}\lambda/(1-\alpha)$, is indeed optimal. Let (c, φ) be an arbitrary admissible control for initial wealth w, and let W be the associated wealth process solving (16). From the Bellman equation (17), Ito's Lemma, and the boundary condition (18), we have

$$J(w, 0) + \int_0^T \beta_t \, dB_t \geq F(W_T), \qquad (27)$$

where $\beta_t = J_w(W_t, t)W_t\varphi_t^\top\sigma$. Since J is nonnegative, the Bellman equation (17) and Ito's Lemma also imply that a nonnegative process M is defined by $M_t = J(w, 0) + \int_0^t \beta_s \, dB_s$. We also know that M is a local martingale (as defined in Appendix D). A nonnegative local martingale is known to be a supermartingale (a fact also stipulated in Appendix D). By taking expectations of each side of (27), this implies that for arbitrary admissible control, $J(w, 0) \geq E[F(W_T)]$.

It remains to show that for the candidate optimal control (c^*, φ^*), we have $J(w, 0) = E[F(W_T)]$, verifying optimality. For the candidate optimal control, the Bellman equation and the same calculations leave us with

$$J(w, 0) + \int_0^T \beta_t \, dB_t = F(W_T), \qquad (28)$$

where equality appears in place of the inequality in (27) because the proposed optimal control achieves the supremum in the Bellman equation. Since $J_w(W_t, t)W_t = e^{\epsilon(T-t)}W_t^\alpha$, it can be seen as an exercise that for the candidate optimal control, β is in $\mathcal{H}^1$, implying by Proposition 5B that the stochastic integral $\int \beta \, dB$ is a martingale. Taking expectations through (28) then leaves $J(w, 0) = E[F(W_T)]$, verifying the optimality of (c^*, φ^*) and confirming that the problem has optimal initial utility $J(w, 0) = e^{\epsilon T}w^\alpha/\alpha$.

D. The Infinite-Horizon Case

The primitives $(A, \mathcal{Y}, \mathcal{C}, g, h, f)$ of an infinite-horizon control problem are just as described in Section 9A, dropping the terminal reward F. The running reward function $f : A \times \mathcal{Y} \times [0, \infty) \to \mathbb{R}$ is usually defined, given a *discount rate* $\rho \in (0, \infty)$, by $f(a, y, t) = e^{-\rho t}v(a, y)$, for some $v : A \times \mathcal{Y} \to \mathbb{R}$.

Given an initial state y in $\mathcal{Y}$, the value of an admissible control c in $\mathcal{C}$ is

$$V^c(y) = E\left[\int_0^\infty e^{-\rho t} v(c_t, Y_t^c)\, dt\right], \tag{29}$$

assuming that the expectation exists, where Y^c is given by (1). The supremum value $V(y)$ is as defined by (2). The finite-horizon Bellman equation (3) is replaced with

$$\sup_{a\in A} \mathcal{D}^a J(y) - \rho J(y) + v(a, y) = 0, \qquad y \in \mathcal{Y}, \tag{30}$$

for J in $C^2(\mathcal{Y})$, where

$$\mathcal{D}^a J(y) = J_y(y)g(a, y) + \frac{1}{2}\mathrm{tr}\left[h(a, y)h(a, y)^\top J_{yy}(y)\right].$$

Rather than the boundary condition (4), one can add technical conditions yielding the so-called *transversality condition*

$$\lim_{T\to\infty} E\left(e^{-\rho T}|J(Y_T^c)|\right) = 0, \tag{31}$$

for any given initial state $Y_0^c = y$ in $\mathcal{Y}$ and any admissible control c. With this, the same arguments and technical assumptions applied in Section 9A imply that a solution J to the Bellman equation (30) defines the value $J(y) = V(y)$ of the problem. The essential difference is the replacement of (7) with

$$J(y) \geq E\left[\int_0^T e^{-\rho t} v(c_t, Y_t^c)\, dt + e^{-\rho T} J(Y_T^c)\right], \qquad T > 0,$$

from which $J(y) \geq V^c(y)$ for an arbitrary admissible control c by taking the limit of the right-hand side as $T \to \infty$, using (31). Similarly, a candidate optimal control is defined in feedback form by a function $C : \mathcal{Y} \to A$ with the property that for each y, the action $C(y)$ solves the Bellman equation (30). Once again, technical conditions on the primitives guarantee the existence of an optimal control, but such conditions are often too restrictive in practice, and the Bellman equation is frequently used more as an aid in conjecturing a solution.

In Merton's problem, for example, with $v(\bar{c}, w) = \bar{c}^\alpha/\alpha$, $\alpha \in (0, 1)$, it is natural to conjecture that $J(w) = Kw^\alpha/\alpha$ for some constant K. With some calculations, the Bellman equation (30) for this candidate value function J leads to $K = \gamma^{\alpha-1}$, where

$$\gamma = \frac{\rho - r\alpha}{1 - \alpha} - \frac{\alpha\lambda^\top(\sigma\sigma^\top)^{-1}\lambda}{2(1 - \alpha)^2}. \tag{32}$$

The associated consumption-portfolio policy (c^*, φ^*) is given by $\varphi_t^* = (\sigma\sigma^\top)^{-1}\lambda/(1-\alpha)$ and $c_t^* = \gamma W_t^*$, where W^* is the wealth process generated by (c^*, φ^*). In order to confirm the optimality of this policy, the transversality condition (31) must be checked, and is satisfied provided $\gamma(1-\alpha) > 0$. This verification is left as an exercise.

E. The Martingale Formulation

The objective now is to use the martingale results of Chapter 6 as the basis of a new method for solving Merton's problem (14). We take the slightly different formulation

$$\sup_{(c,Z,\theta)\in\Gamma(w)} U(c, Z), \tag{33}$$

where

$$\Gamma(w) = \left\{(c, Z, \theta) : (c, Z) \in \widehat{D}, \qquad (c, Z, \theta) \text{ is budget feasible}\right\}, \tag{34}$$

where

$$\widehat{D} = \left\{(c, Z) \in D : E\left(\int_0^T c_t^2 \, dt\right) < \infty \quad \text{and} \quad E(Z^2) < \infty\right\}. \tag{35}$$

Problems (33) and (14) differ only in their integrability restrictions on (c, Z). Under technical conditions, their solutions coincide.

Given the security-price process X of Section 9B, consider the deflated-price process $\widehat{X}$ defined by $\widehat{X}_t = X_t/X_t^0$. We take the finite-horizon setting of Section 9B. For any consumption pair (c, Z), we can also define the deflated consumption pair $(\widehat{c}, \widehat{Z})$ by $\widehat{c}_t = e^{-rt}c_t$ and $\widehat{Z} = e^{-rT}Z$.

Lemma. *Given an initial wealth $w \geq 0$, a strategy (c, Z, θ) is budget feasible given price process X if and only if $(\widehat{c}, \widehat{Z}, \theta)$ is budget feasible given price process $\widehat{X}$, that is,*

$$\theta_t \cdot \widehat{X}_t = w + \int_0^t \theta_s \, d\widehat{X}_s - \int_0^t e^{-rs}c_s \geq 0, \qquad t \in [0, T], \tag{36}$$

and

$$\theta_T \cdot \widehat{X}_T = e^{-rT} Z. \tag{37}$$

Proof: This follows from the Numeraire Invariance Theorem of Section 6B, or alternatively can be verified by direct calculation using Ito's Lemma. ∎

For simplicity, we take the case $N = d$. By Girsanov's Theorem (Appendix D), there is an equivalent martingale measure Q for $\widehat{X}$, defined by

$$E^Q(Z) = E^P(Z\xi_T), \tag{38}$$

for any random variable Z with $E^Q(|Z|) < \infty$, where

$$\xi_t = \exp\left(\nu^\top B_t - \frac{t}{2}\nu^\top \nu\right), \qquad t \in [0, T], \tag{39}$$

and where

$$\nu = \sigma^{-1}\lambda. \tag{40}$$

(The invertibility of σ is implied by our earlier assumption that the rows of σ are linearly independent. The fact that ξ satisfies the Novikov condition and that $\text{var}(\xi_T) < \infty$, as demanded by the definition of an equivalent martingale measure, are easily shown as an exercise.)

Proposition. *Given initial wealth w, (c, Z, θ) is budget feasible, for a consumption choice (c, Z) in $\widehat{D}$, if and only if*

$$E^Q\left(e^{-rT}Z + \int_0^T e^{-rt}c_t\, dt\right) \le w. \tag{41}$$

Proof: Suppose (c, Z, θ) is budget feasible, for (c, Z) in $\widehat{D}$. By the previous lemma, there is some θ in $\mathcal{L}(\widehat{X})$ satisfying (36)–(37), and therefore satisfying

$$w + \int_0^T \theta_t\, d\widehat{X}_t = e^{-rT}Z + \int_0^T e^{-rt}c_t\, dt. \tag{42}$$

Using Jensen's Inequality,

$$E\left[\left(\int_0^T e^{-rt}c_t\, dt\right)^2\right] \le E\left[\left(\int_0^T c_t\, dt\right)^2\right]$$

$$\le E\left(\int_0^T c_t^2\, dt\right) < \infty. \tag{43}$$

The right-hand side of (42) therefore has finite variance under P, as does ξ_T, so the expectation under Q of the right-hand side of (42) is finite. Since $\widehat{X}$ is a martingale under Q, the process M, defined by $M_t = w + \int_0^t \theta_s\, d\widehat{X}_s$, is a local martingale under Q. Moreover, by (36), M is nonnegative, and therefore a supermartingale under Q (Appendix D). Thus $E^Q \left(w + \int_0^T \theta_t \, d\widehat{X}_t \right) \leq w$, and taking expectations under Q through (42) leaves (41).

Conversely, suppose (c, Z) in $\widehat{D}$ satisfies (41), and let M be the Q-martingale defined by

$$M_t = E_t^Q \left(e^{-rT} Z + \int_0^T e^{-rt} c_t \, dt \right), \qquad t \in [0, T].$$

By the martingale representation property of $\widehat{B}$ found in Girsanov's Theorem (Appendix D), there is some $\eta = (\eta^1, \dots, \eta^d)$ with components in $\mathcal{L}^2$ such that

$$M_t = w + \int_0^t \eta_s \, d\widehat{B}_s, \qquad t \in [0, T],$$

where $\widehat{B}_t = B_t - \nu t$ defines a standard Brownian motion in $\mathbb{R}^d$ under Q. From the definitions of ν and $\widehat{B}$,

$$d\widehat{X}_t^i = \widehat{X}_t^i \sigma^i \, d\widehat{B}_t, \qquad 1 \leq i \leq N.$$

Since σ is invertible and $\widehat{X}$ is strictly positive with continuous sample paths, we can choose adapted processes $(\theta^1, \dots, \theta^N)$ such that

$$(\theta_t^1 \widehat{X}_t^1, \dots, \theta_t^N \widehat{X}_t^N) \sigma = \eta_t^\top, \qquad t \in [0, T].$$

This implies that

$$M_t = w + \sum_{i=1}^N \int_0^t \theta_s^i \, dX_s^i.$$

We can also let

$$\theta_t^0 = M_t - \sum_{i=1}^N \theta_t^i \widehat{X}_t^i - \int_0^t e^{-rs} c_s \, ds.$$

Because η has components in $\mathcal{L}^2$, we know that $\theta = (\theta^0, \dots, \theta^N)$ is in $\mathcal{L}(\widehat{X})$. By a calculation using the last two displayed equations and the fact that $X^0 \equiv 1$ (and therefore $\int \theta^0 \, dX^0 \equiv 0$), we know that θ satisfies (36)–(37). Thus, by Lemma 9E, (c, Z, θ) is budget feasible. ∎

From this proposition, problem (33) is equivalent to

$$\sup_{(c,Z) \in \widehat{D}} U(c, Z), \tag{44}$$

subject to

$$E^Q \left(e^{-rT} Z + \int_0^T e^{-rt} c_t \, dt \right) \leq w. \tag{45}$$

F. Martingale Solution

By the Saddle Point Theorem (which can be found in Appendix B) and strict monotonicity of U, the control (c^*, Z^*) solves (44)–(45) if and only if there is a scalar Lagrange multiplier $\gamma > 0$ such that (c^*, Z^*) solves the unconstrained problem

$$\sup_{(c,Z) \in \widehat{D}} U(c, Z) - \gamma E^Q \left(e^{-rT} Z + \int_0^T e^{-rt} c_t \, dt - w \right), \tag{46}$$

with the complementary slackness condition

$$E^Q \left(e^{-rT} Z^* + \int_0^T e^{-rt} c_t^* \, dt \right) = w.$$

Problem (46) is easier to analyze by writing out $U(c, Z)$ explicitly and by using the fact that $E^Q(Z) = E(\xi_T Z)$ for any Z with $E^Q(|Z|) < \infty$. In order to state the resulting form of Merton's problem, let π denote the process defined by $\pi_t = e^{-rt} \xi_t$. (As shown in Section 6J, π may be treated as a state-price deflator.)

Proposition. *There is a trading strategy $\theta^* \in \mathcal{L}(X)$ such that (c^*, Z^*, θ^*) solves Merton's problem (38) if and only if*

$$E \left(\int_0^T \pi_t c_t^* \, dt + \pi_T Z^* \right) = w \tag{47}$$

and there is a constant $\gamma^* > 0$ such that (c^*, Z^*) solves

$$\sup_{(c,Z) \in \widehat{D}} \mathcal{L}(c, Z; \gamma^*), \tag{48}$$

where

$$\mathcal{L}(c, Z; \gamma) = E \left(\int_0^T [u(c_t, t) - \gamma \pi_t c_t] \, dt + F(Z) - \gamma \pi_T Z \right).$$

Proof: We need only show that (45) (with equality) and (47) are equivalent. Then the result follows from Proposition 9E, the Saddle Point Theorem (Appendix B), and the strict monotonicity of either or both of F and

$\{u(\,\cdot\,, t) : t \in [0, T]\}$. By Fubini's Theorem, the fact that c is an adapted process, the law of iterated expectations, and the fact that ξ is a martingale,

$$
E^Q\left(e^{-rT}Z + \int_0^T e^{-rt}c_t\,dt\right) = E\left[\xi_T\left(e^{-rT}Z + \int_0^T e^{-rt}c_t\,dt\right)\right]
$$

$$
= E\left(\xi_T e^{-rT}Z + \int_0^T \xi_T e^{-rt}c_t\,dt\right)
$$

$$
= E\left[\xi_T e^{-rT}Z + \int_0^T E_t(\xi_T e^{-rt}c_t)\,dt\right]
$$

$$
= E\left[\xi_T e^{-rT}Z + \int_0^T e^{-rt}c_t E_t(\xi_T)\,dt\right]
$$

$$
= E\left(\xi_T e^{-rT}Z + \int_0^T e^{-rt}c_t\xi_t\,dt\right)
$$

$$
= E\left(\pi_T Z + \int_0^T \pi_t c_t\,dt\right).
$$

This completes the result. ■

In order to solve the remaining optimization problem (48), it is best to begin by thinking of "E" and "$\int$" as finite sums, in which case the first-order conditions for optimality of $(c^*, Z^*) \gg 0$ for the problem $\sup_{(c,Z)} \mathcal{L}(c, Z; \gamma)$, assuming differentiability, are

$$
u_c(c_t^*, t) - \gamma\pi_t = 0, \qquad t \in [0, T], \tag{49}
$$

and

$$
F'(Z^*) - \gamma\pi_T = 0. \tag{50}
$$

Solving,

$$
c_t^* = I(\gamma\pi_t, t), \qquad t \in [0, T], \tag{51}
$$

and

$$
Z^* = I_F(\gamma\pi_T), \tag{52}
$$

where, as we recall, $I(\,\cdot\,, t)$ inverts $u_c(\,\cdot\,, t)$ and where $I_F = 0$ if $F = 0$ and otherwise I_F inverts F'. We will confirm these conjectured solutions in the proof of the next theorem.

Under strict concavity, the inversions $I(\,\cdot\,, t)$ and I_F are continuous and strictly decreasing. A decreasing function $\hat{w} : (0, \infty) \to \mathbb{R}$ is therefore defined by

$$\widehat{w}(\gamma) = E\left[\int_0^T \pi_t I(\gamma\pi_t, t)\, dt + \pi_T I_F(\gamma\pi_T)\right]. \tag{53}$$

(The expectation may be $+\infty$.) All of this implies that (c^*, Z^*) of (51)–(52) solves (46) provided the required initial investment $\widehat{w}(\gamma)$ is equal to the endowed initial wealth w. This leaves an equation $\widehat{w}(\gamma) = w$ to solve for the "correct" Lagrange multiplier γ^*, and with that an explicit solution (51)–(52) to the optimal consumption policy for Merton's problem.

We can be a little more systematic about the properties of u and F in order to guarantee that $\widehat{w}(\gamma) = w$ can be solved for a unique $\gamma^* > 0$. A strictly concave increasing function $F : \mathbb{R}_+ \to \mathbb{R}$ that is differentiable on $(0, \infty)$ satisfies *Inada conditions* if $\inf_x F'(x) = 0$ and $\sup_x F'(x) = +\infty$. If F satisfies these Inada conditions, then the inverse I_F of F' is well defined as a strictly decreasing continuous function on $(0, \infty)$ whose image is $(0, \infty)$.

Condition A. *Either F is zero or F is differentiable on $(0, \infty)$, strictly concave, and satisfies Inada conditions. Either u is zero or, for all t, $u(\cdot, t)$ is differentiable on $(0, \infty)$, strictly concave, and satisfies Inada conditions. At least one of u and F is nonzero. For each $\gamma > 0$, $\widehat{w}(\gamma)$ is finite.*

Theorem. *Under Condition A, for any $w > 0$, Merton's problem (38) has a solution (c^*, Z^*, θ^*), where (c^*, Z^*) is given by (51)–(52) for a unique $\gamma \in (0, \infty)$.*

Proof: Under Condition A, the Dominated Convergence Theorem implies that $\widehat{w}$ is continuous. Since one or both of $I(\cdot, t)$ and I_F have $(0, \infty)$ as their image and are strictly decreasing, $\widehat{w}$ inherits these two properties. From this, given any initial wealth $w > 0$, there is a unique γ^* with $\widehat{w}(\gamma^*) = w$. Let (c^*, Z^*) be defined by (51)–(52), replacing γ with γ^*. Proposition 9E tells us there is a trading strategy θ^* financing (c^*, Z^*). Let (θ, c, Z) be any budget-feasible choice. Proposition 9E also implies that (c, Z) satisfies (41), which is equivalent by the same arguments used in the proof of Proposition 9F to

$$E\left(\pi_T Z + \int_0^T \pi_t c_t\, dt\right) \le w. \tag{54}$$

The first-order conditions (49) and (50) imply that for all t,

$$u(c_t^*, t) - \gamma^* \pi_t c_t^* \ge u(c_t, t) - \gamma^* \pi_t c_t$$

and that

$$F(Z^*) - \gamma^* \pi_T Z^* \ge F(Z) - \gamma^* \pi_T Z.$$

Integrating these two inequalities and applying (47) and (54) leaves $U(c^*, Z^*) \ge U(c, Z)$, implying the optimality of (c^*, Z^*, θ^*). ∎

For a specific example, we once again consider the case of HARA util-
ity for terminal consumption only, taking $u \equiv 0$ and $F(w) = w^\alpha/\alpha$ for
$\alpha \in (0, 1)$. Then $c^* = 0$ and the calculations above imply that $\widehat{w}(\gamma) =
E\left[\pi_T(\gamma\pi_T)^{1/(\alpha-1)}\right]$. Solving $\widehat{w}(\gamma^*) = w$ for γ^* leaves

$$\gamma^* = w^{\alpha-1} E\left(\pi_T^{\alpha/(\alpha-1)}\right)^{\alpha-1}.$$

It is left as an exercise to check that (52) can be reduced explicitly to

$$Z^* = I_F(\gamma^*\pi_T) = W_T,$$

where

$$dW_t = W_t(r + \overline{\varphi} \cdot \lambda)\, dt + W_t\overline{\varphi}^\top \sigma\, dB_t; \qquad W_0 = w, \tag{55}$$

where $\overline{\varphi} = (\sigma\sigma^\top)^{-1}\lambda/(1-\alpha)$ is the vector of fixed optimal portfolio fractions
found previously from the Bellman equation.

G. A Generalization

We generalize the security-price process $X = (X^0, X^1, \ldots, X^N)$ to be of the
form

$$dX_t^0 = r_t X_t^0\, dt; \qquad X_0^0 > 0,$$

$$dX_t^i = \mu_t^i X_t^i\, dt + X_t^i \sigma_t^i\, dB_t; \qquad X_0^i > 0, \qquad 1 \le i \le N, \tag{56}$$

where r, $\mu = (\mu^1, \ldots, \mu^N)$, and σ^i, for all i, are bounded adapted processes
valued in $\mathbb{R}$, $\mathbb{R}^N$, and $\mathbb{R}^d$, respectively. We assume for simplicity that $N = d$,
that σ^i is the i-th row of a process σ valued in $\mathbb{R}^{d \times d}$ that is nonsingular
almost everywhere. The excess expected returns of the "risky" securities are
defined by an $\mathbb{R}^N$-valued process λ given by $\lambda_t^i = \mu_t^i - r_t$. We assume that
λ is strictly positive, that the process ν defined by $\nu_t = \sigma_t^{-1}\lambda_t$ satisfies the
Novikov condition

$$E\left[\exp\left(\frac{1}{2}\int_0^T \nu_t^\top \nu_t\, dt\right)\right] < \infty, \tag{57}$$

and that $\mathrm{var}(\xi_T) < \infty$, where

$$\xi_t = \exp\left(-\frac{1}{2}\int_0^t \nu_s^\top \nu_s\, ds - \int_0^t \nu_s\, dB_s\right), \qquad t \in [0, T]. \tag{58}$$

A reading of Chapter 6 shows that these assumptions, aside from technical integrability conditions, are of the nature that (a) markets are complete, stemming from the invertibility of σ, and (b) there is no arbitrage,

confirmed by the existence of an equivalent martingale measure Q for the deflated-price processes, defined by $E^Q(Z) = E(\xi_T Z)$.

In this setting, a state-price deflator π is defined by

$$\pi_t = \exp\left(-\int_0^t r_s\, ds\right)\xi_t, \qquad t \in [0, T]. \tag{59}$$

The reformulation of Merton's problem given by Proposition 9F and the form (51)–(52) of the solution (when it exists) still apply, substituting only the state-price deflator π of (59) for that given in the earlier special case of constant r, λ, and σ. Once again, the only serious difficulty to overcome is a solution γ^* to $\widehat{w}(\gamma^*) = w$, where $\widehat{w}$ is again defined by (53). This is guaranteed by Condition A of the previous section. The proof of Theorem 9F thus suffices for the following extension.

Proposition. *Suppose X is defined by (56). Under Condition A, for any $w > 0$, Merton's problem (33) has the optimal consumption policy given by (51)–(52) for a unique scalar γ.*

Although this approach generates an explicit solution for the optimal consumption policy up to an unknown scalar γ, it does not say much about the form of the optimal trading strategy, beyond its existence. The Notes cite sources in which an optimal strategy is represented in terms of the *Malliavin calculus*. The original stochastic control approach, in a Markov setting, gives explicit solutions for the optimal trading strategy in terms of the derivatives of the value function. Although there are few examples in which these derivatives are known explicitly, they can be approximated by a numerical solution of the Hamilton-Jacobi-Bellman equation, by extending the finite-difference methods given in Chapter 11.

H. The Utility Gradient Approach

The martingale approach can be simplified, at least under technical conditions, by adopting the utility gradient approach of Chapter 2. Although conceptually easy, this theory has only been developed to the point of theorems under restrictive conditions and with complicated proofs beyond the scope of this book, so we shall merely sketch out the basic ideas and refer to the Notes for sources with proofs and more details.

We let L_+ denote the set of nonnegative adapted consumption processes satisfying the square-integrability condition $E\left(\int_0^T c_t^2\, dt\right) < \infty$. We adopt a concave utility function $U : L_+ \to \mathbb{R}$. We fix the security-price process X of Section 9G. Fixing the initial wealth w, we say that a consumption process c in L_+ is budget feasible if there is some θ in $\mathcal{H}^2(X)$ such that

$$\theta_t \cdot X_t = w + \int_0^t \theta_s \, dX_s - \int_0^t c_s \, ds, \qquad t \in [0, T], \tag{60}$$

with $\theta_T \cdot X_T = 0$. We have the problem

$$\sup_{c \in A} U(c), \tag{61}$$

where A is the set of budget-feasible consumption processes. If c^* is budget feasible and the gradient $\nabla U(c^*)$ of U at c^* exists, the gradient approach to optimality reviewed in Appendix B leads to the first-order condition for optimality:

$$\nabla U(c^*; c^* - c) \leq 0, \qquad c \in A. \tag{62}$$

This problem is a special case of problem (33) if U is of the form

$$U(c) = E \left[\int_0^T u(c_t, t) \, dt \right]. \tag{63}$$

Other utility functions, such as habit formation and recursive utility (reviewed, in a discrete-time setting, in Exercises 2.8 and 2.9) have been studied in continuous time, so we do not limit our study here to the additive-utility model.

We suppose that c^* is budget feasible and that $\nabla U(c^*)$ exists, with a Riesz representation π in L_+. That is,

$$\nabla U(c^*; c - c^*) = E \left[\int_0^T (c_t - c_t^*)\pi_t \, dt \right], \qquad c \in A. \tag{64}$$

As shown in Appendix F, this is true for the additive model, under conditions, taking $\pi_t = u_c(c_t^*, t)$. Appendix F also gives Riesz representations of the utility gradients of other forms of utility functions, such as continuous-time versions of the habit-formation and recursive utilities considered in Exercises 2.8 and 2.9.

Based on Proposition 2D and the results of Section 9G, it is natural to conjecture that c^* is optimal if and only if π is a state-price deflator. In order to explore this conjecture, we suppose that π is indeed a state-price deflator, meaning in this case that the deflated price process $X^\pi \equiv \pi X$ is a martingale. The Numeraire Invariance Theorem (or direct calculation) implies that $c \in A$ if and only if there is some $\theta \in \mathcal{H}^2(X)$ with

$$\theta_t \cdot X_t^\pi = w\pi_0 + \int_0^t \theta_s \, dX_s^\pi - \int_0^t c_s \, \pi_s \, ds, \qquad t \in [0, T], \tag{65}$$

and $\theta_T \cdot X_T^\pi = 0$. Assuming that any trading strategy θ in $\mathcal{H}^2(X)$ is in $\mathcal{H}^1(X^\pi)$, relation (65) implies that for any c in A, since $\int \theta \, dX^\pi$ is a martingale,

$$E\left(\int_0^T c_t \pi_t \, dt\right) = w\pi_0.$$

This is along the lines of (47). Applying this in particular to c^*, we have

$$\nabla U(c^*; c - c^*) = E\left[\int_0^T \pi_t(c_t - c_t^*) \, dt\right] = 0, \qquad c \in A. \qquad (66)$$

Thus, assuming some technical conditions along the way, we have shown that the first-order conditions for optimality is that X^π is a martingale. We would next like to be able to deduce what c^* must be if $\nabla U(c^*)$ is to have a Riesz representation π with this property.

Since any given deflator π is an Ito process, we can write

$$d\pi_t = \mu_\pi(t) \, dt + \sigma_\pi(t) \, dB_t, \qquad (67)$$

for some $\mu_\pi \in \mathcal{L}^1$ and $\sigma_\pi \in \mathcal{L}(B)$. If X^π is a martingale, then $X^0\pi$ in particular is a martingale, and therefore has a zero-drift process. By Ito's Lemma, this gives us

$$X_t^0 r_t \pi_t + \mu_\pi(t) X_t^0 = 0, \qquad t \in [0, T],$$

which is equivalent to

$$\mu_\pi(t) = -\pi_t r_t, \qquad t \in [0, T]. \qquad (68)$$

Again using Ito's Lemma and the fact that $X^j\pi$ is also to be a martingale for any $j \in \{1, \ldots, N\}$,

$$\mu_t^j X_t^j \pi_t + \mu_\pi(t) X_t^j + X_t^j \sigma_t^j \cdot \sigma_\pi(t) = 0.$$

Combining this with (68) implies that $\sigma_\pi/\pi = \nu$, where ν solves

$$\sigma_t \nu_t = -\lambda_t, \qquad t \in [0, T], \qquad (69)$$

and where $\lambda_t^j = \mu_t^j - r_t$. Together, (68) and (69) yield

$$d\pi_t = -\pi_t r_t \, dt - \pi_t \nu_t \, dB_t,$$

which can be reduced, using Ito's Lemma to calculate $\log(\pi_t)$, to the expression

$$\pi_t = \pi_0 \exp\left(-\int_0^t r_s \, ds\right) \xi_t, \tag{70}$$

where ξ is given by (58). This is an explicit solution for π up to choice of π_0. It coincides with the relationship shown in Chapter 6 between state-price deflators and equivalent martingale measures.

It remains to recover a budget-feasible consumption process c^* with the property that $\nabla U(c^*)$ has a Riesz representation π of the form (70). In the additive case, we have $\pi_t = u_c(c_t^*, t)$, so that $c_t^* = I(\pi_t, t)$, where $I(\cdot, t)$ inverts $u_c(\cdot, t)$. Finally, we need to choose π_0 so that c^* is budget feasible. It suffices by the same numeraire invariance argument made earlier that

$$\pi_0 \, w = E\left(\int_0^T c_t^* \, \pi_t \, dt\right) = E\left[\int_0^T I(\pi_t, t) \pi_t \, dt\right]. \tag{71}$$

Provided $I(\cdot, t)$ has range $(0, \infty)$ for all t, the arguments used in Section 9F can be applied for the existence of π_0 with this property. It is enough, for instance, that ν can be chosen to be bounded, and that I satisfies a uniform growth condition in its first argument. The Notes cite examples of a nonadditive utility function U with the property that for each deflator π in a suitably general class, one can recover a unique consumption process c^* with the property that $\nabla U(c^*)$ has π as its Riesz representation. Subject to regularity conditions, the habit-formation and recursive-utility functions have this property.

For the case of incomplete markets (for which it is not true that $\text{rank}(\sigma) = d$ almost everywhere), all of the above steps can be carried out in the absence of arbitrage, except that there need not be a trading strategy θ^* that finances the proposed solution c^*. Papers cited in the Notes have taken the following approach to this issue. With incomplete markets, there is a family of different ν solving (69). The objective is to choose a solution ν^* with the property that c^* can be financed. This can be done under technical regularity conditions.

Exercises

9.1 For the candidate optimal portfolio control $\varphi_t^* = \overline{\varphi}$ given by (22), verify that (28) is indeed a martingale as asserted.

9.2 Solve Merton's problem in the following cases. Add any regularity conditions that you feel are appropriate.

(A)   Let T be finite, $F = 0$, and $u(c, t) = e^{-\rho t} c^\alpha / \alpha$, $\alpha \in (0, 1)$.

(B)   Let T be finite, $F = 0$, and $u(c, t) = \log c$.

(C)   Let $T = +\infty$ and $u(c, t) = e^{-\rho t} c^\alpha / \alpha$, $\alpha \in (0, 1)$. Verify the solution given by $c_t^* = \gamma W_t^*$ and $\varphi_t^* = (\sigma \sigma^\top)^{-1} \lambda / (1 - \alpha)$, where γ is given by (32). Verify the so-called transversality condition (31) with $\gamma(1 - \alpha) > 0$.

9.3   Extend the example in Section 9D, with $v(\bar{c}, w) = \bar{c}^\alpha / \alpha$, to the case without a riskless security. Add regularity conditions as appropriate.

9.4   The rate of growth of capital stock in a given production technology is determined by a "random shock" process Y solving the stochastic differential equation

$$dY_t = (b - \kappa Y_t)\, dt + k \sqrt{Y_t}\, dB_t; \qquad Y_0 = y \in \mathbb{R}_+, \qquad t \geq 0,$$

where b, κ, and k are strictly positive scalars with $2b > k^2$, and where B is a standard Brownian motion. Let $\mathcal{C}$ be the space of nonnegative adapted consumption processes satisfying $\int_0^T c_t\, dt < \infty$ almost surely for all $T \geq 0$. For each c in $\mathcal{C}$, a capital stock process K^c is defined by

$$dK_t^c = (K_t^c h Y_t - c_t)\, dt + K_t^c \epsilon \sqrt{Y_t}\, dB_t; \qquad K_0^c = x > 0,$$

where h and ϵ are strictly positive scalars with $h > \epsilon^2$. Consider the control problem

$$V(x, y) = \sup_{c \in \mathcal{C}}\; E\left[\int_0^T e^{-\rho t} \log(c_t)\, dt \right],$$

subject to $K_t^c \geq 0$ for all t in $[0, T]$.

(A)   Let $C : \mathbb{R}_+ \times [0, T] \to \mathbb{R}_+$ be defined by

$$C(x, t) = \frac{\rho x}{1 - e^{-\rho(T-t)}},$$

and let K be the solution of the SDE

$$dK_t = [K_t h Y_t - C(K_t, t)]\, dt + K_t \epsilon \sqrt{Y_t}\, dB_t; \qquad K_0 = x > 0.$$

Finally, let c^* be the consumption process defined by $c_t^* = C(K_t, t)$. Show that c^* is the unique optimal consumption control. Hint: Verify that $V(x, y) = J(x, y, 0)$, where J is of the form

$$J(x, y, t) = A_1(t) \log(x) + A_2(t) y + A_3(t), \qquad (x, y, t) \in \mathbb{R}_+ \times \mathbb{R} \times [0, T),$$

where A_1, A_2, and A_3 are (deterministic) real-valued functions of time. State the function A_1 and differential equations for A_2 and A_3.

(B)   State the value function and the optimal consumption control for the infinite-horizon case. Add regularity conditions as appropriate.

9.5   An agent has the objective of maximizing $E[u(W_T)]$, where W_T denotes wealth at some future time T and $u : \mathbb{R} \to \mathbb{R}$ is increasing and strictly concave. The wealth W_T is the sum of the market value of a fixed portfolio of assets and the terminal value of the margin account of a futures trading strategy, as elaborated below. This problem is one of characterizing optimal futures hedging. The first component of wealth is the spot market value of a fixed portfolio $p \in \mathbb{R}^M$ of M different assets whose price processes $S^1, \ldots, S^M$ satisfy the respective stochastic differential equations

$$dS_t^m = \mu_m(t)\, dt + \sigma_m(t)\, dB_t; \qquad t \geq 0; \qquad S_0^m = 1, \qquad m \in \{1, \ldots, M\},$$

where, for each m, $\mu_m : [0, T] \to \mathbb{R}$ and $\sigma_m : [0, T] \to \mathbb{R}^d$ are continuous. There are futures contracts for K assets with delivery at some date $\tau > T$, having futures-price processes $F^1, \ldots, F^k$ satisfying the stochastic differential equations

$$dF_t^k = m_k(t)\, dt + v_k(t)\, dB_t; \qquad t \in [0, T], \qquad 1 \leq k \leq K,$$

where m_k and v_k are continuous on $[0, T]$ into $\mathbb{R}$ and $\mathbb{R}^d$, respectively. For simplicity, we assume that there is a constant short rate r for borrowing or lending. One takes a futures position merely by committing oneself to mark a margin account to market. Conceptually, that is, if one holds a long (positive) position of, say, ten futures contracts on a particular asset and the price of the futures contract goes up by a dollar, then one receives ten dollars from the short side of the contract. (In practice, the contracts are largely insured against default by the opposite side, and it is normal to treat the contracts as default-free for modeling purposes.) The margin account earns interest at the riskless rate (or, if the margin account balance is negative, one loses interest at the riskless rate). We ignore margin calls or borrowing limits. Formally, as described in Section 8C, the futures-price process is actually the cumulative-dividend process of a futures contract; the true price process is zero. Given any bounded adapted process $\theta = (\theta^1, \ldots, \theta^K)$ for the agent's futures-position process, the agent's wealth at time T is $p \cdot S_T + X_T$, where X is the Ito process for the agent's margin account value, defined by $X_0 = 0$ and $dX_t = rX_t\, dt + \theta_t\, dF_t$.

(A)   Set up the agent's dynamic hedging problem for choice of futures-position process θ in the framework of continuous-time stochastic control. State the Bellman equation and first-order conditions. Derive an explicit expression for the optimal futures position θ_t involving the (unknown) value function. Make regularity assumptions such as differentiability and nonsingularity. Hint: Let $W_t = p \cdot S_t + X_t$, $t \in [0, T]$.

(B)   Solve for the optimal policy θ in the case $m \equiv 0$, meaning no expected futures-price changes. Add any regularity conditions needed.

(C)   Solve the problem explicitly for the case $u(w) = -e^{-\alpha w}$, where $\alpha > 0$ is a scalar risk aversion coefficient. Add any regularity conditions needed.

9.6   In the setting of Section 9B, consider the special case of the utility function

$$U(c, Z) = E \left[\int_0^T \log(c_t) \, dt + \sqrt{Z} \right].$$

Obtain a closed-form solution for Merton's problem (14). Hint: The mixture of logarithm and power function in the utility makes this a situation in which the martingale approach has an advantage over the Bellman approach, from which it might be difficult to conjecture a value function. Once the optimal consumption policy is found, do not forget to calculate the optimal portfolio trading strategy.

9.7   Suppose B is a standard Brownian motion and there are two securities with price processes S and β given by

$$dS_t = \mu_t S_t \, dt + \sigma_t S_t \, dB_t; \qquad S_0 > 0$$

$$d\beta_t = r_t \beta_t \, dt; \qquad \beta_0 > 0,$$

where μ, σ, and r are bounded adapted processes with $\mu_t > r_t$ for all t. We take the infinite horizon case, with utility function U defined by

$$U(c) = E \left(\int_0^\infty e^{-\rho t} c_t^\alpha \, dt \right),$$

where $\alpha \in (0, 1)$ and $\rho \in (0, \infty)$. Taking the approach of Section 9H, c^* is, in principle, an optimal choice if and only if

$$E \left(\int_0^\infty \pi_t c_t^* \, dt \right) = w,$$

where $\nabla U(c^*)$ has Riesz representation π, and where S^π and β^π are martingales. Assuming that the solution c^* is an Ito process with

$$dc_t^* = c_t^* \, \mu_t^* \, dt + c_t^* \, \sigma_t^* \, dB_t,$$

we can write

$$d\pi_t = \pi_t \mu_\pi(t) \, dt + \pi_t \sigma_\pi(t) \, dB_t$$

for processes μ_π and σ_π that can be solved explicitly in terms of μ^* and σ^* from Ito's Lemma and the fact that $\pi_t = \alpha e^{-\rho t} c_t^{\alpha-1}$. Assuming that S^π and β^π are indeed martingales, solve for μ^* and σ^* explicitly.

9.8 Verify that, as defined by (38)–(40), Q is indeed an equivalent martingale measure, including the property that $\text{var}(\xi_T) < \infty$.

Notes

Standard treatments of stochastic control in this setting are given by Fleming and Rishel (1975), Krylov (1980), Bensoussan (1983), Lions (1981, 1983), Fleming and Soner (1993), and Davis (1993). Fleming and Soner (1993) develop the notion of *viscosity solutions* of the Hamilton-Jacobi-Bellman equation. Among other advantages of this approach, it allows one to characterize the continuous-time stochastic control problem as the limit of discrete Markov control problems of the sort considered in Chapter 3.

Merton (1969, 1971), in perhaps the first successful application of stochastic control methods in an economics application, formulated and solved the problem described in Section 9B. (Another early example is Mirrlees [1974].) Extensions and improvements of Merton's result have been developed by Aase (1984), Fleming and Zariphopoulou (1991), Karatzas, Lehoczky, Sethi, and Shreve (1986), Lehoczky, Sethi, and Shreve (1983, 1985), Sethi and Taksar (1988), Fitzpatrick and Fleming (1991), Richard (1975), Jacka (1984), Ocone and Karatzas (1991) (who apply the Malliavin calculus), and Merton (1990b).

The martingale approach to optimal investment described in Section 9E has been developed in a series of papers. Principle among these are Cox and Huang (1989) and, subsequently, Karatzas, Lehoczky, and Shreve (1987). This literature includes Cox (1983), Pliska (1986), Cox and Huang (1991), Back (1986), Back and Pliska (1987), Huang and Pagès (1992), Lakner and Slud (1993), Pagès (1987), Jeanblanc-Picqué and Pontier (1990), Richardson (1989), and Shreve and Xu (1990). For applications of duality techniques to markets with constraints, see Cvitanić and Karatzas

(1992, 1993, 1994), He and Pagés (1993), He and Pearson (1991a,b), Karatzas, Lehoczky, Shreve, and Xu (1991), and El Karoui and Quenez (1991).

For problems with mean-variance-criteria in a continuous-time setting, see Ansel and Stricker (1993), Bajeux-Besnainou and Portait (1993), Bossaerts and Hillion (1994), Bouleau and Lamberton (1993), Duffie and Jackson (1990), Duffie and Richardson (1991), Föllmer and Schweizer (1990), Föllmer and Sondermann (1986), Lakner (1994a), and Schweizer (1993a,b, 1994a,b).

For optimality under various habit-formation utilities, see Constantinides (1990), Detemple and Zapatero (1992), Ingersoll (1992), Ryder and Heal (1973), and Sundaresan (1989). A model involving local substitution for consumption was developed by Hindy and Huang (1992, 1993), and Hindy, Huang, and Kreps (1992). See, also, Hindy, Huang, and Zhu (1993b).

Ekern (1993) is an example of a model of irreversible investment. Dixit and Pyndyck (1993) review many other models of optimal production under uncertainty using stochastic control methods.

For developments of recursive utility in continuous-time settings, and the associated technical problem of backward stochastic differential equations, see Ahn (1993), Bergman (1985), Buckdahn (1995), Alvarez and Tourin (1994), Darling (1994), Duffie and Epstein (with Skiadas) (1992a), Duffie and Epstein (1992b), Duffie and Lions (1990), Duffie and Skiadas (1994), Duffie, Schroder, and Skiadas (1993), El Karoui, Peng, and Quenez (1994), Ma (1991a,b, 1993, 1994a), Pardoux and Peng (1990, 1994), Peng (1992, 1993), Svensson (1989), and Uzawa (1968). For the related problem of backward-forward stochastic differential equations see Antonelli (1993), Cvitanić and Ma (1994), Duffie, Geoffard, and Skiadas (1994), Duffie, Ma, and Yong (1993), Ma, Protter, and Yong (1993), and Ma and Yong (1993).

The utility-gradient approach to optimal investment of Section 9H is based on work by Harrison and Kreps (1979), Kreps (1981), Huang (1985a), Foldes (1978, 1979, 1990, 1991a,b,c), Back (1991a), and Duffie and Skiadas (1994), and is extended in these sources to an abstract setting with more general information and utility functions.

For optimal investment problems in the case of transactions costs, see Akian, Menaldi, and Sulem (1993), Alvarez (1991), Arntzen (1994), Chang (1993), Constantinides (1986), Davis and Norman (1990), Davis and Panas (1991), Duffie and Sun (1990), Dumas and Luciano (1989), Edirisinghe, Naik, and Uppal (1991), Fleming, Grossman, Vila, and Zariphopoulou (1989), Jouini and Kallal (1993a,b), Pliska and Selby (1994), Schroder

(1993), Shreve and Soner (1994), Shreve, Soner, and Xu (1991), Vayanos and Vila (1992), and Zariphopoulou (1992). See also the references cited in the Notes of Chapter 6.

For results with incomplete markets, see Adler and Detemple (1988), Cuoco (1994), Cvitanić and Karatzas (1992, 1994), Duffie, Fleming, and Zariphopoulou (1991), Duffie and Zariphopoulou (1993), Dybvig (1989), El Karoui and Jeanblanc-Picqué (1994), He and Pagés (1993), Koo (1991, 1994a,b), Scheinkman and Weiss (1986), and Svensson and Werner (1993).

For the case of short-sales constraints and other forms of portfolio retrictions, see Back and Pliska (1986), Brennan, Schwartz, and Lagnado (1993), Cuoco (1994), Cvitanić and Karatzas (1992, 1994), Dybvig (1994), Fleming and Zariphopoulou (1991), He and Pagés (1993), Hindy (1995), Shirakawa (1994), Vila and Zariphopoulou (1991), Xu and Shreve (1992a,b), and Zariphopoulou (1992, 1994).

On the existence of additive or other particular forms of utility consistent with given asset prices, sometimes called *integrability*, see Bick (1986), He and Huang (1994), He and Leland (1993), Hodges and Carverhill (1992), and Wang (1993a). On turnpike problems, see Cox and Huang (1991, 1992) and Huang and Zariphopoulou (1994). For problems in settings with incomplete information, usually requiring filtering of the state, see Dothan and Feldman (1986), Gennotte (1984), Detemple (1991), Föllmer and Schweizer (1990), Karatzas (1991), Karatzas and Xue (1990), Kuwana (1994), Lakner (1994b,c), Ocone and Karatzas (1991), and Schweizer (1993b).

Quenez (1992) and Karatzas (1989) survey some of the topics in this chapter. Exercise 9.4 is from Cox, Ingersoll, and Ross (1985a).

10
Equilibrium

THIS CHAPTER REVIEWS security market equilibrium in a continuous-time setting and derives several implications for security prices and expected returns. These include Breeden's consumption-based capital asset pricing model (in both complete and incomplete market settings) as well as the Cox-Ingersoll-Ross model of the term structure.

A. The Primitives

As usual, we let $B = (B^1, \ldots, B^d)$ denote a standard Brownian motion in $\mathbb{R}^d$ on a probability space $(\Omega, \mathcal{F}, P)$, and let $\mathbb{F} = \{\mathcal{F}_t : t \geq 0\}$ denote the standard filtration of B. The consumption space is the set L of adapted processes satisfying $E\left(\int_0^T c_t^2 \, dt\right) < \infty$ for some fixed-time horizon $T > 0$.

There are m agents. Agent i is defined by a nonzero consumption endowment process e^i in the set L_+ of nonnegative processes in L, and by a strictly increasing utility function $U_i : L_+ \to \mathbb{R}$.

As in Section 6K, a cumulative-dividend process is a finite-variance process of the form $C = Z + V - W$, where $Z = \int \theta \, dB$ for some $\theta \in \mathcal{L}(B)$, and where V and W are increasing adapted right-continuous processes. For any time t, the jump $\Delta C_t \equiv C_t - C_{t-}$ represents the lump-sum payment at time t. For example, if the security is a unit zero-coupon bond that matures at time τ, then $C_t = 0$, $t < \tau$, and $C_t = 1$, $t \geq \tau$. By convention, any dividend process C satisfies $C_{0-} = C_0 = 0$. For example, a dividend-rate process δ in L defines the cumulative-dividend process $C = V - W$ with $V_t = \int_0^t \max(\delta_s, 0) \, ds$ and $W_t = \int_0^t \max(-\delta_s, 0) \, ds$. There are $N + 1$ securities, numbered 0 through N, with security j defined by a cumulative-dividend process D^j.

Mainly for expositional reasons, we assume that the given dividend processes are measured in nominal units of account, and will shortly define the price process for consumption in terms of the same nominal units of

account. We later normalize by the price of consumption in order to recover continuous-time versions of the utility-based asset pricing results of
Chapter 2. Altogether, the set of primitives of the economy is

$$\mathcal{E} = \big\{(\Omega, \mathcal{F}, \mathbb{F}, P); \; B; \; (e^i, U_i), \qquad 1 \leq i \leq m; \qquad D^j, \, 0 \leq j \leq N \big\}. \quad (1)$$

B. Security-Spot Market Equilibrium

The dividend process $D = (D^0, \ldots, D^N)$ is assigned a price process $X = (X^0, \ldots, X^N)$ such that the gain process $G = D + X$ is an Ito process in $\mathbb{R}^{N+1}$. We treat X_t as the ex-dividend price at time t, that is, the price
without including the current dividend jump ΔD_t. There is also a process p
in L for the price of the single consumption commodity. A trading strategy is
a process $\theta = (\theta^0, \ldots, \theta^N)$ in $\mathcal{H}^2(G)$. Given the consumption-price process
p, a trading strategy θ *finances a consumption process c* if

$$\theta_t \cdot (X_t + \Delta D_t) = \int_0^t \theta_s \, dG_s - \int_0^t p_s c_s \, ds, \qquad t \in [0, \, T], \quad (2)$$

and

$$\theta_T \cdot (X_T + \Delta D_T) = 0. \quad (3)$$

Relation (2) is an accounting restriction, stating that the market value
of the current portfolio is generated entirely by security trading gains, net
of the cost of consumption purchases. The terminal budget constraint (3)
requires that there be no remaining obligations at time T.

Given a security price process X and a consumption price process p,
agent i faces the problem

$$\sup_{(c, \theta) \in \Lambda(i)} \; U_i(c), \quad (4)$$

where $\Lambda(i) = \{(c, \theta) \in L_+ \times \mathcal{H}^2(G) : \theta \text{ finances } c - e^i\}$.

A *security-spot market equilibrium* for the economy $\mathcal{E}$ of (1) is a collection

$$\big\{X; \; p; \qquad (c^i, \theta^i), \qquad 1 \leq i \leq m\big\} \quad (5)$$

such that given the security price process X and the consumption price
process p, for each agent i, (c^i, θ^i) solves (4), and markets clear:

$$\sum_{i=1}^m \theta^i = 0; \qquad \sum_{i=1}^m c^i - e^i = 0.$$

C. Arrow-Debreu Equilibrium

A related notion of equilibrium is one in which any consumption process c in L can be purchased at time zero for some price $\Pi(c)$ that is given by a nonzero linear *price function* $\Pi : L \to \mathbb{R}$. Paralleling the definitions given in Chapter 2, an allocation $(c^1, \ldots, c^m) \in (L_+)^m$ of consumption processes is feasible if $\sum_{i=1}^m c^i \le \sum_{i=1}^m e^i$. An Arrow-Debreu equilibrium is a collection $[\Pi, (c^1, \ldots, c^m)]$ consisting of a price function Π and a feasible allocation $(c^1, \ldots, c^m)$ such that for each i, c^i solves

$$\sup_{c \in L_+} U_i(c) \qquad \text{subject to } \Pi(c) \le \Pi(e^i). \tag{6}$$

Conditions for the existence of an Arrow-Debreu equilibrium are given in Section 10G and in the Notes.

Lemma. *If $\Pi : L \to \mathbb{R}$ is linear and strictly increasing, then there is a unique π in L such that*

$$\Pi(c) = E\left(\int_0^T \pi_t c_t \, dt \right), \qquad c \in L. \tag{7}$$

Moreover, π is strictly positive.

A proof of this continuous-time analogue of Lemma 2C is found in the Notes. Since U_i is strictly increasing by assumption, any Arrow-Debreu equilibrium price function Π is strictly increasing and therefore has a representation of the form (7) for a unique process $\pi \gg 0$, which is known as the Riesz representation of Π.

If feasible, an allocation $(c^1, \ldots, c^m)$ is Pareto optimal if there is no feasible allocation $(b^1, \ldots, b^m)$ such that $U_i(b^i) \ge U_i(c^i)$ for all i, with strict inequality for at least one i.

The First Welfare Theorem. *Any Arrow-Debreu equilibrium allocation is Pareto optimal.*

Proof: Let $[\Pi, (c^1, \ldots, c^m)]$ be an Arrow-Debreu equilibrium, and let π denote the Riesz representation of Π. Suppose $(b^1, \ldots, b^m)$ is a feasible allocation with $U_i(b^i) \ge U_i(c^i)$ for all i, with at least one strict inequality, say for agent j. We need a contradiction to complete the proof. Since $U_j(b^j) > U_j(c^j)$, we know that

$$\Pi(b^j) > \Pi(c^j). \tag{8}$$

If for some i, $\epsilon \equiv \Pi(c^i) - \Pi(b^i) > 0$, we could let

$$\widehat{c}^i = b^i + \frac{\epsilon}{\Pi(\pi)} \pi, \tag{9}$$

from which $\Pi(\hat{c}^i) = \Pi(c^i)$. But then, since U_i is strictly increasing and $\pi > 0$, we would have $U_i(\hat{c}^i) > U_i(c^i)$, which is impossible by the definition of an equilibrium. Thus

$$\Pi(b^i) \geq \Pi(c^i), \qquad 1 \leq i \leq m. \tag{10}$$

Combining (8), (10), and feasibility produces the contradiction

$$\Pi\left(\sum_{i=1}^m e^i\right) \geq \Pi\left(\sum_{i=1}^m b^i\right) > \Pi\left(\sum_{i=1}^m c^i\right) = \Pi\left(\sum_{i=1}^m e^i\right), \tag{11}$$

which proves the result. ∎

The following result is shown with the Separating Hyperplane Theorem in exactly the same manner as for Lemma 1E.

Proposition. *Suppose, for all i, that U_i is concave. Then $(c^1, \ldots, c^m)$ is a Pareto optimal allocation if and only if there is a nonzero vector λ in $\mathbb{R}^m_+$ such that $(c^1, \ldots, c^m)$ solves the problem*

$$\sup_{(b^1,\ldots,b^m)} \sum_{i=1}^m \lambda_i U_i(b^i) \qquad \text{subject to } b^1 + \cdots + b^m \leq e^1 + \cdots + e^m. \tag{12}$$

D. Implementing Arrow-Debreu Equilibrium

In this section we fix an Arrow-Debreu equilibrium $\left[\Pi, (c^1, \ldots, c^m)\right]$ and examine spanning conditions on the cumulative-dividend process D under which there exists a security-spot market equilibrium with the same consumption allocation. We assume throughout the following that $D_t^0 = 0$, $t < T$, with $D_T^0 = 1$, meaning that D^0 is a (nominal) zero-coupon unit bond maturing at T. This assumption can be relaxed at a cost in notational complexity.

An Ito process $M = (M^1, \ldots, M^k)$ in $\mathbb{R}^k$, for some integer $k \geq 1$, is called a *martingale generator* if M is a martingale and if, for any martingale Y, we can write

$$Y_t = Y_0 + \int_0^t \theta_s \, dM_s,$$

for some $\theta \in \mathcal{L}(M)$. For example, the underlying standard Brownian motion B is itself a martingale generator. From this one can verify that M is a martingale generator if and only if $dM_t = \eta_t \, dB_t$, where η is an $\mathbb{R}^{k \times d}$-valued process that is of rank d almost everywhere.

The following spanning condition on the cumulative-dividend process D is unnecessarily restrictive (in a sense discussed in the Notes), but simplifies the following exposition. We will fix the martingale $M(D)$ in $\mathbb{R}^{N+1}$ defined by $M(D)_t = E_t(D_T)$.

Dynamic Spanning Condition. *D^0 is a nominal zero-coupon unit bond maturing at T and $M(D)$ is a martingale generator.*

Obviously, D^0 makes no contribution toward meeting the condition that $M(D)$ is a martingale generator, which therefore requires at least $d+1$ securities. An example of a cumulative dividend process D for which $M(D)$ is a martingale generator is one for which $D_T^j = \int_0^T \sigma_t^j \, dB_t$, where $\sigma^1, \ldots, \sigma^N$ are the rows of a matrix process σ that has rank d almost everywhere. This means that $d+1$ is also a sufficient number of securities.

Theorem. *Suppose that the cumulative-dividend process D satisfies the dynamic spanning condition. Let $[\Pi, (c^1, \ldots, c^m)]$ be an Arrow-Debreu equilibrium. Let p denote the Riesz representation of Π and let*

$$X_t = E_t(D_T - D_t), \qquad t \in [0, T]. \tag{13}$$

If p is bounded, then $\{X; p; (c^i, \theta^i), 1 \le i \le m\}$ is a security-spot market equilibrium for some $(\theta^1, \ldots, \theta^m)$.

Proof: Given the security-price process X defined by (13) and the Dynamic Spanning Condition on D, we know that $G = X + D = M(D)$ is a martingale generator. We pick an arbitrary agent i and let Y be the martingale defined by

$$Y_t = E_t \left[\int_0^T (c_s^i - e_s^i) p_s \, ds \right], \qquad t \in [0, T]. \tag{14}$$

Since $\Pi(c^i - e^i) = 0$ and p is the Riesz representation of Π, we know that $Y_0 = 0$. The dynamic spanning condition implies that $M(D) = G$ is a martingale generator, so that there is some θ in $\mathcal{L}(G)$ with

$$Y_t = \int_0^t \theta_s \, dG_s, \qquad t \in [0, T]. \tag{15}$$

Since p is bounded and c^i and e^i are in L, $E(Y_T^2) < \infty$. Thus $\theta \in \mathcal{H}^2(G)$ by Proposition 5B. Since $G^0 \equiv 1$, $\int \theta \, dG$ is unaffected by redefining θ^0 so that

$$\theta_t^0 = \sum_{j=1}^{N} \left[\int_0^t \theta_s^j \, dG_s^j - \theta_t^j (X_t^j + \Delta D_t^j) \right] - \int_0^t p_s(c_s^i - e_s^i) \, ds. \tag{16}$$

Simple algebra and (14)–(16) imply that $\theta_T \cdot (X_T + \Delta D_T) = 0$ and that

$$\theta_t \cdot (X_t + \Delta D_t) = \int_0^t \theta_s \, dG_s - \int_0^t (c_s^i - e_s^i) \, p_s \, ds, \qquad t \in [0, T]. \qquad (17)$$

That is, θ finances $c^i - e^i$.

If, for some agent i, $\widehat{\theta}$ is a trading strategy financing $\widehat{c} - e^i$ for some consumption process $\widehat{c}$, we claim that $U_i(\widehat{c}) \leq U_i(c^i)$. If, on the contrary, $U_i(\widehat{c}) > U_i(c^i)$, then we have $\Pi(\widehat{c}) > \Pi(c^i) = \Pi(e^i)$ by the properties of an Arrow-Debreu equilibrium, so $E\left[\int_0^T (\widehat{c}_t - e_t^i) \, p_t \, dt\right] > 0$. This, however, is inconsistent with the requirement of the financing condition that

$$0 = \theta_T \cdot (X_T + \Delta D_T) = \int_0^T \widehat{\theta}_t \, dG_t - \int_0^T (\widehat{c}_t - e_t^i) \, p_t \, dt, \qquad (18)$$

as can be seen by taking expectations through (18) and using the fact that $E\left(\int_0^T \widehat{\theta}_t \, dG_t\right) = 0$. Thus (c^i, θ) solves agent i's problem (4).

Let θ^i be chosen in this fashion for each agent $i > 1$, and let $\theta^1 = -\sum_{i=2}^m \theta^i$. It can be checked from the linearity of stochastic integration that θ^1 finances $c^1 - e^1$, so (c^1, θ^1) is a solution to problem (4) for agent 1. By construction, $\sum_{i=1}^m \theta^i = 0$. By the feasibility of $(c^1, \ldots, c^m)$, we conclude that $\{X; \, p; \, (c^i, \theta^i), \, 1 \leq i \leq m\}$ is an equilibrium. ∎

E. Real Security Prices

The equilibrium $\{X; \, p; \, (c^i, \theta^i), \, 1 \leq i \leq m\}$ shown in the last theorem has a nominal security price process X that is "risk-neutral," in the sense of (13). Relative to the price of the consumption commodity, or in *real* terms, security prices are not generally risk-neutral. For example, consider a particular security paying the nominal cumulative-dividend process C defined by $C_t = \int_0^t \delta_s \, ds$, for some nonnegative dividend-rate process δ in L. We let Y denote the nominal price process of this security. By (13), $Y_t = E_t(\int_t^T \delta_s \, ds)$. The *real* price process $\widehat{Y}$, defined by $\widehat{Y}_t = Y_t/p_t$, and real dividend-rate process $\widehat{\delta}$, defined by $\widehat{\delta}_t = \delta_t/p_t$, are therefore related by

$$\widehat{Y}_t = \frac{1}{p_t} E_t\left(\int_t^T p_s \widehat{\delta}_s \, ds\right), \qquad t \in [0, T]. \qquad (19)$$

We can consider a more general cumulative-dividend process C that is increasing and right-continuous, allowing for the payment of lump-sum amounts at points in time, as for a coupon bond. Since the real dividend process $\widehat{C}$ corresponding to C is given by $\widehat{C}_t = \int_0^t p_s^{-1} \, dC_s$, the real price process $\widehat{Y}$ for a security promising the real cumulative-dividend process $\widehat{C}$ is given from (13) by

$$\widehat{Y}_t = \frac{1}{p_t} E_t \left(\int_t^T p_s \, d\widehat{C}_s \right), \qquad t \in [0, T]. \tag{20}$$

A simple example is a real zero-coupon unit bond maturing at some time τ in $(0, T]$. We have $\widehat{C}_t = 0$, $t < \tau$, and $\widehat{C}_t = 1$, $t \geq \tau$. The real bond-price process is then given from (20) by

$$\Lambda_{t,\tau} \equiv \frac{1}{p_t} E_t(p_\tau), \qquad t < \tau, \tag{21}$$

with $\Lambda_{t,\tau} = 0$, $t \geq \tau$. This defines the term structure of interest rates. Although we will have no need for it, the extension of (20) for a cumulative-dividend process $\widehat{C}$ that is an Ito process may be calculated from the general formula given in Chapter 6 for the deflation of Ito dividend processes.

The central issue, to which we now turn, is a characterization of the consumption-price process p. For example, we will give sufficient conditions for p to be an Ito Process. After the above normalization to real prices, this will imply that p is a state-price deflator in the sense of Chapter 6.

F. Optimality with Additive Separable Utility

For most of the remainder of the chapter we will be exploiting the properties of *smooth-additive* utility functions, defined as follows.

Definition. *A utility function* $U : L_+ \to \mathbb{R}$ *is smooth-additive* (u) *if*

$$U(c) = E \left[\int_0^T u(c_t, t) \, dt \right], \tag{22}$$

where $u : \mathbb{R}_+ \times [0, T] \to \mathbb{R}$ *is smooth on* $(0, \infty) \times [0, T]$ *and, for each t in* $[0, T]$, $u(\cdot, t) : \mathbb{R}_+ \to \mathbb{R}$ *is increasing, strictly concave, with an unbounded derivative* $u_c(\cdot, t)$ *on* $(0, \infty)$.

For the purposes of this definition, we call a function "smooth" if it can be extended to an open set with continuous derivatives of any order. (In our applications, the order required will sometimes be as high as three.) A special case of a utility function U that is smooth-additive (u) is that given by $u(c, t) = e^{-\rho t} c^\alpha / \alpha$, with $\alpha < 1$ and $\alpha \neq 0$. If the consumption-price process p is bounded, the Inada condition of unbounded u_c guarantees that consumption will be strictly positive.

Consider the choice problem in an Arrow-Debreu equilibrium with smooth-additive utility:

$$\sup_{c \in L_+} E\left[\int_0^T u(c_t, t)\, dt \right] \qquad \text{subject to } E\left(\int_0^T p_t c_t\, dt \right) \leq w, \qquad (23)$$

where p is the Riesz representation of the equilibrium price function Π and $w > 0$ is the market value $\Pi(\hat{e})$ of the agent's endowment $\hat{e}$. Given the strict monotonicity and concavity of utility, the Saddle Point Theorem implies that a necessary and sufficient condition for c^* to solve (23) is the existence of a Lagrange multiplier $\gamma > 0$ such that c^* solves the unconstrained problem

$$\sup_{c \in L_+} E\left(\int_0^T [u(c_t, t) - \gamma p_t c_t]\, dt \right), \qquad (24)$$

along with the complementary slackness condition $E(\int_0^T p_t c_t^*\, dt) = w$.

Naturally, one can do no better than to maximize $u(c_t, t) - \gamma p_t c_t$ separately for each t and each state of the world. Since $u_c(\cdot, t)$ is unbounded, this implies, for optimal c^*, that $c^* \gg 0$ and that

$$u_c(c_t^*, t) = \gamma p_t, \qquad t \in [0, T]. \qquad (25)$$

In fact, this leads directly to a method for solving (23) that is described in Section 9G, but that is not needed here. Relation (25) gives us our first characterization of the state-price deflator p in the security-spot market equilibrium studied in Sections 10D and 10E. We know, for some $\gamma > 0$, that

$$p_t = \frac{1}{\gamma} u_c(c_t^*, t), \qquad t \in [0, T], \qquad (26)$$

assuming that one of the agents has the optimal consumption process c^* and a utility function that is smooth-additive (u). The fact that the Lagrange multiplier γ is unknown is of no consequence, since $\{\gamma p_t : t \in [0, T]\}$ is also a state-price deflator for any constant $\gamma > 0$. This characterization of the state-price deflator is in terms of an individual agent's consumption process. Now we work toward a like characterization of p in terms of aggregate consumption, which is arguably more easily studied from empirical data.

G. Equilibrium with Smooth-Additive Utility

This section further characterizes state-price deflators under the assumption of smooth-additive utility. A proof of the following theorem is cited in the Notes.

Theorem. *Suppose that the aggregate endowment process e is bounded away from zero and that for each i, U_i is smooth-additive (u_i). Then there is an Arrow-Debreu equilibrium $[\Pi, (c^1, \ldots, c^m)]$ for which Π has a bounded Riesz representation p, and such that for all i, c^i is bounded away from zero.*

Coupling this result with Theorem 10D, we have conditions for the existence of a security-spot market equilibrium under smooth-additive utility.

Corollary. *Suppose, in addition, that D satisfies the dynamic spanning condition. Let X be given by (13). Then there are trading strategies $(\theta^1, \ldots, \theta^m)$ such that $[X; p; (c^i, \theta^i), 1 \le i \le m]$ is a security-spot market equilibrium.*

We fix the equilibrium consumption allocation $(c^1, \ldots, c^m)$ and consumption-price process p of this result for the remainder of this section and the next. By Theorem 10C, $(c^1, \ldots, c^m)$ is a Pareto optimal allocation. By Proposition 10C, there exists a nonzero "weight" vector $\lambda \in \mathbb{R}^m_+$ such that $(c^1, \ldots, c^m)$ solves the problem

$$\sup_{(b^1,\ldots,b^m)} \sum_{i=1}^m \lambda_i E \left[\int_0^T u_i(b_t^i, t) \, dt \right] \qquad \text{subject to } b^1 + \cdots + b^m \le e. \quad (27)$$

Because of the additive nature of utility, one can solve this problem separately for each time t in $[0, T]$ and state ω in Ω. In order to see this, let $u_\lambda : \mathbb{R}_+ \times [0, T] \to \mathbb{R}$ be defined by

$$u_\lambda(y, t) = \sup_{x \in \mathbb{R}^m} \sum_{i=1}^m \lambda_i u_i(x_i, t) \qquad \text{subject to } x_1 + \cdots + x_m \le y. \quad (28)$$

Since $(c^1, \ldots, c^m)$ solves (27), it follows that $[c^1(\omega, t), \ldots, c^m(\omega, t)]$ solves problem (29) for $y = e(\omega, t)$, except perhaps for (ω, t) in a null subset. (A set $A \subset \Omega \times [0, T]$ is *null* if $E(\int_0^T 1_A(t) \, dt) = 0$, where $1_A(t)$ is the random variable whose outcome is 1 if (ω, t) is in A, and is zero otherwise.) This is shown as follows. Suppose not, and let $(b^1, \ldots, b^m)$ be a feasible allocation and A be a non-null subset of $\Omega \times [0, T]$ such that, for all (ω, t) in A,

$$\sum_{i=1}^m \lambda_i u_i [b^i(\omega, t), t] > \sum_{i=1}^m \lambda_i u_i [c^i(\omega, t), t]. \quad (29)$$

Let $(a^1, \ldots, a^m)$ be the feasible allocation defined by

$$a^i(\omega, t) = b^i(\omega, t), \qquad (\omega, t) \in A,$$

$$= c^i(\omega, t), \qquad \text{otherwise.}$$

Then

$$\sum_{i=1}^{m} \lambda_i \, U_i(a^i) > \sum_{i=1}^{m} \lambda_i \, U_i(c^i),$$

contradicting the fact that $(c^1, \ldots, c^m)$ solves (27).

An exercise in applying the implicit function theorem shows that the utility function $U_\lambda : L_+ \to \mathbb{R}$, defined by

$$U_\lambda(c) = E\left[\int_0^T u_\lambda(c_t, t) \, dt\right], \tag{30}$$

is smooth-additive (u_λ). With $y > 0$, the first-order conditions for optimality of x^* in (29) imply that

$$\lambda_i \, u_{ic}(x_i^*, t) = u_{\lambda c}(y, t), \qquad i \in \{1, \ldots, m\}, \tag{31}$$

where the subscript "c" indicates a derivative in the customary way. This implies that, almost everywhere and for all i,

$$\lambda_i u_{ic}(c_t^i, t) = u_{\lambda c}(e_t, t). \tag{32}$$

Joining (32) with the first-order condition (26) for individual optimality implies that the Riesz representation p of Π is given by

$$kp_t = u_{\lambda c}(e_t, t), \qquad t \in [0, T], \tag{33}$$

for a constant $k > 0$ that can be taken to be 1 by rescaling p.

We have thus characterized a nominal consumption price process p in terms of the "marginal utility of a representative agent." It should be kept in mind that the weights $\lambda_1, \ldots, \lambda_m$ generally depend on the original endowment $(e^1, \ldots, e^m)$, and indeed on the particular equilibrium if there is more than one. (Uniqueness of equilibrium is implied by a gross-substitutes condition cited in the Notes.) Despite these limitations, (33) is a useful representation of state prices on intuitive grounds, and the smoothness of u_λ is also important for future applications of Ito's Lemma.

Returning to the security-spot market equilibrium of Theorem 10D, we can rewrite the security valuation equation (20) in the form

$$\widehat{Y}_t = \frac{1}{u_{\lambda c}(e_t, t)} E_t \left[\int_t^T u_{\lambda c}(e_s, s) \, d\widehat{C}_s \right], \qquad t \in [0, T], \tag{34}$$

which should strike a familiar note from a reading of Chapter 2.

H. The Consumption-Based CAPM

Section 10G showed that a nominal consumption price process p is given by $p_t = u_{\lambda c}(e_t, t)$, where u_λ is defined by (29) for some fixed utility weight vector $\lambda \in \mathbb{R}_+^m$. We henceforth assume that e is an Ito process of the form $de_t = \mu_e(t) \, dt + \sigma_e(t) \, dB_t$, which implies by Ito's Lemma and the smoothness of u_λ that p is also an Ito process with

$$dp_t = \mu_p(t) \, dt + \sigma_p(t) \, dB_t, \tag{35}$$

where $\sigma_p(t) = u_{\lambda cc}(e_t, t)\sigma_e(t)$ and

$$\mu_p(t) = u_{\lambda cc}(e_t, t)\mu_e(t) + u_{\lambda ct}(e_t, t) + \frac{1}{2} u_{\lambda ccc}(e_t, t)\sigma_e(t) \cdot \sigma_e(t). \tag{36}$$

In view of (20) and the fact that p is an Ito process, we may view p as a state-price deflator in the sense of Chapter 6. Based on a review of Section 6D, the real short-rate process r must be given by $r_t = -\mu_p(t)/p_t$. We can thus think of the short rate r_t at time t as the expected exponential rate of decline of the representative agent's "marginal utility," which is $p_t = u_{\lambda c}(e_t, t)$. Also from Section 6D, if the cumulative return of a given security is given by an Ito process R, then the fact that p is a state-price deflator implies that

$$\mu_R(t) - r_t = -\frac{1}{p_t}\sigma_R(t) \cdot \sigma_p(t) = \gamma_t \sigma_R(t) \cdot \sigma_e(t), \tag{37}$$

where $\gamma_t \equiv -u_{\lambda cc}(e_t, t)/u_{\lambda c}(e_t, t)$ is the *Arrow-Pratt measure* of risk aversion of $u_\lambda(\cdot, t)$ at e_t. In other words, excess expected returns are increasing in "instantaneous covariance" of returns with aggregate consumption changes, and increasing in "representative risk aversion." Moreover, these relationships are linear. Under stronger technical conditions, Section 10J extends this *consumption-based capital asset pricing model* (CCAPM) to incomplete markets. Within the restrictive setting of smooth-additive utility, the CCAPM is thus quite general. Without going into details, however, its empirical support is weak.

We can also view the CCAPM from a traditional "beta" perspective. The required calculations are shown in Section 6E. Since $\sigma_p(\omega, t)$ and $\sigma_e(\omega, t)$ are co-linear vectors for all (ω, t), the beta calculations in Section 6E apply equivalently to both e and p. These calculations lead to the "beta" formula

$$\mu_R(t) - r_t = \beta_R(t)(\mu_t^* - r_t), \tag{38}$$

where

$$\beta_R(t) = \frac{\sigma_R(t) \cdot \sigma_t^*}{\sigma_t^* \cdot \sigma_t^*} \tag{39}$$

is the instantaneous analogue to the beta coefficient of the CAPM, and where μ^* and σ^* are the drift and diffusion of a return process R^* with the property that $\sigma_t^* = k_t \sigma_e(t)$ for some strictly positive real-valued process k. In the sense of Section 6E, R^* is a return process with perfect instantaneous correlation with the aggregate consumption process e.

I. The CIR Term Structure

We will work out an equilibrium justification of the Cox-Ingersoll-Ross (CIR) model of the term structure that was introduced in Chapter 7. Our starting point is the solution to Exercise 9.4 involving the optimal consumption process δ from a technology with a capital-stock process K. For a given "discount rate" $\rho \in (0, \infty)$, let

$$U(c) \equiv E\left[\int_0^T e^{-\rho t} \log(c_t)\, dt\right], \qquad c \in L_+. \tag{40}$$

The single agent in the economy has the utility function $U : L_+ \to \mathbb{R}$ defined by (40).

For simplicity, we take the Brownian motion B to be one-dimensional. Repeating the solution to Exercise 9.4, the optimal capital-stock process K is the Ito process defined by

$$dK_t = (K_t hY_t - \delta_t)\, dt + K_t \epsilon \sqrt{Y_t}\, dB_t; \qquad K_0 > 0, \tag{41}$$

where

$$\delta_t = \frac{\rho K_t}{1 - e^{-\rho(T-t)}}, \qquad t \in [0, T], \tag{42}$$

and where Y solves the SDE

$$dY_t = (b - \kappa Y_t)\, dt + k\sqrt{Y_t}\, dB_t; \qquad Y_0 > 0, \tag{43}$$

for strictly positive scalars κ, b, k, h, and ϵ such that $2b > k^2$ and $h > \epsilon^2$. We can think of Y as a "shock" process that affects the productivity of capital. The existence and nonnegativity of the process Y is treated in the Notes of Chapter 7. The existence of the process K defined by (41)–(42) follows by expressing K_t in terms of Y, which can be done by expanding $\log(K_t)$ with the aid of Ito's Lemma.

We will start by assuming that the single agent's endowment process e is the optimal "drawdown" rate δ on the capital stock defined by (42). From this point, despite some slight differences in technical assumptions, we can reproduce the asset pricing results developed earlier in the chapter.

The equilibrium proposed here does not fit into the technical framework of the model provided earlier in the chapter because the logarithmic utility function is not "smooth-additive" in the sense defined above. We nevertheless proceed under the assumption that failure of the technical conditions does not invalidate the essential aspects of the model.

We take the state-price deflator p defined in the usual way for the one-agent ($\lambda = 1$) case of $u_\lambda(x, t) = e^{-\rho t} \log x$ by

$$p_t = u_{\lambda c}(\delta_t, t) = \frac{e^{-\rho t}}{\delta_t}, \qquad t \in [0, T). \tag{44}$$

The real price process S of any security promising an increasing right-continuous real cumulative-dividend process $\widehat{C}$ is then given by (22).

With the aid of Ito's Lemma, we have

$$dp_t = (\epsilon^2 - h) Y_t p_t \, dt - p_t \epsilon \sqrt{Y_t} \, dB_t. \tag{45}$$

The short-rate process r is given as in Section 10H by

$$r_t = \frac{-\mu_p(t)}{p_t} = (h - \epsilon^2) Y_t. \tag{46}$$

Since $dr_t = (h - \epsilon^2) \, dY_t$, we calculate

$$dr_t = \kappa(r^* - r_t) \, dt + \sigma_r \sqrt{r_t} \, dB_t, \tag{47}$$

where $r^* = b(h - \epsilon^2)/\kappa$ and $\sigma_r = k\sqrt{h - \epsilon^2}$. This is the form of the short rate assumed in the CIR model of the term structure studied in Section 7G in a "risk-neutral" setting. It is a convenient fact, to be shown shortly, that for the equilibrium state-price deflator p of (45), the associated "risk-neutral" version of the short-rate process is of the same form (47), although with different coefficients.

For $r_t > r^*$, the drift of r is negative; for $r_t < r^*$, the drift of r is positive. We can therefore view r as a *mean-reverting* process, reverting toward r^*. We can be more precise about this, as follows. It has been shown, as indicated in the Notes, that $\bar{r}_t \equiv E(r_t)$ is finite and continuous in t. It follows from Fubini's Theorem (Appendix C) that $E(\int_0^T r_t \, dt) < \infty$, and therefore, by Proposition 5B, that the stochastic integral $\int_0^T \sigma_r \sqrt{r_t} \, dB_t$ has zero expectation. Thus

$$\bar{r}_t = r_0 + E\left[\int_0^t \kappa(r^* - r_s) \, ds\right].$$

Applying Fubini's Theorem again, $\bar{r}_t = r_0 + \int_0^T \kappa(r^* - \bar{r}_s) \, ds$, which is equivalent to the ordinary differential equation

$$\frac{d\bar{r}_t}{dt} = \kappa(r^* - \bar{r}_t); \qquad \bar{r}_0 = r_0,$$

with solution $\bar{r}_t = r^* + (r_0 - r^*)e^{-\kappa t}$. Thus, $E(r_t) \to r^*$ exponentially with t, and r^* is the "long-run mean" of the short-rate process. By using Fubini's Theorem for conditional expectations, we can show likewise that, for any times t and $s \geq t$,

$$E_t(r_s) = r^* + (r_t - r^*)e^{-\kappa(s-t)} \qquad \text{almost surely.}$$

As we know from Chapter 7, in order to price term-structure instruments, it is enough to be able to represent the short-rate process r under an equivalent martingale measure. We can apply Ito's Lemma to represent p in the form

$$p_t = p_0 \exp\left(\frac{h - \epsilon^2/2}{\epsilon^2 - h} \int_0^t r_s \, ds - \frac{\epsilon}{\sqrt{h - \epsilon^2}} \int_0^t \sqrt{r_s} \, dB_s\right). \tag{48}$$

Based on equation (6.15), under technical integrability conditions, which we simply assume, the density process ξ of an equivalent martingale measure Q is given by

$$\begin{aligned}
\xi_t &= \exp\left(\int_0^t r_s \, ds\right)\frac{p_t}{p_0} \\
&= \exp\left(\frac{\epsilon^2/2}{\epsilon^2 - h} \int_0^t r_s \, ds - \frac{\epsilon}{\sqrt{h - \epsilon^2}} \int_0^t \sqrt{r_s} \, dB_s\right).
\end{aligned} \tag{49}$$

From Girsanov's Theorem of Appendix D, a standard Brownian motion $\widehat{B}$ under the equivalent martingale measure Q is defined by

$$d\widehat{B}_t = dB_t + \frac{\epsilon}{\sqrt{h - \epsilon^2}} \sqrt{r_t} \, dt. \tag{50}$$

Thus, under the equivalent martingale measure Q, we can represent the short-rate process r in the same square-root mean-reverting form

$$dr_t = \kappa(r^* - r_t)\, dt + \sigma_r\sqrt{r_t}\left(d\widehat{B}_t + \frac{\epsilon}{\sqrt{h - \epsilon^2}}\sqrt{r_t}\, dt\right)$$

$$= [b(h - \epsilon^2) + (k\epsilon - \kappa)r_t]\, dt + \sigma_r\sqrt{r_t}\, d\widehat{B}_t.$$

In particular, $\Lambda_{t,s} = E_t^Q\left[\exp\left(\int_t^s -r_u\, du\right)\right]$, which is solved explicitly in Section 7G. Chapter 7 gives multifactor extensions, applications to derivative term-structure pricing, and an explicit solution for the "Green's function," or fundamental solution, of the PDE associated with r.

J. The CCAPM without Dynamic Spanning

We can recover a version of the CCAPM without assuming complete markets, although more demanding technical assumptions are required and there is as yet no set of conditions that is sufficient for the existence of equilibrium except in trivial or simple parametric examples. We will pass over most of the technical details, which are handled in papers cited in the Notes, and take as an assumption the first-order conditions for individual optimality.

Section 9H shows that in principle, if the gradient $\nabla U_i(c^i)$ of the utility of agent i at an optimal consumption process c^i exists and has a Riesz representation given by a deflator π^i, then π^i is a state-price deflator. The discrete-time analogue of this result is Proposition 2D. As shown in Appendix F, the gradient of a utility function U that is smooth-additive (u) at a consumption process c that is bounded away from zero has a Riesz representation π given by $\pi_t = u_c(c_t, t)$.

Let us assume that for each agent i, the utility function U_i is smooth-additive (u_i) and that the equilibrium consumption process c^i is an Ito process bounded away from zero, so that

$$dc_t^i = \mu_c^i(t)\, dt + \sigma_c^i(t)\, dB_t,$$

for appropriate processes μ_c^i and σ_c^i. The Riesz representation π^i of $\nabla U_i(c^i)$ exists and is given by $\pi_t^i = u_{ic}(c_t^i, t)$. This implies that π^i is an Ito process, with $d\pi_t^i = \mu_\pi^i(t)\, dt + \sigma_\pi^i(t)\, dB_t$, where

$$\mu_\pi^i(t) = u_{icc}(c_t^i, t)\mu_c^i(t) + u_{ict}(e_t, t) + \frac{1}{2}u_{iccc}(e_t, t)\sigma_c^i(t) \cdot \sigma_c^i(t)$$

and $\sigma_\pi^i(t) = u_{icc}(c_t^i, t)\sigma_c^i(t)$.

From this point, the calculations in Section 10H for the representative agent can be repeated for agent i. This replaces (37) with

$$\mu_R(t) - r_t = \gamma_t^i \sigma_R(t) \cdot \sigma_c^i(t), \tag{51}$$

where $r_t = -\mu_\pi^i(t)/\pi_t^i$, and where $\gamma_t^i = -u_{icc}(c_t^i, t)/u_{ic}(c_t^i, t)$ is the "risk aversion" of agent i at time t. If there exists a return process R with $\sigma_R = 0$, then r is the short-rate process. In any case, r_t is the expected return on any trading strategy whose return process R has $\sigma_R(t) \cdot \sigma_c^i(t) = 0$.

Assuming that there is indeed a short-rate process r, we can divide each side of (51) by γ_t^i and then sum the resulting expression over the m agents. Since $\sigma_e(t) = \sigma_c^1(t) + \cdots + \sigma_c^m(t)$, we get

$$\mu_R(t) - r_t = \Gamma_t \sigma_R(t) \cdot \sigma_e(t), \tag{52}$$

where

$$\Gamma_t \equiv \left(\frac{1}{\gamma_t^1} + \cdots + \frac{1}{\gamma_t^m} \right)^{-1}$$

is referred to as the *market risk aversion*. Thus, (52) extends (37), showing that excess expected rates of return on all securities are proportional to "instantaneous covariance" of returns with aggregate consumption increments, with a "market-risk-aversion" constant of proportionality. A "beta" form of the CCAPM can now be derived, as shown in Section 6E.

Exercises

10.1 Prove Proposition 10C.

10.2 Show the calculations verifying relations (44) through (50).

10.3 Let $\tilde{r} = \{\tilde{r}_t : 0 \le t \le T\}$ be an arbitrary nonnegative bounded adapted process. This question allows you to prove the existence of a continuous-time security-spot market equilibrium with classical preferences in which the short-rate process is $\tilde{r}$.

First, for the model of preferences, suppose there is a single agent with a utility function that is smooth-additive (u), where $u(x, t) = e^{-\rho t} x^\alpha$, for $\alpha \in (0, 1)$. Next, suppose that the consumption endowment process e is defined by $e_t = \exp(Z_t)$, where

$$Z_t = Z_0 + \int_0^t (a + b\tilde{r}_s) \, ds + \int_0^t \sqrt{\tilde{r}_s} \sigma \, dB_s, \tag{53}$$

where a and b are constants, and where σ is a constant vector in $\mathbb{R}^d$.

(A)   Choose the constants a and b so that the equilibrium short-rate process is $\tilde{r}$.

(B)   Suppose there are heterogeneous agents with utility functions defined, for $i \in \{1, \ldots, m\}$, by

$$U_i(c) = E\left(\int_0^T \exp\left[-\int_0^t \rho_i(s)\, ds \right] c_t^\alpha\, dt \right),$$

where ρ_i is a bounded adapted process. The endowment for agent i is a process e^i such that $e = \sum_{i=1}^m e^i$ is the process defined above in terms of $\tilde{r}$. Assume the existence of an equilibrium with dynamic spanning. Calculate the short-rate process r in terms of the vector $\lambda \in \mathbb{R}_+^m$ (of "weights" on the m agents' utility functions) that defines the representative agent.

(C)   Repeat part (B) in the special case that $\rho_i = \bar{\rho}$ for all i, where $\bar{\rho}$ is a constant. Do not assume complete markets (dynamic spanning). That is, calculate the short-rate process once again. Can you choose a and b so that the short-rate process is $\tilde{r}$? Support your answer.

10.4   This is an alternative to the CIR model of the term structure found in Section 10I. In the CIR model, the equilibrium interest rate has an attractive mean-reverting property. Here we derive a less attractive term structure because of a cruder model for adjustment of the capital stock. Although one must make some minor technical assumptions, there is only one natural closed-form solution.

The capital stock K solves the stochastic integral equation

$$K_t = K_0 + \int_0^t (hK_s - \delta_s)\, ds + \int_0^t \epsilon K_s\, dB_s, \qquad t \geq 0,$$

where h and ϵ are strictly positive scalar, B is a standard Brownian motion in $\mathbb{R}$, and $\delta = \{\delta_t : t \geq 0\}$ is a nonnegative dividend process. As in Exercise 9.4, the single firm in question depletes its capital stock K_t at the rate δ_t. We take an infinite-horizon setting and assume that the firm depletes its stock so as to maximize the agent's utility $U(\delta)$, with

$$U(\delta) = E\left(\int_0^\infty e^{-\rho t} \delta_t^\alpha\, dt \right),$$

where $\rho > 0$ is a scalar discount rate and $\alpha \in (0, 1)$.

(A)   Solve the firm's dividend control problem.

The consumer ignores what the firm is trying to do and merely takes it that the firm's common share sells for $\mathcal{S}(K_t)$, $t \geq 0$, where $\mathcal{S}$ is a C^2 strictly increasing function, and that each share pays the dividend process δ that the firm determines. The consumer is free to purchase any number of these shares (or to short-sell them), and is also able to borrow or lend at a short-rate process r given by $r_t = h(K_t)$, for some function h of the current capital stock. These are the only two securities available. The consumer has one share of the firm's stock as an initial endowment. Let W_t denote the consumer's total wealth at any time t in stock and bond. The consumer must choose at any time t the fraction z_t of wealth to hold in the firm's share (with the remainder reinvested continually at the short rate) and must also decide at what rate to consume. (Consumption is the numeraire.)

(B)   Briefly formulate the consumer's portfolio-consumption control problem. Derive the Bellman equation and first-order conditions, assuming differentiability and interior optima.

Choose a stock-pricing function $\mathcal{S}$ and an interest-rate function h at which the consumer optimally holds none of the bond and one share of the firm. In other words:

(C)   State an equilibrium security-price process and an interest-rate process, both as functions of the current capital stock K_t.

(D)   Calculate the initial equilibrium market value of a zero-net-supply bond paying one unit of real wealth at a given time $\tau > 0$. Supply also the equilibrium market value of a *consol*, a pure income bond paying consumption perpetually at a fixed rate of one unit of consumption per unit of time.

(E)   State a differential equation for the equilibrium market value of a security paying dividends at a rate given by a bounded C^2 function f (with bounded derivative) of the current capital stock. Include a boundary condition.

10.5   Consider the following continuous-time analogue to the Markov single-agent asset pricing model of Chapter 4. Let X be the Ito process in $\mathbb{R}^N$ solving the stochastic differential equation

$$dX_t = \nu(X_t) \, dt + \eta(X_t) \, dB_t; \qquad X_0 = x \in \mathbb{R}^N, \tag{54}$$

where $\nu : \mathbb{R}^N \to \mathbb{R}^N$ and $\eta : \mathbb{R}^N \to \mathbb{R}^{N \times d}$ are sufficiently well behaved for existence. There are N securities in total supply of one each, paying dividends according to a bounded measurable function $f : \mathbb{R}^N \to \mathbb{R}^N_+$. That is, security n pays dividends at the rate $f_n(X_t)$ at time t. The security-price process is an Ito process S in $\mathbb{R}^N$. The single agent chooses a nonnegative real-valued bounded adapted consumption process c and a bounded trading strategy $\theta = (\theta^1, \ldots, \theta^k)$. The wealth process $W^{c\theta}$ of an agent initially endowed with all of the securities and adopting the consumption-portfolio strategy (c, θ) is thus given by

$$W_T^{c\theta} = \mathbf{1} \cdot S_0 + \int_0^T [\theta_t \cdot f(X_t) - c_t]\, dt + \int_0^T \theta_t\, dS_t, \qquad T \geq 0,$$

where $\mathbf{1} = (1, 1, \ldots, 1)^\top \in \mathbb{R}^N$. The agent's utility function U is defined by

$$U(c) = E\left[\int_0^\infty e^{-\rho t} u(c_t)\, dt\right],$$

where $\rho \in (0, \infty)$ and $u : \mathbb{R}_+ \to \mathbb{R}$ is increasing and strictly concave. An equilibrium for this economy is a security-price process S such that the problem $\sup_{c,\theta} U(c)$ has a solution (c, θ) with $c_t = \mathbf{1} \cdot f(X_t)$ and $\theta_t = \mathbf{1}$ for all $t \in [0, \infty)$.

(A)   Suppose the security-price process S is given by $S_t = \mathcal{S}(X_t)$ for all t, for some twice continuously differentiable function $\mathcal{S} : \mathbb{R}^N \to \mathbb{R}^N$. Provide the Bellman equation for the agent's stochastic control problem.

(B)   Based on your understanding of this model, give an expression for the term structure of interest rates. That is, provide an expression for the market value at time t of a T-period pure discount bond, which is a zero-net-supply contract to pay one unit of the consumption numeraire at time $t + T$. No proof or explanation is required here. The expression should involve only the primitives of the model, ν, η, d, u, ρ, the initial state $x \in \mathbb{R}^N$, and future states, $X_t, t \geq 0$.

(C)   Provide a PDE for the market value of any security as a necessary condition for an equilibrium, under stated regularity conditions, using the following infinite-horizon version of the Feynman-Kac formula. (We drop the argument $x \in \mathbb{R}^N$ from all functions for simplicity.) We do not supply the "strong regularity conditions" referred to in the result; there is a range of possible assumptions that are cumbersome and mainly of mathematical interest.

A Version of the Feynman-Kac Formula.   *Suppose $R : \mathbb{R}^N \to \mathbb{R}$ and $h : \mathbb{R}^N \to \mathbb{R}$ are measurable, and that (ν, η, h, R) satisfies the strong regularity conditions. Suppose*

$F \in C^2(\mathbb{R}^N)$ satisfies a growth condition. Then F satisfies the partial differential equation $\mathcal{D}F - RF + h = 0$ if and only if

$$F(x) = E\left(\int_0^\infty \exp\left[-\int_0^t R(X_s)\,ds\right] h(X_t)\,dt\right), \qquad x \in \mathbb{R}^N,$$

where $\mathcal{D}F = F_x \nu + \frac{1}{2}\mathrm{tr}(\eta^\top F_{xx}\eta)$.

(D)   Solve for the term structure of interest rates in the special case of $N = 1$ and

$$u(y) = \frac{y^{(\alpha+1)} - 1}{\alpha + 1}, \qquad \alpha \in (-1, 0),$$

$$\nu(x) = Ax, \qquad A \in \mathbb{R}$$

$$\eta(x) = D, \qquad D \in \mathbb{R}^d$$

$$f(x) = e^{bx}, \qquad b \in \mathbb{R}.$$

Also, solve for the current equilibrium short-rate process r in this economy.

(E)   For this last part, a further extension of the Black-Scholes model, we do not take the parametric assumptions of part (D). Suppose the short-rate process is given by $r_t = R(X_t)$ for all t, where $R : \mathbb{R}^N \to \mathbb{R}$, and that the security-price process is given by $S_t = S(X_t)$ for all t, for some twice continuously differentiable function $\mathcal{S} : \mathbb{R}^N \to \mathbb{R}^N$. Give a PDE for the arbitrage-free value of an additional security defined by a dividend process $\{h(X_t) : t \geq 0\}$, where $h : \mathbb{R}^N \to \mathbb{R}$ is bounded and measurable. In particular, state regularity conditions implying redundancy of this additional security. Finally, give a solution to the PDE you suggest, in the form of an expectation, and provide the corresponding regularity conditions.

10.6   This exercise is to verify that the CIR model of the term structure given in Section 10I can be embedded in a stock-market equilibrium with decentralized production decisions. The objective is to construct an equilibrium $[(S, \pi), \delta, (c, \theta)]$ of the following form:

(a) δ is the optimal real output rate process of a firm controlling the capital stock production process and maximizing its share price;
(b) π is a state-price deflator;
(c) S is the real stock-price process of the firm that is taken as given by the agent, and is equal to the share-price process generated as the

market value of the firm's solution to the problem of maximizing its real market value, given the state-price deflator π;

(d) $(c_t, \theta_t) = (\delta_t, 1)$ solves the agent's optimal consumption and trading strategy problem, given (S, δ) as the price process and real dividend-rate process of the firm. (Note that, as opposed to the pure-exchange economy studied in the body of the chapter, for which securities are held in zero net supply, the total supply of the firm's shares is 1. The market clearing condition is thus that the agent optimally holds 1 share in equilibrium.)

(A)   Formally define a stochastic equilibrium consistent with the loose description just given. In particular, state precisely the agent's problem and the firm's problem.

(B)   In the setting of Exercise 9.4, show that the (real) stock-price process $S = K$, the capital-stock process of (41), and the dividend rate δ given by (42) are consistent with equilibrium. Add any technical regularity conditions that you find appropriate. Hint: Be careful about real versus nominal values.

10.7   Given the Markov shock process X of (54) and an equilibrium characterized by Theorem 10G and its corollary, suppose that the aggregate endowment process e is defined by $e_t = g(X_t, t)$, where $g \in C^{2,1}(\mathbb{R}^N \times [0, T])$. Express a state-price deflator p and the short rate r in the form $p_t = \varphi(X_t, t)$ and $r_t = R(X_t, t)$, for measurable functions φ and R on $\mathbb{R}^N \times [0, T]$. Under technical conditions, the density process ξ of an equivalent martingale measure Q for real security prices is defined by $\xi_t = \exp(\int_0^t r_s \, ds) p_t$. Show that $d\xi_t = -\xi_t \Theta(X_t, t) \, dB_t$ for some $\mathbb{R}^d$-valued function Θ on $\mathbb{R}^N \times [0, T]$. Show that there is a standard Brownian motion $\widehat{B}$ in $\mathbb{R}^d$ under Q such that X solves an SDE of the form

$$dX_t = \alpha(X_t, t) \, dt + \eta(X_t, t) \, d\widehat{B}_t,$$

and state the function α. Show that under technical regularity conditions, the price of a security promising a real dividend-rate process of the form $\{h(X_t, t) : t \in [0, T]\}$ is given as the solution to a PDE of the Cauchy type examined in Appendix E. State the PDE.

Notes

The basic framework of this section is standard. Existence of Arrow-Debreu equilibria in infinite-dimensional settings similar to the one treated in this chapter was first shown by Bewley (1972). The first result that applies directly to the case of square-integrable functions, treated here, is due to Mas-Colell (1986a). Recent developments on general equilibrium in infinite-dimensional spaces are surveyed by Mas-Colell and Zame (1992). Theorem 10G is from Duffie and Zame (1989). Other proofs of essentially the same result are given by Araujo and Monteiro (1989), Karatzas, Lakner, Lehoczky, and Shreve (1990), Dana and Pontier (1990), and Dana (1993a,b), who studies the uniqueness of equilibria. An extension showing existence with recursive utility is given in Duffie, Geoffard, and Skiadas (1994). A sense in which this formulation is extremely restrictive is given in Araujo and Monteiro (1987) and Monteiro (1993).

On Pareto optimality in infinite-dimensional economies, see Mas-Colell (1986b). Cuoco and He (1992b) provide a notion of "local" agent weights associated with the locally Pareto optimal allocation of securities to agents.

Lemma 10C is proved as follows. First, L is a Banach lattice under the norm

$$c \mapsto \left[E\left(\int_0^T c_t^2 \, dt \right) \right]^{1/2}.$$

Any increasing linear function $\Pi : L \to \mathbb{R}$ on a Banach lattice L is continuous, as shown, for example, by Aliprantis and Burkinshaw (1985). Under the given norm, L is a Hilbert space with inner product $(p, c) \mapsto E(\int_0^T p_t c_t \, dt)$. Since Π is continuous, there is a unique π in L such that Π has the representation $\Pi(c) = E(\int_0^T \pi_t c_t \, dt)$, based on the same reasoning used in Exercise 1.17. Since Π is strictly increasing, π is strictly positive.

The seminal continuous-time equilibrium asset pricing model is due to Merton (1973a). Section 10C is standard in general equilibrium theory. Section 10D is based on Duffie and Huang (1985) and Duffie (1986). The dynamic spanning condition and the assumption that securities are defined in nominal terms can be weakened, as explained by Duffie and Zame (1989). The remainder of Section 10G is based on Huang (1987a). Section 10H presents Breeden's (1979) consumption-based capital asset pricing model, whose discrete-time antecedent is Rubinstein (1976). The line of proof shown here, however, is from Duffie and Zame (1989). Section 10I is condensed from Cox, Ingersoll, and Ross (1985a).

Karatzas, Lakner, Lehoczky, and Shreve (1990) and Lehoczky and Shreve (1986) have relatively explicit solutions of equilibrium with additive utility. Karatzas, Lehoczky, and Shreve (1991) show the existence of equilibrium with *singular price* behavior, meaning that the state-price deflator is not an Ito process. This implies, for example, that there is no short-rate process. Asset pricing examples with nonadditive utility models are given by Detemple and Zapatero (1991), Sundaresan (1989), and Constantinides (1990), who studied habit-formation utility, and by Duffie and Epstein (1992b), Duffie and Skiadas (1994), Duffie, Schroder, and Skiadas (1993), and Ma (1991b), who give examples with recursive utility. For the impact of disappointment aversion on security valuation, see Bonomo and Garcia (1993). Heaton (1993) examines the implications of time nonseparable preferences and time aggregation of data. See also Campbell (1990).

Section 10J contains Breeden's consumption-based CAPM once again, this time without complete markets. The general line of proof is from Grossman and Shiller (1982) and Back (1991a); the latter has a more general information filtration. For further development of this model, see Cornell (1981) and Madan (1988). Breeden's original proof is based on the assumed existence of smooth solutions to each agent's value function for stochastic control in a Markov setting. Breeden follows Merton (1973a) in this regard. The impact of transactions costs on the consumption-based CAPM is studied by Grossman and Laroque (1989). See also He and Modest (1993). Related results are found in Black (1990), Delgado and Dumas (1993), Dumas and Luciano (1990), and Heston (1990). For an empirical analysis of the consumption-based CAPM, see Breeden, Gibbons, and Litzenberger (1989). For empirical analyses of the Cox, Ingersoll, and Ross (1985a) term-structure model, see Chen and Scott (1992a,b, 1993a), Duffie and Singleton (1994), Gibbons and Ramaswamy (1993), and Pearson and Sun (1994). A discrete-time analogue of the Cox, Ingersoll, and Ross term-structure model is due to Gibbons and Sun (1986). For further analysis in a Markov setting, see Cox, Ingersoll, and Ross (1985a) and Breeden (1986). For more on the CIR term-structure model, and related models, see Chapter 7.

Related models with incomplete information, or heterogeneous beliefs, or asymmetric information are provided by Detemple (1986, 1995), Detemple and Murthy (1994), Dothan and Feldman (1986), Gennotte (1984), Ghysels (1986), and Zapatero (1993a,b).

Dumas (1989) and Delgado and Dumas (1993) work out explicit solutions for examples of equilibrium models with additive utility. Johnson (1994) gives a characterization of state-price deflators.

Chamberlain (1988) gives sufficient conditions for the Capital Asset Pricing Model, based on the market portfolio. Duffie and Epstein (1992b) show that homothetic recursive utility generates a family of two-factor asset pricing models, one factor being the market portfolio, the other being aggregate consumption.

For an equilibrium model of portfolio insurance, see Basak (1992). Föllmer (1993) describes an alternative to the standard general-equilibrium approach to asset pricing. Pham and Touzi (1993) examine an equilibrium model of the risk premium associated with stochastic volatility. For applications to foreign exchange rates, see Nielsen and Saá-Requejo (1992) and Zapatero (1992).

Goldstein and Zapatero (1994) present a model supporting the Vasicek term-structure model. Bick (1986) and Hodges and Carverhill (1992) present models supporting the Black-Scholes option-pricing formula.

Exercise 10.3 is based partly on Heston (1988b). Part (D) of Exercise 10.5 is from Hansen and Singleton (1986). Exercise 10.7 is based on Cox, Ingersoll, and Ross (1985b), Huang (1987a), and Duffie and Zame (1989).

11

Numerical Methods

THIS CHAPTER REVIEWS three numerical approaches to pricing securities in a continuous-time setting: "binomial" approximation, Monte Carlo simulation, and finite-difference solution of the associated partial differential equation.

A. Central Limit Theorems

It is well known that a normal random variable can be represented as the limit of normalized sums of *i.i.d.* binomial random variables. This idea, a version of the Central Limit Theorem, leads to the characterization given in this section of the Black-Scholes option-pricing formula (equation [5.11]) as the limit of the binomial option-pricing formula (equation [2.16]), letting the number of trading periods per unit of time go to infinity. Aside from making an interesting connection between the discrete- and continuous-time settings, this also suggests a numerical recipe for calculating continuous-time arbitrage-free derivative security prices.

A sequence $\{X_n\}$ of random variables *converges in distribution* to a random variable X, denoted $X_n \Rightarrow X$, if, for any bounded continuous function $f : \mathbb{R} \to \mathbb{R}$, we have $E[f(X_n)] \to E[f(X)]$. We could allow X and each of $X_1, X_2, \ldots$ to be defined on different probability spaces. A standard version of the Central Limit Theorem reads along the following lines. A random variable is *standard normal* if it has the standard normal cumulative distribution function.

Central Limit Theorem. Suppose $Y_1, Y_2, \ldots$ is a sequence of independent and identically distributed random variables on a probability space, each with expected value μ and finite variance $\sigma^2 > 0$. For each n, let $Z_n = Y_1 + \cdots + Y_n$. Then, for any *standard normal random variable X,*

$$\frac{Z_n - n\mu}{\sigma\sqrt{n}} \Rightarrow X.$$

A proof can be found in any good book on probability; several are cited in the Notes. This version of the Central Limit Theorem is not general enough to handle convergence of the binomial option-pricing formula of Exercise 2.1 to the Black-Scholes formula. In order to set up the required extension, we say that a collection

$$Y = \{Y_1^n, Y_2^n, \ldots, Y_{k(n)}^n : n \in \{1, 2, \ldots\}\},$$

with $k(n) \to \infty$ as $n \to \infty$, is a *triangular array* if, for each n, $Y_1^n, \ldots, Y_{k(n)}^n$ are independently distributed random variables on some probability space. The following version of the Central Limit Theorem is sufficient for our purposes here, and can be proved as an easy corollary of the Lindeberg-Feller Central Limit Theorem given in Appendix C.

Proposition. *Suppose Y is a triangular array of random variables such that* $Y_1^n, \ldots,$ $Y_{k(n)}^n$ *are bounded in absolute value by a constant* y_n, *with* $y_n \to 0$. *Let* $Z_n = Y_1^n + \cdots + Y_{k(n)}^n$. *If* $E(Z_n) \to \mu$ *and* $\mathrm{var}(Z_n) \to \sigma^2 > 0$, *then* Z_n *converges in distribution to a normally distributed random variable with mean* μ *and variance* σ^2.

B. Convergence from Binomial to Black-Scholes

Recall the setup from Section 5E of the Black-Scholes model for pricing a European put option:

- a probability space on which there is a standard Brownian motion B;
- a stock-price process S defined by $S_t = x \exp(\alpha t + \sigma B_t)$ and a bond-price process β defined by $\beta_t = \beta_0 e^{rt}$, for constants α, σ, and r;
- the put-option payoff $(K - S_T)^+$, defined by the expiration time T and exercise price K.

The solution (5.26) of the arbitrage-free put price is

$$P(x, 0) = E\left[e^{-rT}\left(K - xe^{X_T}\right)^+\right], \tag{1}$$

where $X_t = (r - \sigma^2/2)t + \sigma B_t$ for any $t \leq T$. We can treat X_t as the cumulative continuously compounded return on the stock up to time t, after "risk-neutralizing" the probability measure. This is formalized in Chapter 6, but is apparent in the Feynman-Kac approach explained in Chapter 5.

In the binomial setting of Exercise 2.1, the stock has a binomial return in each period with outcomes D and $U > D$, while a riskless bond has a constant return given by some $R \in (D, U)$. The risk-neutralized probabilistic representation of the put price is given, as with the call-price formula (2.16), by

$$P_0^T = E\left[R^{-T}(K - xe^\rho)^+\right], \tag{2}$$

where $\rho = Y_1 + \cdots + Y_T$, and where $Y_1, \ldots, Y_T$ are *i.i.d.* binomial random variables having outcomes $u = \log(U)$ and $d = \log(D)$ with respective risk-neutral probabilities $p = (R - D)/(U - D)$ and $1 - p$. We can calibrate the binomial stock returns U and D, as well as the bond return R, to our model of the continuous-time stock- and bond-price processes as follows. Obviously, we set the bond return at $R = e^r$. The stock returns U and D require more thought. To maintain some probabilistic similarity between the continuous-time and binomial models, we will explictly model an exogenously given probability q of an up-return U, and choose U and D so that the mean and standard deviation of the continuously compounding stock returns are the same in the two settings. The probability q should not be confused with the "risk-neutralized" probability p constructed from the returns. Let us arbitrarily choose $q = 0.50$, and then select $u = \alpha + \sigma$ and $d = \alpha - \sigma$. With this, the continuously compounding stock returns in both models have mean α and variance σ^2 per unit of time. Many other combinations of q, u, and d would work.

Let "Model n" refer to the binomial model with n trading periods per unit of time and with returns U_n, D_n, and R_n per trading period. We will allow n to approach infinity, always calibrating, as above, the binomial returns to the continuous-time returns. In order to maintain the mean and variance of total returns per unit of time at the continuously compounding levels μ and σ^2, respectively, we reset the per-trading-period continuously compounding returns $u_n = \log(U_n)$ and $d_n = \log(D_n)$ to $u_n = \alpha/n + \sigma/\sqrt{n}$ and $d_n = \alpha/n - \sigma/\sqrt{n}$. We leave q_n fixed at 0.50. With *i.i.d.* returns, the per-unit-of-time mean and variance of the continuously compounding returns are then, respectively,

$$n\left[q_n u_n + (1 - q_n) d_n\right] = \alpha$$

and

$$nq_n(1 - q_n)(u_n - d_n)^2 = \sigma^2,$$

precisely as required. The per-trading-period return on the bond is $R_n = e^{r/n}$. The number of trading periods required for passage of T units of calendar time is Tn. We can therefore rewrite the put-price formula (2) for

Model n as

$$P(n) = E\left(e^{-rT}\left[K - xe^{\rho(n)}\right]^+\right),\tag{3}$$

where $\rho(n) = Y_1^n + \cdots + Y_{Tn}^n$ and where $Y_1^n, \ldots, Y_{Tn}^n$ are *i.i.d.* binomial with outcomes u_n and d_n at respective risk-neutralized probabilities of p_n and $1 - p_n$, where

$$p_n = \frac{R_n - D_n}{U_n - D_n}.\tag{4}$$

The per-unit-of-time risk-neutralized mean and variance of returns are, respectively,

$$M_n = n\left[p_n u_n + (1 - p_n)d_n\right]$$

and

$$V_n = np_n(1 - p_n)(u_n - d_n)^2.$$

An exercise shows that $M_n \to r - \sigma^2/2$ and $V_n \to \sigma^2$. Thus, in risk-neutral terms, $E[\rho(nT)] \to (r - \sigma^2/2)T$ and $\mathrm{var}[\rho(nT)] \to \sigma^2 T$. Because u_n and d_n each converge to zero, the version of the Central Limit Theorem given by Proposition 11A implies that $\rho(n) \Rightarrow X_T$. Because the function $h : \mathbb{R} \to \mathbb{R}$ defined by $h(y) = (K - xe^y)^+$ is bounded and continuous, the binomial put price $P(n)$ of (3) converges to the Black-Scholes put price $P(x, 0)$ given in equation (1) as the number n of trading intervals per unit of time goes to infinity.

The only properties of the put payoff function h used above are its continuity and its boundedness. The same arguments therefore allow one to conclude that for any bounded continuous g, the arbitrage-free price of a claim to $g(S_{Tn})$ in the binomial setting with n trading periods per unit of time converges to the corresponding continuous-time arbitrage-free price $E[e^{-rT}g(Z_T)]$ obtained from the Feynman-Kac formula, where $Z_T = x\exp[(r - \sigma^2/2)T + \sigma B_T]$.

By put-call parity, the binomial call-pricing formula converges to the Black-Scholes call-pricing formula in the same sense. That is, put-call parity implies both that

$$C_n = x + P_n - e^{-rT}K$$

and that

$$C(x, 0) = x + P(x, 0) - e^{-rT}K.$$

Since $P_n \to P(x, 0)$, we have $C_n \to C(x, 0)$.

C. Binomial Convergence for Unbounded Derivative Payoffs

By now, it may be apparent why we began with the case of put options and only then treated calls by put-call parity. The call payoff function $x \mapsto (e^x - K)^+$ is not bounded! By a slightly more tedious argument, we could have shown convergence for the call-price formula directly, without applying put-call parity, by using the following results. This section is not essential and can be skipped on a first reading. Uniformly integrable random variables are defined in Appendix C.

Continuous Mapping Theorem. *Suppose $X_n \Rightarrow X$ and g is a continuous function. Then $g(X_n) \Rightarrow g(X)$.*

Proposition. *Suppose $X_n \Rightarrow X$. If $\{X_n\}$ is uniformly integrable, then $E(X_n) \to E(X)$. Conversely, if $X, X_1, X_2, \ldots$ are nonnegative and have finite expectations with $E(X_n) \to E(X)$, then $\{X_n\}$ is uniformly integrable.*

It can be shown as an exercise that, for $\rho(n)$ as defined in the previous section, the sequence of call payoffs $\{[xe^{\rho(n)} - K]^+\}$ is uniformly integrable, from which the above two results directly imply convergence of the binomial call-price formula to the Black-Scholes formula.

More generally, consider any derivative security with payoff function g such that $\{V_n\}$ is uniformly integrable when defined by $V_n = g[xe^{\rho(n)}]$. Suppose, moreover, that g is continuous and satisfies a polynomial growth condition, as defined in Appendix E, so that the Feynman-Kac pricing formula (5.26) applies. We then have convergence of the binomial price $E(e^{-rT}V_n)$ to the continuous-time price $E[e^{-rT}g(Z_T)]$, where

$$Z_t = x \exp\left[\left(r - \frac{\sigma^2}{2}\right)t + \sigma B_t\right], \qquad t \le T. \tag{5}$$

D. Discretization of Asset Price Processes

The Feynman-Kac solution (5.40) for derivative asset prices is typically difficult to calculate explictly. Sections D through F address the numerical solution of (5.40) by Monte Carlo simulation of a discrete-time approximation of the stochastic differential equation (5.41).

We begin with a probability space on which is defined a standard Brownian motion B in $\mathbb{R}^d$, along with its standard filtration. The SDE to be approximated is assumed to be of the form

$$dX_t = a(X_t, t)\, dt + b(X_t, t)\, dB_t; \qquad X_0 = x \in \mathbb{R}^N, \tag{6}$$

where $a : \mathbb{R}^N \times [0, \infty) \to \mathbb{R}^N$ and $b : \mathbb{R}^N \times [0, \infty) \to \mathbb{R}^{N \times d}$ have, for any k, bounded k-th derivatives. Referring to Appendix E, this is more than enough to ensure the existence of a unique Ito process X in $\mathbb{R}^N$ satisfying (6). A natural scheme for approximating (6) is the *Euler approximation*: For n periods per unit of time, let $\widehat{X}^n$ be the discrete-time $\mathbb{R}^N$-valued process defined on some (possibly different) probability space $(\Omega, \mathcal{F}, P)$ by

$$\widehat{X}^n_{k+1} - \widehat{X}^n_k = \frac{1}{n} a\left(\widehat{X}^n_k, \frac{k}{n}\right) + \frac{1}{\sqrt{n}} b\left(\widehat{X}^n_k, \frac{k}{n}\right) \epsilon_{k+1}; \qquad \widehat{X}^n_0 = x, \quad (7)$$

where $\epsilon_1, \epsilon_2, \dots$ is an *i.i.d.* sequence of standard normal vectors valued in $\mathbb{R}^d$. This is known as the Euler approximation of (6).

Our objective is to approximate an expression of the form $E[f(X_T)]$, where T is a fixed time, X is the solution of (6), and $f : \mathbb{R}^N \to \mathbb{R}$ satisfies a polynomial growth condition (defined in Appendix E) and has derivatives of any order. Our tentative approximation is $f_n = E[f(\widehat{X}^n_{Tn})]$. The issue is: How good is this approximation? Let $e_n = E[f(X_T)] - f_n$ denote the approximation error. It can be shown that $e_n \to 0$. Even better, we can give an *order of convergence*. A sequence $\{y_n\}$ has *order-k convergence* if $y_n n^k$ is bounded in n. The Euler approximation is said to be a *first-order scheme* in that e_n has order-1 convergence. More precisely, there is a constant C such that $e_n + C/n$ has order-2 convergence. The error coefficient C may be positive or negative, and gives a notion of bias in the approximation. Although C is usually unknown, it turns out that C can itself be approximated to first-order by $C_n = 2(f_n - f_{2n})$.

The Notes give a source for these properties of the Euler approximation as well as references to more complicated schemes with order-2 error. For instance, with $N = 1$ and under technical conditions, an order-2 scheme is given by the *Milshtein approximation*. Given μ and σ in $C^2(\mathbb{R})$ such that, for all t, we have $a(x, t) = \mu(x)$ and $b(x, t) = \sigma(x)$, the Milshtein approximation is given by

$$\widehat{X}^n_{k+1} - \widehat{X}^n_k = \frac{1}{n}\left[\mu\left(\widehat{X}^n_k\right) - \frac{1}{2}\sigma\left(\widehat{X}^n_k\right)\sigma'\left(\widehat{X}^n_k\right)\right]$$
$$+ \frac{1}{\sqrt{n}}\sigma\left(\widehat{X}^n_k\right)\epsilon_{k+1} + \frac{1}{2n}\sigma\left(\widehat{X}^n_k\right)\sigma'\left(\widehat{X}^n_k\right)\epsilon^2_{k+1} \quad (8)$$
$$+ \frac{1}{n^{3/2}}\nu\left(\widehat{X}^n_k\right)\epsilon_{k+1} + \frac{1}{n^2}\eta\left(\widehat{X}^n_k\right),$$

where

$$\nu(x) = \frac{1}{2}\mu(x)\sigma'(x) + \frac{1}{2}\mu'(x)\sigma(x) + \frac{1}{4}\sigma(x)^2\sigma''(x)$$

and

$$\eta(x) = \frac{1}{2}\mu(x)\mu'(x) + \frac{1}{4}\mu''(x)\sigma(x)^2.$$

E. Monte Carlo Simulation

Of course, we do not generally know even the approximation $E[f(\widehat{X}^n_{Tn})]$, but we can in turn estimate this quantity by Monte Carlo simulation. The law of large numbers states if $Y_1, Y_2, \ldots$ is an *i.i.d.* sequence of random variables of finite expectations, then $(Y_1 + \cdots + Y_k)/k \to E(Y_1)$ almost surely.

Let $Y_1 = f(\widehat{X}^n_{Tn})$ be defined as above. This is the first simulation of the random variable whose mean is to be computed. For each i, let Y_i be defined in the same manner, with the exception that we substitute a sequence $\epsilon^{(i)}$ of standard normal vectors in $\mathbb{R}^d$ for the original standard normal vector sequence $\epsilon = (\epsilon_1, \ldots, \epsilon_{Tn})$. We let $\epsilon^{(1)}, \epsilon^{(2)}, \ldots$ itself be *i.i.d.* The sequence $Y_1, Y_2, \ldots$ is therefore *i.i.d.*, and qualifies for an application of the law of large numbers, leaving

$$f(n, k) \equiv \frac{Y_1 + \cdots + Y_k}{k} \to E\left[f\left(\widehat{X}^n_{Tn}\right)\right] \qquad \text{almost surely.} \qquad (9)$$

In practice, one often substitutes *pseudo-random* numbers for $\{\epsilon^{(i)}\}$, using some deterministic scheme. There are a number of methods, called *variance reduction techniques*, that can improve the convergence properties of Monte Carlo simulation. For example, rather than choosing $\epsilon^{(1)}, \epsilon^{(2)}, \ldots$ to be *i.i.d.*, one can use $\epsilon^{(i)}$ for even i, and for odd i, let $\epsilon^{(i)} = -\epsilon^{(i-1)}$. This *antithetic sampling* method typically improves the convergence properties of the simulation. Further variance reduction methods are found in sources cited in the Notes.

At this point, (9) gives us an approximation $f(n, k)$ of $E[f(X_T)]$ based on a discrete-time approximation $\widehat{X}^n$ of the Ito process X with n periods per unit of time, and with k simulations of the process $\widehat{X}^n$. The number of additions required to compute $f(n, k)$ is roughly proportional to $N^2 Tnk$. Since N and T are presumably fixed for a given problem, we are concerned about the size of nk, given limited computation time. The Central Limit Theorem will provide us with an asymptotic tradeoff between the number n of time points per unit of time and the number k of simulated sample paths. This is illustrated in the following section, based on research cited in the Notes.

F. Asymptotically Efficient Tradeoff in Simulating SDEs

Consider the following abstract conditions on a sequence $\{Z(1), Z(2), \ldots\}$ of random variables that converges in distribution to some random variable Z. For our problem of calculating $E[f(X_T)]$, we may think of $Z(n)$ as $f(\widehat{X}^n_{Tn})$ and Z as $f(X_T)$.

Condition A. *Let* $\alpha = E(Z)$ *and* $\alpha(n) = E[Z(n)]$.

(i) $Z(n) \Rightarrow Z$ *as* $n \to \infty$.
(ii) $E\left[Z^2(n)\right] \to E(Z^2) < \infty$ *as* $n \to \infty$.
(iii) $\alpha(n) = \alpha + \beta n^{-p} + o(n^{-p})$ *as* $n \to \infty$, *where* $\beta \neq 0$ *and* $p > 0$.

Conditions (i) and (ii) will be sufficient for an application of the Central Limit Theorem. In our application, p is the order of convergence of the discretization scheme and β is a coefficient of the bias of the estimator $\alpha(n)$. For a sequence x_n of nonzero real numbers, the property "$o(x_n)$" means simply that $o(x_n)/x_n$ converges with n to zero. In our application, n is the number of time periods per sample path.

Consider the estimator for $E(Z)$ given by

$$a_n = \frac{1}{k_n} \sum_{i=1}^{k_n} Z_i(n),$$

where $Z_1(n), Z_2(n), \ldots$ is an *i.i.d.* sequence of random variables with the same distribution as $Z(n)$, and k_n is a postive integer that may depend on n. In our application, k_n is the number of sample paths simulated, given n. For our application, the amount of computer resources used to compute a_n is proportional to nk_n. The following result shows that as this computing budget grows to infinity, the approximation error $z_n = a_n - \alpha$ has an asymptotically normal distribution provided k_n grows with n like n^{2p}. If k_n does not grow at this rate, then the asymptotic distribution is "infinite," meaning a loss in efficiency. For instance, with the Euler scheme ($p = 1$), the number of simulations should quadruple (at least asymptotically) with each doubling of the number of time intervals. With a second-order scheme such as (18), the number of simulations should be on the order of the number of time intervals to the fourth power, and so on. Sharper results concerning the asymptotic distribution can be found with the original source for this result, cited in the Notes.

Theorem. *Suppose Condition A holds.*

(A) *If* $k_n/n^{2p} \to +\infty$ *or if* $k_n/n^{2p} \to 0$ *as* $nk_n \to \infty$, *then*

$$(k_n n)^{p/(1+2p)} |a_n - \alpha| \Rightarrow +\infty. \tag{10}$$

(B) *If* k_n/n^{2p} *converges to a nonzero constant* c *as* $nk_n \to \infty$, *then*

$$(k_n n)^{p/(1+2p)} (a_n - \alpha) \Rightarrow \frac{\sigma}{C^{1/2}} W + \beta C^p, \tag{11}$$

where $C = c^{1/(1+2p)}$, W *is standard normal, and* $\sigma^2 = \mathrm{var}(Z)$.

Proof: Note that

$$a_n - \alpha = \frac{1}{k_n} \sum_{i=1}^{k_n} \widehat{Z}_i(n) + \alpha(n) - \alpha,$$

where $\widehat{Z}_i(n) = Z_i(n) - \alpha(n)$. Then,

$$(k_n n)^{p/(1+2p)} (a_n - \alpha) = (k_n n)^{p/(1+2p)} k_n^{-1/2} \left(\sum_{i=1}^{k_n} \frac{\widehat{Z}_i(n)}{\sqrt{k_n}} \right)$$

$$+ (k_n n)^{p/(1+2p)} (\alpha(n) - \alpha).$$

Parts (i) and (ii) of Condition A allow an application of the Lindeberg-Feller Central Limit Theorem (Appendix C). Thus, as $n \to \infty$,

$$\sum_{i=1}^{k_n} \frac{\widehat{Z}_i(n)}{\sqrt{k_n}} \Rightarrow \sigma W,$$

where W is standard normal and $\sigma^2 = \mathrm{var}(Z)$. Applying part (iii) of Condition A and some algebra completes the proof. ∎

G. Estimation of the Feynman-Kac Pricing Solution

Consider the solution given by (5.40) for the price $C(x,0)$ of a derivative asset paying $g(S_T)$ at time T, where S is defined by (5.34) and where the short rate at time t is given by $r(S_t, t)$. To repeat, we have

$$C(x,0) = E[Y_T g(Z_T)], \tag{12}$$

where $Y_t = \exp[\int_0^t -r(Z_s, s)\, ds]$ and where

$$dZ_t = r(Z_t, t) Z_t\, dt + \sigma(Z_t, t)\, dB_t; \qquad Z_0 = x.$$

Since $dY_t = -r(Z_t, t)Y_t \, dt$, the $\mathbb{R}^{N+1}$-valued process X defined by $X_t = (Y_t, Z_t)$ solves an SDE of the same form as (6). We assume that the associated coefficient functions a and b satisfy the technical regularity conditions imposed with (6) of Section 11D. This calls for r to be bounded with bounded derivatives of every order and for σ to have bounded derivatives of every order. The Feynman-Kac solution (12) can be written in the form $E[f(X_T)]$, where $f : \mathbb{R}^{N+1} \to \mathbb{R}$ is defined by $f(y, z_1, \ldots, z_N) = yg(z_1, \ldots, z_N)$. If g has bounded derivatives of every order, then the derivative asset price $C(x, 0)$ can be approximated as suggested in the previous section. (Weaker conditions will suffice.)

The case of options requires special handling. The payoff function g of a call, defined by $g(x) = (x - K)^+$, is not even once differentiable. The "kink" at K is the only issue to overcome. The function g can be satisfactorily approximated by g_α, where, for any $\alpha > 0$,

$$g_\alpha(x) = \frac{x - K + \sqrt{(x - K)^2 + \alpha}}{2}. \tag{13}$$

Indeed, g_α has continuous derivatives of any order, satisfies a growth condition, and converges uniformly and monotonically from above to g as $\alpha \to 0$. The Dominated Convergence Theorem therefore implies that the associated Feynman-Kac solution also converges to $C(x, 0)$ as $\alpha \to 0$.

H. Finite-Difference Methods

This section reviews a simple finite-difference method for the PDE associated with asset prices. After reviewing the basic idea, we will work out an example based on the Cox-Ingersoll-Ross model of the term structure.

We will treat the *Cauchy problem*: Given real-valued functions r, g, h, μ, and σ on $\mathbb{R} \times [0, T]$, find a function f in $C^{2,1}(\mathbb{R} \times [0, T))$ solving

$$\mathcal{D}f(x, t) - r(x, t)f(x, t) + h(x, t) = 0, \qquad (x, t) \in \mathbb{R} \times [0, T), \tag{14}$$

with boundary condition

$$f(x, T) = g(x, T), \qquad x \in \mathbb{R}, \tag{15}$$

where

$$\mathcal{D}f(x, t) = f_t(x, t) + f_x(x, t)\mu(x, t) + \frac{1}{2}\sigma(x, t)^2 f_{xx}(x, t).$$

As we have seen in Chapter 5, we can interpret the solution f to (14)–(15) as the arbitrage-free market value of a security that promises the dividend rate $h(x, t)$ at time t when the state is x, assuming that the security has a terminal value of $g(x, T)$ at time T when the state is x. The short rate is $r(x, t)$ at time t when the state is x, and the "primitive" securities have prices and dividends determining the functions μ and σ in the manner described in Chapter 5. Alternatively, μ and σ could be determined directly from the equilibrium approach shown in Chapter 10 (see Exercise 10.7). Regularity conditions that ensure the existence and uniqueness of solutions are treated in Appendix E, where probabilistic Feynman-Kac solutions are also treated.

The basic idea of the finite-difference method for solving (14)–(15) is to choose a *grid*

$$\{(x_i, t_j) : i \in \{1, \ldots, N\}, \ j \in \{1, \ldots, M\}\} \subset \mathbb{R} \times [0, T],$$

and to find an approximate solution of (14)–(15) in the form of an $N \times M$ matrix F whose (i, j)-element F_{ij} is to be an approximation of $f(x_i, t_j)$. We always take $t_1 = 0$ and $t_M = T$. We take constants Δx and Δt to define the *mesh sizes* of the grid, so that $x_i - x_{i-1} = \Delta x$ for all $i > 1$ and $t_j - t_{j-1} = \Delta t$ for all $j > 1$, as depicted in Figure 11.1. In principle, increasing the number N of space points or $M = T/\Delta t$ of time points increases the accuracy of the approximation, although the convergence and stability properties of finite-difference methods can be a delicate issue. Various finite-difference methods could be suitable for the Cauchy problem, depending on the properties of (μ, σ, r, h, g). We will merely describe one of these, sometimes known as the *Crank-Nicholson method*, which has reasonable properties. We leave a characterization of the accuracy and stability of this and other finite-difference schemes to sources cited in the Notes.

The basis of the Crank-Nicholson method is the following approximation of the derivatives of f given F:

$$f_t(x_i, t_j) \sim \frac{F_{i,j+1} - F_{ij}}{\Delta t}$$

$$f_x(x_i, t_j) \sim \frac{F_{i+1,j+1} - F_{i-1,j+1} + F_{i+1,j} - F_{i-1,j}}{4\Delta x}$$

$$f_{xx}(x_i, t_j) \sim \frac{F_{i+1,j+1} - 2F_{i,j+1} + F_{i-1,j+1} + F_{i+1,j} - 2F_{ij} + F_{i-1,j}}{2(\Delta x)^2}.$$

It may be seen that the Crank-Nicholson method actually takes $(F_{i,j+1} + F_{i,j})/2$ as our approximation of $f(x_i, t_j)$. Accordingly, as we substitute these approximations of the derivatives of f into (14), we obtain at (x_i, t_j), for $1 < i < N$, the expression

$$a_{ij}F_{i-1,j} + b_{ij}F_{ij} + c_{ij}F_{i+1,j} = -a_{ij}F_{i-1,j+1} - \beta_{ij}F_{i,j+1} - c_{ij}F_{i+1,j+1} + e_{ij}, \quad (16)$$

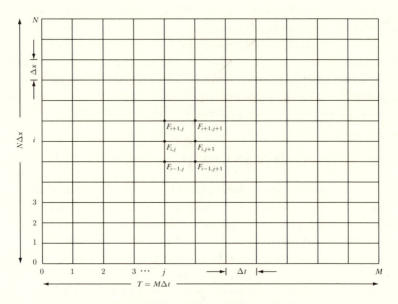

Figure 11.1.   *A Finite-Difference Grid*

where

$$a_{ij} = -\frac{\mu(x_i, t_j)}{4\Delta x} + \frac{\sigma(x_i, t_j)^2}{4(\Delta x)^2}$$

$$b_{ij} = -\frac{r(x_i, t_j)}{2} - \frac{1}{\Delta t} - \frac{\sigma(x_i, t_j)^2}{2(\Delta x)^2}$$

$$c_{ij} = \frac{\mu(x_i, t_j)}{4\Delta x} + \frac{\sigma(x_i, t_j)^2}{4(\Delta x)^2}$$

$$\beta_{ij} = -\frac{1}{\Delta t} + \frac{\sigma(x_i, t_j)^2}{2(\Delta x)^2} + \frac{r(x_i, t_j)}{2}$$

$$e_{ij} = -h(x_i, t_j).$$

Of course, (16) is not defined at $i = 1$ or $i = N$, for which we substitute with
equations of the form

$$b_{1j}F_{1j} + c_{1j}F_{2j} = d_{1j}; \qquad a_{Nj}F_{N-1,j} + b_{Nj}F_{Nj} = d_{Nj}, \tag{17}$$

for suitable coefficients b_{1j}, c_{1j}, d_{1j}, a_{Nj}, b_{Nj}, and d_{Nj} that may depend on the
particular problem at hand.

We can combine (16) and (17) to obtain a backward difference equation for the columns $F_1, F_2, \ldots, F_M$ of F, given by

$$A_j F_j = d_j, \tag{18}$$

with terminal boundary condition

$$F_{iM} = g(x_i, T), \qquad i \in \{1, \ldots, N\}, \tag{19}$$

where A_j is the *tridiagonal matrix* given by

$$A_j = \begin{pmatrix} b_{1j} & c_{1j} & 0 & 0 & 0 & \cdots & 0 \\ a_{2j} & b_{2j} & c_{2j} & 0 & 0 & \cdots & 0 \\ 0 & a_{3j} & b_{3j} & c_{3j} & 0 & \cdots & 0 \\ 0 & 0 & a_{4j} & b_{4j} & c_{4j} & \cdots & 0 \\ \vdots & & & & \ddots & & \vdots \\ 0 & \cdots & 0 & 0 & a_{N-1,j} & b_{N-1,j} & c_{N-1,j} \\ 0 & \cdots & 0 & 0 & 0 & a_{Nj} & b_{Nj} \end{pmatrix} \tag{20}$$

and where $d_j \in \mathbb{R}^N$ is the vector with i-th element

$$d_{ij} = -a_{ij}F_{i-1,j+1} + \beta_{ij}F_{i,j+1} - c_{ij}F_{i+1,j+1} + e_{ij}, \qquad 1 < i < N. \tag{21}$$

Standard algorithms for solving linear equations of the tridiagonal form (18) can be found in off-the-shelf software packages. (Code is provided in Appendix G.) Such algorithms exploit the special structure of A_j, avoiding a "brute-force" calculation of its inverse.

To summarize, the basic finite-difference algorithm (18)–(19) begins by fixing F_M according to the terminal boundary condition (19). Then d_{M-1} is computed from F_M by (21). Then F_{M-1} is computed by solving the tridiagonal equation (18) with $j = M - 1$. Next d_{M-2} is computed from F_{M-1}, (18) is solved for F_{M-2}, and so on, until F_1 is solved. If the functions μ, σ, and r do not depend on the time parameter, then the matrix A_j does not depend on j, and can be computed once before the backward difference solution is propagated. The boundary equations given by (17) usually call for special treatment.

Sources indicated in the Notes treat finite-difference methods for more than one state variable. The number of computations grows exponentially with the number of state variables, as opposed to the linear growth of computations with the Monte Carlo approach. The finite-difference approach can also be more difficult to implement, and its convergence is a more delicate issue. For problems with one or two state variables, however, it is typically the case that the finite-difference approach requires fewer computations in total than the Monte Carlo approach in order to obtain similar accuracy.

I. A Finite-Difference Term-Structure Example

Consider a model for the short rate r given by the stochastic differential equation

$$dr_t = \mu(r_t, t)\, dt + \sigma(r_t, t)\, d\widehat{B}_t; \qquad r_0 \geq 0, \tag{22}$$

where $\widehat{B}$ is a standard Brownian motion under an equivalent martingale measure and where μ and σ satisfy regularity conditions.

Consider the problem of solving for the term structure. For a given time T and any $t < T$, we would like to solve for the price $f(x, t)$ of a security paying one unit of account at time T, when the current time is t and the current short rate is x. Since the short rate is itself the state variable x, and since there are no intermediate dividends to consider, the PDE (14) specializes to

$$\mathcal{D}f(x, t) - xf(x, t) = 0, \tag{23}$$

with boundary condition

$$f(x, T) = 1, \qquad x \in \mathbb{R}. \tag{24}$$

If the functions μ and σ do not depend on t, we can also view $f(x, t)$ as the price at time zero for a unit bond maturing at $T - t$, so the solution of (23)–(24) characterizes the entire term structure up to maturity T.

It would be easy to implement the finite-difference algorithm (18)–(19) directly, although practical considerations often suggest a change of state variables. For example, suppose that μ and σ are continuous and that for all t, we have $\mu(0, t) \geq 0$ and $\sigma(0, t) = 0$. Then the solution of (22) is nonnegative, as indicated in the Notes of Chapter 7. In that case, we can treat the original state space as $[0, \infty)$, and consider a change of state variables, which has been used in the literature cited in the Notes, given by a function $Y : [0, \infty) \to (0, 1]$, with

$$Y(x) = \frac{1}{1 + \gamma x}, \qquad x \in [0, \infty) \tag{25}$$

for some $\gamma > 0$. In other words, the short rate x corresponds to a new state $y = Y(x)$.

We can extend the range of Y to $[0, 1]$ by treating $Y(+\infty)$ as 0. A grid

$$\big\{ (y_i, t_j) : i \in \{1, \ldots, N\}, \ j \in \{1, \ldots, M\} \big\} \subset [0, 1] \times [0, T],$$

with fixed mesh size Δy in the new state variable generates a solution with varying mesh size in the old short-rate state variable x, and with greater grid point concentration at lower interest-rate levels, in a fashion dictated by the coefficient γ. This may be a desirable feature of this change of variables. We take $y_1 = 0$ and $y_N = 1$.

Inverting (25), we can write the short rate as a function of the new state variable given by

$$X(y) = \frac{1-y}{\gamma y}, \qquad y \in (0,1].$$

If we let $\widehat{f}(y, t) = f[X(y), t]$ for all y and t, the PDE (23)–(24) may be written

$$\widehat{Df}(y, t) - X(y)\widehat{f}(y, t) = 0; \qquad \widehat{f}(y, T) = 1, \tag{26}$$

where

$$\widehat{Df}(y, t) = \widehat{f}_y(y, t)\widehat{\mu}(y, t) + \widehat{f}_t(y, t) + \frac{1}{2}\widehat{\sigma}(y, t)^2\widehat{f}_{yy}(y, t),$$

and where, using Ito's Lemma,

$$\widehat{\mu}(y, t) = Y'[X(y)]\mu[X(y), t] + \frac{1}{2}Y''[X(y)]\sigma[X(y), t]^2$$

$$\widehat{\sigma}(y, t) = Y'[X(y)]\sigma[X(y), t].$$

The value equation (26) also applies for other well-behaved changes of variables given by some C^2 function Y with an inverse X. The Notes cite a source proposing a special change of variables with the property that $\widehat{\sigma} \equiv 1$, which has computational advantages.

Solving for an approximation F_{ij} to the bond price $f[X(y_i), t_j]$ is now easily accomplished by the Crank-Nicholson solution (18)–(19) corresponding to (26). Throughout, we take $F_{1j} = 0$, corresponding to a zero bond price at an "infinite" interest rate. This determines the boundary equation of (17) for $i = 1$. For $i = N$, we use the fact that $\sigma(0, t) = 0$ and evaluate (26) at $y = 1$ $(x = 0)$, leaving

$$\widehat{f}_y(1, t)\widehat{\mu}(1, t) + \widehat{f}_t(1, t) = 0.$$

Replacing the usual Crank-Nicholson approximation for $\widehat{f}_y(y_N, t_j)$ with the nonsymmetric approximation

$$\widehat{f}_y(y_N, t_j) \sim \frac{F_{N,j} - F_{N-1,j}}{\Delta y},$$

the boundary equations (17) are then specified by the coefficients $b_{1j} = 1$, $c_{1j} = 0$, $d_{1j} = 0$, and

$$a_{Nj} = -\frac{\widehat{\mu}(1)}{\Delta y}; \qquad b_{Nj} = -\frac{1}{\Delta t} + \frac{\widehat{\mu}(1)}{\Delta y}; \qquad d_{Nj} = -\frac{1}{\Delta t}F_{N,j+1}. \tag{27}$$

For a coupon bond, or any other security promising lump-sum payments during $[0, T]$, the finite-difference equation (18) should be replaced by

$$F_j = F_{j+} + D_j; \qquad A_j F_{j+} = d_j, \tag{18'}$$

where D_j is the vector in $\mathbb{R}^N$ whose i-th element is the lump-sum dividend paid at time t_j if the state is between $x_i - \Delta x/2$ and $x_i + \Delta x/2$, so that we can treat F_{j+} as the ex-dividend approximation and F_j as the cum-dividend approximation. Linear approximations could be made in the obvious fashion if the lump-sum payments do not occur exactly as suggested in terms of the grid points.

Table 11.1 shows the accuracy of this finite-difference scheme for zero-coupon bond prices for the CIR example

$$\mu(x, t) = A(\bar{x} - x); \qquad \sigma(x, t) = C\sqrt{x}, \tag{28}$$

where A, $\bar{x}$, and C are positive constants. The table shows the difference between the exact solution (whose explicit solution for this case is given in Chapter 7) and the approximate solution. This approximation error, as a fraction of the exact solution, is shown in Table 11.1, in parts per million. Computer code for this solution is given in Appendix G.

J. Finite-Difference Algorithms with Early Exercise Options

Suppose the security whose value is to be determined has an early exercise feature, so that at any time t the security can be exercised at a payoff of $g(x, t)$ if the state is x. For example, if the state x represents a primitive security price and the derivative security in question is an American put option at strike K, then $g(x, t) = (K - x)^+$ for all x and t, as discussed in Sections 7E and 7F. With an early exercise feature, it is natural to conjecture that the finite-difference algorithm given in the previous section can be adjusted merely by replacing the backward difference step (18) with

$$F_{ij} = \max\left[\widehat{F}_{ij}, g(x_i, t_j) \right], \qquad i \in \{1, \ldots, N\}, \tag{29}$$

where $\widehat{F}_j$ is the vector in $\mathbb{R}^N$ solving $A_j \widehat{F}_j = d_j$. In other words, at each step, the value of the American security is taken to be the larger of its exercised value and its unexercised value, in line with the anlaysis of Section 3G. Computer code for bond-option prices, based on this algorithm, is shown in Appendix G.

A delicate issue is the convergence, and rate of convergence, of this algorithm (29) to the solution of the associated continuous-time optimal

Table 11.1. *Numerical Error (parts per million)*
of Crank-Nicholson Algorithm for CIR Bond Pricing

Number of State Points	Number of Time Points		
	40	80	160
40	176	186	188
80	35	44	46
120	8	18	20
160	−1	9	11
200	−5	4	6
240	−7	2	4

The instrument priced is a 10-year 7 percent coupon Treasury bond (that is, with semi-annual coupons of 3.5 percent of par). The algorithm is the Crank-Nicholson finite-difference method described in the text. The coefficients used are $A = 0.5$, $\bar{x} = 0.0719$ and $C = 0.1664$. The short rate x is chosen so as to price the bond at par. The parameters are chosen so that, as measured in an instantaneous sense, the initial volatility of the treasury yield is 15 percent. The table shows the difference between the numerical estimate of the bond price and the theoretical price, as a fraction of the theoretical price, in parts per million.

stopping problem that is shown in Section 7E to characterize the American security's true arbitrage-free value. Some of the literature dealing with this convergence issue is cited in the Notes.

K. The Numerical Solution of State Prices

Returning to the setting of the PDE (14)–(15) for security valuation, suppose there are many different securities to be valued, all based on the same functions r, μ, and σ. Only the functions h and g differ from security to security. In this case, given a grid $\{(x_i, t_j)\}$ defined by mesh sizes Δx and Δt, it makes sense to find an approximation Ψ_{ij} of the market value at time 0 of a security that pays $1/\Delta x$ units of account at time t_j in the event that the state is between $x_i + \Delta x/2$ and $x_i - \Delta x/2$. With this, it is reasonable to approximate the market value at time 0 of the security with payoff functions *h* for dividend rate and *g* for terminal value by

$$V(h, g) \equiv \Delta t \Delta x \sum_{j=1}^{M} \left[\sum_{i=1}^{N} \Psi_{ij} h(x_i, t_j) \right] + \Delta x \sum_{i=1}^{N} \Psi_{iM} \, g(x_i, T). \tag{30}$$

We will show how the same finite-difference approach used to calculate *F* in Section H can be modified to calculate the "approximate state prices" specified by Ψ. This is based on the fundamental solution, or "Green's function," of the PDE (14), reviewed in Appendix E. Under technical conditions, for each initial state x^* in $\mathbb{R}$, there is a function $\psi \in C^{2,1}(\mathbb{R} \times (0, T])$ with the following (almost equivalent) properties:

(a) ψ satisfies

$$\mathcal{D}^* \psi(x, t) - r(x, t)\psi(x, t) = 0, \qquad (x, t) \in \mathbb{R} \times (0, T], \tag{31}$$

where

$$\mathcal{D}^* \psi(x, t) = -\psi_t(x, t) - \frac{\partial}{\partial x} \left[\psi(x, t)\mu(x, t) \right] + \frac{1}{2} \frac{\partial^2}{\partial x^2} \left[\sigma(x, t)^2 \psi(x, t) \right],$$

with an initial boundary condition requiring essentially that $\psi(\cdot, t)$ is the density of a measure that converges as $t \to 0$ to a probability measure ν with $\nu(\{x^*\}) = 1$; and

(b) for any (g, h) satisfying technical conditions, the solution f of the PDE (14)–(15) satisfies

$$f(x^*, 0) = \int_0^T \int_{-\infty}^{+\infty} \psi(x, t)h(x, t) \, dx \, dt + \int_{-\infty}^{+\infty} \psi(x, T)g(x, T) \, dx, \tag{32}$$

which is the integral analogous to the sum given by (30).

The PDE (31) is sometimes called the *Fokker-Planck equation*, or the forward Kolmogorov equation, to distinguish it from the backward Kolmogorov equation (14). For the case $r \equiv 0$, one can literally treat $\psi(\cdot, t)$ as the probability density of X_t, where X solves the underlying stochastic differential equation $dX_t = \mu(X_t, t) \, dt + \sigma(X_t, t) \, dB_t$, with $X_0 = x^*$. Much more can be said on this point, as indicated in sources cited in the Notes. The initial boundary condition for (31) stated above corresponds naturally to this interpretation of ψ. An explicit solution for ψ for the Cox-Ingersoll-Ross model (28) is given in Section 7I.

Now, given (32) and the equivalence between (a) and (b), in order to solve for $f(x^*, 0)$ we would like to approximate ψ with a finite-difference solution Ψ of the PDE (31). The same Crank-Nicholson approach can be applied, generating the forward difference equation for the columns $\Psi_1, \Psi_2, \ldots, \Psi_M$ of Ψ given by

$$A_j^* \Psi_j = d_j^*, \tag{33}$$

with boundary condition for a given initial state $x_k = x^*$ of

$$\Psi_{k1} = \frac{1}{\Delta x}; \qquad \Psi_{i1} = 0, \qquad i \neq k, \tag{34}$$

where the tridiagonal matrix A_j^* and the vector d_j^* can be calculated for each j in the same manner as for the backward difference equation, using the Crank-Nicholson approximations for the derivatives of ψ in terms of Ψ. Specifically, for σ twice continuously differentiable with respect to x and μ continuously differentiable with respect to x, we have

$$d_{ij}^* = -a_{ij}^* \Psi_{i-1,j-1} + \beta_{ij}^* \Psi_{i,j-1} - c_{ij}^* \Psi_{i+1,j-1} \tag{35}$$

and

$$A_j^* = \begin{pmatrix} b_{1j}^* & c_{1j}^* & 0 & 0 & 0 & \cdots & 0 \\ a_{2j}^* & b_{2j}^* & c_{2j}^* & 0 & 0 & \cdots & 0 \\ 0 & a_{3j}^* & b_{3j}^* & c_{3j}^* & 0 & \cdots & 0 \\ 0 & 0 & a_{4j}^* & b_{4j}^* & c_{4j}^* & \cdots & 0 \\ \vdots & & & & & \ddots & \vdots \\ 0 & \cdots & 0 & 0 & a_{N-1,j}^* & b_{N-1,j}^* & c_{N-1,j}^* \\ 0 & \cdots & 0 & 0 & 0 & a_{Nj}^* & b_{Nj}^* \end{pmatrix}, \tag{36}$$

where

$$a_{ij}^* = \frac{\mu(x_i, t_j) - 2\sigma(x_i, t_j)\sigma_x(x_i, t_j)}{4\Delta x} + \frac{\sigma(x_i, t_j)^2 + 2\sigma_x(x_i, t_j)\sigma(x_i, t_j)}{4(\Delta x)^2}$$

$$b_{ij}^* = -\frac{1}{\Delta t} - \frac{\sigma(x_i, t_j)^2 + 2\sigma_x(x_i, t_j)\sigma(x_i, t_j)}{2(\Delta x)^2}$$

$$c_{ij}^* = \frac{2\sigma(x_i, t_j)\sigma_x(x_i, t_j) - \mu(x_i, t_j)}{4\Delta x} + \frac{\sigma(x_i, t_j)^2 + 2\sigma_x(x_i, t_j)\sigma(x_i, t_j)}{4(\Delta x)^2}$$

$$\beta_{ij}^* = r(x_i, t_j) + \mu_x(x_i, t_j) - 2\sigma_{xx}(x_i, t_j)\sigma(x_i, t_j) - 2\sigma_x^2(x_i, t_j) - \frac{1}{\Delta t}$$
$$+ \frac{\sigma(x_i, t_j)^2}{2(\Delta x)^2}.$$

The cases of $i = 1$ and $i = N$ again require special consideration.

One begins with the initial condition (34) for Ψ_1, and then propagates the solution forward, calculating Ψ_j at each stage by (33), given d_j^* in terms of Ψ_{j-1}.

Given Ψ, the approximate value of any security with dividend rate h and terminal value g is given by (30). If there is but a single security to value, equation (30) involves an extra set of computations that is not required with the backward approach. With many securities to value, however, the "forward approach" can involve significant savings in computations.

The astute reader will notice that we could have avoided the scaling factors Δx and $1/\Delta x$ in (30) and (34), respectively, in which case Ψ would not be an approximation for ψ, but rather for $\Delta x \psi$.

L. Numerical Solution of the Pricing Semi-Group

In the tridiagonal system (33)–(35), we have $d_j^* = C_j^* \Psi_{j-1}$ for the tridiagonal matrix

$$
C_j^* = \begin{pmatrix}
\beta_{1j}^* & -c_{1j}^* & 0 & 0 & 0 & \cdots & 0 \\
-a_{2j}^* & \beta_{2j}^* & -c_{2j}^* & 0 & 0 & \cdots & 0 \\
0 & -a_{3j}^* & \beta_{3j}^* & -c_{3j}^* & 0 & \cdots & 0 \\
0 & 0 & -a_{4j}^* & \beta_{4j}^* & -c_{4j}^* & \cdots & 0 \\
\vdots & & & & \ddots & & \vdots \\
0 & \cdots & 0 & 0 & -a_{N-1,j}^* & \beta_{N-1,j}^* & -c_{N-1,j}^* \\
0 & \cdots & 0 & 0 & 0 & -a_{Nj}^* & \beta_{Nj}^*
\end{pmatrix}.
$$

Thus (33) can be reexpressed in the recursive form

$$
\Psi_j = \Pi_j \Psi_{j-1}, \tag{37}
$$

where $\Pi_j = (A_j^*)^{-1} C_j^*$. It follows that for any j and $k \geq j$,

$$
\Psi_k = \Pi_{jk} \Psi_j, \tag{38}
$$

where

$$
\Pi_{jk} = \Pi_{j+1} \Pi_{j+2} \cdots \Pi_k, \tag{39}
$$

and where Π_{jj} denotes the identity matrix. The collection $\Pi = \{\Pi_{jk} : 1 \leq j \leq k \leq M\}$ of $N \times N$ matrices is a semi-group since it has the property: Whenever $j \leq k \leq m$, we have $\Pi_{jm} = \Pi_{jk} \Pi_{km}$. We will describe some of the useful properties of the semi-group Π.

First, for any initial state x_k in the grid, the associated approximate state-price matrix Ψ is given by

$$\Psi_j = \Pi_{1j}\Psi_1, \tag{40}$$

where Ψ_1 is given by (34). This means that given the semi-group Π, the state prices associated with any given initial state can be obtained without repeated solution of the tridiagonal equations (37).

Second, given any payoff functions h and g, the $N \times M$ matrix F^* approximating the solution f to (14)–(15) is easily characterized as follows. For any j and $k \geq j$, we have

$$F_j^* = \Pi_{jk}F_k^* + \sum_{m=j+1}^{k} \Pi_{jm}H_m, \tag{41}$$

where H_j is the vector in $\mathbb{R}^N$ with $h(x_i, t_j)\Delta t$ as its i-th element. In particular, (41) applies with $k = M$ and the boundary condition $F_{iM}^* = g(x_i, T)$.

Although solving for the semi-group Π can be computationally intensive, there are obvious compensations. For the case in which μ, σ, and r do not depend on t, the matrices A_j^* and C_j^* do not depend on j, so there is but a single matrix $\overline{\Pi}$ to compute, with $\Pi_j = \overline{\Pi}$ for all j.

The close parallel between (41) and the Markov chain valuation equation (3.17) is not an accident. One can indeed approximate the solution X to the SDE $dX_t = \mu(X_t, t)\,dt + \sigma(X_t, t)\,dB_t$ with that of an N-state Markov chain having transition matrix $q^{(j)}$ at period $j \in \{1, \ldots, M\}$ given by

$$q_{ik}^{(j)} = [1 + r(x_i, t_j)\Delta t]\Pi_{ik}. \tag{42}$$

A source given in the Notes gives the sense of this approximation and further details on this connection between continuous and discrete pricing.

The parallel with the discrete-time case extends to the pricing of American securities. Using the semi-group approach, one can replace the backward difference equation (22) for the American security described in Section 10I with the backward equation

$$F_j^* = \max\left[\Pi_{j+1}(F_{j+1} + H_{j+1}), G_j\right], \tag{43}$$

where the maximum is taken element-wise and where G_j is the vector in $\mathbb{R}^N$ whose i-th element is $g(x_i, t_j)$. Equation (3.21) gives the exact discrete-time version of this American valuation algorithm. Since (43) is simpler than (29), computation of the semi-group Π may be worth the effort if one wishes to price many different American securities.

M. Numerically Fitting the Initial Term Structure

In the context of the term-structure model (22), there are many practical applications in which the initial term structure is given from market data in the form of a vector p in $\mathbb{R}^N$, with p_j denoting the price at time 0 of a unit pure discount bond maturing at t_j. (In practice, p is often obtained from the prices of coupon bonds by spline methods, some cited in the Notes of Chapter 7.) Since a model rarely coincides with reality, the functions μ and σ determining the risk-neutral behavior of the short rate will not, in general, generate a term structure consistent with the market data p. Suppose, however, that for each t, the functions $\mu(\cdot, t)$ and $\sigma(\cdot, t)$ depend on a free parameter $\lambda(t)$. One can imagine choosing the function λ in order to match the solution of the term structure to that given by p. For example, one could extend the CIR model (28) by replacing the constant $\overline{x}$ with $\lambda(t)$, and then choose $\lambda(t_1), \lambda(t_2), \ldots, \lambda(t_M)$ so that the solution given in Section I for the term structure is consistent with p.

One can imagine a number of different numerical approaches to this term-structure matching procedure. One that has been suggested by a source cited in the Notes is based on the numerical solution Ψ for state prices. Using the fact that $\sum_{i=1}^{N} \Psi_{ij}$ approximates p_j, the proposed algorithm for λ is given by the following steps:

(a) Let $j = 2$.

(b) Search for that number $\lambda(t_j)$ such that given Ψ_{j-1}, we have

$$\widehat{p}_j[\lambda(t_j), \Psi_{j-1}] = p_j, \tag{44}$$

where $\widehat{p}_j[\lambda(t_j), \Psi_{j-1}] = \sum_{i=1}^{N} \Psi_j$ is notation indicating the dependence of the solution Ψ_j of (33) on Ψ_{j-1} and $\lambda(t_j)$ given by (35) and (36). This one-dimensional search could be conducted by a Newton-Raphson iterative method.

(c) Let j be increased by 1, and return to step (b) if $j \leq M$. Otherwise, stop.

In order for the numerical search for $\lambda(t_j)$ in step (44) to succeed, and for the solution to be uniquely defined, the model should be such that $\widehat{p}_j(\cdot, \Psi_{j-1})$ is a strictly monotonic continuous function with range $(0, 1)$. This is true for the CIR example given above, in which $\overline{x}$ is replaced in (28) with $\lambda(t)$.

One could match additional parameters to market data on the prices of derivative securities, such as options. The idea is to obtain better "calibration" with the market in order, in principle, to obtain higher accuracy in the pricing of derivative securities. For example, one can extend by taking

λ to be an $\mathbb{R}^2$-valued function specifying 2 free parameters, to be matched against the initial term structure of bond prices as well as the initial "volatility structure" implicit in bond-option prices, an approach taken in papers cited in the Notes.

Of course, with the passage of time, the "matched" model will fall out of calibration, implying that the free parameter vector λ was in fact inappropriate. In typical practice, a new set of free parameters is chosen, and valuation proceeds again. This process of routine reparameterization is theoretically inconsistent (and, to the author's knowledge, has been applied with relatively little econometric sophistication), but seems to some degree unavoidable. The "name of the game" is apparently to specify an accurate term-structure model that is both tractable and relatively stable over time.

Exercises

11.1 Prove Proposition 11A, using the Lindeberg-Feller Central Limit Theorem given in Appendix C.

11.2 Show, as claimed in Section B, that the per-unit-of-time risk-neutralized mean M_n and variance V_n converge to $r - \sigma^2/2$ and σ^2, respectively.

11.3 Show that the sequence $\{[xe^{\rho(n)} - K]^+\}$ of "binomial" call-option payoffs constructed in Section C is uniformly integrable. Hint: Use the converse part of Theorem 11C.

11.4 Show how the Lindeberg-Feller Central Limit Theorem is invoked in order to obtain the limiting Normal distribution asserted in the proof of Theorem 11F.

11.5 Verify the Crank-Nicholson equation (16) from (14) and the Crank-Nicholson derivative approximations.

11.6 (Binomial Approximation of Black-Derman-Toy Term-Structure Model) The continuous-time version of the Black-Derman-Toy model shown in Exercise 7.2 has the short-rate process r given by

$$r_t^c = U(t) \exp\left[\beta(t)\widehat{B}(t)\right],$$

where $\widehat{B}$ is a standard Brownian motion under an equivalent martingale measure and where $U : [0, \infty) \to \mathbb{R}_{++}$ and $\beta : [0, \infty) \to \mathbb{R}_{++}$ are continuously differentiable. The discrete-time version of the Black-Derman-Toy model given in Exercise 3.12 has the short-rate process r given by $r_t^d = a_t \exp(b_t X_t)$, where, for each time $t \in \{0, 1, \ldots\}$, a_t and b_t are strictly positive constants, and X_t is a shock process with the property that under an equivalent martingale measure Q, we have, for all t,

$$Q\left(X_{t+1} - X_t = 1 \mid X_0, \ldots, X_t\right) = Q\left(X_{t+1} - X_t = 0 \mid X_0, \ldots, X_t\right) = \frac{1}{2}.$$

This exercise calls for the construction, at each t, of sequences $\{a_t^n\}$ and $\{b_t^n\}$ of coefficients for the discrete-time Black-Derman-Toy model with the property that for each $t \in \{1, 2, \ldots\}$,

$$r_t^n \equiv a_t^n \exp(b_t^n X_{tn}) \Rightarrow r_t^c,$$

or convergence in distribution of the discrete-time model with n time periods per unit of calendar time to the continuous-time model. Hint: Use the Continuous Mapping Theorem, and the fact that $z \mapsto U(t) \exp(\beta(t)z)$ defines a continuous function on $\mathbb{R}$ into $\mathbb{R}$. We can write

$$r_t^n = U(t) \exp\left[\beta_t \left(X_{tn} b_t^n - \log\left[\frac{a_t^n}{U(t)}\right]\right)\right].$$

Show that it is therefore enough to choose $\{a_t^n\}$ and $\{b_t^n\}$ so that

$$X_{tn} b_t^n - \log\left[\frac{a_t^n}{U(t)}\right] \Rightarrow Z,$$

where Z is normally distributed with mean zero and variance t. Make use of the Central Limit Theorem to design $\{a_t^n\}$ and $\{b_t^n\}$ accordingly.

Notes

Standard references on probability theory include Chung (1974), Chow and Teicher (1978), Billingsley (1986), and Durrett (1991), all of which include the law of large numbers and the Central Limit Theorem. The convergence of the binomial option-pricing formula to the Black-Scholes formula is due to Cox, Ross, and Rubinstein (1979). Extensions of this approach can be found in Amin (1991, 1993b), Cutland, Kopp, and Willinger (1991, 1993b), Duffie (1988b), Duffie and Protter (1988), Nelson and Ramaswamy (1989), Madan, Milne, and Shefrin (1989), Lee (1991), Cutland, Kopp, and Willinger (1991, 1993b), He (1990, 1991), Lamberton and Pagès (1990), Willinger and Tacqu (1991), and Eberlein (1991), among many other papers. For other numerical procedures, see Gerber and Shiu (1994) and Levy, Avellaneda, and Parás (1994).

Section 11D is based on Talay and Tubaro (1990). Milshtein (1974, 1978) introduced second-order schemes such as (8). Talay (1984, 1986, 1990) provides more complicated second-order schemes for discretization of stochastic differential equations in $\mathbb{R}^n$. See also Bernard, Talay, and Tubaro (1993), Chavella (1994), Newton (1990), and Török (1993) in this regard. Section 11F is based on Duffie and Glynn (1992), where additional details may be found. The first edition of this book took a different approach to the tradeoff between number of simulations and number of time steps, based on the Large Deviations Theorem, which is described by Durrett (1991). The smooth approximation g_α in Section 11G of the call payoff function appears in Duffie (1988b), and was related to the author by Stephen Smale. Various applications of the Monte Carlo estimation of derivative asset prices are given by Barraquand (1993), Boyle (1977, 1988, 1990), Boyle, Evnine, and Gibbs (1989), Fournie (1993), and Jones and Jacobs (1986). For the simulation of hedging coefficients, or "deltas" and other derivatives, see Clelow and Carverhill (1992), Broadie and Glasserman (1993), and Kat (1993a). Joy and Boyle (1994) present a "quasi-Monte Carlo" method, with a finance application. Marcet (1993) and Marcet and Marshall (1994) apply Monte Carlo methods to the numerical solution of equilibrium asset pricing in discrete-time economies.

Mitchell and Griffiths (1980), Smith (1985), and Strikwerda (1989) are basic treatments of the finite-difference solution of PDEs. Computer code for the solution of tridiagonal systems of equations such as (18) is given by Press, Flannery, Teukolsky, and Vetterling (1993). An example of a more advanced finite-difference approach is given by Lawson and Morris (1978). Schwartz (1977) introduced the use of finite-difference methods to the solution of asset pricing in finance. The term-structure example of Section 11I is based on Courtadon (1982) and Stanton (1990). Jamshidian (1991c) gives an alternate change of variables under which the diffusion is a constant. The literature in finance is reviewed and summarized by Clelow (1990). The Crank-Nicholson approximation is known as an *implicit* method. Hull and White (1990b) show how the range of the simpler *explicit* methods can be extended. Hull (1993) reviews some of the simpler implicit and explicit methods. Dewynne and Wilmott (1994) provide example applications to exotic options. Barles, Daher, and Romano (1992) examine the general issue of convergence of finite-difference schemes in finance applications. Nelson and Ramaswamy (1989) treat finite-difference methods that are based on replacing the underlying stochastic differential equation with a Markov chain that has binomial transitions, extending the range of application of the binomial approach. Kishimoto (1989) and Stanton (1990), and Stanton and Wallace (1994) numerically solve "path-dependent" security prices, such as mortgage-backed securities. Dengler and Jarrow (1993) examine the implications of variable time steps in numerical option-pricing solutions.

Justification of the valuation algorithm (29) for securities with early exercise options is a delicate issue that is treated by Jaillet, Lamberton, and Lapeyre (1988, 1990). An early variation of this algorithm for the Black-Scholes (log-normal) put option problem is found in Brennan and Schwartz (1977). The methods of Chernoff and Petkau (1984) also give a practical, accurate numerical approximation to the American put value. For further results on the numerical valuation of American-style securities, see Ait Sahlia (1995), Amin (1991), Amin and Khanna (1994), Barraquand and Pudet (1994), Broadie and Detemple (1994), Bunch and Johnson (1993), Büttler (1993), Büttler and Waldvogel (1994), Carr (1994), Carr and Faguet (1994), Gandhi, Kooros, and Salkin (1993b), Lee (1990), and Zhang (1993).

The valuation of securities in terms of state prices also appears in the literature under such labels as *path integrals*, as in Dash (1989), or Green's function, as in Beaglehole (1990) and Beaglehole and Tenney (1990), who calculate the fundamental solution G explicitly for the Cox-Ingersoll-Ross model (28), or Jamshidian (1991c). The idea of using pricing semi-groups goes back at least to Garman (1985). See, also, Huang (1985c).

The issue of matching parameters to the initial term structure apparently originated with Ho and Lee (1986) in their "binomial" model of the term structure. Subsequent work in this vein can be found in Black, Derman, and Toy (1990), Dybvig (1988), Heath, Jarrow, and Morton (1990, 1992a,b), Hull and White (1990a, 1994), and Jamshidian (1991c). Further references are given in the Notes of Chapter 7. The Newton-Raphson search, and other numerical optimization techniques, can be found in Luenberger (1984) and Press, Flannery, Teukolsky, and Vetterling (1993).

An important topic that we have not treated is numerical solution of dynamic programming problems. Examples in the literature include Judd (1989), Tauchen and Hussey (1991), and Gagnon and Taylor (1986), who treat discrete-time models. Fitzpatrick and Fleming (1991), Fleming and Soner (1993), and Prigent (1994) treat convergence of optimal policies from discrete to continuous time using viscosity methods. A particular application involving a free boundary that arises with investment under durability is treated by Hindy, Huang, and Zhu (1993a,b).

Eydeland (1994a,b) provides alternative numerical methods for some of the derivative valuation problems addressed here. Bouleau and Lépingle (1994) is a general treatment of numerical methods for stochastic problems.

Appendixes

A

Probability—The Finite-State Case

SUPPOSE Ω is a finite set. A *tribe* on Ω is a collection $\mathcal{F}$ of subsets of Ω that includes the empty set $\emptyset$ and that satisfies the following two conditions:

(a) if B is in $\mathcal{F}$, then its *complement* $\{\omega \in \Omega : \omega \notin B\}$ is also in $\mathcal{F}$;

(b) if A and B are in $\mathcal{F}$, their union $A \cup B$ is in $\mathcal{F}$.

A tribe $\mathcal{F}$ is also known as an *algebra* or *field*, among other terms. When Ω is to be thought of as the states of the world, the elements of $\mathcal{F}$ are called *events*. Conditions (a) and (b) allow for simple logical rules regarding the probabilities of events. Specifically, a *probability measure* is a function $P : \mathcal{F} \rightarrow [0, 1]$ satisfying $P(\emptyset) = 0$, $P(\Omega) = 1$, and, for any disjoint events A and B,

$$P(A \cup B) = P(A) + P(B).$$

Under P, an event B has *probability* $P(B)$. A pair $(\Omega, \mathcal{F})$ consisting of a finite set Ω and a tribe $\mathcal{F}$ on Ω is called a measurable space. With the addition of a probability measure P on $\mathcal{F}$, the triple $(\Omega, \mathcal{F}, P)$ is a called a *probability space*.

Fixing a measurable space $(\Omega, \mathcal{F})$, a *random variable* is a function $X : \Omega \rightarrow \mathbb{R}$ with the following property: For any $x \in \mathbb{R}$, the set $\{\omega \in \Omega : X(\omega) = x\}$ is in $\mathcal{F}$. Intuitively, X is a random variable if, for any possible outcome x, we will know whether X has this outcome from knowing the outcomes (true or false) of the events in $\mathcal{F}$. If X is a random variable with respect to $(\Omega, \mathcal{F})$, we also say that X is $\mathcal{F}$-*measurable*.

Since Ω is finite, for any random variable X there are events $B_1, \ldots, B_n$ and some α in $\mathbb{R}^n$ such that $X = \alpha_1 1_{B_1} + \cdots + \alpha_n 1_{B_n}$, where the *indicator function* 1_B for an event B is defined by $1_B(\omega) = 1$ for ω in B, and $1_B(\omega) = 0$

otherwise. Given a probability measure P, the *expectation* of X is then defined by

$$E(X) = \alpha_1 P(B_1) + \cdots + \alpha_n P(B_n), \tag{A.1}$$

merely the probability-weighted average of the outcomes.

For a probability space $(\Omega, \mathcal{F}, P)$ with Ω finite, if $\mathcal{G}$ is a tribe on Ω that is contained by $\mathcal{F}$, then $\mathcal{G}$ represents in some sense "less information," and is known as a *sub-tribe* of $\mathcal{F}$. For any $\mathcal{F}$-measurable random variable X, the *conditional expectation* of X given a sub-tribe $\mathcal{G}$ of $\mathcal{F}$ is defined as any $\mathcal{G}$-measurable random variable Y, the property $E(XZ) = E(YZ)$ for any $\mathcal{G}$-measurable random variable Z. We let $E(X \mid \mathcal{G})$ denote this the conditional expectation. The *law of iterated expectations* states that if $\mathcal{G}$ is a sub-tribe of another sub-tribe $\mathcal{H}$, then for any random variable X, $E[E(X \mid \mathcal{H}) \mid \mathcal{G}] = E(X \mid \mathcal{G})$.

If Y is a nonnegative random variable with $E(Y) = 1$, then we can create a new probability measure Q from the old probability measure P by defining $Q(B) = E(1_B Y)$ for any event B. In this case, we write $\frac{dQ}{dP} = Y$, and call Y the *Radon-Nikodym derivative* of Q with respect to P. It also follows that for any random variable X,

$$E^Q(X) = E^P(YX),$$

where E^Q denotes expectation under Q, and likewise for E^P. If $Q(B) > 0$ whenever $P(B) > 0$, and vice versa, then P and Q are said to be *equivalent measures*; they have the same events of probability zero.

If $\mathcal{G}$ is a sub-tribe of $\mathcal{F}$ and Q is equivalent to P, then

$$E^Q(Z \mid \mathcal{G}) = \frac{1}{E^P(\xi \mid \mathcal{G})} E^P(\xi Z \mid \mathcal{G}), \tag{A.2}$$

where $\xi = \frac{dQ}{dP}$.

The tribe *generated* by a set Z of random variables is the smallest sub-tribe, often denoted $\sigma(Z)$, with respect to which each random variable in Z is measurable. It is enough to think of $\sigma(Z)$ as the set of events that can be ascertained as true or false by observing the outcomes of all of the random variables in Z.

Suppose there are multiple periods given by a set $\mathcal{T}$ of times such as $\{0, 1, \ldots, T\}$ or $\{0, 1, \ldots\}$. A *filtration* $\mathbb{F} = \{\mathcal{F}_t : t \in \mathcal{T}\}$ of sub-tribes of $\mathcal{F}$ is usually given, as described in Section 2A. We always assume that $\mathcal{F}_t \subset \mathcal{F}_s$ whenever $t \leq s$. Given $\mathbb{F}$, a *stopping time* is a random variable τ taking values in $\mathcal{T} \cup \{+\infty\}$ such that for any time t in $\mathcal{T}$, the event $\{\omega \in \Omega : \tau(\omega) \leq t\}$ is in $\mathcal{F}_t$. The event $\tau = +\infty$ is allowed for convenience. For example, if two processes X and Y are not the same, then the stopping time $\tau = \inf\{t :$

$X_t \neq Y_t$} has a strictly positive probability of being finite valued, but may also have a strictly positive probability of being $+\infty$. (We follow the usual convention that the infimum of the empty set is $+\infty$.) A stopping time τ is nontrivial if $P(\tau = +\infty) < 1$. A martingale can be defined as in Section 2A, or alternatively as any $\mathbb{F}$-adapted process X such that for any finite-valued stopping time τ, we have $E(X_\tau) = E(X_1)$.

The tribe $\mathcal{F}_\tau$ of events known at a finite-valued stopping time τ, allows us to define the conditional expectation $E_\tau(\cdot) \equiv E(\cdot \mid \mathcal{F}_\tau)$. We define $\mathcal{F}_\tau$ to include any event A with the property that for any time t, the event $A \cap \{\omega : \tau(\omega) \leq t\}$ is in $\mathcal{F}_t$.

A *supermartingale* is an adapted process X with the property that $X_t \geq E_t(X_s)$ for all t and $s \geq t$. It is known that a supermartingale X can be decomposed as the sum $X = M - A$, where M is a martingale and A is an increasing process with $A_0 = 0$. Likewise, a *submartingale* is an adapted process X with the property that $X_t \leq E_t(X_s)$ for all t and $s \geq t$. It is known that a submartingale X can be decomposed as the sum $X = M + A$, where M is a martingale and A is an increasing process with $A_0 = 0$.

B
Separating Hyperplanes and Optimality

THIS APPENDIX REVIEWS some applications of the following basic well-known result. Good basic references are Rockafellar (1970) and Luenberger (1984).

Separating Hyperplane Theorem. *Suppose that A and B are convex disjoint subsets of $\mathbb{R}^n$. There is some nonzero linear functional F such that $F(x) \leq F(y)$ for each x in A and y in B. Moreover, if x is in the interior of A or y is in the interior of B, then $F(x) < F(y)$.*

Our first application of the Separating Hyperplane Theorem is a special case for separation of cones that is applied in Theorem 1A.

Linear Separation of Cones. *Suppose M and K are closed convex cones in $\mathbb{R}^n$ that intersect precisely at zero. If K does not contain a linear subspace other than $\{0\}$, then there is a nonzero linear functional F such that $F(x) < F(y)$ for each x in M and each nonzero y in K.*

Proof: We can assume without loss of generality that $K \neq \{0\}$. We will show that the nonzero elements of K are contained by an open convex set J, disjoint with M. Then the result follows from the Separating Hyperplane Theorem.

Let C be the convex hull (that is, the set of all convex combinations) of $\{y \in K : \|y\| = 1\}$. Since K does not contain a nontrivial linear subspace, and since K and M are closed and intersect only at zero,

$$\epsilon \equiv \inf\{\|y + \widehat{y} - m\| : y \in K, \widehat{y} \in C, m \in M\} > 0.$$

Let

$$J = \{y + \lambda(\hat{y} + z) : y \in K, y \neq 0, \hat{y} \in C, \lambda \in (0, \infty), \|z\| < \epsilon\}.$$

It is easy to check that J is convex, open, and disjoint from M. ∎

Our next application of the Separating Hyperplane Theorem is the Saddle Point Theorem for optimality. A *concave program* is a triple (U, X, g) of the form

$$\sup_{x \in X} U(x) \qquad \text{subject to } g(x) \leq 0, \tag{B.1}$$

where X is a convex subset of some vector space, $U : X \to \mathbb{R}$ is concave, and $g : X \to \mathbb{R}^m$ is convex for some integer m. The *Lagrangian* for (U, X, g) is the function $\mathcal{L} : X \times \mathbb{R}^m_+ \to \mathbb{R}$ defined by $\mathcal{L}(x, \lambda) = U(x) - \lambda \cdot g(x)$. A pair (x_0, λ_0) in $X \times \mathbb{R}^m_+$ is a *saddle point* of $\mathcal{L}$ if, for all (x, λ) in $X \times \mathbb{R}^m_+$, we have $\mathcal{L}(x, \lambda_0) \leq \mathcal{L}(x_0, \lambda_0) \leq \mathcal{L}(x_0, \lambda)$. If (x_0, λ_0) is a saddle point, we often term λ_0 a *Lagrange multiplier* for problem (B.1). The following version of the conditions for optimality is proved with the Separating Hyperplane Theorem. The existence of some $\underline{x}$ in X with $g(\underline{x}) \ll 0$ is known as the *Slater condition*.

Saddle Point Theorem. *Let (U, X, g) be a concave program.*

  I. *(Necessity) Suppose the Slater condition is satisfied. If x_0 solves (B.1), then there exists $\lambda_0 \in \mathbb{R}^m_+$ such that (x_0, λ_0) is a saddle point of the Lagrangian $\mathcal{L}$. Moreover, $\lambda_0 \cdot g(x_0) = 0$, which is called the complementary slackness condition.*

  II. *(Sufficiency) If (x_0, λ_0) is a saddle point of $\mathcal{L}$, then x_0 solves (B.1).*

Proof: For the first part of the result, let $L = \mathbb{R} \times \mathbb{R}^m$, with subsets

$$A = \{(r, z) : \exists x \in X; r \leq U(x), z \geq g(x)\}$$

and

$$B = \{(r, z) : r > U(x_0), z \ll 0\},$$

which are both convex. By the fact that x_0 solves (B.1), the sets A and B are disjoint. By the Separating Hyperplane Theorem, there is a linear functional $F : L \to \mathbb{R}$ such that $F(v) < F(w)$ for each v in A and w in B. It follows, for any v in A and w in the closure of B, that $F(v) \leq F(w)$. There is some scalar α and λ in $\mathbb{R}^m$ such that for any (r, z) in L, we have $F(r, z) = \alpha r + \lambda \cdot z$. Using the Slater condition, we can check that $\alpha < 0$ and $\lambda \geq 0$. Let $\lambda_0 = -\lambda/\alpha$. It follows, using the fact that $[U(x_0), 0]$ is in both A and the closure of B, that (x_0, λ_0) is a saddle point, and that complementary slackness holds.

  The second part of the result is easy to show. ∎

Now we turn to first-order conditions for optimality. Consider

$$\sup_{x \in X} U(x), \tag{B.2}$$

where X is a convex subset of a vector space L and $U : X \to \mathbb{R}$ is some function. We are interested in necessary and sufficient conditions for x^* to solve (B.2). For $x \in X$, let

$$F(x) = \{y \in L : \exists \epsilon \in (0,1), \quad x + \alpha y \in X, \quad \alpha \in [0, \epsilon]\},$$

the set of *feasible directions* from x. The derivative of U at some x in X in the direction $y \in F(x)$, if it exists, is defined as the limit

$$\delta U(x; y) \equiv \lim_{\alpha \downarrow 0} \frac{U(x + \alpha y) - U(x)}{\alpha}. \tag{B.3}$$

This is sometimes known as the *directional* or *Gateaux* derivative. If $y \mapsto \delta U(x; y)$ defines a linear function on $F(x)$, this function is called the *gradient* of U at x, and is denoted $\nabla U(x)$. In that case, we write $\nabla U(x; y) = \delta U(x; y)$ for the value of $\nabla U(x)$ at y. For example, if $U : \mathbb{R}^n \to \mathbb{R}$ is a differentiable function, then the gradient $\nabla U(x)$ exists at any x and $\nabla U(x; y) = \partial U(x) \cdot y$, where $\partial U(x)$ is the vector of partial derivatives of U at x.

Suppose x^* solves (B.2) and $\nabla U(x^*)$ exists. Then $\nabla U(x^*; y) \leq 0$ for all y in $F(x^*)$, for if not, there is some feasible direction y with $\nabla U(x^*; y) > 0$, in which case there is some $\alpha > 0$ with $U(x + \alpha y) - U(x) > 0$, which contradicts the optimality of x^*. If $F(x^*)$ is the entire vector space L, it follows that $\nabla U(x^*) \equiv 0$ is necessary for the optimality of x^*, for if $\nabla U(x^*; y) < 0$, then $-y$ is a feasible direction of strict improvement.

If U is concave, $\nabla U(x^*)$ exists, and $F(x^*) = L$, then it is both necessary and sufficient for the optimality of x^* that $\nabla U(x^*) \equiv 0$. Necessity has been shown. For sufficiency, concavity of U implies that for any x and $y \in X$,

$$U(y) - U(x) \leq \nabla U(x; y - x). \tag{B.4}$$

Taking $x = x^*$, we have $U(y) \leq U(x^*)$ for all y. There are extensions of these results to the case of nondifferentiable U.

C

Probability—The General Case

THIS APPENDIX EXTENDS the definitions of Appendix A to handle probability spaces with possibly infinitely many distinct events. We also add some useful general results, such as the Dominated Convergence Theorem, the Central Limit Theorem, and Fubini's Theorem. Standard references are Billingsley (1986) and Chung (1974).

Given a set Ω of states, a *tribe* on Ω is a collection $\mathcal{F}$ of subsets of Ω that includes the empty set $\emptyset$ and that satisfies the following two conditions:

(a) if B is in $\mathcal{F}$, then its *complement* $\{\omega \in \Omega : \omega \notin B\}$ is also in $\mathcal{F}$;
(b) for any sequence $\{B_1, B_2, \ldots\}$ in $\mathcal{F}$, the union $B_1 \cup B_2 \cup \cdots$ is in $\mathcal{F}$.

A tribe is also known in this general context as a *σ-algebra* or *σ-field*. For any collection $\mathcal{A}$ of subsets of Ω, the tribe *generated* by $\mathcal{A}$ is the intersection of all tribes containing $\mathcal{A}$. An important example is to take $\Omega = \mathbb{R}^n$ and to let $\mathcal{F}$ be the tribe generated by the open sets of $\mathbb{R}^n$. In this case, $\mathcal{F}$ is known as the *Borel* tribe on $\mathbb{R}^n$, and is denoted $\mathcal{B}(\mathbb{R}^n)$.

Suppose Ω is a set with tribe $\mathcal{F}$. A *random variable* is a function $X : \Omega \to \mathbb{R}$ with the following property: For any set A in the Borel tribe $\mathcal{B}(\mathbb{R})$, the set $\{\omega \in \Omega : X(\omega) \in A\}$ is in $\mathcal{F}$. A *probability measure* is a function $P : \mathcal{F} \to [0, 1]$ satisfying $P(\emptyset) = 0$, $P(\Omega) = 1$, and, for any sequence $B_1, B_2, \ldots$ of disjoint events,

$$P(B_1 \cup B_2 \cup \cdots) = \sum_{n=1}^{\infty} P(B_n).$$

The triple $(\Omega, \mathcal{F}, P)$ is a probability space.

An event B is said to be *almost sure* if $P(B) = 1$. For example, "$X = Y$ *almost surely*" means, in formal notation, that $P(\{\omega \in \Omega : X(\omega) = Y(\omega)\}) = 1$. We sometimes write instead, more informally, that "$P(X = Y) = 1$." It is our practice throughout to take "$X = Y$" to mean merely that $X = Y$ almost surely, but the phrase "almost surely" is sometimes added for emphasis.

Given a probability space $(\Omega, \mathcal{F}, P)$, a *null set* is a subset of an event of zero probability. In order to assign zero probability to null sets, the probability space can be *completed*, which means that we can replace $\mathcal{F}$ with the tribe $\mathcal{F}^{\sim}$ generated by the union of $\mathcal{F}$ and the set of all null sets. The probability measure P then extends uniquely to a probability measure $P^{\sim}$ on $(\Omega, \mathcal{F}^{\sim})$ with the property that $P^{\sim}(A) = P(A)$ for all A in $\mathcal{F}$ and $P^{\sim}(A) = 0$ for any null set A. The space $(\Omega, \mathcal{F}^{\sim}, P^{\sim})$ is called the *completion* of $(\Omega, \mathcal{F}, P)$.

Suppose X is a random variable that can be written as a linear combination, $X = \alpha_1 1_{B_1} + \cdots + \alpha_n 1_{B_n}$, of indicator functions. In this case, X is called *simple*. As in the finite-state case, the *expectation* of X given a probability measure P on $(\Omega, \mathcal{F})$ is defined by

$$E(X) = \alpha_1 P(B_1) + \cdots + \alpha_n P(B_n),$$

merely the probability-weighted average of the outcomes. If X is not necessarily simple, but is a nonnegative random variable, then the expectation of X is defined as

$$E(X) \equiv \sup_{Y \in \mathcal{S}} E(Y) \qquad \text{subject to } Y \leq X, \tag{C.1}$$

where $\mathcal{S}$ is the set of simple random variables. More generally, any random variable X may be written as $X = X^+ - X^-$, where $X^+ \equiv \max(X, 0)$ and $X^- \equiv \max(-X, 0)$; that is, X is the difference between its positive and negative parts. If both $E(X^+)$ and $E(X^-)$ are finite, then X is said to be *integrable*, and its expectation is defined by

$$E(X) \equiv E(X^+) - E(X^-), \tag{C.2}$$

which coincides with the definition for simple random variables when X is itself simple. If X^+ is integrable and X^- is not, we define $E(X) = -\infty$, and symmetrically define $E(X) = +\infty$ when X^- is integrable and X^+ is not.

Fixing a probability space $(\Omega, \mathcal{F}, P)$, a sequence $\{X_n\}$ of random variables *converges in distribution* to a random variable X if, for any bounded continuous $f : \mathbb{R} \to \mathbb{R}$, we have $E[f(X_n)] \to E[f(X)]$. The sequence $\{X_n\}$ *converges in probability* to X if, for all $\epsilon > 0$, $P(|X_n - X| \geq \epsilon) \to 0$. The sequence $\{X_n\}$ converges almost surely to X if there is an event B of probability 1 such that $X_n(\omega) \to X(\omega)$ for all ω in B. The definition of convergence in distribution extends as given to the case of X_n defined on a (possibly different) probability space $(\Omega_n, \mathcal{F}_n, P_n)$ for each n.

Dominated Convergence Theorem. *Suppose $\{X_n\}$ is a sequence of random variables on a probability space with $|X_n| \leq Y$ for all n, where Y is a random variable with*

$E(|Y|) < \infty$. *Suppose, almost surely, or in probability, or in distribution, that* X_n *converges to* X. *Then* $E(X_n) \to E(X)$.

Convergence almost surely implies convergence in probability, which in turn implies convergence in distribution, so we could have stated the Dominated Convergence Theorem just for convergence in distribution and had the same result.

A sequence $\{X_n\}$ of random variables on a given probability space is *independently distributed* if, for any finite subset $\{X_1, \ldots, X_k\}$ and any bounded measurable functions $f_i : \mathbb{R} \to \mathbb{R}$, $1 \leq i \leq k$, we have

$$E[f_1(X_1)f_2(X_2)\cdots f_k(X_k)] = E[f_1(X_1)]E[f_2(X_2)]\cdots E[f_k(X_k)].$$

A sequence $\{X_n\}$ of random variables on a given probability space is *uniformly integrable* if

$$\lim_{\alpha \to \infty} \sup_n E(Y_{\alpha n}) = 0,$$

where $Y_{\alpha n}(\omega) = |X_n(\omega)|$ if $|X_n(\omega)| \geq \alpha$ and otherwise $Y_{\alpha n}(\omega) = 0$.

We next describe a version of the Central Limit Theorem. For this, we define

$$Y = \left\{ Y_1^n, Y_2^n, \ldots, Y_{k(n)}^n : n \in \{1, 2, \ldots\} \right\},$$

with $k(n) \to \infty$, to be a *triangular array* if, for each n, $Y_1^n, \ldots, Y_{k(n)}^n$ are independently distributed random variables on some probability space. For any constant $\epsilon > 0$, let $U(\epsilon)$ denote the "ϵ-truncated" triangular array defined by $U_j^n(\epsilon) = 0$ for $|Y_j^n| \leq \epsilon$ and $U_j^n(\epsilon) = Y_j^n$ for $|Y_j^n| > \epsilon$. The array Y satisfies the *Lindeberg-Feller condition* if, for any $\epsilon > 0$,

$$\lim_{n \to \infty} \text{var}\left[U_1^n(\epsilon) + \cdots + U_{k(n)}^n(\epsilon) \right] = 0.$$

The Lindeberg-Feller Central Limit Theorem. *Suppose Y is a triangular array of random variables, all with zero expectations, satisfying the Lindeberg-Feller condition. For each n, let $Z_n = Y_1^n + \cdots + Y_{k(n)}^n$ and let $s_n^2 = \text{var}(Z_n)$. If $s_n^2 \to \sigma^2 > 0$, then Z_n converges in distribution to a Normal random variable with mean zero and variance σ^2.*

For any integrable random variable X, the *conditional expectation* of X given a sub-tribe $\mathcal{G}$ of $\mathcal{F}$ is denoted $E(X \mid \mathcal{G})$, and is defined as any $\mathcal{G}$-measurable random variable Y with the property $E(XZ) = E(YZ)$ for any $\mathcal{G}$-measurable random variable Z such that XZ is integrable. The existence of this conditional expectation is assured, but we do not show that here. The *law of iterated expectations* applies as in the finite-state case.

As in the finite-state setting, Q and P are equivalent probability measures on $(\Omega, \mathcal{F})$ if, for any event A, $P(A) = 0$ if and only if $Q(A) = 0$. In this case, there is always a strictly positive random variable ξ called the *Radon-Nikodym* derivative of Q with respect to P, with the following property: If Z is such that $E^Q(|Z|) < \infty$, then $E^Q(Z) = E^P(\xi Z)$. Under the same assumptions, if $\mathcal{G}$ is a sub-tribe of $\mathcal{F}$, then

$$E^Q(Z \mid \mathcal{G}) = \frac{1}{E^P(\xi \mid \mathcal{G})} E^P(\xi Z \mid \mathcal{G}). \tag{C.3}$$

It is common to denote ξ by $\frac{dQ}{dP}$.

If there are multiple periods, we fix a set of times denoted $\mathcal{T}$, usually with $\mathcal{T} = \{0, 1, \ldots, T\}$, or $\mathcal{T} = \{0, 1, \ldots\}$, or $\mathcal{T} = [0, T]$, or $\mathcal{T} = [0, \infty)$. A filtration $\mathbb{F} = \{\mathcal{F}_t : t \in \mathcal{T}\}$ of sub-tribes of $\mathcal{F}$ is usually given, as in the finite-state case. We always assume that $\mathcal{F}_t \subset \mathcal{F}_s$ whenever $t \leq s$.

For the case $\mathcal{T} = [0, T]$ or $[0, \infty)$, we often require a family $X = \{X_t : t \in \mathcal{T}\}$ of random variables to be measurable when treated as a function $X : \Omega \times \mathcal{T} \to \mathbb{R}$. "Measurable" here means *product measurable*, sometimes called *jointly measurable*, that is, measurable with respect to the smallest tribe on $\Omega \times \mathcal{T}$ containing all sets of the form $A \times B$, where $A \in \mathcal{F}$ and B is in the Borel tribe on $\mathcal{T}$. In fact, we always take it as a matter of definition, given at the beginning of Chapter 5, that a *process* $X : \Omega \times \mathcal{T} \to \mathbb{R}$ is product measurable so as to avoid continually referring to product measurability.

A process X is *adapted* if, for all t, the random variable X_t is measurable with respect to $\mathcal{F}_t$. A *martingale* is an adapted process X that is *integrable*, in the sense that X_t is integrable for each t, and such that $E(X_t \mid \mathcal{F}_s) = X_s$ whenever $t \geq s$.

A *stopping time* is a random variable $\tau : \Omega \to \mathcal{T}$ with the property that for each time t, the event $\{\omega : \tau(\omega) \geq t\}$ is in $\mathcal{F}_t$. As in the finite-state case, a martingale can also be defined as an adapted integrable process such that for any bounded stopping time τ, we have $E(X_\tau) = E(X_0)$.

Fubini's Theorem states the following. Suppose $(\Omega, \mathcal{F}, P)$ is a probability space and $X : \Omega \times [0, T] \to \mathbb{R}$ is product measurable. If

$$E\left(\int_0^T |X_t| \, dt\right) < \infty,$$

then $E\left(\int_0^T X_t \, dt\right) = \int_0^T E(X_t) \, dt$. That is, we can reverse the order of the expectation and the time integral. More generally, if $\mathcal{G}$ is a sub-tribe of $\mathcal{F}$, then the conditions above for Fubini's Theorem imply that

$$E\left(\int_0^T X_t \, dt \,\middle|\, \mathcal{G}\right) = \int_0^T E(X_t \mid \mathcal{G}) \, dt \qquad \text{almost surely.} \qquad (C.4)$$

Fubini's Theorem also applies as stated with $T = +\infty$. This version can be found in Ethier and Kurtz (1986: 74).

D
Stochastic Integration

THIS APPENDIX SUMMARIZES the definition of the stochastic integral and reviews two useful related results, Girsanov's Theorem and the Martingale Representation Theorem. Standard references are Chung and Williams (1990), Karatzas and Shreve (1988), and Revuz and Yor (1991). For the case of a general information filtration, see Protter (1990).

We fix a standard Brownian motion $B = (B^1, \ldots, B^d)$ in $\mathbb{R}^d$ on a complete probability space $(\Omega, \mathcal{F}, P)$, as well as the standard filtration $\mathbb{F} = \{\mathcal{F}_t : t \geq 0\}$ of B, as defined in Section 5I. We remind the reader that a "process" has been defined for the purposes of this book as a jointly measurable function on $\Omega \times [0, \infty)$ into some Euclidean space. We also recall that B is defined by the fact that it is an $\mathbb{R}^d$-valued process with continuous sample paths such that

(a) $P(B_0 = 0) = 1$;

(b) for any times t and $s > t$, $B_s - B_t$ is normally distributed in $\mathbb{R}^d$ with mean zero and covariance matrix $(s - t)I$;

(c) for any times $t_0, \ldots, t_n$ with $0 < t_0 < t_1 < \cdots < t_n < \infty$, the random variables $B(t_0), B(t_1) - B(t_0), \ldots, B(t_n) - B(t_{n-1})$ are independently distributed.

Finally, recall that $\mathcal{F}_t$ is the tribe (often called the σ-algebra) generated by the union of the tribe $\sigma(B_s : 0 \leq s \leq t)$ and the null sets of $\mathcal{F}$.

In order to define the stochastic integral, we fix a time interval $[0, T]$ and take M to be one of the processes $B^1, \ldots, B^d$, say B^i. An adapted process $\theta : \Omega \times [0, T] \to \mathbb{R}$ is *simple* if there is a partition of $[0, T]$ given by times $0 = t_0 < t_1 < \cdots < t_N = T$ such that for all $n > 0$,

$$\theta(t) = \theta(t_n), \qquad t \in (t_{n-1}, t_n].$$

For a simple process θ, it is natural to define the stochastic integral $\int \theta \, dM$, at any time $t \in [t_n, t_{n+1})$, for any $n < N$, by

$$\int_0^t \theta_s \, dM_s \equiv \sum_{i=0}^{n-1} \theta(t_{i+1}) \left[M(t_{i+1}) - M(t_i) \right] + \theta(t_{n+1}) \left[M(t) - M(t_n) \right].$$

For $t = t_N = T$, we let $\int_0^T \theta_s \, dM_s = \sum_{i=0}^{N-1} \theta(t_{i+1}) \left[M(t_{i+1}) - M(t_i) \right]$. We let $\mathcal{L}$ denote the set of adapted processes. We recall the notation from Chapter 5:

$$\mathcal{L}^1 = \left\{ \theta \in \mathcal{L} : \int_0^T |\theta_t| \, dt < \infty \ a.s. \right\}$$

$$\mathcal{L}^2 = \left\{ \theta \in \mathcal{L} : \int_0^T \theta_t^2 \, dt < \infty \ a.s. \right\}$$

$$\mathcal{H}^2 = \left\{ \theta \in \mathcal{L}^2 : E \left(\int_0^T \theta_t^2 \, dt \right) < \infty \right\}.$$

An important fact that we shall not prove here is that for any $\theta \in \mathcal{H}^2$, there is a sequence $\{\theta_n\}$ of adapted simple processes approximating θ in the sense that

$$E \left(\int_0^T [\theta_n(t) - \theta(t)]^2 \, dt \right) \to 0.$$

It also turns out that for each θ in $\mathcal{H}^2$, there is a unique random variable Y_θ with the property that for any such sequence $\{\theta_n\}$ approximating θ,

$$E \left(\left[Y_\theta - \int_0^T \theta_n(t) \, dM_t \right]^2 \right) \to 0.$$

(To be more precise, Y_θ is uniquely defined in the sense that if another random variable Y has the same property, then $Y = Y_\theta$ almost surely.) This random variable Y_θ is denoted $\int_0^T \theta_t \, dM_t$. Since T and $M = B^i$ are arbitrary, we have defined the stochastic integral $\int_0^T \theta_t \, dB_t \equiv \sum_{i=1}^d \int_0^T \theta_t^i \, dB_t^i$ for any $\theta = (\theta^1, \ldots, \theta^d)$ in $(\mathcal{H}^2)^d$ and any T. The fact that this definition of the stochastic integral is possible, and the fact that the process $\int \theta \, dB$ satisfies the properties laid out in Chapter 5, are both shown, for example, in Karatzas and Shreve (1988: Sec. 3.2). In particular, this stochastic integral is defined so that every sample path is continuous. Karatzas and Shreve have taken special care to extend the usual definition of $\int \theta \, dB$ for "progressively measurable" θ in $(\mathcal{H}^2)^d$ to allow any θ in $(\mathcal{H}^2)^d$.

In the text of the book we sometimes need to define a stochastic integral for an integrand in $(\mathcal{L}^2)^d$ but *not* in $(\mathcal{H}^2)^d$. That is, we wish to define $\int \theta \, dB \equiv \sum_i \int \theta^i \, dB^i$ for some given $\theta = (\theta^1, \ldots, \theta^d) \in (\mathcal{L}^2)^d$. This is done as follows. For any given positive integer n, let $\tau(n) = \inf\{t : \int_0^t \theta_s \cdot \theta_s \, ds = n\}$. Let $\theta_t^{(n)} = \theta_t 1_{t \leq \tau(n)}$. Then $\theta^{(n)}$ is in $(\mathcal{H}^2)^d$, so we can define $\int \theta^{(n)} \, dB$. Since θ is in $(\mathcal{L}^2)^d$, we know that $\tau(n) \to T$ almost surely, and we can therefore define $\int_0^t \theta_s \, dB_s$ for any t in $[0, T]$ as the limit of $\int_0^t \theta_s^{(n)} \, dB_s$ as $n \to \infty$.

Bick and Willinger (1994) point out that for some of the applications treated in this book, such as the Black-Scholes option-pricing formula, the stochastic integral simplifies to the usual Stieltjes integral.

We will sometimes need to work with the notion of a *local martingale*, an adapted process X with the property that there exists an increasing sequence $\tau(n)$ of stopping times converging to T almost surely such that for each n, the *stopped process* $X^{\tau(n)}$ is a martingale when defined by $X_t^{\tau(n)} = X_{\min(t,\tau(n))}$. For example, in the previous paragraph, since $\int \theta^{(n)} \, dB$ is a martingale (Proposition 5B), $\int \theta \, dB$ is a local martingale. Of course, a martingale is a local martingale.

A *supermartingale* is an adapted integrable process X with the property that for any times t and $s > t$, $E_t(X_s) \leq X_t$. A *right-continuous process* is a process X such that for all $t < T$, we have $X_t = \lim_{s \downarrow t} X_s$, that is, whose sample paths are continuous from the right. For example, any stochastic integral is right-continuous since its sample paths are continuous! The following two results are frequently applied:

(a) A nonnegative local martingale is a supermartingale.
(b) *Doob-Meyer Decomposition:* A right-continuous supermartingale X may be expressed in the form $X = M - A$, where M is a martingale and A is an increasing adapted process with $A_0 = 0$.

The Martingale Representation Theorem. *If M is a local martingale, then there exists θ in $(\mathcal{L}^2)^d$ such that*

$$M_t = M_0 + \int_0^t \theta_s \, dB_s, \qquad t \geq 0. \tag{D.1}$$

The following result is closely related, as can be seen from the sketch of its proof.

Dudley's Theorem. *Fix $T > 0$ and let X be any $\mathcal{F}_T$-measurable random variable. Suppose $d = 1$ or $E(|X|) < \infty$. Then there exists a constant x and some θ in $(\mathcal{L}^2)^d$ such that*

$$X = x + \int_0^T \theta_t \, dB_t \qquad almost \; surely. \tag{D.2}$$

We can give the proof for $E(|X|) < \infty$. In that case $\{M_t = E_t(X), t \geq 0\}$ is a martingale with $M_0 = x \equiv E(X)$ and $M_T = X$. Then (D.2) follows from (D.1). The proof for $d = 1$, as well as that of the Martingale Representation Theorem, are standard and can be found, for example, in Karatzas and Shreve (1988) or Protter (1990).

We move now to Girsanov's Theorem, which deals with the construction of a Brownian motion under a change of probability measure. We restrict ourselves for the remainder of the appendix to a fixed time horizon $T < \infty$. In particular, the probability space is $(\Omega, \mathcal{F}_T, P)$ and the standard filtration $\mathbb{F} = \{\mathcal{F}_t : 0 \leq t \leq T\}$ of $B = \{B_t : 0 \leq t \leq T\}$ are as previously defined, with all defining conditions restricted to $[0, T]$. A vector $\theta = (\theta^1, \ldots, \theta^d)$ of processes in $\mathcal{L}^2$ satisfies *Novikov's condition* if

$$E\left[\exp\left(\frac{1}{2}\int_0^T \theta_s \cdot \theta_s \, ds\right)\right] < \infty. \tag{D.3}$$

Proposition. *If θ satisfies Novikov's condition, then a martingale ξ^θ is defined by*

$$\xi_t^\theta = \exp\left(-\int_0^t \theta_s \, dB_s - \frac{1}{2}\int_0^t \theta_s \cdot \theta_s \, ds\right), \qquad t \in [0, T].$$

Suppose θ satisfies Novikov's condition. Because ξ^θ is a martingale and $\xi_0^\theta = 1$, we know that $E(\xi_T^\theta) = 1$. Since ξ_T^θ is strictly positive, we saw in Appendix C that an equivalent probability measure $Q(\theta)$ can be defined by

$$\frac{dQ(\theta)}{dP} = \xi_T^\theta.$$

It is sometimes useful to exploit Ito's Lemma and write $d\xi_t^\theta = -\xi_t^\theta \theta_t \, dB_t$.

Girsanov's Theorem. *Given $\theta \in (\mathcal{L}^2)^d$, suppose that ξ^θ is a martingale. (Novikov's condition suffices.) Then a standard Brownian motion B^θ that is a martingale under $Q(\theta)$ is defined by*

$$B_t^\theta = B_t + \int_0^t \theta_s \, ds, \qquad 0 \leq t \leq T. \tag{D.4}$$

Moreover, B^θ has the martingale representation property under $Q(\theta)$. That is, for any local $Q(\theta)$-martingale M, there is some φ in $(\mathcal{L}^2)^d$ such that

$$M_t = M_0 + \int_0^t \varphi_s \, dB_s^\theta, \qquad t \leq T.$$

The martingale representation aspect of Girsanov's Theorem is not usually emphasized, but is particularly useful in finance applications. By direct calculation, Girsanov's Theorem has the following useful corollary.

Corollary. *Let X be an Ito process in $\mathbb{R}^N$ of the form*

$$X_t = x + \int_0^t \mu_s \, ds + \int_0^t \sigma_s \, dB_s, \qquad 0 \le t \le T.$$

Suppose $\nu = (\nu^1, \dots, \nu^N)$ is a vector of processes in $\mathcal{L}^1$ such that there exists some θ in $(\mathcal{L}^2)^d$ satisfying

$$\sigma_t \theta_t = \mu_t - \nu_t, \qquad 0 \le t \le T.$$

If ξ^θ is a martingale (Novikov's condition suffices), then X is also an Ito process with respect to $(\Omega, \mathcal{F}, \mathbb{F}, Q(\theta))$, and

$$X_t = x + \int_0^t \nu_s \, ds + \int_0^t \sigma_s \, dB_s^\theta, \qquad 0 \le t \le T.$$

In short, Girsanov's Theorem gives us a way to adjust probability assessments so that a given Ito process can be rewritten as an Ito process with almost arbitrary drift.

For any probability measure Q equivalent to P, we can define a martingale M by

$$M_t = E_t \left(\frac{dQ}{dP} \right), \qquad t \le T.$$

The Martingale Representation Theorem implies that there is some $\varphi \in (\mathcal{L}^2)^d$ such that $dM_t = \varphi_t \, dB_t$. In particular, M is a continuous process. Since Q is equivalent to P, we know that M is a strictly positive process, allowing us to define θ in $(\mathcal{L}^2)^d$ by $\theta_t = \varphi_t / M_t$. It follows that $M = \xi^\theta$, and that $Q = Q(\theta)$. Given the unique decomposition property of Ito processes, this implies the following convenient result.

Diffusion Invariance Principle. *Let X be an Ito process with $dX_t = \mu_t \, dt + \sigma_t \, dB_t$. If X is a martingale with respect to an equivalent probability measure Q, then there is a standard Brownian motion $\widehat{B}$ in $\mathbb{R}^d$ under Q such that $dX_t = \sigma_t \, d\widehat{B}_t, \ t \in [0, T]$.*

E

SDEs, PDEs, and the
Feynman-Kac Formula

THIS APPENDIX TREATS the existence of solutions to stochastic differential equations (SDEs) and shows how SDEs can be used to represent solutions to partial differential equations (PDEs) of the parabolic type. Standard references include Karatzas and Shreve (1988) and Chung and Williams (1990).

As usual, a standard Brownian motion B in $\mathbb{R}^d$ is given on some probability space $(\Omega, \mathcal{F}, P)$, along with the standard filtration $\mathbb{F}$ of B, as defined in Chapter 5. An SDE is an expression of the form

$$dX_t = \mu(X_t, t)\, dt + \sigma(X_t, t)\, dB_t, \tag{E.1}$$

where $\mu : \mathbb{R}^N \times [0, \infty) \rightarrow \mathbb{R}^N$ and $\sigma : \mathbb{R}^N \times [0, \infty) \rightarrow \mathbb{R}^{N \times d}$ are given functions. We are interested in conditions on μ and σ under which, for each x in $\mathbb{R}^N$, there is a unique Ito process X satisfying (E.1) with $X_0 = x$. In this case, we say that X solves (E.1) with initial condition x. A process such as X is often called a *diffusion*, although there is no generally accepted definition for "diffusion." By saying "unique," we mean as usual that any other Ito process with the same properties is equal to X almost everywhere. A unique solution in this sense is sometimes called a *strong solution*. We will have no need for what is known as a *weak solution*.

Sufficient conditions for a solution to (E.1) are *Lipschitz* and *growth* conditions on μ and σ. In order to explain these, we first define a norm on matrices by letting $\|A\| = [\operatorname{tr}(AA^\top)]^{1/2}$ for any matrix A. (This coincides with the usual Euclidean norm when A has one row or column.) We then say that σ satisfies a Lipschitz condition in x if there is a constant k such that for any x and y in $\mathbb{R}^N$ and any time t,

$$\|\sigma(x, t) - \sigma(y, t)\| \leq k\|x - y\|. \tag{E.2}$$

Similarly, σ satisfies a growth condition in x if there is a constant k such that for any x in $\mathbb{R}^N$ and any time t,

$$\|\sigma(x, t)\|^2 \leq k(1 + \|x\|^2). \tag{E.3}$$

Note that these conditions apply *uniformly in* t, in that the constants apply for all t simultaneously. The same conditions (E.2) and (E.3), substituting μ for σ, define Lipschitz and growth conditions, respectively, on μ.

SDE Proposition. *Suppose μ and σ are measurable and satisfy Lipschitz and growth conditions in x. Then, for each x in $\mathbb{R}^N$, there is a unique Ito process X in $\mathbb{R}^N$ satisfying the SDE (E.1) with initial condition x. Moreover, X is a Markov process, and for each time t there is a constant C such that*

$$E\left(\|X_t\|^2\right) \leq Ce^{Ct}\left(1 + \|x\|^2\right).$$

The conclusion that X is a Markov process can be strengthened to the conclusion that X is a strong Markov process, a property that we do not define here. One can weaken somewhat the Lipschitz conditions for solutions to (E.1). We say that σ is *locally Lipschitz* in x if, for each positive constant K, there is a constant k such that (E.2) is satisfied for all t and for all x and y bounded in norm by K.

SDE Theorem. *Suppose μ and σ are measurable, satisfy growth conditions in x, and are locally Lipschitz in x. Then, for each x in $\mathbb{R}^N$, there is a unique Ito process X in $\mathbb{R}^N$ satisfying the SDE (E.1) with initial condition x. Moreover, X is a Markov process. If, in addition, μ and σ are continuous functions, then X is a finite-variance process.*

Even these weaker conditions do not cover the case of "square root" diffusions, of the sort used in the Cox-Ingersoll-Ross model in Chapters 7 and 9. For this special case, we can rely on the following result for the one-dimensional case ($N = d = 1$) due to Yamada and Watanabe (1971), reported in Karatzas and Shreve (1988: 291). It is enough that μ is continuous and satisfies a Lipschitz condition in X, and that σ is continuous with the property that

$$|\sigma(x, t) - \sigma(y, t)| \leq \rho(|x - y|),$$

for all x and y and all t, where $\rho : [0, \infty) \to [0, \infty)$ is a strictly increasing function with $\rho(0) = 0$ such that for any $\epsilon > 0$,

$$\int_{(0,\epsilon)} \rho^{-2}(x)\, dx = +\infty.$$

It is enough to take $\rho(x) = \sqrt{x}$, which covers the CIR model (taking $\sigma(x) = 0, x < 0$). While even these weak conditions are further weakened by Yamada and Watanabe (1971), it should be noted that there are counterexamples to the uniqueness of solutions for the case $\sigma(x) = |x|^\alpha$ for $\alpha < 1/2$.

These SDE existence results can be gleaned from such sources as Ikeda and Watanabe (1981), Karatzas and Shreve (1988), Chung and Williams (1990), Revuz and Yor (1991), or Friedman (1975). The conditions of these results also imply that for any given time τ and any x in $\mathbb{R}^N$, there is a unique Ito process X satisfying (E.1) for $t \geq \tau$ with $X_t = x$, $t \leq \tau$. In this case, we say that X solves (E.1) with initial condition x at time τ.

An important special case of the SDE is the *linear stochastic differential equation*

$$dX_t = [a(t)X_t + b(t)]\, dt + c(t)\, dB_t, \tag{E.4}$$

where $a : [0, \infty) \to \mathbb{R}^{N \times N}$, $b : [0, \infty) \to \mathbb{R}^N$, and $c : [0, \infty) \to \mathbb{R}^{N \times d}$ are continuous. We can express the solution to a linear SDE quite explicitly. First, let Φ denote the solution of the ordinary differential equation

$$\frac{d\Phi(t)}{dt} = a(t)\Phi(t), \qquad \Phi(0) = I_{N \times N}.$$

It can be shown that for all t, the matrix $\Phi(t)$ is nonsingular, and the solution of (E.4) is

$$X_t = \Phi(t)\left[X_0 + \int_0^t \Phi^{-1}(s)b(s)\, ds + \int_0^t \Phi^{-1}(s)c(s)\, dB_s \right], \qquad t \geq 0.$$

In particular, X is *Gaussian*, meaning that for any finite times $t_1, \ldots, t_k$, $\{X(t_1), \ldots, X(t_k)\}$ has a joint normal distribution. For any t, the mean vector $m(t)$ and covariance matrix $V(t)$ for X_t are given as solutions to the ordinary differential equations

$$\frac{dm(t)}{dt} = a(t)m(t) + b(t), \qquad m_0 = X_0$$

$$\frac{dV(t)}{dt} = a(t)V(t) + V(t)a(t)^\top + c(t)c(t)^\top, \qquad V(0) = 0.$$

Further details, and generalizations, can be found in Karatzas and Shreve (1988).

We next consider the *Cauchy problem,* for given $T > 0$: Find $f \in C^{2,1}(\mathbb{R}^N \times [0, T))$ solving

$$\mathcal{D}f(x, t) - r(x, t)f(x, t) + h(x, t) = 0, \qquad (x, t) \in \mathbb{R}^N \times [0, T), \qquad \text{(E.5)}$$

with the boundary condition

$$f(x, T) = g(x), \qquad x \in \mathbb{R}^N, \qquad \text{(E.6)}$$

where

$$\mathcal{D}f(x, t) = f_t(x, t) + f_x(x, t)\mu(x, t) + \frac{1}{2}\text{tr}\left[\sigma(x, t)\sigma(x, t)^\top f_{xx}(x, t)\right], \qquad \text{(E.7)}$$

and where $r : \mathbb{R}^N \times [0, T] \to \mathbb{R}$, $h : \mathbb{R}^N \times [0, T] \to \mathbb{R}$, $g : \mathbb{R}^N \to \mathbb{R}$, $\mu : \mathbb{R}^N \times [0, T] \to \mathbb{R}^N$, and $\sigma : \mathbb{R}^N \times [0, T] \to \mathbb{R}^{N \times d}$.

The Feynman-Kac solution to (E.5)–(E.6), should it exist, is given by

$$f(x, t) = E^{x,t}\left[\int_t^T \varphi_{t,s}\, h(X_s, s)\, ds + \varphi_{t,T}\, g(X_T)\right], \qquad \text{(E.8)}$$

where

$$\varphi_{t,s} = \exp\left[-\int_t^s r(X_\tau, \tau)\, d\tau\right],$$

and where $E^{x,t}$ indicates that X is assumed to solve the SDE (E.1) with initial condition x at time t. The term "Feynman-Kac" is widely considered a misnomer in that it originally refers to the probabilistic representation of the solution to a narrower class of parabolic equations than the Cauchy problem. Typically, (E.8) would be called a *probabilistic solution* of the PDE (E.5)–(E.6).

Momentarily putting aside the delicate issue of existence of solutions to the Cauchy problem, the Feynman-Kac representation of a given solution is itself not difficult to verify under technical assumptions. In order to see this, suppose that X solves (E.1) and that f is a solution to the Cauchy problem. For an arbitrary (x, t) in $\mathbb{R}^N \times [0, T]$, let Y be the Ito process defined by $Y_s = f(x, t)$, $s < t$, and

$$Y_s = f(X_s, s)\varphi_{t,s}, \qquad s \in [t, T],$$

where X solves (E.1) with initial condition x at time t. By Ito's Lemma,

$$Y_T = f(x, t) + \int_t^T \varphi_{t,s} [Df(X_s, s) - r(X_s, s)f(X_s, s)]\ ds$$
$$+ \int_t^T \varphi_{t,s} f_x(X_s, s)\sigma(X_s, s)\ dB_s.$$

Taking expectations through each side, rearranging, and assuming enough technical conditions for integrability and (from Proposition 5B) for the integral with respect to B to be a martingale, we have

$$f(x, t) = E^{x,t} \left(\varphi_{t,T} f(X_T, T) - \int_t^T \varphi_{t,s} [Df(X_s, s) - r(X_s, s)f(X_s, s)]\ ds \right),$$

from which (E.8) follows with substitution of (E.5) and (E.6). Sufficient technical conditions are

(a) all of r, g, h, μ, σ, and f are continuous;
(b) the solution f satisfies a *polynomial growth condition* in x, meaning that for some positive constants M and ν,

$$|f(x, t)| \le M (1 + \|x\|^{\nu}), \qquad (x, t) \in \mathbb{R}^N \times [0, T];$$

(c) g and h are each either nonnegative or satisfy a polynomial growth condition in x;
(d) r is nonnegative; and
(e) μ and σ satisfy Lipschitz and growth conditions in x.

We state this more formally:

Proposition. *Suppose conditions (a)–(e) above are satisfied and that f solves* (E.5)–(E.6). *Then* (E.5)–(E.6) *is solved by* (E.8). *There is no other solution to* (E.5)–(E.6) *that satisfies a polynomial growth condition.*

A proof is found in Karatzas and Shreve (1988: 366). Reducing the PDE solution to an expectation in this fashion can sometimes ease the computation of the solution, as is the case for the Black-Scholes formula. The expectation can also can be used as the basis for a numerical solution by Monte Carlo methods, a topic considered in Chapter 11. The Feynman-Kac approach can also be applied to other types of parabolic and elliptic PDEs.

The previous proposition does not resolve whether or not a solution to the PDE actually exists. For this, stronger technical conditions are typically imposed. Different sets of conditions are available in the literature; we will give some of these from different sources. A function $F : \mathbb{R}^N \to \mathbb{R}^K$ is *Hölder continuous* if there is some $\alpha \in (0, 1]$ such that

$$\sup_{x,y,\ x \neq y} \frac{\|F(x) - F(y)\|}{\|x - y\|^\alpha} < \infty.$$

A function has a property (such as Hölder continuity) *locally* if it has the property when restricted to any compact subset of its domain.

Condition 1. *The functions μ, σ, g, h, and r are all continuous and*

    (a) μ and σ are bounded and locally Lipschitz in (x, t);

    (b) σ is Hölder continuous in x, uniformly in t;

    (c) r is bounded and, locally: r is Hölder continuous in x uniformly in t;

    (d) h is Hölder continuous in x, uniformly in t, and satisfies a polynomial growth condition in x;

    (e) $\sigma\sigma^\top$ is uniformly parabolic, in that there is some scalar $\epsilon > 0$ such that the eigenvalues of $\sigma(x, t)\sigma(x, t)^\top$ are larger than ϵ for all $(x, t) \in \mathbb{R}^N \times [0, T]$; and

    (f) g satisfies a polynomial growth condition.

We can substitute strong smoothness conditions for some of the stringent bounding and uniform ellipticity properties of Condition 1.

Condition 2. *All of μ, σ, g, r, and h satisfy a Lipschitz condition in x, and r is nonnegative. All of μ, σ, g, r, h, μ_x, σ_x, g_x, r_x, h_x, μ_{xx}, σ_{xx}, g_{xx}, r_{xx}, and h_{xx} exist, are continuous, and satisfy a growth condition in x.*

Theorem. *Under Condition 1 or Condition 2, there is a unique solution of* (E.5)– (E.6) *that satisfies a polynomial growth condition in x, and this solution is given by* (E.8).

Condition 1 is from Friedman (1975), while Condition 2 is a special case from Krylov (1980). Kuwana (1993) offers improvements on Krylov's result.

Unfortunately, neither Condition 1 nor Condition 2 includes the exact case of the Black-Scholes option-pricing formula, simply because the option payoff is not differentiable in the stock price.

Under technical conditions on μ, σ, and r, there is a function $G : \mathbb{R}^N \times [0, T] \times \mathbb{R}^N \times [0, T] \to \mathbb{R}$, called the *fundamental solution* of (E.5)–(E.6), or sometimes the *Green's function*, that has the following useful properties:

(a) For any $(x_0, t_0) \in \mathbb{R}^N \times [0, T)$, the function ψ defined by $\psi(x, t) = G(x_0, t_0, x, t)$ is in $C^{2,1}(\mathbb{R}^N \times (t_0, T])$ and solves the PDE

$$\mathcal{D}^* \psi(x, t) - r(x, t)\psi(x, t) = 0, \qquad (x, t) \in \mathbb{R}^N \times (t_0, T], \quad \text{(E.9)}$$

where

$$\mathcal{D}^* \psi(x, t) = - \psi_t(x, t) - \sum_{i=1}^{N} \frac{\partial}{\partial x_i} [\psi(x, t)\mu_i(x, t)]$$

$$+ \frac{1}{2} \sum_{i=1}^{N} \sum_{j=1}^{N} \frac{\partial^2}{\partial x_i x_j} [a_{ij}(x, t)\psi(x, t)],$$

where $a(x, t) = \sigma(x, t)\sigma(x, t)^\top$. The PDE (E.9) is sometimes called the *Fokker-Planck equation*, or the *forward Kolmogorov equation*, distinguishing it from the *backward Kolmogorov equation* (E.5)–(E.6).

(b) Under technical conditions on g and h, the solution to (E.5)–(E.6) is given by

$$f(x_0, t_0) = \int_{t_0}^{T} \int_{\mathbb{R}^N} G(x_0, t_0, x, t) h(x, t) \, dx \, dt$$

$$+ \int_{\mathbb{R}^N} G(x_0, t_0, x, T) g(x) \, dx. \qquad \text{(E.10)}$$

A sufficient set of technical conditions, as well as boundary conditions for (E.9), are given by Friedman (1964, 1975). Knowledge of the fundamental solution G is valuable since particular solutions of the PDE (E.5)–(E.6) can be computed from (E.10) for each of a number of different cases for g and h. In the case of $N = 1$, numerical solution of G is treated by a finite-difference approach given in Chapter 10.

Further work on probabilistic solutions of PDEs has been done by Freidlin (1985).

F
Calculation of Utility Gradients

THIS APPENDIX GIVES some examples of the calculation of utility gradients in a continuous-time setting. Further examples are found in Duffie and Skiadas (1994).

First recall the Mean Value Theorem: If $f : [a, b] \to \mathbb{R}$ is continuous on the interval $[a, b]$ and has a derivative on (a, b), then there is some $c \in (a, b)$ such that $f(b) - f(a) = f'(c)(b - a)$.

We fix a probability space and the time interval $[0, T]$. A process $c : \Omega \times [0, T] \to \mathbb{R}$ is *square-integrable* if $E\left(\int_0^T c_t^2 \, dt\right) < \infty$. Let L denote the space of square-integrable processes and L_+ the space of nonnegative processes in L. We recall from Appendix B that the gradient of a function $U : L_+ \to \mathbb{R}$, when well defined at $c \in L_+$, is given by

$$\nabla U(c; h) = \lim_{\alpha \to 0} \frac{U(c + \alpha h) - U(c)}{\alpha}, \qquad h \in F(c),$$

where $F(c)$ is the set of feasible directions at c.

Consider first the additive-utility function U defined by

$$U(c) = E\left[\int_0^T u(c_t, t) \, dt\right],$$

where u is continuous and, for each t, $u(\cdot, t)$ is continuously differentiable on $(0, \infty)$ with a derivative $u_c(\cdot, t)$ satisfying a growth condition $|u_c(y, t)| \le k + ky$, for some constant k independent of t. Let $c \in L_+$ and $h \in F(c)$. Let $\{\alpha_n\}$ be any sequence of strictly positive scalars smaller than 1 and converging to zero. For each n, ω, and t, let $\zeta_{n,t}(\omega)$ be chosen, by the Mean Value Theorem, so that

$$u_c\left[c_t(\omega) + \zeta_{n,t}(\omega), t\right] \alpha_n h_t(\omega) = u\left[c_t(\omega) + \alpha_n h_t(\omega), t\right] - u\left[c_t(\omega), t\right].$$

In fact, this can be done so that ζ_n is a process in L_+. It follows that for all n,

$$\left| \frac{u(c_t + \alpha_n h_t, t) - u(c_t, t)}{\alpha_n} \right| = |u_c(c_t + \zeta_{n,t}, t) h_t|$$

$$\leq (k + k|c_t + \zeta_{n,t}|)|h_t|$$

$$\leq (k + k|c_t| + k\alpha_n|h_t|)|h_t|$$

$$\leq y_t \equiv (k + k|c_t| + |h_t|)|h_t|.$$

Moreover, $E\left(\int_0^T |y_t| \, dt \right) < \infty$ by the Cauchy-Schwartz inequality since both c and h are in L. The Dominated Convergence Theorem implies that

$$\lim_{n \to \infty} \frac{U(c + \alpha_n h) - U(c)}{\alpha} = E\left[\int_0^T \lim_n u_c(c_t + \zeta_{n,t}, t) h_t \, dt \right]$$

$$= E\left[\int_0^T u_c(c_t, t) h_t \, dt \right],$$

since $\zeta_{n,t}(\omega)$ converges with n to 0 for all (ω, t). Thus, for any $h \in F(c)$,

$$\nabla U(c; h) = E\left(\int_0^T \pi_t h_t \, dt \right),$$

where $\pi_t = u_c(c_t, t)$. This implies that the gradient of U at c exists and has the Riesz representation π.

Suppose, for any $\epsilon > 0$, that u_c satisfies the growth condition given above restricted to $(\epsilon, \infty) \times [0, T]$, but not necessarily on the whole domain $[0, \infty) \times [0, T]$. This is important, for example, in dealing with Inada conditions, as in the example $u(x, t) = e^{-\rho t} x^\alpha$. In that case, the above calculations extend to obtain the same solution for utility gradients so long as the given consumption process c is bounded away from zero. That is, suppose for some $\epsilon > 0$ that $c_t \geq \epsilon$ for all t. In order to be a feasible direction, $c + \delta h \geq 0$ for some $\delta \in (0, 1)$, so $c + \alpha h$ must be bounded away from zero for all $\alpha \in (0, \delta/2)$, and all of the above calculations carry through to this case. This situation covers the equilibrium described by Theorem 10G, in which the consumption process c^i of an arbitrary agent i is indeed bounded away from zero.

We now extend this approach to calculating utility gradients to a continuous-time versions of recursive and habit-forming utilities. For these, we need to fix a filtration $\mathbb{F} = \{\mathcal{F}_t : t \in [0, T]\}$ of tribes. In order to avoid spelling out abstract technical conditions on $\mathbb{F}$, we take $\mathbb{F}$ to be the standard filtration of a given standard Brownian motion in $\mathbb{R}^d$. We let $f : \Omega \times [0, T] \times \mathbb{R}^n \times \mathbb{R} \to \mathbb{R}$ be a jointly measurable function satisfying the following conditions:

(a) $f(\cdot, \cdot, z, v)$ is an adapted process, for each fixed (z, v).
(b) uniform Lipschitz condition in utility: There exists a constant K such that $|f(\omega, t, z, u) - f(\omega, t, z, v)| \leq K|u - v|$, for all (ω, t, z, u, v).
(c) uniform growth condition: There exists a constant K such that for all (ω, t, z), we have $|f(\omega, t, z, 0)| \leq K(1 + \|z\|)$.

The function f is a "felicity" function. Its first and second generic arguments, "ω" and "t," allow dependence of felicity on state and time. The third "z" argument allows dependence on current or past consumption through n different variables. The final argument, "v," allows dependence of felicity on utility itself. The additive model has felicity $f(\omega, t, z, v) = u(z, t)$, where z stands for current consumption. Fixing a given consumption process c in L_+, we wish to define a utility process V, an Ito Process whose current level V_t corresponds to current utility for remaining consumption. For example, with the additive model, we have $V_t = E_t \left[\int_t^T u(c_s, s) \, ds \right]$. In general, we will define the utility for c with felicity f to be $U(c) = V_0$.

We use the following existence result of Duffie and Epstein (with Skiadas) (1992a).

Theorem. *Given any $Z = (Z_1, \ldots, Z_n)$ in L^n, there is a unique process V such that*

$$V_t = E_t \left(\int_t^T f(s, Z_s, V_s) \, ds \right), \qquad t \in [0, T].$$

In writing "$f(s, Z_s, V_s)$," we have suppressed ω from the notation.

For the continuous-time case of recursive utility, called *stochastic differential utility*, developed in Duffie and Epstein (with Skiadas) (1992a), this result is applied with $n = 1$ and $Z = c$, the consumption process. For the continuous-time version of habit-formation model, developed by Ryder and Heal (1973) and Sundaresan (1989), and applied by Constantinides (1990) and Detemple and Zapatero (1991, 1992), we take $n = 2$ and let

$$Z_{1t} = c_t$$

$$Z_{2t} = Z_{20} + \int_0^t H(c_s, Z_s) \, ds, \qquad t \in [0, T],$$

for some measurable $H : \mathbb{R}^2 \to \mathbb{R}$ that is uniformly Lipschitz in its second argument and satisfies a growth condition in its first argument. It is not difficult to extend this example to cases in which H is state and time dependent. We can compute the Riesz representation of the gradients of the new utilities just defined. For this, we assume that f is continuously differentiable with respect to (z, v), and that there exists a constant K such that

$$\|f_z(w, t, z, v)\| \leq K(1 + \|z\|), \qquad (w, t, z, v) \in [0, T] \times \Omega \times \mathbb{R}^n \times \mathbb{R},$$

where, here and below, subscripts denote partial derivatives with respect to the indicated arguments. For the habit-formation case, we also assume that H is continuously differentiable, that its partial derivative h_c with respect to consumption satisfies a uniform growth condition,[1] and that h_z is bounded.

With these new utilities, and under the stated assumptions, for any strictly positive consumption process c we again have a utility gradient of the form

$$\nabla U(c; h) = E\left(\int_0^T \pi_t h_t \, dt \right),$$

for a Riesz representation π that is given for stochastic differential utility by

$$\pi_t = Y_t f_z(t, Z_t, V_t),$$

where $Y_t \equiv \exp\left(\int_0^t f_v(s, Z_s, V_s) \, ds \right)$, and for habit-formation utility by

$$\pi_t = Y_t \left[E_t \left(\int_t^T f_z(s, Z_s, V_s) \exp\left(\int_s^t (f_v(u) + h_z(u)) \, du \right) ds \right) h_c(t) + f_c(t) \right],$$

where the obvious arguments have been omitted. Proofs of these gradient representations, and extensions to more general models, can be found in Duffie and Skiadas (1994).

Another formulation of habit formation is suggested by Hindy and Huang (1992), extending the work of Hindy, Huang, and Kreps (1992). Their model is incorporated into this setting by taking $n = 1$ and $Z_t = \int_0^t k_{t-s} \, dC_s$, where k is a bounded adapted process and C is an increasing right-continuous adapted process defining *cumulative consumption*. For the

---

[1]That is, there is a constant K such that $|h_c(c, z)| \leq K(1 + |c|)$ for all (c, z).

case of absolutely continuous cumulative consumption, we have $C_t = \int_0^t c_s \, ds$ for some $c \in L_+$. In general, consumption may occur with "lumps." A gradient calculation for this case is given by Duffie and Skiadas (1994).

G

Finite Difference Computer Code

THIS APPENDIX GIVES computer code written in C by Ravi Myneni and revised by Michael Boulware, at the author's direction, for the numerical solution of coupon-bond and coupon-bond option prices for the Cox-Ingersoll-Ross model of the term structure, using the Crank-Nicholson finite-difference algorithm given in Chapter 11. Zero-coupon bond prices, of course, are also given directly in terms of the explicit solution shown in Chapter 7, from which coupon-bond prices can be computed by treating a coupon bond as a portfolio of zero-coupon bonds of different maturities. This code is merely for the pedagogic purposes of Chapter 11, and is not intended for commerical or other uses. Although this code has been successfully applied by the author to various examples, neither the author, Ravi Myneni, nor Michael Boulware accept any liability for any losses related to its use, or misuse, for any purpose. This code is "faster" than that of the first edition.

The code should be linked with the following copyrighted subroutines from *Numerical Recipes in C*, by Press, Flannery, Teukolsky, and Vetterling (1993).

    (a) `ivector( )`,
    (b) `dvector( )`,
    (c) `free_ivector( )`,
    (d) `free_dvector( )`.

These subroutines are also supplied on a diskette normally sold with copies of *Numerical Recipes in C*. Neither the author of this book nor Ravi Myneni accept any liability for the use or misuse of these subroutines.

The code requires the use of so-called "include" files. Because such files vary from system to system, they are not included here.

```
/****************************************************************
This code was written by Ravi Myneni under the direction
of the author, and revised by Michael Boulware.
****************************************************************/
#define MAX(a,b) (a,b, a > b ? a : b)
  fdi_bond_option(number_space_points,number_time_points,parameters,
                  coupon,par,bond_maturity,option_maturity,call_put,
                  american_european,strike,spot_rates,bond_prices,
                  accrued_interest,option_prices)
   /**********************************************************************
fdi_bond_option() is an implicit finite difference algorithm
        for valuing bond options in the CIR model with constant speed
        of adjustment, long term mean and volatility parameters.
--------------------------------------------------------------------
int    number_time_points  = number of time points
                (Note: actual number of temporal steps is one less.)
int    number_space_points = number of space points
                (Note: actual number of spatial steps is one less.)
        double *parameters       = model parameters vector:
                                   0 <-> speed of adjustment
                                   1 <-> long term mean
                                   2 <-> volatility parameter
        double coupon            = coupon rate (annual % par)
        double par               = bond's par value (%)
double bond_maturity       = bond time to maturity (in years)
double option_maturity     = option time to maturity (in years)
        char   call_put          = call ('C') or put ('P')
        char   american_european = american ('A') or european ('E')
        double strike            = option strike on flat price
        double *spot_rates       = vector of spot rates
        double *bond_prices      = vector of flat bond prices
        double *accrued_interest  = accrued interest on bond
        double *option_prices    = vector of option prices
--------------------------------------------------------------------
   **********************************************************************/
  int number_space_points,number_time_points;
  double *parameters,coupon,par,bond_maturity,option_maturity,strike;
  char call_put,american_european;
  double *spot_rates,*bond_prices,*accrued_interest,*option_prices;
 {
   int error;
   int i,j,k,option_expiration_period,*coupon_flows,*ivector();
   double r,s,t,semi_annual_coupon,accrued,*mu,*sigma,gamma;
   double *a,*b,*c,*y_bond,*y_option,*dvector();
   double time_delta,space_delta;
   void free_ivector(),free_dvector();
   /**** Some useful checks ****/
   if (number_space_points < 10  number_space_points > 3000)
     { printf("! number_space_points out of bounds\n"); return(1); }
   if (number_time_points < 10  number_time_points > 5000)
     { printf("! number_time_points out of bounds\n"); return(2); }
   if (bond_maturity < 2.0/365.0  bond_maturity > 50.0)
     { printf("! bond_maturity invalid\n"); return(3); }
   if (option_maturity < 1.0/365.0  option_maturity > 50.0)
     { printf("! option_maturity invalid\n"); return(4); }
   if (option_maturity >= bond_maturity)
     { printf("! option_maturity exceeds bond_maturity\n"); return(5); }
   if (strike < 0.0)
     { printf("! strike is negative\n"); return(6); }
   /**** Initialization of parameters ****/
   space_delta= 1.0 / (double)(number_space_points-1);
   time_delta= bond_maturity / (double)(number_time_points-1);
   if (time_delta >= 0.5)
     { printf("! number_space_points too small\n"); error= 7; goto fre; }
   gamma= 12.5;
   /**** Calculation of semi-annual coupon ****/
```

```
semi_annual_coupon= coupon * par / 200.0;
/**** Calculation of option expiration node ****/
option_expiration_period= (int)((option_maturity / time_delta) + 0.5);
if (option_expiration_period == 0  option_expiration_period ==
number_time_points-1)
  { printf("! option_maturity out of bounds\n"); error= 8; goto fre; }
/**** Allocation of memory ****/
a= dvector(0,number_space_points-1);
b= dvector(0,number_space_points-1);
c= dvector(0,number_space_points-1);
y_bond= dvector(0,number_space_points-1);
y_option= dvector(0,number_space_points-1);
mu= dvector(0,number_space_points-1);
sigma= dvector(0,number_space_points-1);
coupon_flows= ivector(0,number_time_points-1);
/**** Calculation of semi-annual coupon nodes ****/
for (j=number_time_points-1,i=0 ; j >= 0 ; j--)
    {
      k= (int)(((double)(i)*0.5 / time_delta) + 0.5);
      if (j == number_time_points-k-1)
        { coupon_flows[j]= 1; i++; }
      else
        { coupon_flows[j]= 0; }
    }
/**** Initialization of terminal bond price ****/
for (i=0 ; i < number_space_points ; i++)
  { bond_prices[i]= par; }
/**** Calculation of pde parameters ****/
for (i=1 ; i < number_space_points ; i++)
  {
    error= fdi_sdv(i,gamma,space_delta,parameters,&spot_rates[i],&mu[i],
    &sigma[i]);
    if (error)
      { printf("! error %d occurred in fdi_sdv()\n",error); error= 9; goto fre;
  }
  }
/**** Main valuation loop until option expiration ****/
for (j=number_time_points-1 ; j > option_expiration_period ; j--)
  {
    /**** Addition of semi-annual coupon ****/
    if (coupon_flows[j])
      {
        for (i=0 ; i < number_space_points ; i++)
    { bond_prices[i] += semi_annual_coupon; }
      }
    /**** Highest spot rate case is treated differently ****/
    spot_rates[0]= 1.0e+12;
    a[0]= 0.0;
    b[0]= 1.0;
    c[0]= 0.0;
    if (j == number_time_points-1)
      { y_bond[0]= bond_prices[0] / time_delta; }
    else
      { y_bond[0]= 0.0; }
    /**** Lowest spot rate case is also treated differently ****/
    a[number_space_points-1]= -mu[number_space_points-1] / space_delta;
    b[number_space_points-1]= mu[number_space_points-1] / space_delta
                            - 1.0 / time_delta;
    c[number_space_points-1]= 0.0;
    y_bond[number_space_points-1]= -bond_prices[number_space_points-1] /
                                   time_delta;
    /**** Now do the intermediate points ****/
    for (i=1 ; i < number_space_points-1 ; i++)
      {
        r= mu[i] / (4.0 * space_delta);
        s= sigma[i] / (2.0 * pow(space_delta,2.0));
```

```
          a[i]= (s - r);
          b[i]= -((1.0 / time_delta) + (2.0 * s) + 0.5*spot_rates[i]);
          c[i]= (s + r);
          y_bond[i]= (r - s) * bond_prices[i-1] + ((2.0 * s) -
          (1.0 / time_delta) - 0.5*spot_rates[i])
                    * bond_prices[i] - (r + s) * bond_prices[i+1];
        }
    /**** Solution of tridiagonal system ****/
    tridagm(a,b,c,bond_prices,y_bond,number_space_points);
    }
/**** Initialization of terminal value of option ****/
if (coupon_flows[option_expiration_period])
  { accrued= 0.0; }
else
  {
    for (i=option_expiration_period ; !coupon_flows[i] ; i++) {;}
    accrued= (1.0 - ((double)(i - option_expiration_period)
            * time_delta / 0.5)) * semi_annual_coupon;
  }
for (i=0 ; i < number_space_points ; i++)
    {
      if (call_put == 'C'  call_put == 'c')
        { option_prices[i]= MAX(bond_prices[i]-accrued-strike,0.0); }
      else
        { option_prices[i]= MAX(strike-bond_prices[i]+accrued,0.0); }
    }
/**** Main valuation loop until initial period ****/
for (j=option_expiration_period ; j > 0 ; j--)
    {
    /**** Addition of semi-annual coupon ****/
    if (coupon_flows[j])
        {
          for (i=0 ; i < number_space_points ; i++)
    { bond_prices[i] += semi_annual_coupon; }
        }
    /**** Highest spot rate case is treated differently ****/
    spot_rates[0]= 1.0e+12;
    a[0]= 0.0;
    b[0]= 1.0;
    c[0]= 0.0;
    if (j == number_time_points-1)
        {
          y_bond[0]= bond_prices[0] / time_delta;
          y_option[0]= option_prices[0] / time_delta;
        }
    else
        {
          y_bond[0]= 0.0;
          y_option[0]= 0.0;
        }
    /**** Lowest spot rate case is also treated separately ****/
    a[number_space_points-1]= -mu[number_space_points-1] / space_delta;
    b[number_space_points-1]= mu[number_space_points-1] / space_delta
                            - 1.0 / time_delta;
    c[number_space_points-1]= 0.0;
    y_bond[number_space_points-1]= -bond_prices[number_space_points-1] /
                                    time_delta;
    y_option[number_space_points-1]= -option_prices[number_space_points-1] /
                                    time_delta;
    /**** Now do the intermediate points ****/
    for (i=1 ; i < number_space_points-1 ; i++)
        {
          r= mu[i] / (4.0 * space_delta);
          s= sigma[i] / (2.0 * pow(space_delta,2.0));
          a[i]= (s - r);
          b[i]= -((1.0 / time_delta) + (2.0 * s) + 0.5*spot_rates[i]);
```

```
                  c[i]= (s + r);
                  y_bond[i]= (r - s) * bond_prices[i-1] + ((2.0 * s) -
                  (1.0 / time_delta) -0.5*spot_rates[i])
                              * bond_prices[i] - (r + s) * bond_prices[i+1];
                  y_option[i]= (r - s) * option_prices[i-1] + ((2.0 * s) -
                  (1.0 / time_delta) -0.5*spot_rates[i])
                                 * option_prices[i] - (r + s) * option_prices[i+1];
            }
        /**** Solution of tridiagonal system ****/
        tridagm(a,b,c,bond_prices,y_bond,number_space_points);
        tridagm(a,b,c,option_prices,y_option,number_space_points);
        /**** American feature is handled by the Wald-Bellman equation ****/
        if (american_european == 'A'  american_european == 'a')
           {
             if (coupon_flows[j-1])
               { accrued= 0.0; }
             else
               {
                  for (i=j-1 ; !coupon_flows[i] ; i++) {;}
                  accrued= (1.0 - ((double)(i - j + 1)
                          * time_delta / 0.5)) * semi_annual_coupon;
               }
             for (i=0 ; i < number_space_points ; i++)
               {
                  if (call_put == 'C'  call_put == 'c')
                    { option_prices[i]= MAX(option_prices[i],bond_prices[i]-accrued-
strike); }
                  else
                    { option_prices[i]= MAX(option_prices[i],strike-bond_prices[i]+
                      accrued); }
               }
          }
       }
     if (coupon_flows[0])
       { *accrued_interest= 0.0; }
     else
       {
          *accrued_interest= (1.0 - ((double)(coupon_flows[0]) * time_delta
                         / 0.5)) * semi_annual_coupon;
          for (i=0 ; i < number_space_points ; i++)
   { bond_prices[i] -= *accrued_interest; }
       }
     /**** Cleanup ****/
     error= 0;
   fre:
     free_dvector(a,0,number_space_points-1);
     free_dvector(b,0,number_space_points-1);
     free_dvector(c,0,number_space_points-1);
     free_dvector(y_bond,0,number_space_points-1);
     free_dvector(y_option,0,number_space_points-1);
     free_dvector(mu,0,number_space_points-1);
     free_dvector(sigma,0,number_space_points-1);
     free_ivector(coupon_flows,0,number_time_points-1);
     return(error);
   }
fdi_sdv(position,gamma,space_delta,parameters,spot_rate,mu,sigma)
   /*****************************************************************************
fdi_sdv() computes the coefficients for fdi_bond_option().
-------------------------------------------------------------------------
long    position   = position along the space axis.
        double gamma      = scaling factor (usually 12.5).
        double space_delta = one interval of space axis.
        double *parameters       = model parameters vector:
                                   0 <-> speed of adjustment
                                   1 <-> long term mean
                                   2 <-> volatility parameter
```

```
        double *spot_rate  = spot rate (in decimal).
        double *mu         = drift rate modified by gamma (in decimal).
        double *sigma      = variance modified by gamma (in decimal).
------------------------------------------------------------------------
    ***********************************************************************/
int position;
double gamma,space_delta,*parameters,*spot_rate,*mu,*sigma;
{
  int error;
  int i,j,k;
  double r,s,y;
      /**** Some useful checks ****/
      if (position < 0)
        { printf("! position invalid\n"); return(1); }
      if (gamma < 1.0  gamma > 100.0)
        { printf("! gamma out of bounds\n"); return(2); }
      if (space_delta <= 0)
        { printf("! space_delta invalid\n"); return(3); }
      /**** Compute spot rate ****/
      y= (double)(position) * space_delta;
      *spot_rate= (1.0 - y)/ (gamma * y);
      /**** Useful calculation ****/
      s= *spot_rate * pow(parameters[2],2.0);
      /**** Compute drift ****/
      r= parameters[0] * (parameters[1] - *spot_rate);
      r *= -gamma * pow(y,2.0);
      r += pow(gamma,2.0) * pow(y,3.0) * s;
      *mu= r;
      /**** Compute variance/2.0 ****/
      r= 0.5 * pow(gamma,2.0) * pow(y,4.0) * s;
      *sigma= r;
  return(0);
}
tridagm(a,b,c,x,y,number)
  /***********************************************************************
        tridagm() is a variant  Numerical Recipes' routine of the same name.
------------------------------------------------------------------------
    ***********************************************************************/
  long number;
  double *a,*b,*c,*x,*y;
{
  int error;
  int i,j,k;
  double r,s,t,bet,*gam,*vec;
  double *dvector();
  gam= dvector(0,number-1);
  if (b[0] == 0.0)
    { error= 1; goto fre; }
  x[0]= y[0] / (bet=b[0]);
  for (j=1 ; j < number ; j++)
    {
        gam[j]= c[j-1] / bet;
        bet= b[j] - a[j] * gam[j];
        if (bet == 0.0)
          { error= 2; goto fre; }
        x[j]= (y[j] -a[j] * x[j-1]) / bet;
    }
  for (j=(number-2) ; j >= 0 ; j--)
    { x[j] -= gam[j+1] * x[j+1]; }
  error= 0;
 fre:
  free_dvector(gam,0,number-1);
  return(error);
}
```

Bibliography

Aase, K. (1984). "Optimum Portfolio Diversification in a General Continuous Time Model." *Stochastic Processes and Their Application* 18: 81–98.

Abel, A. (1986). "Stock Prices under Time-Varying Dividend Risk: An Exact Solution in an Infinite-Horizon General Equilibrium Model." Wharton School, University of Pennsylvania.

Acharya, S., and D. Madan. (1993a). "Arbitrage-Free Econometric Option Pricing Models in an Incomplete Market with a Locally Risky Discount Factor." Federal Reserve Board.

———. (1993b). "Idiosyncratic Risk, Borrowing Constraints and Asset Prices." Barnard College.

Adler, M., and J. Detemple. (1988). "On the Optimal Hedge of a Non-Traded Cash Position." *Journal of Finance* 43: 143–153.

Ahn, H. (1993). "A Review on Stochastic Differential Utility." Mathematics Department, Purdue University.

Ait Sahlia, F. (1995). "Optimal Stopping and Weak Convergence Methods for Some Problems in Financial Economics." Ph.D. diss., Operations Research Department, Stanford University.

Ait Sahalia, Y. (1992). "Nonparametric Pricing of Interest Rate Derivative Securities." Graduate School of Business, University of Chicago.

Aiyagari, S., and M. Gertler. (1990). "Asset Returns with Transaction Costs and Uninsured Individual Risk: A Stage III Exercise." Working Paper 454. Federal Reserve Bank of Minneapolis.

Akahari, J. (1993). "Some Formulas for a New Type of Path-Dependent Option." Working Paper. Department of Mathematics, University of Tokyo.

Akian, M., J.-L. Meñaldi, and A. Sulem. (1993). "On an Investment-Consumption Model with Transaction Costs." Working Paper. INRIA, Rocquencourt, France.

Aliprantis, C., and O. Burkinshaw. (1985). *Positive Operators*. Orlando: Academic Press.

Allegretto, W., G. Barone-Adesi, and R. Elliott. (1993). "Numerical Evaluation of the Critical Price and American Options." Department of Mathematics, University of Alberta.

Allingham, M. (1991). "Existence Theorems in the Capital Asset Pricing Model." *Econometrica* 59: 1169–1174.

Alvarez, O. (1991). "Gestion de Portefeuille Avec Coût de Transaction." École Polytechnique.

Alvarez, O., and A. Tourin. (1994). "Viscosity Solutions of Nonlinear Integro-Differential Equations." Université de Paris IX-Dauphine.

Amaro de Matos, J. (1993). "MSM Estimators of American Option Pricing Models." INSEAD, Fontainebleau, France.

Amin, K. (1991). "On the Computation of Continuous Time Option Prices Using Discrete Approximations." *Journal of Financial and Quantitative Analysis* 26: 477–495.

———. (1993a). "Jump-Diffusion Option Valuation in Discrete-Time." *Journal of Finance* 48: 1833–1863.

———. (1993b). "Option Valuation with Systematic Stochastic Volatility." *Journal of Finance* 48: 881–910.

Amin, K., and J. Bodurtha. (1995). "Discrete-Time Valuation of American Options with Stochastic Interest Rates." *Review of Financial Studies* 8: 193–234.

Amin, K., and R. Jarrow. (1993). "Pricing Options on Risky Assets in a Stochastic Interest Rate Economy." *Mathematical Finance* 2: 217–237.

Amin, K., and A. Khanna. (1994). "Convergence of American Option Values from Discrete to Continuous-Time Financial Models." *Mathematical Finance* 4: 289–304.

Amin, K., and A. Morton. (1994). "Implied Volatility Functions in Arbitrage-Free Term Structure Models." *Journal of Financial Economics* 35: 141–180.

Amin, K., and V. Ng. (1993). "Options Valuation with Systematic Stochastic Volatility." *Journal of Finance* 48: 881–909.

Ansel, J., and Stricker, C. (1992). "Quelques Remarques sur un theoreme de Yan." Université de Franche-Comté.

———. (1993). "Couverture des actifs contingents." Laboratoire de Mathématiques - URA CNRS 741, UFR Science et Techniques.

———. (1994). "Lois de Martingale, Densités et Decomposition de Föllmer Schweizer." Université de Franche-Comté.

Antonelli, F. (1993). "Backward-Forward Stochastic Differential Equations." *Annals of Applied Probability* 3: 777-793.

Apelfeld, R., and A. Conze. (1990). "The Term Structure of Interest Rates: The Case of Imperfect Information." Department of Economics, University of Chicago.

Araujo, A., and P. Monteiro. (1987). "Generic Non-Existence of Equilibria in Finance Models." *Journal of Mathematical Economics* 20: 489–501.

———. (1989). "Equilibrium Without Uniform Conditions." *Journal of Economic Theory* 48: 416–427.

Arnold, L. (1974). *Stochastic Differential Equations: Theory and Applications.* New York: Wiley.

Arntzen, H. (1994). "Solution to a Class of Stochastic Investment Problems involving Finite Variation Controls." Mathematics Institute, University of Oslo.

Arrow, K. (1951). "An Extension of the Basic Theorems of Classical Welfare Economics." In J. Neyman, *Proceedings of the Second Berkeley Symposium on Mathematical Statistics and Probability,* pp. 507–532. Berkeley: University of California Press.

———. (1953). "Le Rôle des valeurs boursières pour la repartition la meillure des risques." *Econometrie.* Colloq. Internat. Centre National de la Recherche Scientifique 40 (Paris 1952), pp. 41–47; discussion, pp. 47–48, C.N.R.S. (Paris 1953). English Translation in *Review of Economic Studies* 31 (1964): 91–96.

———. (1970). *Essays in the Theory of Risk Bearing.* London: North-Holland.

Arrow, K., and G. Debreu. (1954). "Existence of an Equilibrium for a Competitive Economy." *Econometrica* 22: 265–290.

Artzner, P. (1995). "Approximate Completeness with Multiple Martingale Measures." *Mathematical Finance* 5: 1–12.

Artzner, P., and F. Delbaen. (1990a). "'Finem Lauda' or the Risk of Swaps." *Insurance: Mathematics and Economics* 9: 295–303.

———. (1990b). "Term Structure of Interest Rates: The Martingale Approach." *Advances in Applied Mathematics* 10: 95–129.

———. (1992). "Credit Risk and Prepayment Option." *ASTIN Bulletin* 22: 81–96.

———. (1993). "Optional and Dual Predictable Projections in Finance and Insurance." Université Louis Pasteur, Strasbourg, France.

———. (1994). "Default Risk Insurance and Incomplete Markets." Université Louis Pasteur, Strasbourg, France.

Artzner, P., and D. Heath. (1990). "Completeness and Non-Unique Pricing." Department of Operations Research, Cornell University.

Au, K., and D. Thurston. (1993). "Markovian Term Structure Movements." School of Banking and Finance, University of New South Wales.

Avellaneda, M., and A. Parás. (1994). "Hedging Derivatives in the Presence of Transaction Costs: Non-Linear Diffusion Equation, Obstacle Problems and Non-Markovian Strategies." Courant Institute of Mathematical Sciences, New York University.

Babbs, S. (1991). "A Family of Ito Process Models for the Term Structure of Interest Rates." Financial Options Research Centre, University of Warwick.

Babbs, S., and M. Selby. (1993). "Pricing by Arbitrage in Incomplete Markets." Financial Options Research Centre, University of Warwick.

Babbs, S., and N. Webber. (1994). "A Theory of the Term Structure with an Official Short Rate." Midland Global Markets and University of Warwick.

Bachelier, L. (1900). "Théorie de la Speculation." *Annales Scientifiques de L'École Normale Supérieure* 3d ser., 17: 21–88. Translation in *The Random Character of Stock Market Prices,* ed. Paul Cootner, pp. 17–79. Cambridge, Mass.: MIT Press, 1964.

Back, K. (1986). "Securities Market Equilibrium without Bankruptcy: Contingent Claim Valuation and the Martingale Property." Research Paper 683. Center for Mathematical Studies in Economics and Management Science, Northwestern University.

———. (1991a). "Asset Pricing for General Processes." *Journal of Mathematical Economics* 20: 371–396.

———. (1991b). "Term Structure Notes." Washington University, St. Louis.

Back, K., and S. Pliska. (1986). "Discrete versus Continuous Trading in Securities Markets with Net Worth Constraints." Working Paper 700. Center for Mathematical Studies in Economics and Management Science, Northwestern University.

———. (1987). "The Shadow Price of Information in Continuous Time Decision Problems." *Stochastics* 22: 151–186.

———. (1991). "On the Fundamental Theorem of Asset Pricing with an Infinite State Space." *Journal of Mathematical Economics* 20: 1–18.

Backus, D., S. Foresi, and S. Zin. (1994). "Arbitrage Opprtunities in Arbitrage-Free Models of Bond Pricing." Stern School of Business, New York University and NBER (National Bureau of Economic Research).

Backus, D., and S. Zin. (1994). "Reverse Engineering the Yield Curve." NBER.

Bajeux-Besnainou, I., and R. Portait. (1992). "Pricing Derivative Securities with a Multi-Factor Model of the Yield Curve." Working Paper. ESSEC, Cergy-Pontoise, France.

———. (1993). "Dynamic Asset Allocation in a Mean-Variance Framework." ESSEC and Laboratoire d'Econométrie de L'École Polytechnique.

Bajeux-Besnainou, I., and J.-C. Rochet. (1992). "Dynamic Spanning: Are Options an Appropriate Investment?" Working Paper. ESSEC, Cergy-Pontoise, France.

Balasko, Y. (1989). *Foundations of the Theory of General Equilibrium.* New York: Academic Press.

Balasko, Y., and D. Cass. (1986). "The Structure of Financial Equilibrium with Exogenous Yields: The Case of Incomplete Markets." *Econometrica* 57: 135–162.

Balasko, Y., D. Cass, and P. Siconolfi. (1990). "The Structure of Financial Equilibrium with Exogenous Yields: The Case of Restricted Participation." *Journal of Mathematical Economics* 19: 195–216.

Balduzzi, P. (1994). "A Second Factor in Bond Yields." Department of Finance, Stern School of Business, New York University.

Ball, C. (1994). "Unit Roots and the Estimation of Interest Rate Dynamics." Owen Graduate School of Management, Vanderbilt University.

Ball, C., and A. Roma. (1994). "Stochastic Volatility Option Pricing." *Journal of Financial and Quantitative Analysis* 29: 589–607.

Ball, C., and W. Torous. (1994). "Regime Shifts in Short-Term Interest Rate Dynamics." Owen Graduate School of Management, Vanderbilt University.

Banz, R., and M. Miller. (1978). "Prices for State-Contingent Claims: Some Evidence and Applications." *Journal of Business* 51: 653-672.

Barles, G., J. Burdeau, M. Romano, and N. Samsoen. (1993). "Estimation de la frontière libre des options américaines au voisinage de l'echéance." *Comtes Rendus de l'Academie de Science de Paris* 316-I: 171–174.

Barles, G., C. Daher, and M. Romano. (1992). "Convergence of Numerical Schemes for Parabolic Equations Arising in Finance Theory." Cahier 9244, CEREMADE, Université de Paris.

Barles, G., M. Romano, and N. Touzi. (1993). "Contingent Claims and Market Completeness in a Stochastic Volatility Model." Département de Mathématiques, Université de Tours, France.

Barone, E., and S. Risa. (1994). "Valuation of Floaters and Options on Floaters under Special Repo Rates." Instituto Mobiliare Italiano, Rome.

Barone-Adesi, G., and R. Elliott. (1991). "Approximations for the Values of American Options." *Stochastic Analysis and Applications* 9: 115–131.

Barraquand, J. (1993). "Numerical Valuation of High Dimensional Multivariate European Securities." Digital Research Laboratory, Paris.

Barraquand, J., and T. Pudet. (1994). "Pricing of American Path-Dependent Contingent Claims." Digital Research Laboratory, Paris.

Bartle, R. (1976). *The Elements of Real Analysis* (2d ed.). New York: Wiley.

Basak, S. (1992). "A General Equilibrium Model of Portfolio Insurance." Graduate School of Industrial Administration, Carnegie Mellon University.

Baz, J., and M. Pascutti. (1994). "The Pricing of Swap Covenants: Analysis and Applications." Harvard Business School, Harvard University.

Beaglehole, D. (1990). "Tax Clienteles and Stochastic Processes in the Gilt Market." Graduate School of Business, University of Chicago.

Beaglehole, D., and M. Tenney. (1990). "General Solutions of Some Interest Rate Contingent Claim Pricing Equations." *Journal of Fixed Income* 1: 69–84.

Becker, R., and J. Boyd. (1992). "Recursive Utility: Discrete Time Theory." Department of Economics, Indiana University.

Beckers, S. (1981). "Standard Deviations Implied in Option Process as Predictors of Future Stock Price Variability." *Journal of Banking and Finance* 5: 363–382.

Bekaert, G., R. Hodrick, and D. Marshall. (1994). "The Implications of First-Order Risk Aversion for Asset Market Risk Premiums." Graduate School of Business, Stanford University.

Bellman, R. (1957). *Dynamic Programming*. Princeton, N.J.: Princeton University Press.

Bensoussan, A. (1983). "Lectures on Stochastic Control." In S. Mitter and A. Moro, *Nonlinear Filtering and Stochastic Control,* Lecture Notes in Mathematics 972, pp. 1–62. New York: Springer-Verlag.

———. (1984). "On the Theory of Option Pricing." *Acta Applicandae Mathematicae* 2: 139–158.

Bensoussan, A., M. Crouhy, and D. Galai. (1992). "Black-Scholes Approximation of Complex Option Values: The Cases of European Compound Call Options and Equity Warrants." Université de Paris, Dauphine, and INRIA, France.

Benveniste, L., and J. Scheinkman. (1979). "On the Differentiability of the Value Function in Dynamic Models of Economics." *Econometrica* 47: 727–732.

Berardi, A., and M. Esposito. (1994). "A Base Model for Multifactor Specifications of the Term Structure." Economic Research Department, Banca Commerciale Italiana.

Bergman, Y. (1985). "Time Preference and Capital Asset Pricing Models." *Journal of Financial Economics* 14: 145–159.

———. (1991). "Option Pricing with Differential Interest Rates: Arbitrage Bands Beget Arbitrage Ovals." School of Business, Hebrew University, Jerusalem.

Berk, J. (1992). "The Necessary and Sufficient Conditions that Imply the CAPM." Faculty of Commerce, University of British Columbia, Canada.

Berk, J. and H. Uhlig. (1993). "The Timing of Information in a General Equilibrium Framework." *Journal of Economic Theory* 59: 275–287.

Bernard, P., D. Talay, and L. Tubaro. (1993). "Rate of Convergence of a Stochastic Particle Method for the Kolmogorov Equation with Variable Coefficients." INRIA, Sophia-Antipolis, France.

Bertsekas, D. (1976). *Dynamic Programming and Stochastic Control.* New York: Academic Press.

Bertsekas, D., and S. Shreve. (1978). *Stochastic Optimal Control: The Discrete Time Case.* New York: Academic Press.

Bewley, T. (1972). "Existence of Equilibria in Economies with Infinitely Many Commodities." *Journal of Economic Theory* 4: 514–540.

———. (1982). "Thoughts on Volatility Tests of the Intertemporal Asset Pricing Model." Department of Economics, Northwestern University.

Bick, A. (1986). "On Viable Diffusion Price Processes." *Journal of Finance* 45: 673–689.

———. (1988). "Producing Derivative Assets with Forward Contracts." *Journal of Financial and Quantitative Analysis* 2: 153–160.

———. (1993). "Quadratic Variation Based Dynamic Strategies." Faculty of Business Administration, Simon Fraser University, Vancouver, Canada.

———. (1994). "Futures Pricing via Futures Strategies." Faculty of Business Administration, Simon Fraser University, Vancouver, Canada.

Bick, A., and H. Reisman. (1993). "Generalized Implied Volatility." Faculty of Business Administration, Simon Fraser University, Vancouver, Canada.

Bick, A., and W. Willinger. (1994). "Dynamic Spanning without Probabilities." *Stochastic Processes and Their Applications* 50: 349–374.

Billingsley, P. (1986). *Probability and Measure* (2d ed.). New York: Wiley.

Black, F. (1972). "Capital Market Equilibrium with Restricted Borrowing." *Journal of Business* 45: 444–454.

———. (1976). "The Pricing of Commodity Contracts." *Journal of Financial Economics* 3: 167–179.

———. (1990). "Mean Reversion and Consumption Smoothing." *Review of Financial Studies* 3: 107–114.

———. (1993). "Exploring General Equilibrium." Goldman, Sachs and Company, New York.

Black, F., E. Derman, and I. Kani. (1992). "A Two-Factor Model of Interest Rates." Goldman, Sachs and Company, New York.

Black, F., E. Derman, and W. Toy. (1990). "A One-Factor Model of Interest Rates and Its Application to Treasury Bond Options." *Financial Analysts Journal*: January–February, 33–39.

Black, F., and P. Karasinski. (1991). "Bond and Option Pricing when Short Rates are Lognormal." *Financial Analysts Journal*: July–August, 52–59.

Black, F., and M. Scholes. (1973). "The Pricing of Options and Corporate Liabilities." *Journal of Political Economy* 81: 637–654.

Blackwell, D. (1965). "Discounted Dynamic Programming." *Annals of Mathematical Statistics* 36: 226–235.

Blume, L., D. Easley, and M. O'Hara. (1982). "Characterization of Optimal Plans for Stochastic Dynamic Programs." *Journal of Economic Theory* 28: 221–234.

Bollerslev, T., R. Chou, and K. Kroner. (1992). "ARCH Modeling in Finance: A Review of the Theory and Empirical Evidence." *Journal of Econometrics* 52: 5–59.

Bonomo, M., and R. Garcia. (1993). "Disappointment Aversion as a Solution to the Equity Premium and the Risk-Free Rate Puzzles." CRDE Working Paper 2793. Université de Montréal.

Bossaerts, P. (1990). "Modern Term Structure Theory." California Institute of Technology, Pasadena.

Bossaerts, P., and P. Hillion. (1994). "Local Parametric Analysis of Hedging in Discrete Time." California Institute of Technology, Pasadena, and Tilburg University, The Netherlands.

Bottazzi, J.-M. (1995). "Existence of Equilibria with Incomplete Markets: The Case of Smooth Returns." *Journal of Mathematical Economics* 24: 59–72.

Bottazzi, J.-M., and T. Hens. (1993). "Excess Demand Funtions and Incomplete Markets." CERMSEM, Harvard University.

Bottazzi, J-M., T. Hens, and A. Löffler. (1994). "Market Demand Functions in the CAPM." Delta, Université de Paris.

Bouleau, N., and D. Lamberton. (1993). "Residual Risks and Hedging Strategies in Markovian Markets." CERMA-ENPC, Paris, France.

Bouleau, N., and D. Lépingle. (1994). *Numerical Methods for Stochastic Processes*. New York: Wiley.

Boyle, P. (1977). "Options: A Monte Carlo Approach." *Journal of Financial Economics* 4: 323–338.

————. (1988). "A Lattice Framework for Option Pricing with Two State Variables." *Journal of Financial and Quantitative Analysis* 23: 1–12.

————. (1990). "Valuation of Derivative Securities Involving Several Assets Using Discrete Time Methods." Accounting Group, University of Waterloo, Waterloo, Canada.

Boyle, P., J. Evnine, and S. Gibbs. (1989). "Numerical Evaluation of Multivariate Contingent Claims." *Review of Financial Studies* 2: 241–250.

Boyle, P., and T. Vorst. (1992). "Options Replication in Discrete Time with Transaction Costs." *Journal of Finance* 47: 271–293.

Brace, A., and M. Musiela. (1994a). "A Multifactor Gauss Markov Implementation of Heath, Jarrow, and Morton." *Mathematical Finance* 4: 259–284.

———. (1994b). "Swap Derivatives in a Gaussian HJM Framework." Treasury Group, Citibank, Sydney, Australia.

Bray, M. (1994a). "The Arbitrage Pricing Theory is Not Robust 1: Variance Matrices and Portfolio Theory in Pictures." London School of Economics.

———. (1994b). "The Arbitrage Pricing Theory is Not Robust 2: Factor Structure and Factor Pricing." London School of Economics.

Breeden, D. (1979). "An Intertemporal Asset Pricing Model with Stochastic Consumption and Investment Opportunities." *Journal of Financial Economics* 7: 265–296.

———. (1986). "Consumption, Production, Inflation and Interest Rates." *Journal of Financial Economics* 16: 3–39.

Breeden, D., M. Gibbons, and R. Litzenberger. (1989). "Empirical Tests of the Consumption Oriented CAPM." *Journal of Finance* 44: 231–262.

Breeden, D., and R. Litzenberger. (1978). "Prices of State-Contingent Claims Implicit in Option Prices." *Journal of Business* 51: 621–651.

Brennan, M., and E. Schwartz. (1977). "The Valuation of American Put Options." *Journal of Finance* 32: 449–462.

———. (1979). "A Continuous Time Approach to the Pricing of Bonds." *Journal of Banking and Finance* 3: 133–155.

———. (1980a). "Conditional Predictions of Bond Prices and Returns." *Journal of Finance* 35: 405–419.

———. (1980b). "Analyzing Convertible Bonds." *Journal of Financial and Quantitative Analysis* 10: 907–929.

———. (1982). "An Equilibrium Model of Bond Pricing and a Test of Market Efficiency." *Journal of Financial and Quantitative Analysis* 17: 301–329.

Brennan, M., E. Schwartz, and R. Lagnado. (1993). "Strategic Asset Allocation." Anderson School of Management, University of California, Los Angeles.

Broadie, M., and J. Detemple. (1995). "American Capped Call Options on Dividend-Paying Assets." *Review of Financial Studies* 8: 161–191.

———. (1993a). "Bounds and Approximations for American Option Values." Graduate School of Business, Columbia University.

———. (1993b). "The Valuation of American Options on Multiple Assets." Graduate School of Business, Columbia University.

————. (1994). "American Option Valuation: New Bounds, Approximations, and a Comparison of Existing Methods." Graduate School of Business, Columbia University. Forthcoming in *Review of Financial Studies*.

Broadie, M., and P. Glasserman. (1993). "Estimating Security Price Derivatives Using Simulation." Graduate School of Business, Columbia University. Forthcoming in *Management Science*.

Brock, W. (1979). "An Integration of Stochastic Growth Theory and the Theory of Finance, Part I: The Growth Model." In J. Green and J. Scheinkman, *General Equilibrium, Growth, and Trade*, pp. 165–192. New York: Academic Press.

————. (1982). "Asset Prices in a Production Economy." In J. McCall, *The Economics of Information and Uncertainty*, pp. 1–46. Chicago: University of Chicago Press.

Brown, D., and M. Gibbons. (1985). "A Simple Econometric Approach for Utility-Based Asset Pricing Models." *Journal of Finance* 40: 359–381.

Brown, D., P. DeMarzo, and C. Eaves. (1993a). "Computing Equilibria when Asset Markets are Incomplete." Department of Economics, Stanford University. Forthcoming in *Econometrica*.

————. (1993b). "Computing Zeros of Sections Vector Bundles Using Homotopies and Relocalization." Department of Operations Research, Stanford University. Forthcoming in *Mathematics of Operations Research*.

Brown, R., and S. Schaefer. (1993). "Interest Rate Volatility and the Shape of the Term Structure." *Philosophical Transactions of the Royal Society: Physical Sciences and Engineering* 347: 449–598.

————. (1994). "The Term Structure of Real Interest Rates and the Cox, Ingersoll, and Ross Model." *Journal of Financial Economics* 35: 3–42.

Broze, L., O. Scaillet, and J.-M. Zakoïan. (1993). "Testing for Continuous-Time Models of the Short-Term Interest Rate." CORE, Louvain-la-Neuve, Belgium.

Buckdahn, R. (1995). "BSDE with Non-Square Integrable Terminal Value—FBSDE with Delay." Faculté des Sciences, Département de Mathématiques, Université de Bretagne Occidentale, Brest, France.

Bunch, D., and H. Johnson. (1993). "A Simple and Numerically Efficient Valuation Method for American Puts Using a Modified Geske-Johnson Approach." *Journal of Finance* 47: 809–816.

Buono, M., R. Gregory-Allen, and U. Yaari. (1992). "The Efficacy of Term Structure Estimation Techniques: A Monte Carlo Study." *Journal of Fixed Income* 2: 52–63.

Büttler, H.-J. (1993). "Evaluation of Callable Bonds: Finite Difference Methods, Stability and Accuracy." Swiss National Bank, Zürich.

Büttler, H.-J., and J. Waldvogel. (1994). "Pricing Callable Bonds by Means of Green's Function." Swiss National Bank, Zürich. Forthcoming in *Mathematical Finance.*

Campbell, J. (1984). "Bond and Stock Returns in a Simple Exchange Model." Department of Economics, Princeton University.

———. (1986). "A Defense of Traditional Hypotheses about the Term Structure of Interest Rates." *Journal of Finance* 41: 183–193.

———. (1990). "Intertemporal Asset Pricing without Consumption." Department of Economics, Princeton University.

Campbell, J., A. Lo, and A. MacKinlay. (1994). "The Econometrics of Financial Markets." Research Program in Computational Finance, Massachusetts Institute of Technology.

Carr, P. (1989). "European Option Valuation When Carrying Costs are Unknown." Johnson Graduate School of Management, Cornell University.

———. (1991). "Deriving Derivatives of Derivative Securities." Johnson Graduate School of Management, Cornell University.

———. (1993a). "Valuing Bond Futures and the Quality Option." Johnson Graduate School of Management, Cornell University.

———. (1993b). "European Put Call Symmetry." Johnson Graduate School of Management, Cornell University.

———. (1994). "On Approximations for the Values of American Options." Johnson Graduate School of Management, Cornell University.

Carr, P., and R.-R. Chen. (1993). "Valuing Bond Futures and the Quality Option." Johnson Graduate School of Management, Cornell University.

Carr, P., and K. Ellis. (1994). "Non-Standard Valuation of Barrier Options." Johnson Graduate School of Management, Cornell University.

Carr, P., and D. Faguet. (1994). "Fast Accurate Valuation of American Options." Johnson Graduate School of Management, Cornell University.

Carr, P., and R. Jarrow. (1990). "The Stop-Loss Start-Gain Paradox and Option Valuation: A New Decomposition into Intrinsic and Time Value." *Review of Financial Studies* 3: 469–492.

Carr, P., R. Jarrow, and R. Myneni. (1992). "Alternative Characterizations of American Put Options." *Mathematical Finance* 2: 87–106.

Carverhill, A. (1988). "The Ho and Lee Term Structure Theory: A Continuous Time Version." Working Paper 88–85. Financial Options Research Centre, University of Warwick.

———. (1990). "A Survey of Elementary Techniques for Pricing Options on Bonds and Interest Rates." Working Paper 90-9. Financial Options Research Centre, University of Warwick.

————. (1991). "The Term Structure of Interest Rates and Associated Options: Equilibrium versus Evolutionary Models." Working Paper 91-21. Financial Options Research Centre, University of Warwick.

————. (1994). "A Simplified Exposition of the Heath, Jarrow, and Morton Model." Department of Finance, University of Science and Technology, Hong Kong.

Carverhill, A., and K. Pang. (1995). "Efficient and Flexible Bond Option Valuation in the Heath Jarrow and Morton Framework." Department of Finance, University of Science and Technology, Hong Kong.

Cass, D. (1984). "Competitive Equilibria in Incomplete Financial Markets." Center for Analytic Research in Economics and the Social Sciences, University of Pennsylvania.

————. (1989). "Sunspots and Incomplete Financial Markets: The Leading Example." In G. Feiwel, *The Economics of Imperfect Competition and Employment: Joan Robinson and Beyond*, pp. 677–693. London: Macmillan.

————. (1991). "Incomplete Financial Markets and Indeterminacy of Financial Equilibrium." In J.-J. Laffont, *Advances in Economic Theory*. Cambridge: Cambridge University Press, pp. 263–288.

Chae, S. (1988). "Existence of Equilibria in Incomplete Markets." *Journal of Economic Theory* 44: 9–18.

Chamberlain, G. (1988). "Asset Pricing in Multiperiod Securities Markets." *Econometrica* 56: 1283–1300.

Chan, K.-C., A. Karolyi, F. Longstaff, and A. Saunders. (1992). "An Empirical Comparison of Alternative Models of the Short-Term Interest Rate." *Journal of Finance* 47: 1209–1227.

Chan, Y.-K. (1992). "Term Structure as a Second Order Dynamical System, and Pricing of Derivative Securities." Bear Stearns and Company, New York.

Chang, F.-R. (1993). "Adjustment Costs, Optimal Investment and Uncertainty." Department of Economics, Indiana University.

Chapman, D. (1994). "Habit Formation, Consumption, and State-Prices." Department of Finance, Graduate School of Business, University of Texas at Austin.

Charretour, F., R. Elliott, R. Myneni, and R. Viswanathan. (1992). "American Option Valuation Notes." Oberwohlfach Institute, Oberwohlfach, Germany.

Chavella, D. (1994). "Numerical Error in Monte Carlo Simulations of Log-Normal Processes." BARRA, Oakland, California.

Chen, L. (1994). "Stochastic Mean and Stochastic Volatility: A Three-Factor Model of the Term Structure of Interest Rates and Its Application to the Pricing of Interest Rate Derivatives: Part I." Harvard Business School, Harvard University.

Chen, R.-R., and L. Scott. (1993b). "Pricing Interest Rate Futures Options with Futures-Style Margining." *Journal of Futures Markets* 13: 15–22.

―――. (1992a). "Pricing Interest Rate Options in a Two-Factor Cox-Ingersoll-Ross Model of the Term Structure." *Review of Financial Studies* 5: 613–636.

―――. (1992b). "Maximum Likelihood Estimation for a Multi-Factor Equilibrium Model of the Term Structure of Interest Rates." Department of Finance, Rutgers University.

―――. (1993a). "Multi-Factor Cox-Ingersoll-Ross Models of the Term Structure: Estimates and Tests from a State-Space Model Using a Kalman Filter." Department of Finance, Rutgers University.

Chen, Z.-W. (1994). "Viable Costs and Equilibrium Prices in Frictional Securities Markets." Graduate School of Business, University of Wisconsin.

Cheng, S. (1991). "On the Feasibility of Arbitrage-Based Option Pricing When Stochastic Bond Price Processes Are Involved." *Journal of Economic Theory* 53: 185–198.

Cherian, J., and R. Jarrow. (1993). "Options Markets, Self-Fulfilling Prophecies, and Implied Volatilities." School of Management, Boston University.

Cherif, T., N. El Karoui, R. Myneni, and R. Viswnathan. (1995). "Arbitrage Pricing and Hedging of Quanto Options and Interest Rate Claims with Quadratic Gaussian State Variables." Working Paper. Laboratoire de Probabilités, Université de Paris, VI.

Chernoff, H., and A. Petkau. (1984). "Numerical Methods for Bayes Sequential Decisions Problems." Technical Report 34. Statistics Center, Massachusetts Institute of Technology.

Cherubini, U. (1993). "The Orthogonal Polynomial Approach to Contingent Claim Pricing." Banco Commerciale Italiana, Ufficio Studi, Milan.

Cherubini, U., and M. Esposito. (1992). "Using Pearson's System to Characterize Diffusion Processes: A Note." Banco Commerciale Italiana, Ufficio Studi, Milan.

―――. (1993). "Options in and on Interest Rate Futures Contracts: Results from Martingale Pricing Theory." Banco Commerciale Italiana, Ufficio Studi, Milan.

Chesney, M., R.-J. Elliott, and R. Gibson. (1993). "Analytical Solution for the Pricing of American Bond and Yield Options." *Mathematical Finance* 3: 277–294.

Chew, S.-H. (1983). "A Generalization of the Quasilinear Mean with Applications to the Measurement of Income Inequality and Decision Theory Resolving the Allais Paradox." *Econometrica* 51: 1065–1092.

————. (1989). "Axiomatic Utility Theories with the Betweenness Property." *Annals of Operations Research* 19: 273–298.

Chew, S.-H., and L. Epstein. (1991). "Recursive Utility under Uncertainty." In A. Khan and N. Yannelis, *Equilibrium Theory with an Infinite Number of Commodities.* New York: Springer-Verlag, pp. 353–369.

Cheyette, O. (1992). "Markov Representation of the Heath-Jarrow-Morton Model." BARRA, Oakland, California.

Chow, Y., and H. Teicher. (1978). *Probability Theory: Independence Interchangeability Martingales.* New York: Springer-Verlag.

Christensen, B. J. (1991). "Statistics for Arbitrage-Free Asset Pricing." Department of Finance, New York University.

Christensen, P. (1987). "An Intuitive Approach to the Harrison and Kreps Concept of Arbitrage Pricing for Continuous Time Diffusions." Department of Management, Odense University, Denmark.

Chuang, C. (1994). "Joint Distribution of Brownian Motion and Its Maximum, with a Generalization to Correlated BM and Applications to Barrier Options." Department of Statistics, Stanford University.

Chung, K. L. (1974). *A Course in Probability Theory* (2d ed.). New York: Academic Press.

Chung, K. L., and R. Williams. (1990). *An Introduction to Stochastic Integration* (2d ed.). Boston: Birkhäuser.

Citanna, A., A. Kajii, and A. Villanacci. (1994). "Constrained Suboptimality in Incomplete Markets: A General Approach and Two Applications." Center for Analytic Research in Economics and the Social Sciences, University of Pennsylvania.

Citanna, A., and A. Villanacci. (1993). "On Generic Pareto Improvement in Competitive Economies with Incomplete Asset Structure." Center for Analytic Research in Economics and the Social Sciences, University of Pennsylvania.

Clark, S. (1993). "The Valuation Problem in Arbitrage Price Theory." *Journal of Mathematical Economics* 22: 463–478.

Clelow, L. (1990). "Finite Difference Techniques for One and Two Dimensional Option Valuation Problems." Financial Options Research Center, University of Warwick.

Clelow, L., and A. Carverhill. (1992). "Efficient Monte Carlo Valuation and Hedging of Contingent Claims." Financial Options Research Centre, University of Warwick.

Coleman, T., L. Fisher, and R. Ibbotson. (1992). "Estimating the Term Structure of Interest Rates from Data that Include the Prices of Coupon Bonds." *Journal of Fixed Income*: September, 85–116.

Constantinides, G. (1982). "Intertemporal Asset Pricing with Heterogeneous Consumers and without Demand Aggregation." *Journal of Business* 55: 253–267.

———. (1986). "Capital Market Equilibrium with Transactions Costs." *Journal of Political Economy* 94: 842–862.

———. (1989). "Theory of Valuation: Overview and Recent Developments." In S. Bhatt and G. Constantinides, *Theory of Valuation, Frontiers of Modern Financial Theory*, pp. 1–23. Totowa, N.J.: Rowman and Littlefield.

———. (1990). "Habit Formation: A Resolution of the Equity Premium Puzzle." *Journal of Political Economy* 98: 519–543.

———. (1992). "A Theory of the Nominal Term Structure of Interest Rates." *Review of Financial Studies* 5: 531–552.

———. (1993). "Option Pricing Bounds with Transactions Costs." Graduate School of Business, University of Chicago.

Constantinides, G., and D. Duffie. (1991). "Asset Pricing with Heterogeneous Consumers." Graduate School of Business, Stanford University. Forthcoming in *Journal of Political Economy*.

Conze, A., and R. Viswanathan. (1991a). "Probability Measures and Numeraires." CEREMADE, Université de Paris.

———. (1991b). "Path Dependent Options: The Case of Lookback Options." *Journal of Finance* 5: 1893–1907.

Cooper, I., and A. Mello. (1991). "The Default Risk of Swaps." Sloan School of Management, Massachusetts Institute of Technology.

———. (1992). "Pricing and Optimal Use of Forward Contracts with Default Risk." Department of Finance, London Business School, University of London.

Cornell, B. (1981). "The Consumption Based Asset Pricing Model." *Journal of Financial Economics* 9: 103–108.

Courtadon, G. (1982). "The Pricing of Options on Default-Free Bonds." *Journal of Financial and Quantitative Analysis* 17: 75–100.

Cox, J. (1983). "Optimal Consumption and Portfolio Rules When Assets Follow a Diffusion Process." Working Paper 658. Graduate School of Business, Stanford University.

Cox, J., and C.-F. Huang. (1988). "Options Pricing and Its Applications." In S. Bhattacharya and G. Constantinides, *Frontiers of Financial Theory*. Totowa, N.J.: Rowman and Littlefield, pp. 272–288.

———. (1989). "Optimal Consumption and Portfolio Policies When Asset Prices Follow a Diffusion Process." *Journal of Economic Theory* 49: 33–83.

———. (1991). "A Variational Problem Arising in Financial Economics with an Application to a Portfolio Turnpike Theorem." *Journal of Mathematical Economics* 20: 465–488.

———. (1992). "A Continuous-Time Portfolio Turnpike Theorem." *Journal of Economic Dynamics and Control* 16: 491-508.

Cox, J., J. Ingersoll, and S. Ross. (1980). "An Analysis of Variable Rate Loan Contracts." Graduate School of Business, Stanford University.

——. (1981a). "A Re-examination of Traditional Hypotheses about the Term Structure of Interest Rates." *Journal of Finance* 36: 769–799.

——. (1981b). "The Relation between Forward Prices and Futures Prices." *Journal of Financial Economics* 9: 321–346.

——. (1985a). "A Theory of the Term Structure of Interest Rates." *Econometrica* 53: 385–408.

——. (1985b). "An Intertemporal General Equilibrium Model of Asset Prices." *Econometrica* 53: 363–384.

Cox, J., and S. Ross. (1976). "The Valuation of Options for Alternative Stochastic Processes." *Journal of Financial Economics* 3: 145–166.

Cox, J., S. Ross, and M. Rubinstein. (1979). "Option Pricing: A Simplified Approach." *Journal of Financial Economics* 7: 229–263.

Cox, J., and M. Rubinstein. (1985). *Options Markets*. Englewood Cliffs, N.J.: Prentice-Hall.

Cuoco, D. (1994). "Optimal Policies and Equilibrium Prices with Portfolio Cone Constraints and Stochastic Labor Income." Wharton School, University of Pennsylvania.

Cuoco, D., and H. He. (1992a). "Dynamic Aggregation and Computation of Equilibria in Finite-Dimensional Economies with Incomplete Financial Markets." Haas School of Business, University of California, Berkeley.

——. (1992b). "Dynamic Equilibrium in Infinite-Dimensional Economies with Incomplete Financial Markets." The Wharton School, University of Pennsylvania.

Cutland, N., P. Kopp, and W. Willinger. (1991). "A Nonstandard Approach to Option Pricing." *Mathematical Finance* 1: 1–38.

——. (1993a). "Stock Price Returns and the Joseph Effect: Fractional Version of the Black-Scholes Model." *Mathematics Research Reports* 6(12), School of Mathematics, University of Hull, England.

——. (1993b). "From Discrete to Continuous Financial Models: New Convergence Results for Options Pricing." *Mathematical Finance* 3: 101–124.

Cvitanić, J., and I. Karatzas. (1992). "Convex Duality in Constrained Portfolio Optimization." *Annals of Applied Probability* 2: 767–818.

——. (1993). "Hedging Contingent Claims with Constrained Portfolios." *Annals of Applied Probability* 3: 652–681.

——. (1994). "On Portfolio Optimization under 'Drawdown' Constraints." Institute for Mathematics and Its Applications, University of Minnesota.

Cvitanić, J., and J. Ma. (1994). "Hedging Options for a Large Investor and Forward-Backward SDEs." Department of Statistics, Columbia University.

Daher, C., M. Romano, and G. Zacklad. (1992). "Détermination du prix de produits optionnels obligatoires à partir d'un modèle multifacteurs de la courbe des taux." Caisse Autonome de Refinancement, Paris.

Dai, Q. (1994). "Implied Green's Funtion in a No-Arbitrage Markov Model of the Instantaneous Short Rate." Graduate School of Business, Stanford University.

Daigler, R. (1993). *Financial Futures Markets.* New York: Harper Collins.

Dalang, R., A. Morton, and W. Willinger. (1990). "Equivalent Martingale Measures and No-Arbitrage in Stochastic Securities Market Models." *Stochastics and Stochastics Reports* 29: 185–201.

Dana, R.-A. (1993a). "Existence, Uniqueness and Determinacy of Arrow-Debreu Equilibria in Finance Models." *Journal of Mathematical Economics* 22: 563–580.

———. (1993b). "Existence and Uniqueness of Equilibria when Preferences are Additively Separable." *Econometrica* 61: 953–958.

Dana, R.-A., and M. Jeanblanc-Picqué. (1994). *Marchés financiers en temps continu: valorisation et équilibre.* Paris: Economica.

Dana, R.-A., and M. Pontier. (1990). "On the Existence of a Stochastic Equilibrium." Université de Paris VI, Paris.

Danesi, V., J.-P. Garcia, V. Genon-Catalot, and J.-P. Laurent. (1993). "Parameter Estimation for Yield Curve Models Using Contrast Methods." Université Marne-La-Valeé, Noisy-Le-Grand, France.

Darling, R. (1994). "Constructing Gamma-Martingales with Prescribed Limit, Using Backward SDE." Université de Provence, Marseilles.

Das, S. (1993a). "Jump-Hunting Interest Rates." Department of Finance, New York University.

———. (1993b). "Mean Rate Shifts and Alternative Models of the Interest Rate: Theory and Evidence." Department of Finance, New York University.

Dash, J. (1989). "Path Integrals and Options-I." Financial Strategies Group, Merrill Lynch Capital Markets, New York.

Dassios, A. (1994). "The Distribution of the Quantiles of a Brownian Motion with Drift and the Pricing of Related Path-Dependent Options." Department of Statistics, London School of Economics.

Davis, M. (1993). "Review of 'Controlled Markov Processes and Viscosity Solutions' by W. Fleming and H. Soner. Forthcoming in *AMS Bulletin.*" Imperial College, University of London.

Davis, M., and M. Clark. (1993). "Analysis of Financial Models including Transactions Costs." Imperial College, University of London.

Davis, M., and A. Norman. (1990). "Portfolio Selection with Transaction Costs." *Mathematics of Operations Research* 15: 676–713.

Davis, M., and V. Panas. (1991). "European Option Pricing with Transaction Costs." Proceedings of the Thirtieth IEEE Conference on Decision and Control, Brighton, December, pp. 1299–1304.

Davis, M., V. Panas, and T. Zariphopoulou. (1993). "European Option Pricing with Transaction Costs." *SIAM Journal of Control and Optimization* 31: 470–493.

Debreu, G. (1953). "Une economie de l'incertain." Electricité de France, Paris.

————. (1954). "Valuation Equilibrium and Pareto Optimum." *Proceedings of the National Academy of Sciences* 40: 588–592.

————. (1959). *Theory of Value.* Cowles Foundation Monograph 17. New Haven, Conn.: Yale University Press.

————. (1972). "Smooth Preferences." *Econometrica* 40: 603–615; Corrigendum 44 (1976): 831–832.

————. (1982). "Existence of Competitive Equilibrium." In K. Arrow and M. Intriligator, *Handbook of Mathematical Economics*, Vol. II, pp. 697–743. Amsterdam: North-Holland.

Decamps, J.-P., and J.-C. Rochet. (1993). "A Variational Approach for Pricing Options and Corporate Bonds." GREMAQ, Université des Sciences Sociales, Toulouse, France.

Deelstra, G., and F. Delbaen. (1994a). "Long-Term Returns in Stochastic Interest Rate Models." Department of Mathematics, Vrije Universiteit Brussel.

————. (1994b). "Existence of Solutions of Stochastic Differential Equations Related to the Bessel Process." Department of Mathematics, Vrije Universiteit Brussel.

Dekel, E. (1987). "Asset Demands without the Independence Axiom." Department of Economics, University of California, Berkeley.

Delbaen, F. (1992). "Representing Martingale Measures when Asset Prices are Continuous and Bounded." *Mathematical Finance* 2: 107–130.

————. (1993). "Consols in the CIR Model." *Mathematical Finance* 3: 125–134.

Delbaen, F., P. Monat, W. Schachermayer, M. Schweizer, and C. Stricker. (1994). "Inégalités de normes avec poids et fermeture d'un espace d'intégrales stochastiques." *Comtes Rendus de l'Academie de Science de Paris* 319I: 1079–1081.

Delbaen, F., and W. Schachermayer. (1992). "Arbitrage and Free Lunch with Bounded Risk for Unbounded Continuous Processes." Department of Mathematics, University of Vienna.

————. (1993). "A General Version of the Fundamental Theorem of Asset Pricing." Working Paper. Department of Mathematics, University of Vienna.

————. (1994a). "Arbitrage Possibilities in Bessel Processes and Their Relations to Local Martingales." Department of Mathematics, Vrije Universiteit Brussel.

————. (1994b). "The No-Arbitrage Property under a Choice of Numéraire." Department of Mathematics, Vrije Universiteit Brussel.

————. (1994c). "Attainable Claims with p'th Moments." Department of Mathematics, Vrije Universiteit Brussel.

————. (1994d). "The Existence of Absolutely Continuous Local Martingale Measures." Department of Mathematics, Vrije Universiteit Brussel.

Delbaen, F., and H. Shirakawa. (1994). "A Note on the No Arbitrage Condition for International Financial Markets." Department of Mathematics, Vrije Universiteit Brussel.

Delgado, F., and B. Dumas. (1993). "How Far Apart Can Two Riskless Interest Rates Be?." Fuqua School of Business, Duke University.

Demange, G., and J.-C. Rochet. (1992). *Methodes mathématiques de la finance.* Paris: Economica.

DeMarzo, P. (1988). "An Extension of the Modigliani-Miller Therorem to Stochastic Economics with Incomplete Markets." *Journal of Economic Theory* 45: 353–369.

DeMarzo, P., and B. Eaves. (1993). "A Homotopy, Grassmann Manifold, and Relocalization for Computing Equilibria of GEI." Hoover Institute, Stanford University.

de Munnik, J. (1992). *The Valuation of Interest Rate Derivative Securities.* Amsterdam: Tinbergen Institute.

Dengler, H., and R. Jarrow. (1993). "Option Pricing Using a Binomial Model with Random Time Steps." Mathematics Department and Johnson Graduate School of Management, Cornell University.

Derman, E., and I. Kani. (1994). "Riding on the Smile." *Risk* 7 (February): 32–39.

Detemple, J. (1986). "Asset Pricing in a Production Economy with Incomplete Information." *Journal of Finance* 41: 383–391.

Detemple, J. (1991). "Further Results on Asset Pricing with Incomplete Information." *Journal of Economic Dynamics and Control* 15: 425–454.

————. (1995). "Asset Pricing in an Intertemporal Noisy Rational Expectations Equilibrium." Sloan School of Management, Massachusetts Institution of Technology.

Detemple, J., and S. Murthy. (1994). "Intertemporal Asset Pricing with Heterogeneous Beliefs." *Journal of Economic Theory* 62: 294–320.

Detemple, J., and L. Selden. (1991). "A General Equilibrium Analysis of Option and Stock Market Interactions." *International Economic Review* 32: 279–303.

Detemple, J., and F. Zapatero. (1991). "Asset Prices in an Exchange Economy with Habit Formation." *Econometrica* 59: 1633–1658.

——. (1992). "Optimal Consumption-Portfolio Policies with Habit Formation." *Mathematical Finance* 2: 251–274.

Dewynne, J., and P. Wilmott. (1994). "Exotic Options: Mathematical Models and Computation." Department of Mathematics, Southampton University.

Dezhbakhsh, H. (1994). "Foreign Exchange Forward and Futures Prices: Are They Equal?" *Journal of Financial and Quantitative Analysis* 1: 75–87.

Diament, P. (1993). "Semi-Empirical Smooth Fit to the Treasury Yield Curve." Graduate School of Business, Columbia University.

Dixit, A., and R. Pindyck. (1993). *Investment under Uncertainty.* Princeton: Princeton University Press.

Donaldson, J., and R. Mehra. (1984). "Comparative Dynamics of an Equilibrium Intertemporal Asset Pricing Model." *Review of Economic Studies* 51: 491–508.

Donaldson, J., T. Johnson, and R. Mehra. (1987). "The Behavior of the Term Structure of Interest Rates in a Real Business Cycle Model." Graduate School of Business, Columbia University.

Dothan, M. (1978). "On the Term Structure of Interest Rates." *Journal of Financial Economics* 7: 229–264.

——. (1990). *Prices in Financial Markets.* New York: Oxford University Press.

Dothan, M., and D. Feldman. (1986). "Equilibrium Interest Rates and Multiperiod Bonds in a Partially Observable Economy." *Journal of Finance* 41: 369–382.

Drèze, J. (1971). "Market Allocation under Uncertainty." *European Economic Review*, Winter, 1970–71: 133–165.

Duan, J.-C. (1995). "The Garch Option Pricing Model." *Mathematical Finance* 5: 13–32.

Duan, J.-C., and J.-G. Simonato. (1993). "Estimating Exponential-Affine Term Structure Models." Department of Finance, McGill University and CIRANO.

Duffee, G. (1994). "On the Changing Behavior of the Treasury Bill Yield Curve." Federal Reserve Board, Washington, D.C.

Duffie, D. (1985). "Predictable Representation of Martingale Spaces and Changes of Probability Measure." In J. Azéma and M. Yor, *Séminaires de probabilité XIX, Lecture Notes in Mathematics Number 1123, pp. 278–285.* New York: Springer-Verlag.

————. (1986). "Stochastic Equilibria: Existence, Spanning Number, and the 'No Expected Financial Gain from Trade' Hypothesis." *Econometrica* 54: 1161–1184.

————. (1987). "Stochastic Equilibria with Incomplete Financial Markets." *Journal of Economic Theory* 41: 405–416, Corrigendum 49 (1989): 384.

————. (1988a). "An Extension of the Black-Scholes Model of Security Valuation." *Journal of Economic Theory* 46: 194–204.

————. (1988b). *Security Markets: Stochastic Models.* Boston: Academic Press.

————. (1989). *Futures Markets.* Englewood Cliffs, N.J.: Prentice-Hall.

————. (1992). "The Nature of Incomplete Markets." In J.-J. Laffont, *Advances in Economic Theory.* Cambridge: Cambridge University Press, pp. 214–262.

————. (1993). "Special Repo Rates." Graduate School of Business, Stanford University.

Duffie, D., and L. Epstein (With C. Skiadas). (1992a). "Stochastic Differential Utility." *Econometrica* 60: 353-394.

Duffie, D., and L. Epstein. (1992b). "Asset Pricing with Stochastic Differential Utility." *Review of Financial Studies* 5: 411–436.

Duffie, D., W. Fleming, and T. Zariphopoulou. (1991). "Hedging in Incomplete Markets with HARA Utility." Forthcoming in *Journal of Economic Dynamics and Control.*

Duffie, D., and M. Garman. (1991). "Intertemporal Arbitrage and the Markov Valuation of Securities." *Cuadernos economicos de ICE* 49: 37–60.

Duffie, D., J. Geanakoplos, A. Mas-Colell, and A. McLennan. (1994). "Stationary Markov Equilibria." *Econometrica* 62: 745–781.

Duffie, D., P.-Y. Geoffard, and C. Skiadas. (1994). "Efficient and Equilibrium Allocations with Stochastic Differential Utility." *Journal of Mathematical Economics* 23: 133–146.

Duffie, D., and P. Glynn. (1992). "Efficient Monte Carlo Estimation of Security Prices." Research Paper. Graduate School of Business, Stanford University. Forthcoming in *Annals of Applied Probability.*

Duffie, D., and M. Harrison. (1993). "Arbitrage Pricing of Russian Options and Perpetual Lookback Options." *Annals of Applied Probability* 3: 641–651.

Duffie, D., and C.-F. Huang. (1985). "Implementing Arrow-Debreu Equilibria by Continuous Trading of Few Long-Lived Securities." *Econometrica* 53: 1337–1356.

————. (1986). "Multiperiod Security Markets with Differential Information: Martingales and Resolution Times." *Journal of Mathematical Economics* 15: 283–303.

Duffie, D., and M. Huang. (1994). "Swap Rates and Credit Quality." Graduate School of Business, Stanford University.

Duffie, D., and M. Jackson. (1990). "Optimal Hedging and Equilibrium in a Dynamic Futures Market." *Journal of Economic Dynamics and Control* 14: 21–33.

Duffie, D., and R. Kan. (1992). "A Yield-Factor Model of Interest Rates." Research Paper. Graduate School of Business, Stanford University.

Duffie, D., and P.-L. Lions. (1990). "PDE Solutions of Stochastic Differential Utility." *Journal of Mathematical Economics* 21: 577–606.

Duffie, D., J. Ma, and J. Yong. (1993). "Black's Consol Rate Conjecture." Forthcoming in *Annals of Applied Probability.*

Duffie, D., and P. Protter. (1988). "From Discrete to Continuous Time Finance: Weak Convergence of the Financial Gain Process." *Mathematical Finance* 2: 1–16.

Duffie, D., and H. Richardson. (1991). "Mean-Variance Hedging in Continuous Time." *Annals of Applied Probability* 1: 1–15.

Duffie, D., M. Schroder, and C. Skiadas. (1993). "A Model of Price Dependence on the Timing of the Resolution of Uncertainty." Research Paper. Kellogg School, Northwestern University.

Duffie, D., M. Schroder, and C. Skiadas. (1994). "Recursive Valuation of Defaultable Securities and the Timing of the Resolution of Uncertainty." Research Paper. Kellogg School, Northwestern University.

Duffie, D., and W. Shafer. (1985). "Equilibrium in Incomplete Markets I: A Basic Model of Generic Existence." *Journal of Mathematical Economics* 14: 285–300.

———. (1986a). "Equilibrium in Incomplete Markets II: Generic Existence in Stochastic Economies." *Journal of Mathematical Economics* 15: 199–216.

———. (1986b). "Equilibrium and the Role of the Firm in Incomplete Markets." Graduate School of Business, Stanford University.

Duffie, D., and K. Singleton. (1993). "Simulated Moments Estimation of Markov Models of Asset Prices." *Econometrica* 61: 929–952.

———. (1994). "Modeling Term Structures of Defaultable Bonds." Graduate School of Business, Stanford University.

———. (1995). "An Econometric Model of the Term Structure of Interest Rate Swap Yields." Graduate School of Business, Stanford University.

Duffie, D., and C. Skiadas. (1994). "Continuous-Time Security Pricing: A Utility Gradient Approach." *Journal of Mathematical Economics* 23: 107–132.

Duffie, D., and R. Stanton. (1988). "Pricing Continuously Resettled Contingent Claims." *Journal of Economic Dynamics and Control* 16: 561–574.

Duffie, D., and T.-S. Sun. (1990). "Transactions Costs and Portfolio Choice in a Discrete-Continuous Time Setting." *Journal of Economic Dynamics and Control* 14: 35–51.

Duffie, D., and W. Zame. (1989). "The Consumption-Based Capital Asset Pricing Model." *Econometrica* 57: 1279–1297.

Duffie, D., and T. Zariphopoulou. (1993). "Optimal Investment with Undiversifiable Income Risk." *Mathematical Finance* 3: 135–148.

Dumas, B. (1989). "Two-Person Dynamic Equilibrium in the Capital Market." *Review of Financial Studies* 2: 157–188.

Dumas, B., and E. Luciano. (1989). "An Exact Solution to a Dynamic Portfolio Choice Problem under Transactions Costs." Wharton School, University of Pennsylvania.

Dunn, K., and K. Singleton. (1986). "Modeling the Term Structure of Interest Rates under Nonseparable Utility and Durability of Goods." *Journal of Financial Economics* 17: 27–55.

Dupire, B. (1992). "Arbitrage Pricing with Stochastic Volatility." Société Générale, Division Options, Paris, France.

———. (1994). "Pricing with a Smile." *Risk* (January) 7: 18–20.

Durrett, R. (1991). *Probability: Theory and Examples*. Belmont, California: Wadsworth Publishing Co.

Dybvig, P. (1988). "Bond and Bond Option Pricing Based on the Current Term Structure." School of Business, Washington University, St. Louis.

———. (1989). "Hedging Nontraded Wealth." School of Business, Washington University, St. Louis.

———. (1994). "Duesenberry's Ratcheting of Consumption: Optimal Dynamic Consumption and Investment Given Intolerance for Any Decline in Standard of Living." School of Business, Washington University, St. Louis.

Dybvig, P., and C.-F. Huang. (1988). "Nonnegative Wealth, Absence of Arbitrage, and Feasible Consumption Plans." *Review of Financial Studies* 1: 377–401.

Dybvig, P., J. Ingersoll, and S. Ross. (1994). "Long Forward and Zero-Coupon Rates Can Never Fall." School of Business, Washington University, St. Louis.

Dynkin, E., and A. Yushkevich. (1979). *Controlled Markov Processes*. Berlin, New York: Springer-Verlag.

Eberlein, E. (1991). "On Modelling Questions in Security Valuation." Institut für Mathematische Stochastik, Universität Freiburg.

Edirisinghe, C., V. Naik, and R. Uppal. (1991). "Optimal Replication of Options with Transactions Costs." College of Business, University of Tennessee. Forthcoming in *Journal of Financial and Quantitative Analysis*.

Ekern, S. (1993). "Entry and Exit Decisions with Restricted Reversibility." Working Paper. Norwegian School of Economics, Bergen.

El Karoui, N., and H. Geman. (1991). "A Probabilistic Approach to the Valuation of General Floating Rate Notes." Laboratoire de Probabilités, Université de Paris VI.

El Karoui, N., and M. Jeanblanc-Picqué. (1994). "Optimisation of Consumption with Labor Income." Laboratoire de Probabilités, Université de Paris VI.

El Karoui, N., M. Jeanblanc-Picqué, and R. Viswanathan. (1991). "On the Robustness of the Black-Scholes Equation." LAMM, École Normale Supérieure de Cachan, France.

El Karoui, N., and V. Lacoste. (1992). "Multifactor Models of the Term Structure of Interest Rates." Laboratoire de Probabilités, Université de Paris VI.

El Karoui, N., C. Lepage, R. Myneni, N. Roseau, and R. Viswanathan. (1991a). "The Valuation and Hedging of Contingent Claims with Gaussian Markov Interest Rates." Laboratoire de Probabilités, Université de Paris VI.

————. (1991b). "The Pricing and Hedging of Interest Rate Claims: Applications." Laboratoire de Probabilités, Université de Paris VI.

El Karoui, N., R. Myneni, and R. Viswanathan. (1992). "Arbitrage Pricing and Hedging of Interest Rate Claims with State Variables I: Theory." Laboratoire de Probabilités, Université de Paris VI.

El Karoui, N., S. Peng, and M. Quenez. (1994). "Backward Stochastic Differential Equations in Finance." Laboratoire de Probabilités, Université de Paris VI.

El Karoui, N., and M. Quenez. (1991). "Evaluation dans les marchés incomplets et programmation dynamique." Laboratoire de Probabilités, Université de Paris VI.

————. (1993). "Dynamic Programming and Pricing of Contingent Claims in an Incomplete Market." Laboratoire de Probabilités, Université de Paris VI.

El Karoui, N., and J.-C. Rochet. (1989). "A Pricing Formula for Options on Coupon Bonds." October, Laboratoire de Probabilités, Université de Paris VI.

Elliott, R. (1982). *Stochastic Calculus and Applications.* New York: Springer-Verlag.

Engle, R. (1982). "Autoregressive Conditional Heteroskedasticity with Estimates of the Variance of United Kingdom Inflation." *Econometrica* 50: 987–1008.

Epstein, L. (1988). "Risk Aversion and Asset Prices." *Journal of Monetary Economics* 22: 179–192.

————. (1992). "Behavior under Risk: Recent Developments in Theory and Application." In J.-J. Laffont, *Advances in Economic Theory.* Cambridge: Cambridge University Press, pp. 1–63.

Epstein, L., and T. Wang. (1994). "Intertemporal Asset Pricing under Knightian Uncertainty." *Econometrica* 62: 283–322.

Epstein, L., and S. Zin. (1989). "Substitution, Risk Aversion and the Temporal Behavior of Consumption and Asset Returns I: A Theoretical Framework." *Econometrica* 57: 937–969.

————. (1991). "The Independence Axiom and Asset Returns." Department of Economics, University of Toronto.

Ethier, S., and T. Kurtz. (1986). *Markov Processes: Characterization and Convergence.* New York: Wiley.

Eydeland, A. (1994a). "A Spectral Algorithm for Pricing Interest Rate Options." Department of Mathematics, University of Massachusetts.

————. (1994b). "A Fast Algorithm for Computing Integrals in Function Spaces: Financial Applications." Fuji Capital Markets Corporation, New York.

Feller, W. (1951). "Two Singular Diffusion Problems." *Annals of Mathematics* 54: 173–182.

Fisher, M., D. Nychka, and D. Zervos. (1994). "Fitting the Term Structure of Interest Rates with Smoothing Splines." Working Paper. Board of Governors of the Federal Reserve Board, Washington D.C.

Fitzpatrick, B., and W. Fleming. (1991). "Numerical Methods for Optimal Investment—Consumption Models." *Mathematics of Operations Research* 16: 823–841.

Fleming, J., and R. Whaley. (1994). "The Value of Wildcard Options." *Journal of Finance* 1: 215–236.

Fleming, W., S. Grossman, J.-L. Vila, and T. Zariphopoulou. (1989). "Optimal Portfolio Rebalancing with Transaction Costs." Department of Applied Mathematics, Brown University.

Fleming, W., and R. Rishel. (1975). *Deterministic and Stochastic Optimal Control.* Berlin: Springer-Verlag.

Fleming, W., and H. Soner. (1993). *Controlled Markov Processes and Viscosity Solutions.* New York: Springer-Verlag.

Fleming, W., and T. Zariphopoulou. (1991). "An Optimal Investment/Consumption Model with Borrowing Constraints." *Mathematics of Operations Research* 16: 802–822.

Flesaker, B. (1993). "Testing the Heath-Jarrow-Morton/Ho-Lee Model of Interest Rate Contingent Claims Pricing." *Journal of Financial and Quantitative Analysis* 28: 483–495.

Florenzano, M., and P. Gourdel. (1993). "Incomplete Markets in Infinite Horizon: Debt Constraints versus Node Prices." CNRS-CEPREMAP, Paris.

————. (1994). "T-Period Economies with Incomplete Markets." *Economics Letters* 44: 91–97.

Foldes, L. (1978). "Martingale Conditions for Optimal Saving-Discrete Time." *Journal of Mathematical Economics* 5: 83–96.

————. (1979). "Optimal Saving and Risk in Continuous Time." *Review of Economic Studies* 46: 39–65.

————. (1990). "Conditions for Optimality in the Infinite-Horizon Portfolio-Cum-Saving Problem with Semimartingale Investments." *Stochastics and Stochastics Reports* 29: 133–170.

————. (1991a). "Certainty Equivalence in the Continuous-Time Portfolio-Cum-Saving Model." In M.H.A. Davis and R. Elliott, *Applied Stochastic Analysis*. London: Gordon and Breach.

————. (1991b). "Existence and Uniqueness of an Optimum in the Infinite-Horizon Portfolio-cum-Saving Model with Semimartingale Investments." L.S.E. Financial Markets Group Discussion Paper 109, London School of Economics.

————. (1991c). "Optimal Sure Portfolio Plans." *Mathematical Finance* 1: 15–55.

Föllmer, H. (1981). "Calcul d'Ito Sans Probabilités." In J.Azéma and M.Yor, *Séminaire de Probabilités XV, Lecture Notes in Mathematics* 850, pp. 143–150. Berlin: Springer-Verlag.

Föllmer, H. (1993). "A Microeconomic Approach to Diffusion Models for Stock Prices." *Mathematical Finance* 1: 1–23.

Föllmer, H., and M. Schweizer. (1990). "Hedging of Contingent Claims under Incomplete Information." In M.. Davis and R. Elliott, *Applied Stochastic Analysis*. London: Gordon and Breach, pp. 389–414.

Föllmer, H., and D. Sondermann. (1986). "Hedging of Non-Redundant Contingent Claims." In A. Mas-Colell and W. Hildenbrand, *Contributions to Mathematical Economics*, pp. 205–223. Amsterdam: North-Holland.

Fournie, E. (1993). "Statistiques des diffusions ergodiques avec applications en finance." Ph.D. diss., Université de Nice-Sophia Antipolis.

Fournie, E., and D. Talay. (1993). "Application de la statistique des diffusions a un modele de taux d'interet." INRIA, Sophia Antipolis, France.

Frachot, A. (1993). "Factor Models of Domestic and Foreign Interest Rates with Stochastic Volatilities." Working Paper. Banque de France, Paris.

Frachot, A., D. Janci, and V. Lacoste. (1993). "Factor Analysis of the Term Structure: A Probabilistic Approach." Working Paper. Banque de France, Paris.

Frachot, A., and J.-P. Lesne. (1993a). "Econometrics of Linear Factor Models of Interest Rates." Working Paper. Banque de France, Paris.

————. (1993b). "Factor Models of Interest Rates with Stochastic Volatilities." Working Paper. Banque de France, Paris.

————. (1993c). "Expectations Hypotheses and Stochastic Volatilities." Working Paper. Banque de France, Paris.

Freedman, D. (1983). *Markov Chains*. New York: Springer-Verlag.

Freidlin, M. (1985). *Functional Integration and Partial Differential Equations*. Princeton, N.J.: Princeton University Press.

Friedman, A. (1964). *Partial Differential Equations of the Parabolic Type*. Englewood Cliffs, N.J.: Prentice-Hall.

————. (1975). *Stochastic Differential Equations and Applications, Vol. I*. New York: Academic Press.

Gabay, D. (1982). "Stochastic Processes in Models of Financial Markets." In *Proceedings of the IFIP Conference on Control of Distributed Systems, Toulouse*. Toulouse, France: Pergamon Press.

Gagnon, J., and J. Taylor. (1986). "Solving and Estimating Stochastic Equilibrium Models with the Extended Path Method." Department of Economics, Stanford University.

Gale, D. (1960). *The Theory of Linear Economic Models*. New York: McGraw-Hill.

Gallant, R., and H. White. (1988). *A Unified Theory of Estimation and Inference for Nonlinear Dynamic Models*. New York: Basil Blackwell.

Gandhi, S., A. Kooros, and G. Salkin. (1993a). "Average-Price Options, An Analytic Approach." Imperial College, University of London.

————. (1993b). "An Improved Analytic Approximation for American Option Pricing." Imperial College, University of London.

Garman, M. (1985). "Towards a Semigroup Pricing Theory." *Journal of Finance* 40: 847–861.

Geanakoplos, J. (1990). "An Introduction to General Equilibrium with Incomplete Asset Markets." *Journal of Mathematical Economics* 19: 1–38.

Geanakoplos, J., and A. Mas-Colell. (1989). "Real Indeterminacy with Financial Assets." *Journal of Economic Theory* 47: 22–38.

Geanakoplos, J., and H. Polemarchakis. (1986). "Existence, Regularity, and Constrained Suboptimality of Competitive Allocations when the Asset Market Is Incomplete." In W. Heller and D. Starrett, *Essays in Honor of Kenneth J. Arrow, Volume III*, pp. 65–96. Cambridge: Cambridge University Press.

Geanakoplos, J., and W. Shafer. (1990). "Solving Systems of Simultaneous Equations in Economics." *Journal of Mathematical Economics* 19: 69–94.

Geman, H., N. El Karoui, and J.-C. Rochet. (1991). "Probability Changes and Option Pricing." Laboratoires de Probabilités, Université de Paris VI.

Geman, H., and M. Yor. (1993). "Bessel Processes, Asian Options and Perpetuities." *Mathematical Finance* 3: 349–375.

Gennotte, G. (1984). "Continuous-Time Production Economies under Incomplete Information I: A Separation Theorem." Working Paper 1612–1684. Sloan School, Massachusetts Institute of Technology.

Gerber, H., and E. Shiu. (1994). "Option Pricing by Esscher Transforms." *Transactions of the Society of Actuaries* 46: 51–92.

Geske, R. (1979). "The Valuation of Compound Options." *Journal of Financial Economics* 7: 63–81.

Geske, R., and H. Johnson. (1984). "The American Put Option Valued Analytically." *Journal of Finance* 39: 1511–1524.

Ghysels, E. (1986). "Asset Prices in an Economy with Latent Technological Shocks - Econometric Implications of a Discrete Time General Equilibrium Model." Department of Economics and Centre de Recherche et Développement en Économique, Université de Montréal.

Gibbons, M., and K. Ramaswamy. (1993). "A Test of the Cox-Ingersoll-Ross Model of The Term Structure of Interest Rates." *Review of Financial Studies* 6: 619–658.

Gibbons, M., and T. Sun. (1986). "The Term Structure of Interest Rates: A Simple Exposition of the Cox, Ingersoll, and Ross Model." Graduate School of Business, Stanford University.

Gihman, I., and A. Skorohod. (1972). *Stochastic Differential Equations.* Berlin: Springer-Verlag.

Gilles, C., and S. LeRoy. (1991). "On the Arbitrage Pricing Theory." *Economic Theory* 1: 213–230.

———. (1992a). "Bubbles and Charges." *International Economic Review* 33: 323-339.

———. (1992b). "Stochastic Bubbles in Markov Economies." Board of Governors of The Federal Reserve System, Washington, D.C.

Giovannini, A., and P. Weil. (1989). "Risk Aversion and Intertemporal Substitution in the Capital Asset Pricing Model." National Bureau of Economic Research, Cambridge, Massachusetts.

Girotto, B., and F. Ortu. (1993). "Existence of Equivalent Martingale Measures in Finite Dimensional Securities Markets." Department of Applied Mathematics, Università di Trieste, Italy.

———. (1994). "Consumption and Portfolio Policies with Incomplete Markets and Short-Sale Contraints in the Finite-Dimensional Case: Some Remarks." *Mathematical Finance* 4: 69–73.

Goldman, B., H. Sosin, and M. Gatto. (1979). "Path Dependent Options: 'Buy at the Low, Sell at the High'." *Journal of Finance* 34: 1111–1127.

Goldstein, R., and F. Zapatero. (1994). "General Equilibrium with Constant Relative Risk Aversion and Vasicek Interest Rates." Haas School of Business, University of California, Berkeley.

Goldys, B., M. Musiela, and D. Sondermann. (1994). "Lognormality of Rates and Term Structure Models." School of Mathematics, University of New South Wales.

Gorman, W. (1953). "Community Preference Fields." *Econometrica* 21: 63–80.

Gottardi, P. (1995). "An Analysis of the Conditions for the Validity of the Modigliani-Miller Theorem with Incomplete Markets." *Economic Theory* 5: 191–208.

Gottardi, P., and T. Hens. (1994). "The Survival Assumption and Existence of Competitive Equilibria when Asset Markets are Incomplete." Department of Economics, University of Venice.

Gourieroux, C., and J.-P. Laurent. (1994). "Estimation of a Dynamic Hedging." CREST and CEPREMAP, Paris.

Gourieroux, C., and O. Scaillet. (1994). "Estimation of the Term Structure from Bond Data." CREST and CEPREMAP, Paris.

Grannan, E., and G. Swindle. (1992). "Minimizing Transaction Costs of Option Hedging Strategies." Department of Statistics, University of California, Santa Barbara.

Grauer, F., and R. Litzenberger. (1979). "The Pricing of Commodity Futures Contracts, Nominal Bonds, and Other Risky Assets under Commodity Price Uncertainty." *Journal of Finance* 44: 69–84.

Grinblatt, M. (1994). "An Analytic Solution for Interest Rate Swap Spreads." Anderson Graduate School of Management, University of California, Los Angeles.

Grinblatt, M., and N. Jegadeesh. (1993). "The Relative Pricing of Eurodollar Futures and Forward Contracts." Anderson Graduate School of Management, University of California, Los Angeles.

Grodal, B., and K. Vind. (1988). "Equilibrium with Arbitrary Market Structure." Department of Economics, University of Copenhagen.

Grossman, S., and G. Laroque. (1989). "Asset Pricing and Optimal Portfolio Choice in the Presence of Illiquid Durable Consumption Goods." *Econometrica* 58: 25–52.

Grossman, S., and R. Shiller. (1982). "Consumption Correlatedness and Risk Measurement in Economies with Non-Traded Assets and Heterogeneous Information." *Journal of Financial Economics* 10: 195–210.

Grundy, B., and Z. Wiener. (1995). "Theory of Rational Optional Pricing: II." The Wharton School, University of Pennsylvania.

Gul, F., and O. Lantto. (1992). "Betweenness Satisfying Preferences and Dynamic Choice." Graduate School of Business, Stanford University.

Haan, W. (1994). "Heterogeneity, Aggregate Uncertainty and the Short Interest Rate: A Case Study of Two Solution Techniques." Department of Economics, University of California, San Diego.

Hahn, F. (1992). "A Remark on Incomplete Markets Equilibrium." Department of Economics, Cambridge University.

———. (1994). "On Economies with Arrow Securities." Department of Economics, Cambridge University.

Hakansson, N. (1970). "Optimal Investment and Consumption Strategies under Risk for a Class of Utility Functions." *Econometrica* 38: 587–607.

———. (1974). "Convergence to Isoelastic Utility and Policy in Multiperiod Portfolio Choice." *Journal of Financial Economics* 1: 201–224.

Hansen, L. (1982). "Large Sample Properties of Generalized Method of Moments Estimators." *Econometrica* 50: 1029–1054.

Hansen, L., and R. Jaganathan. (1990). "Implications of Security Market Data for Models of Dynamic Economies." *Journal of Political Economy* 99: 225–262.

Hansen, L., and S. Richard. (1987). "The Role of Conditioning Information in Deducing Testable Restrictions Implied by Dynamic Asset Pricing Models." *Econometrica* 55: 587–614.

Hansen, L., and T. Sargent. (1990). "Recursive Linear Models of Dynamic Economies." Department of Economics, University of Chicago.

Hansen, L., and K. Singleton. (1982). "Generalized Instrumental Variables Estimation of Nonlinear Rational Expectations Models." *Econometrica* 50: 1269–1286.

———. (1983). "Stochastic Consumption, Risk Aversion, and the Temporal Behavior of Asset Returns." *Journal of Political Economy* 91: 249–265.

———. (1986). "Efficient Estimation of Linear Asset Pricing Models with Moving Average Errors." Department of Economics, University of Chicago.

Hara, C. (1993). "A Role of Redundant Assets in the Presence of Transaction Costs." Sloan School of Management, Massachusetts Institute of Technology.

———. (1994). "Marginal Rates of Substitution for Uninsurable Risks with Constraint-Efficient Asset Structures." Center for Operations Research and Econometrics, Université Catholique de Louvain.

Harris, M. (1987). *Dynamic Economic Analysis.* New York: Oxford University Press.

Harrison, M. (1985). *Brownian Motion and Stochastic Flow Systems.* New York: Wiley.

Harrison, M., and D. Kreps. (1979). "Martingales and Arbitrage in Multiperiod Securities Markets." *Journal of Economic Theory* 20: 381–408.

Harrison, M., and S. Pliska. (1981). "Martingales and Stochastic Integrals in the Theory of Continuous Trading." *Stochastic Processes and Their Applications* 11: 215–260.

Hart, O. (1975). "On the Optimality of Equilibrium when the Market Structure Is Incomplete." *Journal of Economic Theory* 11: 418–430.

Harvey, A., E. Ruiz, and N. Shephard. (1992). "Multivariate Stochastic Variance Models." Department of Statistical and Mathematical Sciences, London School of Economics.

Harvey, A., and N. Shephard. (1993). "The Econometrics of Stochastic Volatility." Department of Statistical and Mathematical Sciences, London School of Economics.

He, H. (1990). "Convergence from Discrete- to Continuous-Time Contingent Claims Prices." *Review of Financial Studies* 3: 523–546.

———. (1991). "Optimal Consumption-Portfolio Policies: A Convergence from Discrete to Continuous Time Models." *Journal of Economic Theory* 55: 340–363.

He, H., and C. Huang. (1994). "Consumption-Portfolio Policies: An Inverse Optimal Problem." *Journal of Economic Theory* 62: 294-320.

He, H., and H. Leland. (1993). "On Equilibrium Asset Price Processes." *Review of Financial Studies* 6: 593–617.

He, H., and D. Modest. (1993). "Market Frictions and Consumption-Based Asset Pricing." Haas School of Business, University of California at Berkeley.

He, H., and H. Pagés. (1993). "Labor Income, Borrowing Constraints, and Equilibrium Asset Prices." *Economic Theory* 3: 663-696.

He, H., and N. Pearson. (1991a). "Consumption and Portfolio Policies with Incomplete Markets: The Infinite-Dimensional Case." *Journal of Economic Theory* 54: 259–305.

———. (1991b). "Consumption and Portfolio Policies with Incomplete Markets and Short-Sale Contraints: The Finite-Dimensional Case." *Mathematical Finance* 1: 1–10.

Heath, D., R. Jarrow, and A. Morton. (1990). "Bond Pricing and the Term Structure of Interest Rates: A Discrete Time Approximation." *Journal of Financial and Quantitative Analysis* 25: 419–440.

———. (1992a). "Bond Pricing and the Term Structure of Interest Rates: A New Methodology for Contingent Claims Valuation." *Econometrica* 60: 77–106.

———. (1992b). "Contingent Claim Valuation with a Random Evolution of Interest Rates." Operations Research Department, Cornell University.

Heaton, J. (1993). "The Interaction between Time-Nonseparable Preferences and Time Aggregation." *Econometrica* 61: 353–386.

Heaton, J., and D. Lucas. (1992). "The Effects of Incomplete Insurance Markets and Trading Costs in a Consumption-Based Asset Pricing Model." *Journal of Economic Dynamics and Control* 16: 601–620.

Hellwig, M. (1991). "Rational Expectations Equilibria in Sequence Economies with Symmetric Information: The Two Period Case. Forthcoming in *Journal of Mathematical Economics*." University of Basel.

Hemler, M. (1987). "The Quality Delivery Option in Treasury Bond Futures Contracts." Graduate School of Business, University of Chicago.

Henrotte, P. (1991). "Transactions Costs and Duplication Strategies." Graduate School of Business, Stanford University.

———. (1994). "Multiperiod Equilibrium with Endogenous Price Uncertainty." Groupe HEC, Département de Finance et Economie, Jouy en Josas, France.

Hens, T. (1991). "Structure of General Equilibrium Models with Incomplete Markets." Ph.D. diss., Department of Economics, University of Bonn.

Hernandez, A., and M. Santos. (1994). "Competitive Equilibria for Infinite-Horizon Economies with Incomplete Markets." Centro de Investigación Económica, ITAM, Mexico City.

Heston, S. (1988a). "Generalized Interest Rate Processes for the Goldman, Sachs, and Company Mortgage Valuation Model." Graduate School of Industrial Administration, Carnegie-Mellon University.

———. (1988b). "Testing Continuous Time Models of the Term Structure of Interest Rates." Graduate School of Industrial Administration, Carnegie-Mellon University.

———. (1989). "Discrete Time Versions of Continuous Time Interest Rate Models." Graduate School of Industrial Administration, Carnegie-Mellon University.

———. (1990). "Sticky Consumption, Optimal Investment, and Equilibrium Asset Prices." School of Organization and Management, Yale University.

———. (1993). "A Closed-Form Solution for Options with Stochastic Volatility with Applications to Bond and Currency Options." *Review of Financial Studies* 6: 327–344.

Heynen, R., and H. Kat. (1993). "Volatility Prediction: A Comparison of the Sochastic Volatility, GARCH(1,1) and EGARCH(1,1) Models." Department of Operations Research, Erasmus University Rotterdam.

Heynen, R., A. Kemna, and T. Vorst. (1994). "Analysis of the Term Structure of Implied Volatilities." *Journal of Financial and Quantitative Analysis* 1: 31–57.

Hildenbrand, W., and P. Kirman. (1989). *Introduction to Equilibrium Analysis* (2d ed.). Amsterdam: North-Holland Elsevier.

Hindy, A. (1995). "Viable Prices in Financial Markets with Solvency Constraints." *Journal of Mathematical Economics* 24: 105–136.

Hindy, A., and C.-F. Huang. (1992). "Intertemporal Preferences for Uncertain Consumption: A Continuous Time Approach." *Econometrica* 60: 781–802.

———. (1993). "Optimal Consumption and Portfolio Rules with Local Substitution." *Econometrica* 61: 85–122.

Hindy, A., C.-F. Huang, and D. Kreps. (1992). "On Intertemporal Preferences in Continuous Time: The Case of Certainty." *Journal of Mathematical Economics* 21: 401–440.

Hindy, A., C.-F. Huang, and H. Zhu. (1993a). "Numerical Analysis of a Free Boundary Singular Control Problem in Financial Economics." Research Paper 1267. Graduate School of Business, Stanford University.

———. (1993b). "Optimal Consumption and Portfolio Rules with Durability and Habit Formation." Graduate School of Business, Stanford University.

Hindy, A., and M. Huang. (1993). "Asset Pricing with Linear Collateral Constraints." Graduate School of Business, Stanford University.

Hirsch, M., M. Magill, and A. Mas-Colell. (1990). "A Geometric Approach to a Class of Equilibrium Existence Theorems." *Journal of Mathematical Economics* 19: 95-106.

Ho, T., and S. Lee. (1986). "Term Structure Movements and Pricing Interest Rate Contingent Claims." *Journal of Finance* 41: 1011–1029.

Hobson, D., and C. Rogers. (1993). "Models of Endogenous Stochastic Volatility." Judge Institute of Management Studies, Cambridge University.

Hodges, S., and A. Carverhill. (1992). "The Characterization of Economic Equilibria Which Support Black-Scholes Options Pricing." Financial Options Research Centre, University of Warwick.

Hofmann, N., E. Platen, and M. Schweizer. (1992). "Option Pricing under Incompleteness and Stochastic Volatility." Department of Mathematics, University of Bonn.

Hogan, M. (1993a). "The Lognormal Interest Rate Model and Eurodollar Futures." Working Paper. Citibank, New York.

———. (1993b). "Problems in Certain Two-Factor Term Structure Models." *Annals of Applied Probability* 3: 576–581.

Honda, T. (1992). "Equilibrium in Incomplete Real Asset Markets with Dispersed Forecast Functions." Engineering-Economic Systems Department, Stanford University.

Hong, C., and L. Epstein. (1989). "Non-Expected Utility Preferences in a Temporal Framework with an Application to Consumption-Savings Behaviour." Department of Political Economy, Johns Hopkins University.

Howe, M.A., and B. Rustem. (1994a). "Minimax Hedging Strategy." Financial Options Research Centre, University of Warwick.

———. (1994b). "Multi-Period Minimax Hedging Strategies." Financial Options Research Centre, University of Warwick.

Huang, C.-F. (1985a). "Information Structures and Viable Price Systems." *Journal of Mathematical Economics* 14: 215–240.

———. (1985b). "Information Structures and Equilibrium Asset Prices." *Journal of Economic Theory* 31: 33–71.

———. (1985c). "Discussion on 'Towards a Semigroup Pricing Theory'." *Proceedings of the Journal of Finance* 40: 861–862.

———. (1987a). "An Intertemporal General Equilibrium Asset Pricing Model: The Case of Diffusion Information." *Econometrica* 55: 117–142.

———. (1987b). "Continuous Time Stochastic Processes." In J. McCall, *The New Palgrave: A Dictionary of Economic Theory and Doctrine.* London: Macmillan Press.

———. (1994). *Theory of Financial Markets.* Forthcoming from Oxford University Press.

Huang, C.-F., and R. Litzenberger. (1988). *Foundations for Financial Economics.* Amsterdam: North-Holland.

Huang, C.-F., and H. Pagès. (1992). "Optimal Consumption and Portfolio Policies with an Infinite Horizon: Existence and Convergence." *Annals of Applied Probability* 2: 36–64.

Huang, C.-F., and T. Zariphopoulou. (1994). "Further Results on Continuous-Time Portfolio Turnpike Theorem." Fixed Income Derivatives Research, Goldman, Sachs and Company, New York.

Huang, P., and H. Wu. (1994). "Competitive Equilibrium of Incomplete Markets for Securities with Smooth Payoffs." *Journal of Mathematical Economics* 23: 219–234.

Hull, J. (1993). *Options, Futures, and Other Derivative Securities* (2d ed.). Englewood Cliffs, N.J.: Prentice-Hall.

Hull, J., and A. White. (1987). "The Pricing of Options on Assets with Stochastic Volatilities." *Journal of Finance* 2: 281–300.

———. (1990a). "Pricing Interest Rate Derivative Securities." *Review of Financial Studies* 3: 573–592.

———. (1990b). "Valuing Derivative Securities Using the Explicit Finite Difference Method." *Journal of Financial and Quantitative Analysis* 25: 87–100.

———. (1992). "The Price of Default." *Risk* 5: 101–103.

———. (1993). "One-Factor Interest-Rate Models and the Valuation of Interest-Rate Derivative Securities." *Journal of Financial and Quantitative Analysis* 28: 235–254.

————. (1994). "Numerical Procedures for Implementing Term Structure Models." Faculty of Management, University of Toronto.

————. (1995). "The Impact of Default Risk on the Prices of Options and Other Derivative Securities." *Journal of Banking and Finance* 19: 299–322.

Husseini, S., J. Lasry, and M. Magill. (1990). "Existence of Equilibrium with Incomplete Markets." *Journal of Mathematical Economics* 19: 39–68.

Ikeda, N., and S. Watanabe. (1981). *Stochastic Differential Equations and Diffusion Processes.* Amsterdam: North-Holland.

Ingersoll, J. (1977). "An Examination of Corporate Call Policies on Convertible Securities." *Journal of Finance* 32: 463–478.

————. (1987). *Theory of Financial Decision Making.* Totowa, N.J.: Rowman and Littlefield.

————. (1992). "Optimal Consumption and Portfolio Rules with Intertemporally Dependent Utility of Consumption." *Journal of Economic Dynamics and Control* 16: 681–712.

Jacka, S. (1984). "Optimal Consumption of an Investment." *Stochastics* 13: 45–60.

————. (1991). "Optimal Stopping and the American Put." *Mathematical Finance* 1: 1–14.

Jaillet, P., D. Lamberton, and B. Lapeyre. (1988). "Inéquations variationelles et théorie des options." *Comtes rendus de l'academie de sciences de Paris* 307: 961–965.

————. (1990). "Variational Inequalities and the Pricing of American Options." CERMA-ENPC, La Courtine, France.

Jakobsen, S. (1992). "Prepayment and the Valuation of Danish Mortgage-Backed Bonds." Ph.D. diss., Aarhaus School of Business, Denmark.

Jamshidian, F. (1989a). "An Exact Bond Option Formula." *Journal of Finance* 44: 205–209.

————. (1989b). "Closed-Form Solution for American Options on Coupon Bonds in the General Gaussian Interest Rate Model." Financial Strategies Group, Merrill Lynch Capital Markets, New York.

————. (1989c). "Free Boundary Formulas for American Options." Financial Strategies Group, Merrill Lynch Capital Markets, New York.

————. (1989d). "The Multifactor Gaussian Interest Rate Model and Implementation." Financial Strategies Group, Merrill Lynch Capital Markets, New York.

————. (1991a). "Bond and Option Evaluation in the Gaussian Interest Rate Model." *Research in Finance* 9: 131–170.

————. (1991b). "Commodity Option Evaluation in the Gaussian Futures Term Structure Model." *Review of Futures Markets* 10: 324-346.

———. (1991c). "Forward Induction and Construction of Yield Curve Diffusion Models." *Journal of Fixed Income* 1 (June): 62–74.

———. (1992). "A Simple Class of Square-Root Interest Rate Models." Fuji International Finance PLC, London.

———. (1993a). "Bond, Futures, and Option Evaluation in the Quadratic Interest Rate Model." Fuji International Finance PLC, London.

———. (1993b). "Options and Futures Evaluation with Deterministic Volatilities." *Mathematical Finance* 3: 149–159.

———. (1993c). "Hedging and Evaluating Diff Swaps." Fuji International Finance PLC, London.

———. (1994). "Hedging Quantos, Differential Swaps and Ratios." *Applied Mathematical Finance* 1: 1–20.

Jamshidian, F., and M. Fein. (1990). "Closed Form Solutions for Oil Futures and European Options in the Gibson-Schwartz Model: A Comment." Financial Strategies Group, Merrill Lynch Capital Markets, New York.

Jarrow, R. (1988). *Finance Theory.* Englewood Cliffs, N.J.: Prentice-Hall.

Jarrow, R., D. Lando, and S. Turnbull. (1993). "A Markov Model for the Term Structure of Credit Risk Spreads." Johnson Graduate School of Management, Cornell University.

Jarrow, R., and D. Madan. (1991). "A Characterization of Complete Security Markets on a Brownian Filtration." *Mathematical Finance* 1: 31–44.

———. (1994). "Valuing and Hedging Contingent Claims on Semimartingales." Johnson Graduate School of Management, Cornell University.

Jarrow, R., and A. Rudd. (1983). *Option Pricing.* Homewood, Ill.: Richard D. Irwin.

Jarrow, R., and S. Turnbull. (1991). "A Unified Approach for Pricing Contingent Claims on Multiple Term Structures." Johnson Graduate School of Management, Cornell University.

———. (1992). "The Pricing and Hedging of Options on Financial Securities Subject to Credit Risk: The Discrete Time Case." Johnson Graduate School of Management, Cornell University.

———. (1994). "Delta, Gamma and Bucket Hedging of Interest Rate Derivatives." *Applied Mathematical Finance* 1: 21–48.

———. (1995). "Pricing Options on Financial Securities Subject to Default Risk." *Journal of Finance* 50: 53–86.

Jeanblanc-Picqué, M., and M. Pontier. (1990). "Optimal Portfolio for a Small Investor in a Market Model with Discontinuous Prices." *Applied Mathematics and Optimization* 22: 287–310.

Johnson, B. (1994). "Dynamic Asset Pricing Theory: The Search for Implementable Results." Engineering-Economic Systems Department, Stanford University.

Johnson, H. (1987). "Options on the Maximum or the Minimum of Several Assets." *Journal of Financial and Quantitative Analysis* 22: 277–283.

Johnson, H., and D. Shanno. (1987). "The Pricing of Options when the Variance is Changing." *Journal of Financial and Quantitative Analysis* 22: 143–151.

Johnson, H., and R. Stulz. (1987). "The Pricing of Options with Default Risk." *Journal of Finance* 42: 267–280.

Jones, R., and R. Jacobs. (1986). "History Dependent Financial Claims: Monte Carlo Valuation." Department of Finance, Simon Fraser University, Vancouver, Canada.

Jorgensen, P. L. (1994a). "American Option Pricing." School of Business, Institute of Management, University of Aarhaus, Denmark.

―――. (1994b). "American Bond Option Pricing in One-Factor Spot Interest Rate Models." Institute of Management, University of Aarhaus, Denmark.

Jouini, E., and H. Kallal. (1991). "Martingales, Arbitrage, and Equilibrium in Security Markets with Transactions Costs." Department of Economics, University of Chicago. Forthcoming in *Journal of Economic Theory*.

―――. (1993a). "Efficient Trading Strategies in the Presence of Market Frictions." CREST-ENSAE, Paris.

―――. (1993b). "Portfolio Choice and Market Frictions." ENSAE, and Laboratoire d'Econométrie de l'Ecole Polytechnique, Paris, France.

Joy, C., and P. Boyle. (1994). "Quasi-Monte Carlo Methods in Numerical Finance." Enron Capital and Trade Resources, Houston, Texas.

Judd, K. (1989). "Minimum Weighted Residual Methods for Solving Dynamic Economic Models." Hoover Institution, Stanford University.

Kabanov, Y., and D. Kramkov. (1993). "No-Arbitrage and Equivalent Martingale Measures: An Elementary Proof of the Harrison-Pliska Theorem." Central Economics and Mathematics Institute, Moscow.

―――. (1995). "Asymptotic Arbitrage on Large Financial Markets." Central Economics and Mathematics Institute, Moscow.

Kajii, A. (1994). "Anonymity and Optimality of Competitive Equilibrium when Markets are Incomplete." *Journal of Economic Theory* 64: 115–129.

Kakutani, S. (1941). "A Generalization of Brouwer's Fixed-Point Theorem." *Duke Mathematical Journal* 8: 451–459.

―――. (1993). "Gradient of the Representative Agent Utility when Agents have Stochastic Recursive Preferences." Graduate School of Business, Stanford University. Forthcoming in *Journal of Mathematical Economics*.

Kan, R. (1995). "Structure of Pareto Optima when Agents Have Stochastic Recursive Preferences." *Journal of Economic Theory* 66: 626–631.

Kandori, M. (1988). "Equivalent Equilibria." *International Economic Review* 29: 401–417.

Karatzas, I. (1987). "Applications of Stochastic Calculus in Financial Economics." Graduate School of Business, Columbia University.

———. (1988). "On the Pricing of American Options." *Applied Mathematics and Optimization* 17: 37–60.

———. (1989). "Optimization Problems in the Theory of Continuous Trading." *SIAM Journal of Control and Optimization* 27: 1221–1259.

———. (1991). "A Note on Utility Maximization under Partial Obervations." *Mathematical Finance* 1: 57–70.

———. (1993). "IMA Tutorial Lectures 1–3: Minneapolis." Department of Statistics, Columbia University.

Karatzas, I., and S.-G. Kou. (1994). "On the Pricing of Contingent Claims under Constraints." Department of Statistics, Columbia University.

Karatzas, I., P. Lakner, J. Lehoczky, and S. Shreve. (1990). "Equilibrium in a Simplified Dynamic, Stochastic Economy with Heterogeneous Agents." Department of Mathematics, Carnegie-Mellon University.

Karatzas, I., J. Lehoczky, S. Sethi, and S. Shreve. (1986). "Explicit Solution of a General Consumption/Investment Problem." *Mathematics of Operations Research* 11: 261–294.

Karatzas, I., J. Lehoczky, and S. Shreve. (1987). "Optimal Portfolio and Consumption Decisions for a 'Small Investor' on a Finite Horizon." *SIAM Journal of Control and Optimization* 25: 1157–1186.

———. (1991). "Equilibrium Models with Singular Asset Prices." *Mathematical Finance* 1/3: 11–30.

Karatzas, I., J. Lehoczky, S. Shreve, and G.-L. Xu. (1991). "Martingale and Duality Methods for Utility Maximization in Incomplete Markets." *SIAM Journal of Control and Optimization* 29: 702–730.

Karatzas, I., and S. Shreve. (1988). *Brownian Motion and Stochastic Calculus.* New York: Springer-Verlag.

———. (1995). "Methods of Mathematical Finance." Chapters 1–3, Draft Manuscript, Department of Mathematics, Carnegie-Mellon University, Pittsburgh.

Karatzas, I., and X.-X. Xue. (1990). "Utility Maximization in a Financial Market with Partial Observations." Department of Mathematics, Rutgers University.

Kat, H. (1993a). "Replicating Ordinary Call Options in an Imperfect Market: A Stochastic Simulation Study." Derivatives Department, MeesPierson N.V., Amsterdam.

————. (1993b). "Hedging Lookback and Asian Options." Derivatives Department, MeesPierson N.V., Amsterdam.

Kehoe, T., and D. K. Levine. (1993). "Debt-Constrained Asset Markets." *Review of Economic Studies* 60: 865–888.

Kennedy, D. (1994). "The Term Structure of Interest Rates as a Gaussian Random Field." *Mathematical Finance* 4: 247–258.

Kim, I. (1990). "The Analytic Valuation of American Options." *Review of Financial Studies* 3: 547–572.

Kim, J. (1992). "A Martingale Analysis of the Term Structure of Interest Rates." Graduate School of Industrial Administration, Carnegie-Mellon University.

————. (1993). "A Discrete-Time Approximation of a One-Factor Markov Model of the Term Structure of Interest Rates." Graduate School of Industrial Administration, Carnegie-Mellon University.

————. (1994). "A Model of the Term Structure of Interest Rates with the Time-Variant Market Price of Risk." Graduate School of Industrial Administration, Carnegie-Mellon University.

Kind, P., R. Liptser, and W. Runggaldier. (1991). "Diffusion Approximation in Past Dependent Models and Applications to Option Pricing." *Annals of Applied Probability* 1: 379–405.

Kishimoto, N. (1989). "A Simplified Approach to Pricing Path Dependent Securities." Fuqua School of Business, Duke University.

Kocherlakota, N. (1990). "On the Discount Factor in 'Growth' Economies." *Journal of Monetary Economics* 25: 43–47.

Koedijk, K., F. Nissen, P. Schotman, and C. Wolff. (1994). "The Dynamics of Short-Term Interest Rate Volatility Reconsidered." Limburg Institute of Financial Economics, University of Limburg.

Koo, H.-K. (1991). "Consumption and Portfolio Choice with Uninsurable Income Risk." Department of Economics, Princeton University.

————. (1994a). "Consumption and Portfolio Selection with Labor Income I: Evaluation of Human Capital." Olin School of Business, Washington University, St.Louis.

————. (1994b). "Comsumption and Portfolio Selection with Labor Income II: The Life Cycle-Permanent Income Hypothesis." Olin School of Business, Washington University, St.Louis.

Koopmans, T. (1960). "Stationary Utility and Impatience." *Econometrica* 28: 287–309.

Kopp, P. (1984). *Martingales and Stochastic Integrals.* Cambridge: Cambridge University Press.

Korn, R. (1992). "Contingent Claim Valuation in a Market with a Higher Interest Rate for Borrowing than for Lending." Department of Mathematics, Johannes Gutenberg-Universität Mainz.

Krasa, S., and Werner, J. (1991). "Equilibria with Options: Existence and Indeterminacy." *Journal of Economic Theory* 54: 305–320.

Kraus, A., and R. Litzenberger. (1975). "Market Equilibrium in a Multiperiod State Preference Model with Logarithmic Utility." *Journal of Finance* 30: 1213–1227.

Kraus, A., and M. Smith. (1993). "A Simple Multifactor Term Structure Model." *Journal of Fixed Income* 19: 19–23.

Kreps, D. (1979). "Three Essays on Capital Markets." Technical Report 298. Institute for Mathematical Studies in the Social Sciences, Stanford University.

———. (1981). "Arbitrage and Equilibrium in Economies with Infinitely Many Commodities." *Journal of Mathematical Economics* 8: 15–35.

———. (1982). "Multiperiod Securities and the Efficient Allocation of Risk: A Comment on the Black-Scholes Option Pricing Model." In J. McCall, *The Economics of Uncertainty and Information*, pp. 203–232. Chicago: University of Chicago Press.

———. (1988). *Notes on the Theory of Choice*. Boulder, Colo., and London: Westview Press.

———. (1990). *A Course in Microeconomic Theory*. Princeton, N.J.: Princeton University Press.

Kreps, D., and E. Porteus. (1978). "Temporal Resolution of Uncertainty and Dynamic Choice." *Econometrica* 46: 185–200.

Kydland, F. E., and E. Prescott. (1991). "Indeterminacy in Incomplete Market Economies." *Economic Theory* 1: 45–62.

Krylov, N. (1980). *Controlled Diffusion Processes*. New York: Springer-Verlag.

Kunitomo, N. (1993). "Long-Term Memory and Fractional Brownian Motion in Financial Markets." Faculty of Economics, University of Tokyo.

Kurz, M. (1992). "Asset Prices with Rational Beliefs." Department of Economics, Stanford University.

———. (1993). "General Equilibrium with Endogenous Uncertainty." Department of Economics, Stanford University.

Kusuoka, S. (1992a). "Arbitrage and Martingale Measure." Research Institute for Mathematical Sciences, Kyoto University.

———. (1992b). "Consistent Price System when Transaction Costs Exist." Research Institute for Mathematical Sciences, Kyoto University.

———. (1993). "Limit Theorem on Option Replication Cost with Transaction Costs." Department of Mathematics, University of Tokyo.

Kuwana, Y. (1994). "Optimal Consumption/Investment Decisions with Partial Observations," Ph.D. diss. Statistics Department, Stanford University.

Lakner, P. (1993a). "Martingale Measures for a Class of Right-Continuous Processes." *Mathematical Finance* 3: 43–54.

————. (1993b). "Equivalent Local Martingale Measures and Free Lunch in a Stochastic Model of Finance with Continuous Trading." Statistics and Operation Research Department, New York University.

————. (1994a). "Minimization of the Expected Squared Difference of a Random Variable and Stochastic Integrals with a Given Integrator." Statistics and Operation Research Department, New York University.

————. (1994b). "Utility Maximization with Partial Information." Statistics and Operation Research Department, New York University.

————. (1994c). "Optimal Investment Processes for Utility Maximazation Problems with Restricted Information." Statistics and Operation Research Department, New York University.

Lakner, P., and E. Slud. (1993). "Optimal Consumption by a Bond Investor: The Case of Random Interest Rate Adapted to a Point Process." Graduate School of Business, New York University.

Lamberton, D. (1993). "Convergence of the Critical Price in the Approximation of American Options." *Mathematical Finance* 3: 179–190.

Lamberton, D., and B. Lapeyre. (1991). *Introduction au calcul stochastique appliqué à la finance.* Paris: Ellipses.

Lamberton, D., and G. Pagès. (1990). "Sur l'approximation des réduites." *Annales de l'Institut Henri Poincaré* 26: 331–355.

Lamoureux C., and W. Lastrapes. (1993). "Forecasting Stock-Return Variance: Toward an Understanding of Stochastic Implied Volatilities." *Review of Financial Studies* 6: 293–327.

Lando, D. (1993). "A Continuous-Time Markov Model of the Term Structure of Credit Risk Spreads." Statistics Center, Cornell University.

————. (1994a). "On Cox Processes and Credit Risky Bonds." Statistics Center, Cornell University.

————. (1994b). "Three Essays on Contingent Claims Pricing." Ph.D. diss., Statistics Center, Cornell University.

Langetieg, T. (1980). "A Multivariate Model of the Term Structure." *Journal of Finance* 35: 71–97.

Lawson, J., and J. Morris. (1978). "The Extrapolation of First Order Methods for Parabolic Partial Differential Equations I." *SIAM Journal of Numerical Analysis* 15: 1212–1224.

Lee, J.-J. (1990). "The Valuation of American Calls." Graduate School of Business, Stanford University.

————. (1991). "A Note on Binomial Approximation for Contingent Securities." Graduate School of Business, Stanford University.

Lee, B., and B. Ingram. (1991). "Simulation Estimation of Time-Series Models." *Journal of Econometrics* 47: 197–205.

Lehoczky, J., S. Sethi, and S. Shreve. (1983). "Optimal Consumption and Investment Policies Allowing Consumption Constraints and Bankruptcy." *Mathematics of Operations Research* 8: 613–636.

———. (1985). "A Martingale Formulation for Optimal Consumption/Investment Decision Making." In G. Feichtinger, *Optimal Control and Economic Analysis 2*, pp. 135–153. Amsterdam: North-Holland.

Lehoczky, J., and S. Shreve. (1986). "Explicit Equilibrium Solutions for a Multi-Agent Consumption/Investment Problem." Technical Report 384. Department of Statistics, Carnegie-Mellon University.

Leland, H. (1985). "Option Pricing and Replication with Transactions Costs." *Journal of Finance* 40: 1283–1301.

———. (1993). "Long-Term Debt Value, Bond Covenants, and Optimal Capital Structure." Institution of Business and Economic Research, University of California, Berkeley.

LeRoy, S. (1973). "Risk Aversion and the Martingale Property of Asset Prices." *International Economic Review* 14: 436–446.

Levental, S., and A. Skorohod. (1994). "A Necessary and Sufficient Condition for Absence of Arbitrage with Tame Portfolios." School of Business, Michigan State University.

Levhari, D., and T. Srinivasan. (1969). "Optimal Savings under Uncertainty." *Review of Economic Studies* 59: 153–165.

Levine, D. (1989). "Infinite Horizon Equilibria with Incomplete Markets." *Journal of Mathematical Economics* 18: 357–376.

Levine, D., and W. Zame. (1992). "Debt Constraints and Equilibium in Infinite Horizon Economies with Incomplete Markets." Department of Economics, Johns Hopkins University. Forthcoming in *Journal of Mathematical Economics*.

Levy, A., M. Avellaneda, and A. Parás. (1994). "A New Approach for Pricing Derivative Securities in Markets with Uncertain Volatilities: A 'Case Study' on the Trinomial Tree." Courant Institute of Mathematical Sciences, New York University.

Li, A., P. Ritchken, and L. Sankarasubramaniam. (1993). "Lattice Models for Pricing American Interest Rate Claims." Working Paper. First National Bank of Chicago, New York.

Lintner, J. (1965). "The Valuation of Risky Assets and the Selection of Risky Investment in Stock Portfolios and Capital Budgets." *Review of Economics and Statistics* 47: 13–37.

Lions, P.-L. (1981). "Control of Diffusion Processes in R^N." *Communications in Pure and Applied Mathematics* 34: 121–147.

———. (1983). "Optimal Control of Diffusion Processes." Université de Paris IX, Dauphine.

Litterman, R., and J. Scheinkman. (1988). "Common Factors Affecting Bond Returns." Goldman Sachs, Financial Strategies Group, New York.

Litzenberger, R. (1992). "Swaps: Plain and Fanciful." *Journal of Finance* 47: 831-850.

Löffler, A. (1994). "Variance Aversion Implies μ–σ^2–Criterion." Graduiertenkolleg des FB Wirtschaftswissenschaften, Berlin.

Longstaff, F. (1990). "The Valuation of Options on Yields." *Journal of Financial Economics* 26: 97–121.

Longstaff, F., and E. Schwartz. (1992a). "Interest Rate Volatility and the Term Structure: A Two-Factor General Equilibrium Model." *Journal of Finance* 47: 1259–1282.

―――. (1992b). "Valuing Risky Debt: A New Approach." Anderson Graduate School of Management, University of California, Los Angeles.

―――. (1993). "Implementing of the Longstaff-Schwartz Interest Rate Model." Anderson Graduate School of Management, University of California, Los Angeles.

Lu, S., and G. Yu. (1993). "Valuation of Options under Stochastic Volatility: The Garch Diffusion Approach." Department of Mathematics, University of Michigan.

Lucas, D. (1991). "Asset Pricing with Undiversifiable Income Risk and Short Sales Constraints: Deepening the Equity Premium Puzzle." Kellogg School of Management, Northwestern University.

Lucas, R. (1978). "Asset Prices in an Exchange Economy." *Econometrica* 46: 1429–1445.

Luenberger, D. (1969). *Optimization by Vector Space Methods*. New York: Wiley.

―――. (1984). *Introduction to Linear and Nonlinear Programming* (2d ed.). Reading, Mass.: Addison-Wesley.

―――. (1995). *Microeconomic Theory*. New York: McGraw-Hill.

Luttmer, E. (1991). "Asset Pricing in Economies with Frictions." Department of Economics, University of Chicago.

Ma, C. (1991a). "Market Equilibrium with Heterogeneous Recursive-Utility-Maximizing Agents." *Economic Theory* 3: 243–266.

―――. (1991b). "Valuation of Derivative Securities with Mixed Poisson-Brownian Information and with Recursive Utility." Department of Economics, University of Toronto.

―――. (1993). "Intertemporal Recursive Utility in the Presence of Mixed Poisson-Brownian Uncertainty." Department of Economics, McGill University.

―――. (1994a). "Attitudes toward the Timing of Resolution of Uncertainty and Existence of Resursive Utility." Department of Economics, McGill University.

————. (1994b). "Discrete-Time Model of Asset Pricing in Incomplete Market: Ge Approach with Recursive Utility." Department of Economics, McGill University.

Ma, J., P. Protter, and J. Yong. (1993). "Solving Forward-Backward Stochastic Differential Equations Explicitly—A Four Step Scheme." Institute for Mathematics and Its Applications, University of Minnesota.

Ma, J., and J. Yong. (1993). "Solvability of Forward-Backward SDEs and the Nodal Set of Hamilton-Jacobi-Bellman Equations." Institute for Mathematics and its Applications, University of Minnesota.

Machina, M. (1982). "'Expected Utility' Analysis without the Independence Axiom." *Econometrica* 50: 277–323.

Madan, D. (1988). "Risk Measurement in Semimartingale Models with Multiple Consumption Goods." *Journal of Economic Theory* 44: 398–412.

Madan, D., F. Milne, and H. Shefrin. (1989). "The Multinomial Option Pricing Model and Its Brownian and Poisson Limits." *Review of Financial Studies* 2: 251–266.

Madan, D., and H. Unal. (1993). "Pricing the Risks of Default." College of Business, University of Maryland.

Magill, M., and M. Quinzii. (1993). "Incomplete Markets over an Infinite Horizon: Long-Lived Securities and Speculative Bubbles." University of Southern California. Forthcoming in *Journal of Mathematical Economics.*

————. (1994a). "Infinite Horizon Incomplete Markets." *Econometrica* 62: 853–880.

————. (1994b). *Theory of Incomplete Markets.* Forthcoming: MIT Press.

Magill, M., and W. Shafer. (1990). "Characterisation of Generically Complete Real Asset Structures." *Journal of Mathematical Economics* 19: 167–194.

————. (1991). "Handbook of Mathematical Economics, Volume 4." In Hildenbrand, W., and H. . Sonnenschein, *Incomplete Markets.* Amsterdam: North-Holland, pp. 1523–1614.

Malliaris, A. (1982). *Stochastic Methods in Economics and Finance.* Amsterdam: North-Holland.

Mankiw, G. (1986). "The Equity Premium and the Concentration of Aggregate Shocks." *Journal of Financial Economics* 17: 211–219.

Marcet, A. (1993). "Simulation Analysis of Dynamic Stochastic Models: Applications to Theory and Estimation." Department of Economics, Universitat Pompeu Fabra, Barcelona.

Marcet, A., and D. Marshall. (1994). "Solving Nonlinear Rational Expectations Models by Parameterized Expectations: Convergence to Stationary Solutions." Universitat Pompeu Fabra, Department of Economics, Barcelona.

Marcet, A., and K. Singleton. (1991). "Optimal Consumption and Savings Decisions and Equilibrium Asset Prices in a Model with Heterogeneous Agents Subject to Portfolio Constraints." Carnegie-Mellon University and Graduate School of Business, Stanford University.

Margrabe, W. (1978). "The Value of an Option to Exchange One Asset for Another." *Journal of Finance* 33: 177–186.

Marimon, R. (1987). "Kreps' 'Three Essays on Capital Markets' Almost Ten Years Later." Department of Economics, University of Minnesota. Forthcoming in *Revista Espanola de Economia.*

Marsh, T. (1994). "Term Structure of Interest Rates and the Pricing of Fixed Income Claims and Bonds." Haas School of Business, University of California, Berkeley.

Mas-Colell, A. (1985). *The Theory of General Economic Equilibrium—A Differentiable Approach.* Cambridge: Cambridge University Press.

————. (1986a). "The Price Equilibrium Existence Problem in Topological Vector Lattices." *Econometrica* 54: 1039–1054.

————. (1986b). "Valuation Equilibrium and Pareto Optimum Revisited." In W. Hildenbrand and A. Mas-Colell, *Contributions to Mathematical Economics,* pp. 317–332. Amsterdam: North-Holland.

————. (1987). "An Observation on Geanakoplos and Polemarchakis." Department of Economics, Harvard University.

————. (1991). "Indeterminacy in Incomplete Market Economies." *Economic Theory* 1: 45–62.

Mas-Colell, A., and P. Monteiro. (1991). "Self-Fulfilling Equilibria: An Existence Theorem for a General State Space." Department of Economics, Paper 2, Harvard University, Economic Theory Discussion. Forthcoming in *Journal of Mathematical Economics.*

Mas-Colell, A., and W. Zame. (1992). "Equilibrium Theory in Infinite Dimensional Spaces." In W. Hildenbrand and H. Sonnenschein, *Handbook of Mathematical Econonomics, Vol. 4,* pp. 1835–1898. Amsterdam: North-Holland.

McFadden, D. (1986). "A Method of Simulated Moments for Estimation of Discrete Response Models without Numerical Integration." Department of Economics, Massachusetts Institute of Technology.

McKean, H. (1965). "Appendix: Free Boundary Problem for the Heat Equation Arising from a Problem in Mathematical Economics." *Industrial Management Review* 6: 32–39.

McKenzie, L. (1954). "On Equilibrium in Graham's Model of World Trade and Other Competitive Systems." *Econometrica* 22: 147–161.

McManus, D. (1984). "Incomplete Markets: Generic Existence of Equilibrium and Optimality Properties in an Economy with Futures Markets." Department of Economics, University of Pennsylvania.

Mehra, R., and E. Prescott. (1985). "The Equity Premium: A Puzzle." *Journal of Monetary Economics* 15: 145–161.

Mehrling, P. (1990). "Heterogeneity, Incomplete Markets, and the Equity Premium." Department of Economics, Barnard College and Columbia University.

Melino, A., and S. Turnbull. (1990). "Pricing Foreign Currency Options with Stochastic Volatility." *Journal of Econometrics* 45: 239-265.

Merton, R. (1969). "Lifetime Portfolio Selection under Uncertainty: The Continuous Time Case." *Review of Economics and Statistics* 51: 247–257.

———. (1971). "Optimum Consumption and Portfolio Rules in a Continuous Time Model." *Journal of Economic Theory* 3: 373–413; Erratum 6 (1973): 213–214.

———. (1973a). "An Intertemporal Capital Asset Pricing Model." *Econometrica* 41: 867–888.

———. (1973b). "The Theory of Rational Option Pricing." *Bell Journal of Economics and Management Science* 4: 141–183.

———. (1974). "On the Pricing of Corporate Debt: The Risk Structure of Interest Rates." *Journal of Finance* 29: 449–470.

———. (1976). "Option Pricing when the Underlying Stock Returns are Discontinuous." *Journal of Financial Economics* 5: 125–144.

———. (1977). "On the Pricing of Contingent Claims and the Modigliani-Miller Theorem." *Journal of Financial Economics* 5: 241–250.

———. (1990a). "Capital Market Theory and the Pricing of Financial Securities." In B. Friedman and F. Hahn, *Handbook of Monetary Economics*, pp. 497–581. Amsterdam: North-Holland.

———. (1990b). *Continuous-Time Finance.* Oxford: Basil Blackwell.

———. (1993). "On Continuous and Discrete Time Option Pricing: Approximations and Their Interpretation." Dipartimento di Matematica Pura ed Applicata, Universitá di Padova.

———. (1994a). "Influence of Mathematical Models in Finance on Practice: Past, Present and Future." *Philosophical Transactions of the Royal Society, Series A* 347: 451–464.

———. (1994b). "On the Mathematics and Economics Assumptions of Continuous-Time Models." Sloan School of Management, Massachusetts Institute of Technology.

Milshtein, G. (1974). "Approximate Integration of Stochastic Differential Equations." *Theory of Probability and Its Applications* 3: 557–562.

———. (1978). "A Method of Second-Order Accuracy Integration of Stochastic Differential Equations." *Theory of Probability and Its Applications* 23: 396–401.

Miltersen, K. (1993). "Pricing of Interest Rate Contingent Claims: Implementing the Simulation Approach." Department of Management, Odense University.

———. (1994). "An Arbitrage Theory of the Term Structure of Interest Rates." *Annals of Applied Probability* 4: 953–967.

Miltersen, K., K. Sandmann, and D. Sondermann. (1994). "Closed Form Solutions for Term Structure Derivations with Log-Normal Interest Rates." Department of Management, Odense University, Denmark.

Mirrlees, J. (1974). "Optimal Accumulation under Uncertainty: The Case of Stationary Returns to Investment." In J. Drèze, *Allocation under Uncertainty: Equilibrium and Optimality*, pp. 36–50. New York: Wiley.

Mitchell, A., and D. Griffiths. (1980). *The Finite Difference Method in Partial Differential Equations.* New York: John Wiley.

Miura, R. (1992). "A Note on Look-Back Options Based on Order Statistics." *Hitotsubashi Journal of Commerce and Management* 27: 15–28.

Modigliani, F., and M. Miller. (1958). "The Cost of Capital, Corporation Finance, and the Theory of Investment." *American Economic Review* 48: 261–297.

Monat, P., and C. Stricker. (1993a). "Décomposition de Föllmer-Schweizer et Fermeture de $G_T(\Theta)$." Département de Mathématiques, Université Franche-Comté, France.

———. (1993b). "Follmer-Schweizer Decomposition and Closedness of $G_T(\Theta)$." Laboratoire de Mathématiques, URA CNRS 741, Paris, France.

Monteiro, P. (1991). "A New Proof of the Existence of Equilibrium in Incomplete Markets Economies." Forthcoming in *Journal of Mathematical Economics*, Universidade Federal do Rio de Janeiro and Harvard University.

———. (1993). "Inada's Condition Imply Equilibrium Existence is Rare." Department of Economics, Universidade Federal do Rio de Janeiro.

Müller, S. (1985). *Arbitrage Pricing of Contingent Claims.* Lecture Notes in Economics and Mathematical Systems, vol. 254. New York: Springer-Verlag.

Musiela, M. (1994a). "Stochastic PDEs and Term Structure Models." Department of Mathematics, University of New South Wales, Sydney.

———. (1994b). "Nominal Annual Rates and Lognormal Volatility Structure." Department of Mathematics, University of New South Wales, Sydney.

Musiela, M., and D. Sondermann. (1994). "Different Dynamical Specifications of the Term Structure of Interest Rates and Their Implications." Department of Mathematics, University of New South Wales, Sydney.

Myneni, R. (1992a). "The Pricing of the American Option." *Annals of Applied Probability* 2: 1–23.

———. (1992b). "Continuous-Time Relationships Between Futures and Forward Prices." Graduate School of Business, Stanford University.

Naik, V. (1993). "Asset Prices in Dynamic Production Economies with Time Varying Risk." Faculty of Commerce and Business Administration, University of British Columbia.

Naik, V., and M. Lee. (1993). "The Yield Curve and Bond Options Prices with Discrete Shifts in Economic Regimes." University of British Columbia.

Naik, V., and R. Uppal. (1992). "Leverage Constraints and the Optimal Hedging of Stock and Bond Options." Faculty of Commerce and Business Administration, University of British Columbia.

Negishi, T. (1960). "Welfare Economics and Existence of an Equilibrium for a Competitive Economy." *Metroeconometrica* 12: 92–97.

Nelson, D. (1990). "ARCH Models as Diffusion Appoximations." *Journal of Econometrics* 45: 7–38.

———. (1991). "Conditional Heteroskedasticity in Asset Returns: A New Approach." *Econometrica* 59: 347–370.

———. (1992). "Filtering and Forecasting with Misspecified ARCH Models I." *Journal of Econometrics* 52: 61–90.

Nelson, D., and K. Ramaswamy. (1989). "Simple Binomial Processes as Diffusion Approximations in Financial Models." *Review of Financial Studies* 3: 393–430.

Nelson, J., and S. Schaefer. (1983). "Innovations in Bond Portfolio Management: Duration Analysis and Immunization." In G. Bierwag, G. Kaufman, and A. Toevs, *The Dynamic of the Term Structure and Alternative Portfolio Immunization Strategies.* Greenwich: JAI Press.

Newton, N. (1990). "Asymptotically Efficient Runge-Kutta Methods for a Class of Ito and Stratonovich Equations." Department of Electrical Engineering, University of Essex.

Nielsen, L.T. (1990a). "Equilibrium in CAPM without a Riskless Asset." *Review of Economic Studies* 57: 315–324.

———. (1990b). "Existence of Equilibrium in CAPM." *Journal of Economic Theory* 52: 223–231.

———. (1993a). "Two-Fund Separation and Equilibrum." INSEAD, Fontainebleau, France.

———. (1993b). "Robustness of the Market Model." *Economic Theory* 3: 365-370.

Nielsen, L. T., and J. Saá-Requejo. (1992). "Exchange Rate and Term Structure Dynamics and the Pricing of Derivative Securities." Working Paper. INSEAD, Fontainebleau, France.

Nielsen, L. T., J. Saá-Requejo, and P. Santa-Clara. (1993). "Default Risk and Interest Rate Risk: The Term Structure of Credit Spreads." Working Paper. INSEAD, Fontainebleau, France.

Ocone, D., and I. Karatzas. (1991). "A Generalized Clark Representation Formula, with Application to Optimal Portfolios." *Stochastics and Stochastics Reports* 34: 187–220.

Ōhashi, K. (1991). "A Note on the Terminal Date Security Prices in a Continuous Time Trading Model with Dividends." *Journal of Mathematical Economics* 20: 219–224.

Øksendal, B. (1985). *Stochastic Differential Equations*. Berlin: Springer-Verlag.

Oliveira, D. (1994). "Arbitrage Pricing of Integral Options." Instituto de Matemática Pura e Applicada, Rio de Janeiro.

O'Nan, M. (1976). *Linear Algebra* (2d ed.). New York: Harcourt Brace Jovanovich.

Pagès, H. (1987). "Optimal Consumption and Portfolio Policies when Markets are Incomplete." Department of Economics, Massachusetts Institute of Technology.

Pakes, A., and D. Pollard. (1986). "The Asymptotics of Simulation Estimators." Department of Economics, University of Wisconsin.

Pan, W.-H. (1992). "A Second Welfare Theorem for Constrained Efficient Allocations in Incomplete Markets." Department of Economics, University of Rochester.

———. (1993). "Constrained Efficient Allocations in Incomplete Markets: Characterization and Implementation." Department of Economics, University of Rochester.

Pardoux, E., and S. Peng. (1990). "Adapted Solution of a Backward Stochastic Differential Equation." *Systems and Control Letters* 14: 55–61.

———. (1994). "Some Backward Stochastic Differencial Equations with Non-Lipschitz Coefficients." Department of Mathematics, Université de Provence.

Pearson, N., and T.-S. Sun. (1994). "An Empirical Examination of the Cox, Ingersoll, and Ross Model of the Term Structure of Interest Rates using the Method of Maximum Likelihood." *Journal of Finance* 54: 929–959.

Pedersen, H., and E. Shiu. (1993). "Pricing of Options on Bonds by Binomial Lattices and by Diffusion Processes." Investment Policy Department, Great-West Life Assurance Company.

Pedersen, H., E. Shiu, and A. Thorlacius. (1989). "Arbitrage-Free Pricing of Interest Rate Contingent Claims." *Transactions of the Society of Actuaries* 41: 231–265.

Peng, S. (1992). "Backward Stochastic Differential Equations and Applications to Optimal Control." Department of Mathematics, Shandong University.

————. (1993). "Adapted Solution of Backward Stochastic Equations and Related Partial Differential Equations." Department of Mathematics, Shandong University.

Pennacchi, G. (1991). "Identifying the Dynamics of Real Interest Rates and Inflation: Evidence Using Survey Data." *Review of Financial Studies* 4: 53–86.

Pham, H., and N. Touzi. (1993). "Intertemporal Equilibrium Risk Premia in a Stochastic Volatility Model." CREST, Paris.

Platen, E., and M. Schweizer. (1994). "On Smile and Skewness." School of Mathematical Sciences Centre for Mathematics and Its Applications, The Australian National University, Canberra.

Platten, I. (1993). "Non-linear General Equilibrium Models of the Term Structure: Comments and Two-factor Generalization." University De Mons-Hainaut, Mons, Belgium.

Pliska, S. (1986). "A Stochastic Calculus Model of Continuous Trading: Optimal Portfolios." *Mathematics of Operations Research* 11: 371–382.

Pliska, S., and M. Selby. (1994). "On a Free Boundary Problem that Arises in Portfolio Management." Financial Options Research Centre, University of Warwick.

Polemarchakis, H., and P. Siconolfi. (1991). "Competitive Equilibria without Free Disposal or Nonsatiation." Research Paper 9115. CORE, Université Catholique de Louvain.

Polemarchakis, H., and B. Ku. (1990). "Options and Equilibrium." *Journal of Mathematical Economics* 19: 107–112.

Pollard, D. (1984). *Convergence of Stochastic Processes.* New York: Springer-Verlag.

Prescott, E., and R. Mehra. (1980). "Recursive Competitive Equilibrium: The Case of Homogeneous Households." *Econometrica* 48: 1365–1379.

Press, W., B. Flannery, S. Teukolsky, and W. Vetterling. (1993). *Numerical Recipes in C: The Art of Scientific Computing* (2d ed.). Cambridge: Cambridge University Press.

Prigent, J.-L. (1994). "From Discrete to Continuous Time Finance: Weak Convergence of the Optimal Financial Trading Strategies." Institute of Mathematical Research of Rennes, University of Rennes.

Prisman, E. (1985). "Valuation of Risky Assets in Arbitrage Free Economies with Frictions." Department of Finance, University of Arizona.

Protter, P. (1990). *Stochastic Integration and Differential Equations.* New York: Springer-Verlag.

Pye, G. (1966). "A Markov Model of the Term Structure." *Quarterly Journal of Economics* 81: 61–72.

Quenez, M.-C. (1992). "Méthodes de controle stochastique en finance." Ph.D. diss., Laboratoires de Probabilités, Université de Paris VI.

Radner, R. (1967). "Equilibre des marchés a terme et au comptant en cas d'incertitude." *Cahiers d'Econométrie* 4: 35–52.

―――. (1972). "Existence of Equilibrium of Plans, Prices, and Price Expectations in a Sequence of Markets." *Econometrica* 40: 289–303.

Rady, S. (1993). "State Prices Implicit in Valuation Formula for Derivative Securities: A Martingale Approach." London School of Economics.

Ramaswamy, K., and S. Sundaresan. (1986). "The Valuation of Floating-Rate Instruments, Theory and Evidence." *Journal of Financial Economics* 17: 251–272.

Reisman, H. (1986). "Option Pricing for Stocks with a Generalized Log-Normal Price Distribution." Department of Finance, University of Minnesota.

Renault, E., and N. Touzi. (1992a). "Option Hedging and Implicit Volatilities." GREMAQ, Toulouse, France.

―――. (1992b). "Stochastic Volatility Models: Statistical Inference from Implied Volatilities." GREMAQ IDEI, Toulouse, and CREST, Paris, France.

Repullo, R. (1986). "On the Generic Existence of Radner Equilibria when There Are as Many Securities as States of Nature." *Economics Letters* 21: 101–105.

Revuz, D. (1975). *Markov Chains.* Amsterdam: North-Holland.

Revuz, D., and M. Yor. (1991). *Continuous Martingales and Brownian Motion.* New York: Springer-Verlag.

Ricciardi, L., and S. Sato. (1988). "First-Passage-Time Density and Moments of the Ornstein-Uhlenbeck Process." *Journal of Applied Probability* 25: 43–57.

Rich, D. (1993). "The Valuation of Black-Scholes Options Subject to Intertemporal Default Risk." Department of Finance, Virginia Polytechnic Institute.

Richard, S. (1975). "Optimal Consumption, Portfolio, and Life Insurance Rules for an Uncertain Lived Individual in a Continuous Time Model." *Journal of Financial Economics* 2: 187–203.

―――. (1978). "An Arbitrage Model of the Term Structure of Interest Rates." *Journal of Financial Economics* 6: 33–57.

―――. (1994). "A Model of the Term Structure of Interest Rates with Volatility Proportional to the Cube of the Short Rate." Miller, Anderson and Sherrerd, Philadelphia.

Richard, S., and R. Roll. (1989). "Prepayments on Fixed-Rate Mortgage-Backed Securities." *Journal of Portfolio Management* 15: 73–82.

Richardson, H. (1989). "A Minimum Variance Result in Continuous Trading Portfolio Optimization." *Management Science* 35: 1045–1055.

Ritchken, P., and L. Sankarasubramaniam. (1992). "Valuing Claims when Interest Rates Have Stochastic Volatility." Department of Finance, University of Southern California.

———. (1993). "On Finite State Markovian Representations of the Term Structure." Department of Finance, University of Southern California.

Rockafellar, R.T. (1970). *Convex Analysis.* Princeton, N.J.: Princeton University Press.

Rogers, C. (1993a). "Equivalent Martingale Measures and No-Arbitrage." Department of Mathematics, Queen Mary and Westfield College, University of London.

———. (1993b). "Which Model for Term-Structure of Interest Rates Should One Use." Department of Mathematics, Queen Mary and Westfield College, University of London.

Rogers, C., and Z. Shi. (1994). "The Value of an Asian Option" Queen Mary and Westfield College, Department of Mathematics, University of London.

Rogers, C., and W. Stummer. (1994). "How Well Do One-Factor Models Fit Bond Prices?" School of Mathematical Sciences, University of Bath.

Rogers, C., and D. Williams. (1987). *Diffusions, Markov Processes, and Martingales: Ito Calculus.* New York: Wiley.

Ross, S. (1976). "The Arbitrage Theory of Capital Asset Pricing." *Journal of Economic Theory* 13: 341–60.

———. (1978). "A Simple Approach to the Valuation of Risky Streams." *Journal of Business* 51: 453–475.

———. (1987). "Arbitrage and Martingales with Taxation." *Journal of Political Economy* 95: 371–393.

———. (1989). "Information and Volatility: The Non-Arbitrage Martingale Approach to Timing and Resolution Irrelevancy." *Journal of Finance* 64: 1–17.

Rothschild, M. (1986). "Asset Pricing Theories." In W. Heller and D. Starrett, *Uncertainty, Information and Communication—Essays in Honor of Kenneth J. Arrow,* vol. 3, pp. 97–128. Cambridge: Cambridge University Press.

Royden, H. (1968). *Real Analysis* (2d ed.). New York: Macmillan.

Rubinstein, M. (1974a). "A Discrete-Time Synthesis of Financial Theory." Working Paper 20. Haas School of Business, University of California, Berkeley.

———. (1974b). "An Aggregation Theorem for Securities Markets." *Journal of Financial Economics* 1: 225–244.

————. (1976). "The Valuation of Uncertain Income Streams and the Pricing of Options." *Bell Journal of Economics* 7: 407–425.

————. (1987). "Derivative Assets Analysis." *Economics Perspectives* 1: 73–93.

————. (1992). "Guiding Force." In Peter Field, *From Black-Scholes to Black Holes.* pp. 39–48, London: Risk Magazine.

————. (1994). "Implied Binomial Trees." *Journal of Finance* 49: 771–818.

————. (1995). "As Simple as One, Two, Three." *Risk* 8: 44–47.

Rudin, W. (1973). *Functional Analysis.* New York: McGraw-Hill.

Ryder, H., and G. Heal. (1973). "Optimal Growth with Intertemporally Dependent Preferences." *Review of Economic Studies* 40: 1–31.

Saà-Requejo, J. (1993). "The Dynamics of the Term Structure of Risk Premia in Foreign Exchange Markets." Working Paper. INSEAD, Fontainebleau, France.

Samuelson, P. (1969). "Lifetime Portfolio Selection by Dynamic Stochastic Programming." *Review of Economics and Statistics* 51: 239–246.

Sandmann, K., and D. Sondermann. (1993). "On the Stability of Lognormal Interest Rate Models." Department of Mathematics, University of Bonn.

Santos, M. (1991). "Smoothness of the Policy Function in Discrete Time Economic Models." *Econometrica* 59: 1365–1382.

————. (1994). "Smooth Dynamics and Computation in Models of Economic Growth." *Journal of Economic Dynamics and Control* 18: 879–895.

Santos, M., and M. Woodford. (1994). "Rational Asset Pricing Bubbles." Department of Economics, Universdad Carlos III, Madrid.

Schachermayer, W. (1992). "A Hilbert-Space Proof of the Fundamental Theorem of Asset Pricing." *Insurance Mathematics and Economics* 11: 249–257.

————. (1993). "A Counterexample to Several Problems in the Theory of Asset Pricing." *Mathematical Finance* 3: 217–230.

————. (1994). "Martingale Measures for Discrete-Time Processes with Infinite Horizon." *Mathematical Finance* 4: 25–56.

Schaefer, S., and E. Schwartz. (1984). "A Two-Factor Model of the Term Structure: An Approximate Analytical Solution." *Journal of Financial and Quantitative Analysis* 19: 413–423.

Scheinkman, J. (1989). "Market Incompleteness and the Equilibrium Valuation of Assets." In S. Bhattacharya and G. Constantinides, *Theory of Valuation, Frontiers of Financial Theory*, pp. 45–51. Totowa, N.J.: Rowman and Littlefield.

Scheinkman, J., and L. Weiss. (1986). "Borrowing Constraints and Aggregate Economic Activity." *Econometrica* 54: 23–45.

Schroder, M. (1993). "Optimal Portfolio Selection with Transactions Costs." Working Paper. Finance Department, Northwestern University.

Schwartz, E. (1977). "The Valuation of Warrants: Implementing a New Approach." *Journal of Financial Economics* 4: 79–94.

Schweizer, M. (1992). "Martingale Densities for General Asset Prices." *Journal of Mathematical Economics* 21: 363–378.

————. (1993a). "Approximating Random Variables by Stochastic Integrals." Department of Mathematics, University of Bonn.

————. (1993b). "Risk-Minimizing Hedging Strategies under Restricted Information." Department of Mathematics, University of Bonn.

————. (1994a). "A Projection Result for Semimartingales." Department of Mathematics, University of Bonn.

————. (1994b). "Hedging and the CAPM." Department of Mathematics, University of Bonn.

Scott, L. (1987). "Option Pricing when the Variance Changes Randomly: Theory, Estimation, and Application." *Journal of Financial and Quantitative Analysis* 4: 419-438.

————. (1992). "Stock Market Volatility and the Pricing of Index Options: An Analysis of Implied Volatilities and the Volatility Risk Premium in a Model with Stochastic Interest Rates and Volatility." Department of Finance, University of Georgia.

————. (1993). "Pricing Stock Options in a Jump-Diffusion Model with Stochastic Volatility and Interest Rates: Applications of Fourier Inversion Methods." Department of Finance, University of Georgia.

Selby, M., and S. Hodges. (1987). "On the Evaluation of Compound Options." *Management Science* 33: 347–355.

Selby, M., and C. Strickland. (1993). "Computing the Fong and Vasicek Pure Discount Bond Price Formula." FORC Preprint 93/42, October 1993, University of Warwick.

Selden, L. (1978). "A New Representation of Preference over 'Certain × Uncertain' Consumption Pairs: The 'Ordinal Certainty Equivalent' Hypothesis." *Econometrica* 46: 1045–1060.

Sethi, S., and M. Taksar. (1988). "A Note on Merton's 'Optimum Consumption and Portfolio Rules in a Continuous-Time Model'." *Journal of Economic Theory* 46: 395–401.

Shannon, C. (1993). "Determinacy in Infinite Horizon Exchange Economies." Department of Economics, University of California, Berkeley.

Sharpe, W. (1964). "Capital Asset Prices: A Theory of Market Equilibrium under Conditions of Risk." *Journal of Finance* 19: 425–442.

————. (1985). *Investments* (3d ed.). Englewood Cliffs, N.J.: Prentice-Hall.

Shepp, L., and A. N. Shiryaev. (1993). "The Russian Option: Reduced Regret." *Annals of Applied Probability* 3: 631–640.

Shimko, D. (1993). "Bounds of Probability." *Risk* 6 (April): 33–37.

Shirakawa, H. (1994). "Optimal Consumption and Portfolio Selection with Incomplete Markets and Upper and Lower Bound Constraints." *Mathematical Finance* 4: 1–24.

Shreve, S., and M. Soner. (1994). "Optimal Investment and Consumption with Transaction Costs." *Annals of Applied Probability* 4: 609–692.

Shreve, S., M. Soner, and G.-L. Xu. (1991). "Optimal Investment and Consumption with Two Bonds and Transaction Costs." *Mathematical Finance* 1: 53–84.

Siegel, D., and D. Siegel. (1990). *Futures Markets*. Orlando: The Dryden Press.

Singleton, K. (1987). "Specification and Estimation of Intertemporal Asset Pricing Models." In B. Friedman and F. Hahn, *Handbook of Monetary Economics*, vol. 1, pp. 583–626. Amsterdam: North-Holland.

Skiadas, C. (1991a). "Time-Consistent Choice and Preferences for Information." Operations Research Department, Stanford University.

———. (1991b). "Conditioning and Aggregation of Preferences." Operations Research Department, Stanford University.

Smith, G. (1985). *Numerical Solution of Partial Differential Equations: Finite Difference Methods* (3d ed.). Oxford: Clarendon Press.

Soner, M., E. Shreve, and J. Cvitanić. (1994). "There Is No Nontrivial Hedging Portfolio for Option Pricing with Transaction Costs." Institute for Mathematics and Its Applications, University of Minnesota.

Stambaugh, R. (1988). "The Information in Forward Rates: Implications for Models of the Term Structure." *Journal of Financial Economics* 21: 41–70.

Stanton, R. (1990). "Rational Prepayment and the Valuation of Mortgage-Backed Securities." Graduate School of Business, Stanford University. Forthcoming in *Review of Financial Studies*.

Stanton, R., and N. Wallace. (1994). "ARM Wrestling: Valuing Adjustable Rate Mortgages Indexed to the Eleventh District Cost of Funds." Haas School of Business, University of California, Berkeley. Forthcoming in *Journal of the American Real Estate and Urban Economics Association*.

Stapleton, R., and M. Subrahmanyam. (1978). "A Multiperiod Equilibrium Asset Pricing Model." *Econometrica* 46: 1077–1093.

Stokey, N., and R. Lucas. (1989). *Recursive Methods in Economic Dynamics (with Ed Prescott)*. Cambridge, Massachusetts: Harvard University Press.

Stoll, H., and R. Whaley. (1993). *Futures and Options: Theory and Applications*. Cincinnati: Southwestern.

Streufert, P. (1991a). "Existence and Characterization Results for Stochastic Dynamic Programming." Research Paper 91–109. Department of Economics, University of California, San Diego.

––––––. (1991b). "Nonnegative Stochastic Dynamic Preferences." Research Paper 91–110. Department of Economics, University of California, San Diego.

––––––. (1991c). "Ordinal Dynamic Programming." Research Paper 9104. Department of Economics, University of Wisconsin, Madison.

Stricker, C. (1984). "Integral Representation in the Theory of Continuous Trading." *Stochastics and Stochastic Reports* 13: 249–265.

––––––. (1990). "Arbitrage et Lois de Martingale." *Annales de l'Institut Henri Poincaré* 26: 451–460.

Strikwerda, J. (1989). *Finite Difference Schemes and Partial Differential Equations.* Belmont, California: Wadsworth.

Stroock, D., and S.R.S. Varadhan. (1979). *Multidimensional Diffusion Processes.* New York: Springer-Verlag.

Stulz, R. (1982). "Options on the Minimum or the Maximum of Two Risky Assets: Analysis and Applications." *Journal of Financial Economics* 10: 161–185.

Sun, T.-S. (1992). "Real and Nominal Interest Rates: A Discrete-Time Model and its Continuous-Time Limit." *Review of Financial Studies* 5: 581–612.

Sundaresan, S. (1989). "Intertemporally Dependent Preferences in the Theories of Consumption, Portfolio Choice and Equilibrium Asset Pricing." *Review of Financial Studies* 2: 73–89.

––––––. (1991). "Valuation of Swaps." In S. Khoury, *Recent Development in International Banking and Finance.* Amsterdam: North Holland.

Svensson, L. E. O. (1989). "Portfolio Choice with Non-Expected Utility in Continuous Time." *Economic Letters* 30: 313–317.

Svensson, L. E. O., and M. Dahlquist. (1993). "Estimating the Term Structure of Interest Rates with Simple and Complex Functional Forms: Nelson and Siegel vs. Longstaff and Schwartz." Institute for International Economic Studies, Stockholm University.

Svensson, L. E. O., and I. Werner. (1993). "Non-Traded Assets in Incomplete Markets." *European Economic Review* 37: 1149-1168.

Talay, D. (1984). "Efficient Numerical Schemes for the Approximation of Expectations of Functionals of S.D.E." In H. Korezlioglu, G. Mazziotto, and J. Szpirglas, *Filtering and Control of Random Processes: Lecture Notes in Control and Information Sciences 61.* New York: Springer-Verlag, pp. 294–313.

––––––. (1986). "Discrétiation d'une equation différentielle stochastique et calcul approché d'espérances de fonctionelles de la solution." *Mathematical Modeling and Numerical Analysis* 20: 141–179.

———. (1990). "Second Order Discretization Schemes of Stochastic Differential Systems for the Computation of the Invariant Law." Institut National de Recherche en Informatique et en Automatique, Sophia Antipolis, France.

Talay, D., and L. Tubaro. (1990). "Expansion of the Global Error for Numerical Schemes Solving Stochastic Differential Equations." Research Paper 1069. Institut National de Recherche en Informatique et en Automatique, Sophia Antipolis, France.

Tauchen, G., and R. Hussey. (1991). "Quadrature-Based Methods for Obtaining Approximate Solutions to the Integral Equations of Nonlinear Rational Expectations Models." *Econometrica* 59: 371–396.

Taylor, S. (1994). "Modeling Stochastic Volatility: A Review and Comparative Study." *Mathematical Finance* 4: 183-204.

Telmer, C. (1990). "Asset Pricing and Incomplete Markets." Department of Economics, Queen's University.

Török, C. (1993). "Numerical Solution of Linear Stochastic Differential Equations." Department of Mathematics, Technical University of Kosice.

Touzi, N. (1993). "Modèles Volatilité Stochastique." Ph.D. diss., CEREMADE, Université de Paris IX, Dauphine.

———. (1995). "American Options Exercise Boundary when the Volatility Changes Randomly." CEREMADE, Université de Paris IX, Dauphine.

Turnbull, S. (1993). "Pricing and Hedging Diff Swaps." School of Business, Queen's University.

———. (1994). "Interest Rate Digital Options and Range Notes." School of Business, Queen's University.

Xu, G.-L., and S. Shreve. (1992a). "A Duality Method for Optimal Consumption and Investment under Short-Selling Prohibition. I. General Market Coefficients." *Annals of Applied Probability* 2: 87–112.

———. (1992b). "A Duality Method for Optimal Consumption and Investment under Short-Selling Prohibition. II. Constant Market Coefficients." *Annals of Applied Probability* 2: 314-328.

Uzawa, H. (1968). "Time Preference, the Consumption Function and Optimal Asset Holdings." In J. Wolfe, *Value, Capital and Growth: Papers in Honor of Sir John Hicks*, pp. 485–504. Chicago: Aldine.

Van Horne, J. (1993). *Financial Market Rates and Flows* (4th ed.). Englewood Cliffs: Prentice-Hall.

Van Moerbeke, P. (1976). "On Optimal Stopping and Free Boundary Problems." *Archive for Rational Mechanics and Analysis* 60: 101–148.

Varian, H. (1984). *Microeconomic Analysis* (2d ed.). New York: Norton.

Vasicek, O. (1977). "An Equilibrium Characterization of the Term Structure." *Journal of Financial Economics* 5: 177–188.

Vayanos, D., and J.-L. Vila. (1992). "Equilibrium Interest Rate and Liquidity Premium Under Proportional Transactions Costs." Sloan School of Management, Massachusetts Institute of Technology.

Vila, J.-L., and T. Zariphopoulou. (1991). "Optimal Consumption and Portfolio Choice with Borrowing Constraints." Sloan School of Management, Massachusetts Institute of Technology.

Walras, L. (1874–1877). *Eléments d'économie politique pure* (4th ed.). Lausanne: L. Corbaz, English translation of the definitive edition by W. Jaffé, *Elements of Pure Economics*. London: Allen and Unwin, (1954).

Wang, S. (1991). "Is Kreps-Porteus Utility Distinguishable from Intertemporal Expected Utility." Department of Economics, University of Toronto.

———. (1993a). "The Integrability Problem of Asset Prices." *Journal of Economic Theory* 59: 199–213.

———. (1993b). "The Local Recoverability of Risk Aversion and Intertemporal Substitution." *Journal of Economic Theory* 59: 333–363.

Webber, N. (1990). "The Term Structure of Spot Rate Volatility and the Behavior of Interest Rate Processes." Financial Options Research Centre, University of Warwick.

———. (1992). "The Consistency of Term Structure Models: The Short Rate, the Long Rate, and Volatility." Financial Options Research Centre, University of Warwick.

Weil, P. (1992). "Equilibrium Asset Prices with Undiversifiable Labor Income Risk." *Journal of Economic Dynamics and Control* 16: 769–790.

Werner, J. (1985). "Equilibrium in Economies with Incomplete Financial Markets." *Journal of Economic Theory* 36: 110–119.

———. (1991). "On Constrained Optimal Allocations with Incomplete Markets." *Economic Theory* 1: 205–209.

Whalley, A. E., and P. Wilmott. (1994). "Optimal Hedging of Options with Small but Arbitrary Transaction Cost Structure." Mathematical Institute, Oxford University.

Wiggins, J. (1987). "Option Values under Stochastic Volatility: Theory and Empirical Estimates." *Journal of Financial Economics* 19: 351–372.

Willinger, W., and M. Tacqu. (1989). "Pathwise Stochastic Integration and Application to the Theory of Continuous Trading." *Stochastic Processes and Their Applications* 32: 253–280.

Willinger, W., and M. Tacqu. (1991). "Toward a Convergence Theory for Continuous Stochastic Securities Market Models." *Mathematical Finance* 1: 55–100.

Wilmott, P., J. Dewynne, and S. Howison. (1993). *Option Pricing: Mathematical Models and Computation*. Oxford: Oxford Financial Press.

Yamada, T., and S. Watanabe. (1971). "On the Uniqueness of Solutions of Stochastic Differential Equations." *Journal of Mathematics of Kyoto University* 11: 155–167.

Yamazaki, A. (1991). "Equilibrium in Economies with Incomplete Markets and Outside Money: Transactions Costs and Existence." Department of Economics, Hitotsubashi University.

Yor, M. (1991). "On Some Exponential Functionals of Brownian Motion." Laboratoires de Probabilités, Université de Paris VI.

———. (1993). "The Distribution of Brownian Quantiles." Laboratoires de Probabilités, Université de Paris VI.

Yu, G. (1993). "Essays on the Valuation of American Options." Stern School of Business, New York University.

Zapatero, F. (1992). "Equilibrium Asset Prices and Exchange Rates." Haas School of Business, University of California, Berkeley.

———. (1993a). "Effects of Financial Innovations on Market Volatility when Beliefs are Heterogeneous." Haas School of Business, University of California, Berkeley.

———. (1993b). "Interest Rates with Converging Heterogeneous Reliefs." Haas School of Business, University of California at Berkeley.

Zariphopoulou, T. (1992). "Investment-Consumption Models with Transactions Costs and Markov-Chain Parameters." *SIAM Journal on Control and Optimization* 30: 613–636.

———. (1994). "Consumption-Investment Models with Constraints." Department of Mathematics, University of Wisconsin. Forthcoming in *SIAM Journal on Control and Optimization*.

Zhang, X. (1993). "Options américaines et modèles de diffusion avec sauts." *Comtes Rendus de l'Academie de Science de Paris* 317: 857–862.

———. (1994). "Numerical Analysis of American Option Pricing in a Jump-Diffusion Model." CERMA, URA-CNRS 1502, E.N.P.C, Paris, France.

Zheng, C.-C. (1994). "Pricing Interest Rates Contingent Claims by a Pricing Kernel." NationsBank, New York.

Zhou, Y.-Q. (1993). "The Global Structure of Equilibrium Manifold in Incomplete Markets." Department of Economics, Columbia University.

Symbol Glossary

$\overline{\mathbb{R}} = \mathbb{R} \cup \{-\infty, +\infty\}$, xv

$x > 0$, xvi

$x \geq 0$, xvi

$x \gg 0$, xvi

$x \mapsto F(x)$, xvi

$\partial U(c^*)$, 5

$\text{corr}(\cdot)$, 12

$\partial f(a, b)$, 14

$\partial^2 U(c^i)$, 14

$(\cdot \mid \cdot)$, 17

G^π, 23, 118

$\nabla U(c^*; c)$, 25, 277

$\nabla U(c^*)$, 25, 210, 277

E^Q, 28

$(x - K)^+$, 36

$\max(x, y)$, 55

$\mathcal{U}F$, 65

$\int \theta \, dB$, 82, 286

$\mathbb{F}$, 82

$\text{var}_t(\cdot)$, 84

$\mathcal{H}^1$, 84, 92

$\mathcal{H}^2$, 84, 92

$\mathcal{L}^1$, 84, 92

$\mathcal{L}^2$, 82, 92

$\text{cov}_t(\cdot)$, 93

$\mathcal{L}(S)$, 85

$\mathcal{H}^2(S)$, 85

$\int \theta \, dS$, 85

$\mathcal{D}$, 93

$\mathcal{L}(X)$, 93

$\mathcal{H}^2(X)$, 93

$\text{tr}(A)$, 93

$\int \theta \, dX$, 93

X^π, 103

$\underline{\Theta}(X)$, 104

R^θ, 106

$\mathcal{H}^2(G)$, 117

ΔV, 118

D^θ, 120

$L^2(P)$, 121

$\emptyset$, 271

$\sigma(Z)$, 272

Author Index

Subject Index

About the Author

Darrell Duffie is Professor of Finance at the Graduate School of Business, Stanford University. He is the author of *Security Markets* and *Futures Markets*.